THE SECULAR PARADOX

SECULAR STUDIES

General Editor: Phil Zuckerman

Losing Our Religion: How Unaffiliated Parents Are Raising Their Children
Christel J. Manning

Race in a Godless World: Atheism, Race, and Civilization, 1850–1914
Nathan G. Alexander

The Varieties of Nonreligious Experience: Atheism in American Culture
Jerome P. Baggett

The Secular Paradox: On the Religiosity of the Not Religious
Joseph Blankholm

The Secular Paradox

On the Religiosity of the Not Religious

Joseph Blankholm

NEW YORK UNIVERSITY PRESS
New York

NEW YORK UNIVERSITY PRESS
New York
www.nyupress.org

© 2022 by New York University
All rights reserved

References to Internet websites (URLs) were accurate at the time of writing. Neither the author nor New York University Press is responsible for URLs that may have expired or changed since the manuscript was prepared.

Library of Congress Cataloging-in-Publication Data
Names: Blankholm, Joseph, author.
Title: The secular paradox : on the religiosity of the not religious / Joseph Blankholm.
Description: New York : New York University Press, [2022] | Series: Secular studies | Includes bibliographical references and index.
Identifiers: LCCN 2021036242 | ISBN 9781479809493 (hardback) | ISBN 9781479809509 (paperback) | ISBN 9781479809523 (ebook) | ISBN 9781479809516 (ebook other)
Subjects: LCSH: Secularism. | Religion—Philosophy.
Classification: LCC BL2747.8 .B56 2022 | DDC 211/.6—dc23
LC record available at https://lccn.loc.gov/2021036242

New York University Press books are printed on acid-free paper, and their binding materials are chosen for strength and durability. We strive to use environmentally responsible suppliers and materials to the greatest extent possible in publishing our books.

Manufactured in the United States of America

10 9 8 7 6 5 4 3 2 1

Also available as an ebook

To the Figueroas

CONTENTS

Introduction: A Strange Ambivalence — 1

1. Belief — 23
2. Community — 57
3. Ritual — 103
4. Conversion — 144
5. Tradition — 185

Epilogue: The Helmet of Mambrino — 221

Acknowledgments — 225

Notes — 229

Bibliography — 261

Index — 289

About the Author — 297

Introduction

A Strange Ambivalence

Religion versus *Religion*

On a chilly Sunday morning in April 2013, I sat in the parlor of a large brick house in a suburb of New York City. Outside were acres of bare trees and dead grass still waiting for the warmth of spring. The men and women I met wore comfortable shoes, and their clothes were made from fabrics like corduroy and moleskin. Among them were a chemist, a professor, a doctor, and an artist. All of them were white, and most were over fifty. While we sipped coffee and ate cake, they asked me polite questions about who I am and where I am from. Several had gone to graduate school in New York, and before moving to Westchester, one had lived near my apartment in Manhattan. They asked me about my research and wanted to know the questions that kept me up at night. One man recommended a book about cosmology and another a podcast about quantum physics. Before I could ask, they guessed what a researcher would like to know. I learned about the religions they grew up in, their careers, and their families, and they told me their reasons for joining their community. As our conversation was winding down, Sunday School ended, and a group of children ran through the room looking for cake. I wandered after them in search of the kind man who had offered to drive me home.

For the previous hour and a half, around forty of us had sat in rows of folding chairs in a room on the opposite side of the house. We had attended a program that included music, discussion, and quiet contemplation, as well as a "Platform," or prepared speech, titled "Faith for Faithless Times." The Platform was a jeremiad for a society in peril and offered us deliverance from the consumerism and hedonism that dominate our culture. "I assume that at least some of you have joined a community here, and not necessarily a religion," the speaker told us. "I'm here to press the point that this [Ethical Culture] society is part of a religion—with a philosophy." Attending services on Sundays is not enough. To save ourselves and to save the world, he implored, we need to embrace the philosophy that this religion offers. And yet religion can also be dangerous: "I offer religion as the problem. . . . It's one of the mental blocks causing the trouble."

By "religion" he meant two different things—one good and one bad—though he rarely distinguished between them. "Traditional religion," as he sometimes called it, "failed" to see humans for what they really are, embedded "in an interrelational web of minds." While "religion sees humans as part of God's creation," he said he prefers "science," which "sees humans as part of nature." "Rather than being diplomatic and nice, I think it's time, at least among ourselves, to admit that organized religion, as distinct from us, which is disorganized religion"—and here he had to pause for laughter—"organized religion has reached its limit at making human beings a better people." Ethics are thus key to the right kind of religion:

> Since making people good is supposedly one of the primary excuses for the existence of any particular religion, it's time to unpack more energetically our radically different approach to religion and offer it more definitely as not merely an alternative but as a replacement for the failed religions that continue to play a part in screwing up our world and screwing up humankind. Religion should help people be good, but often, it does the opposite.

The "God idea," as he called it, "spreads through culture and hurts mankind." By contrast, "Ethical Humanist religion" offers "a way out of that mentality." Paradoxically, Ethical Culture offers a religion that is an alternative to religion.

All secular people face tough choices. They need to avoid anything that feels too religious, and they struggle to name what they share with others who are secular. How nonbelievers define religion influences the minutiae of their lives, though their definitions are usually implicit. A broad definition and a strong aversion to religion can make a ritual as commonplace as a wedding feel uncomfortable. Even for secular people with a narrow definition and a tolerant indifference, a passing reference to God can be cringe-worthy. The boundaries that feel right to some secular people do not feel right to others. As they disagree about how much religion is too much, nonbelievers effect distinct ways of being secular. The Ethical Culture movement stands at one extreme in its self-proclaimed religiosity; antireligion groups like the Freedom From Religion Foundation stand at another. Whether nonbelievers should even form groups based on their shared beliefs is one of many potential rifts that divides them. Secular people's efforts to avoid religion and the creative ways in which they embrace it generate the diversity in American secularism.

This book makes sense of secular people's strange ambivalence toward religion. Though being secular means being not religious, it also means participating in a secular tradition and sharing ways of life with other secular people. The secular paradox is the tension between what secular people do not share and what they have in common—between avoiding religion and embracing something like it. This book is an ethnographic study of the effects of the secular paradox on the everyday lives of very secular people in the United States. It is also a study of the paradox's origin and an attempt to bring those who read it to a new understanding of secularism.

Though I focus mostly on secular activists and nonbelievers who participate in groups with one another, all secular people live with the secular paradox. Very secular people illuminate the paradox well because they embody its contradictions more than people who are not as ardent in their secularism. The awkwardness of very secular people's ambivalence makes a strong demand for explanation and reveals important aspects of being secular that are easily overlooked when trying to understand less intensely secular people, such as the religiously indifferent. By investigating the beliefs, practices, feelings, and ways of belonging that emerge from very secular people's ambivalent relationship with religion, I show the paradox's influence on everyone who shares secular beliefs and anyone who feels like some parts of life are too religious.

Nonbelievers who mis-fit secularism provide the most telling clues about its oddity because they belie the simple story in which secular is not religious. The lives of secular people of color, secular women, and secular people who have rejected religions other than Christianity reveal the predominant whiteness and maleness of American secularism and the specific kinds of religion the secular is not. Secular misfits' insistence on their secularity and their growing participation in America's secular movement are changing what it means to be secular and revealing aspects of secularism that have long been assumed and gone unnoticed. Throughout this book, I rely heavily on secular misfits' insights to explain the secular paradox. Their voices are prominent in all its chapters because they are not just part of the secular paradox's story; they are the ones who tell it best. Understanding power from the outside in reveals its workings better than inheriting it ever could.

I began this book with an anecdote about Ethical Culture because it is paradigmatic of American secularism in its extreme rejection and embrace of religion and in its overwhelming whiteness. Ethical Culture is also the oldest continuously active secular movement in the United States. It was founded in the nineteenth century, and its blend of secular and religious, if telling, can sometimes seem anachronistic. The year 1876 is etched into the stone facade of the New York Society for Ethical Culture, which stands at the corner of Sixty-Eighth Street and Central Park West, though the building was not erected until 1910.[1] The earlier date marks when Felix Adler, the movement's founder, first began to organize a community of like-minded nonbelievers.

Adler was the son of Samuel Adler, rabbi of New York City's Temple Emanu-El, which was then the wealthiest congregation in the United States and one of the leading Reform synagogues.[2] Rabbi Adler groomed his son to follow in his footsteps at Emanu-El, but when the younger Adler returned from completing his doctorate at the University of Heidelberg in 1873, it was clear that his ideas about divinity were no longer in step with his father's congregation. Adler's Ethical Culture was nontheistic and indebted to the transcendental idealism of Immanuel Kant.[3] It was part of a larger freethought movement that flourished in the United States in the decades following the Civil War.[4] Adler was deeply engaged with this larger movement, having served as president of the Free Religious Association from 1878 to 1882.[5] Calling Ethical Culture secular, even today, fails to capture the movement's flexibility and its ambivalence toward religion. Several Ethical Leaders I spoke with paraphrased a quote from one of Adler's lectures to explain the line they walk: "The Ethical Movement is religious to those who are religiously-minded and to those who interpret its work religiously, and it is simply ethical to those who are not so minded."[6] Ethical Culture societies remain strong communities for nontheistic people whose embrace of religion and secularism exceeds tidy labels.

Some nonbeliever groups are communities whose members meet in person, like Ethical Culture societies. There are around fourteen hundred of these local communities throughout the United States.[7] Other groups I focus on in this book are national organizations with diffuse membership or small groups with paid staff, dedicated to lobbying or legal activism. Though many of the very secular people I met participate in face-to-face secular communities, some told me they would never join a secular community because they consider them too religious. These secular people are striving for secular purity and want to avoid anything that resembles religion, including a like-minded community of nonbelievers. I encounter this notion of secular purity often when explaining my research to acquaintances and colleagues, some of whom consider a nonbeliever organization a contradiction in terms. In the words of one self-described atheist, "The idea that you're building an entire organization based on what you don't believe, to me, sounds like an offense against sensibility."[8] From his perspective, organized nonbelievers are paradoxical. Atheism only negates, and a community for nonbelievers is insufficiently secular.

"Purity" and "pollution" are useful concepts for understanding secular people's aversion to religion. They help us understand the anxiety about religion that secular people feel, which is visceral and affective, often prior to conscious reflection. For secular people, religious pollution poses a danger to secular purity. The stronger a secular person's belief in the need for secular purity, the stronger their aversion to religion and the more intense the anxiety of its proximity.[9] Purity and pollution help demonstrate how difficult secular purity is to achieve. Avoiding all religious pollution means living in religion's remainder. Defining religion broadly makes secular purity unlikely or even impossible.[10] Can secular people celebrate Christmas? Can they meditate or practice yoga? Can they get married in a church? Can they even visit a church? What do secular people need to avoid at their weddings to maintain their secularity—or at their memorial services? Can a secular person be spiritual or have faith? Do secular people believe in things or have a set of beliefs they share?

These are tough questions. They arise from the weirdness of being secular, which means avoiding something that is everywhere and at the same time embracing it, albeit reluctantly. This push and pull—this ambivalence—is what it feels like to be secular.[11] This book explores this feeling. It shares stories and reflections from the lives of very secular people. It documents both their struggle to avoid religion and the many ways they are, for lack of a better term, so religious. Their ambivalence is not confusion. It originates with the secular paradox. Understanding the origin and effects of the paradox offers an exit to the endless cycle of negation and affirmation it demands. This book argues for an understanding of secularism that includes both halves of being secular: absolutely not religious and surprisingly religion-like.[12]

Naming Secular People

Members of Ethical Culture are not the only ones struggling for words. Everyone in the United States who joins a group for avowedly secular people is hard-pressed to name what they believe and how they live. Scholars face this challenge, as well, and I am no different.[13] In this book, I rely mostly on two terms: "nonbeliever" and "secular." By "nonbeliever," I mean an ellipsis: a person who lacks belief in God, gods, or the supernatural. Organized nonbelievers are those who organize *qua* nonbelievers. Some of those with whom I spoke do not consider themselves nonbelievers because they prefer to avoid any negative terminology. Instead they describe themselves with more affirming terms like "humanist" and "freethinker." No one label is used by all nonbelievers who form communities. Most identify with several labels, which can also include "nontheist," "agnostic," "naturalist," or "rationalist," among others. Secular activists use the term "nonbeliever" frequently, and it is less aligned with particular factions than terms like "humanist" and "atheist." The same is true of "secular." Though nearly all of the nonbelievers I spoke with consider themselves "secular," some avoid the label, and only a few adopt it as their primary identity. Relying on the term "secular" also helps this book join a robust, growing conversation. "Secular" and "secularism" can describe secular people, the separation of church and state, and the creation and regulation of religion.[14] "Nonbelievers" and "secular" are efficacious umbrella categories, but they are necessarily imperfect.

In recent years, the American Religious Identification Survey and surveys conducted by Pew Research have drawn attention to the religious "nones," a shorthand term for Americans who, when asked by pollsters, state that they have no religious affiliation.[15] Research has shown that this group is deeply heterogeneous and includes atheists and agnostics, the spiritual but not religious, the religiously indifferent, and those who identify with a religion intermittently.[16] This is because religious affiliation is just one part of a larger category, religiosity, which includes not only how people belong but also how they believe and behave. Belief, behavior, and belonging capture most aspects of people's religiosity, so they are useful categories for social scientists researching religion. The "nones," or the religiously unaffiliated, are literally a surplus category of an increasingly outmoded way of taxonomizing religious life.

Survey options like Christian, Catholic, Muslim, and Jewish used to capture the vast majority of the US population's religious affiliation, but around a quarter of Americans no longer fit within these divisions and subdivisions.[17] Critical studies of "religion" as a term and concept have shown that even though the Latin *religio* antedates Christianity, Christian culture structures what people mean when they talk about religion today.[18] Christianity shapes our world even if we are not Christian. Belief, behavior, and belonging are abstracted ways of describing elements of Christianity, such as creeds, church membership, and prayer, which have broadened to include equivalents in non-Christian cultures. Christianity provided the template for what religion is, and over centuries, merchants and missionaries identified analogues in other cultures and effected the so-called world religions, often to the benefit of colonial and postcolonial empires, like that of the United States.[19]

The rise of the "nones" reflects a weakening of Christian culture as a template for organizing life.[20] The same is true of other negative surplus categories like "nonbelieving" and "nonpracticing" but also positive terms like "spirituality," which can sometimes describe noninstitutional or individualized religiosity.[21] That more and more people fit poorly into the categories abstracted from Christian religiosity does not necessarily mean that these people are anti-Christian or that they have converted to another religion. Social scientists recognize that people are living in ways that are kind of religious but also kind of secular, and they are inventing new ways to measure religiosity because how people believe, behave, and belong matters a great deal for understanding related areas of life, like politics and economics.[22]

One straightforward strategy for making these abstract categories work better is to name and describe the ways in which secular people believe, behave, and belong that are equivalent to religion. Many organized nonbelievers have adopted this strategy, in part because it makes them legible in a Christian-centered culture like the United States. Terms like "humanist," "secular humanist," and "freethinker" signal a shared worldview and avoid the religious connotations of identifying with a "faith" or a "tradition." "Worldview" is an old term that abstracts beyond "belief" to include secular perspectives.[23] "Ideology" can do some of the same work, but it bears more negative connotations.[24] Both "worldview" and "ideology" are belief-centered terms in need of other categories to account for behaviors and ways of belonging that are equivalent to religion but not religious. For instance, "community" functions as a secular abstraction from "congregation," "leadership" abstracts from "clergy," and "life-cycle rituals" can describe everything from weddings and funerals to baptisms and christenings. Social scientists and secular people use these abstractions to compare religious and nonreligious people without eliding meaningful distinctions between them.

For some secular people, abstracting from Christianity's salient distinctions in order to create equivalence for the purposes of comparison only reinscribes the basic structures of Christianity. Remaining within Christianity's organizing logic buttresses the state-based forms of governance that coevolved with Christianity. These structures continue to give disproportionate political and economic benefits to Christians and those who most resemble them by analogy.[25] In this view, abstraction fails to secularize sufficiently and perpetuates Christianity by another name.[26] A number of scholars have recognized the ways in which secularism is structured by Protestantism and even intensifies certain of its features, such as iconoclasm, skepticism toward ritual, and an emphasis on beliefs.[27] For these and other scholars, "secularism" can be a name for the state-based governance of religion according to a Christian model, even in non-Christian countries like Egypt.[28] "Secularity" can be a way to describe the broader, non-state-based "set of concepts, norms, sensibilities, and dispositions that characterize secular societies and subjectivities."[29]

Whether and how to challenge this latent Christian bias is a difficult question. German philosophers Hans Blumenberg and Karl Löwith famously debated whether Christianity's structuring influence on the modern world made the latter de facto Christian, even if it appeared to have become secular.³⁰ For Löwith, Christian influence runs deep, and a return to the concepts and values of pre-Christian Europe is the only way to liberate contemporary culture. For Blumenberg, Christianity has influenced the ways in which secular modern people ask questions, but it does not determine their answers. At the core of their debate lies the question of what is distinctive about Christianity: its truth claims or the ways it frames the world and determines what questions are important.³¹ Whether the structural influence of Christianity makes something Christian is a vitally important question for anyone trying to purify the secular—or any other tradition—of Christian influence. Secular people wrestle with how they should relate to religion, so they provide a wide range of responses to this question, which by definition plagues the modern and the secular.³²

Paradoxically, I take a both/and approach to secularism and religion. Though scholars who argue that Christianity has strongly influenced secular culture are correct, trying to escape the orbit of Christianity's gravity, while still speaking English in an Anglophone culture, is Sisyphean at best and at worst Icarian.³³ Christianity's gravity is weakening, evidently,³⁴ but its influence remains strong. European languages bear traces of Christianity even if those who speak them have sought to avoid its influence. For a long time, I avoided pointing out to secular activists that "good-bye" is a contracted and corrupted version of "God be with ye." I assumed that a person needs to be aware of linguistic impurity for it to harm them. When I finally did, an activist responded immediately, "I have to stop staying 'good-bye.'" Many organized nonbelievers avoid exclaiming "Oh my God!" or saying "Bless you" when someone sneezes. For secular people of all kinds, talking about non-Christian things with language and concepts deeply influenced by Christianity is a real challenge.

To understand the profound awkwardness of being secular, we need to make our words and concepts speak in new ways that sometimes contradict the inheritance from which they emerge. Scholars of secularism like Elizabeth Hurd have argued that we must fracture and reassemble the concept of religion and its close relatives like secularism, spirituality, and superstition.³⁵ Sociologist of religion Andrew McKinnon has made a similar point: "Defining religion in a way that bears little or no resemblance to common sense definitions can be important for 'recontextualizing' phenomena, and developing new understandings of various phenomena. This is an indispensable component of sociological studies—as long as we do not think we are defining what religion (really!) is."[36] Fracturing and reassembling requires that we continue to borrow from everyday language, which remains structured by Christianity's salient categories. It also means adopting more critical approaches that use genealogical methods to interrogate structural influence. This means trying to think otherwise, which is to say, other than Christian, and especially other than Protestant. Good social science needs to get critical distance from its terms by using them in ways that fit what they describe but that also call our attention to the history of power that makes them fit. By exploring the secular religiosity of very secular people and using the terms "religious" and "secular" in ways that both make sense and surprise, I try to do just that. I take seriously the paradox captured in flip phrases like "evangelical atheist" and "secular fundamentalist." I inquire into its consequences and the reasons we inherit it.

Stylistically, readers will probably find that I ask words to do too much. This is intentional, to try to draw lessons from language's limits. Secular people who do religion-like things are especially difficult to categorize, and their challenge to description tells a fascinating story about a symbolic inheritance that struggles to see them as anything other than awkward and paradoxical. As my visit to the Ethical Culture Society of Northern Westchester makes plain, organized nonbelievers in the United States struggle to understand themselves and be understood. In many conversations I had with people who identify as both secular and religious, only context indicated whether religion was the good kind or the bad kind: one is religious but not *religious*; one is part of a religion but not *religion*.

The self-descriptions that secular people have developed are deeply instructive for anyone looking for ways to overcome latent Christian biases and modes of governance that perpetuate them. They also hold lessons for anyone looking for new ways to use Christian-based categories like belief, behavior, and belonging to describe non-Christian people. Very secular people have robust, often ambiguous vocabularies for dealing with their constitutive challenge. Adopting these vocabularies will not resolve the difficulties we face when talking about religion or secularism, but observing their creation and the reasons for it can bring us into a new relationship with our own ways of using words. As I try to show throughout this book, we try, and we fail; our mistakes help us understand the world and one another better. Our confusion is instructive. The lack of clarity holds the truth; what is misunderstood and read between the lines is real and must be layered on the literal truth.

The particular labels that secular people use to describe themselves can divide or unify depending on who uses them and how. Some labels are negative because they point to beliefs that nonbelievers deny rather than affirm. Atheists, like nonbelievers, deny that God, gods, and the supernatural are real. Agnostics with a knowledge of the term's philosophical meaning do not affirm the existence of the supernatural, but they acknowledge that the limits of empiricism prevent them from making strongly certain statements about reality because science can only falsify hypotheses. Some secular people prefer "agnostic" simply because it sounds more polite than "atheist." Other terms describe what nonbelievers believe in. Humanists emphasize that humans are the source of meaning in the world, and they alone are responsible for the future of humanity. Most humanists consider themselves secular, and a small minority also consider themselves religious. Some religious humanists are more comfortable identifying as nontheists than atheists, so "nontheists" is the preferred term of the Secular Coalition for America, a lobbying group that aims to unify nonbelievers.

In the nineteenth century, "freethinkers" named not only atheists and agnostics but also Spiritualists, anarchists, and people studying Eastern religions. Today, freethinkers are usually antireligious atheists, though in a few cases secular people have told me they use "freethinker" like "agnostic," as a polite alternative to "atheist." Ongoing debates over what these labels mean erase any stable point of reference because adopting a label means taking a side. Nearly every self-descriptor carries with it a decades- or even centuries-long dispute over its proper meaning. A scholar's adoption of a certain label necessarily situates that scholar within these debates, leaving no outside from which to name. Rather than enter the fray and pick a side, this book uses several different terms and explains what they mean to organized nonbelievers. It also explains why new labels keep forming.

I have adopted most of my strategic approach to naming from the secular people I spent time with, who sometimes consider themselves religious, sometimes not religious, and sometimes something in between.[37] Researching this book has changed how I think about religion and the secular, and one of my goals is to share with those who read it ways to make everyday language more capable of describing those non-Christian parts of the world that Christianity continues to structure, even if it holds less power than it once did. Naming secular people is both what this book does and what it investigates. Of course, I want to inform readers about nonbeliever groups in the United States, the people who join them, and the ways in which they understand themselves and their place in the world. But I also want to perform a work on readers by introducing new ways of thinking about religion and secularism—by taking their meanings beyond their limits.[38] I write now as an experiment, and though perhaps it will fail, I hope this book can be judged not only for what it describes but also for what it accomplishes.

Finding and Studying Secular People

This book relies on extensive ethnographic fieldwork among a network of leaders and activists who run the United States' major nonbeliever organizations. These leaders and activists responded promptly to my inquiries, introduced me to other activists, invited me to their workshops and private meetings, and sacrificed many hours of their time to talk with me, not only during interviews but also over meals and drinks. Many will find their voices and their ideas reflected in this book, and I remain grateful for their participation and support. These leaders and activists comprise a diffuse network, so I adopted a multisited approach and traveled throughout the United States in order to be with them in person.[39] From June 2010 through November 2013 and again during the summers of 2016, 2017, and 2018, I was a participant observer at dozens of lectures, conferences, private meetings, workshops, and social gatherings of local and national nonbeliever organizations. To visit their headquarters and conferences, I traveled to California, Louisiana, Ohio, Massachusetts, Michigan, Minnesota, New Jersey, New York, Washington DC, and Wisconsin. Needing to identify relevant nonbeliever organizations and study their ongoing activities, I analyzed hundreds of emails, blog posts, Facebook posts, and postings to online forums, as well as dozens of newsletters, magazines, and postings to Google discussion groups.

From April 2012 through January 2013, I conducted sixty-five in-depth interviews with the leaders, former leaders, and members of these groups.

From 2016 through 2018, I conducted thirty-seven more interviews and visited several more field sites in order to pursue my lingering questions in more depth. All in all, this book relies on more than a hundred interviews, dozens of site visits, and innumerable hours spent in the interesting ethnographic business of hanging out. Whenever possible, I conducted interviews in person and, ideally, at the headquarters of the organization for which an individual worked. Some groups do not have offices, and some of the people I interviewed were no longer involved with secular activism, so I interviewed them at cafes and restaurants and, occasionally, at their homes or another location they found convenient. In some cases, I conducted interviews over the phone with leaders and activists I had met in person but whom I was unable to interview while we were in the same city. Nine of those I interviewed over the phone I have never met face-to-face. Other people I have met many times and spoken with for hours, but we have never sat down for a recorded interview. Only once did I conduct a group interview, when I met with two Humanistic Jews at a Starbucks Cafe in a suburb of Minneapolis. Most people I interviewed I reached by chain referral, either through formal introduction or through recommendation and the use of publicly available contact information. Interviews were semistructured and covered a wide range of topics, including organizational and personal history, interorganizational cooperation, and the constellation of labels used by nonbelievers. During the first hour or so of an interview, I tried to avoid priming those with whom I spoke and stuck mostly to a structured interview schedule. After that first hour, I often engaged my research participants in cotheorizing. Many of those I interviewed are extremely intelligent, have published books and articles on secularism, and have reflected deeply on their lives and the subject of my research. Their thoughtful insights have been invaluable in shaping this book's presentation of their world.

Conforming with ethnographic norms, I have guaranteed the anonymity of those with whom I spoke by assigning them pseudonyms and changing their identifying biographical details, even when research participants have given me permission to use their real names. Many leaders and activists were frank with me during interviews, and most aired grievances of one kind or another about other members of their tight-knit national community. Because I remain uninterested in muckraking and personal drama, this book benefits from the luxury of not needing to expose such details, except under a cloud of anonymity and only to further its central argument. Because many of the leaders of these organizations are public figures who can be identified easily with only a small number of details, I have disguised certain biographical characteristics and insisted on using general terms like "leader" and "activist," rather than specific titles like "executive director," "president," or "director of public policy." When a person's primary income has come from an organization, I have generally favored the term "leader," and when a person has been affiliated with a group but not considered an employee, I have favored the terms "activist," "group member," or "community member." That said, in a few instances, I have used these terms interchangeably in order to obscure the identity of an interviewee, especially when quoting a former employee or presenting a potentially inflammatory statement. In order to streamline the telling of certain illustrative anecdotes, I have simplified some events and consolidated separate instances into single, dense stories. Writing this book, I have tried to capture behaviors, turns of phrase, and interactions that are typical among America's organized nonbelievers. I suspect that those who are part of these groups will find my examples familiar and unremarkable, and I hope the way that I have framed them will offer some insights that can serve as thanks for all they have shared with me.

This book focuses almost entirely on nonbeliever organizations with a national presence, many of which have local chapters throughout the United States. Though some of these groups have existed for many decades, several were formed in the past few years, and new groups appear all the time. The largest groups include the Center for Inquiry, the American Humanist Association, the Secular Student Alliance, the Freedom From Religion Foundation, American Atheists, the Secular Coalition for America, the Ethical Culture movement, the Unitarian Universalist Humanist Association, and the Society for Humanistic Judaism. Smaller organizations include Black Nonbelievers, Hispanic American Freethinkers, Foundation Beyond Belief, Secular Woman, and Ex-Muslims of North America.

All these groups have different organizational structures and aims. While some are more interested in forming communities, others focus entirely on activism and advocacy. The Center for Inquiry, for instance, is an umbrella organization that includes the Council for Secular Humanism, the Richard Dawkins Foundation for Reason and Science, and the Committee for Skeptical Inquiry, each of which has a different mission and constituency. The American Ethical Union is a less centralized organization that unites the more than twenty independent Ethical Culture societies throughout the United States. The Freedom From Religion Foundation (FFRF) has a range of programs that it runs from its offices in Madison, Wisconsin, though with the help of its large team of lawyers, it primarily provides legal support for nonbelievers. FFRF has more than twenty local chapters, but the leaders in Madison emphasized to me that the local groups began at the grassroots level, and the national organization has no formal role in their governance. This hands-off approach is typical of groups that have a strong aversion to religion because they seek to avoid structures they consider authoritarian or dogmatic. Despite these differences among national groups, many organized nonbelievers I met are members of multiple communities in their local area and affiliate with several national organizations. The landscape of organized nonbelief reflects a combination of strategic pragmatism and strong beliefs about the appropriate attitude toward religion.

This book focuses specifically on *organized* nonbelievers for reasons that also have a lot to do with pragmatism and intellectual commitment. When I first began to consider what an anthropology of atheism or secularism would look like, it was 2009, and I was a graduate student at Columbia University. My initial attempts to study secular people were inclusive and nearly aimless. Living in New York City and being at a university, I was so surrounded by secular people that a man who is now a close friend came out to me as Christian after meeting me several times and sharing a few drinks. The challenge of studying secular people soon became clear: Who counts, and how do I study them in a systematic, empirically rigorous way? My own identity provided little help in structuring the break between self and other ostensibly required for anthropological inquiry. Despite what strangers think when they meet that most ridiculous of doctors, a doctor of religion, I am a secular person in more senses than one. Thus, at the start of my research, my challenge was twofold: How do I identify secular people, and how do I alienate myself sufficiently enough to make what I am an object of study?

To tackle the first challenge, I made the practical decision to look for the most committed secular people I could find. Many of these were involved with secular groups, but some were not. Soon I realized there was an entire world of organized secularism that had been continuously active for more than a century. Through a scholar's eyes, the groups I encountered looked strangely religious despite their opposition to religion. My confusion cemented my focus on secular people who join communities because they posed a problem I became obsessed with figuring out. As it turns out, secular people who form groups are doing things that seriously challenge many of the big ideas about religion that we in American culture inherit. I knew I was onto something fascinating, and I had to pursue it.[40]

My decision to focus on nonbelievers who organize themselves was practical in two ways. I could delimit who counts for the purposes of my study, and I could pursue the strangeness of the secular-religious until I managed to make sense of it. Though this book hardly answers all of the important questions relating to secular people, it relies on my research and the research of others, including many recent studies, in order to provide a vocabulary and framework for understanding who secular people are and why being secular can feel so weird at times.

The problem of how to deal with my own secular identity might seem more challenging, but this book's thesis is an argument for why it is not. Inasmuch as the secular is not what it appears to be and inasmuch as it is shot through with its ostensible other, it provides the loose thread of its own undoing to anyone willing to pull it. Its history and genealogy lead into a disorienting hall of mirrors. These seemingly infinite reflections are a condition of being secular, so documenting that condition performs the work of self-estrangement that is so important to social scientific inquiry.[41] I hope those who read this book can share with me the numerous odd epiphanies that I have experienced while conducting years of research among secular people. Indeed, I have discovered what I have to come to call, only half in jest, my subterranean religion. Whether we are secular is entirely a matter of dispute—and that conflict is at the heart of being secular.

A Generative Tension within Secularism

There is a surprising variety of names for secular people. This variety stems from nonbelievers' ambivalence toward religion, which is their desire to both reject it and preserve something like it. Affirmative labels like "humanist" can emphasize the beliefs, practices, and ways of belonging that nonbelievers share with one another. Negative labels like "atheist" can emphasize the bad parts of religion that they seek to avoid. The work of affirming what nonbelievers share and emphasizing what they deny is the generative tension that secularism carries within its semantic and conceptual sediment. Secular ambivalence structures what it means to be secular.

Most secular people I spoke with strike a balance that works for them. They reject the things that seem too religious, and they embrace the religion-like things they find important and useful, though sometimes ignoring their uncanny religiosity. This same tension exists within atheism, which is both an old Christian term for heresy and, since the late eighteenth century, a name for the beliefs of nonbelievers. Because secular people face a choice between rejecting religion and embracing something like it, they often disagree about where to draw the line between secular and religious. Those who dissent from the existing options found new groups, invent new labels, and create new ways of being secular. Secular people's ambivalence toward religion is highly productive, and tracing its effects is crucial for understanding what it means to be secular in the United States today.

Sometimes secular people negotiate their antagonistic drives consciously, either as individuals or in conversation with one another. At other times their reactions are visceral and not up for debate.[42] Nonbelievers develop particular ways of thinking, speaking, and being secular by deciding, consciously or unconsciously, which things are too religious and need to be avoided. This in turn shapes the structures and activities of the groups they form. The numerous ways in which secular and religious can be distinct, overlapping, or analogous become points of contention and delimit the boundaries that separate one way of being a nonbeliever from another. Successfully avoiding religion, or even just the wrong kind of religion, requires ongoing reflection on what religion is and how much its pollution sullies the secular. Everyone I spoke with described how, over time, what they reject has changed, sometimes toward a purer secular and sometimes toward the hybridity of secular religion. To be secular means to struggle, in ways big and small, with being not religious. None of the people I met during my fieldwork—and no secular people in the rest of my life—have resolved this ambivalence. Declaring it resolved by calling secular people "religious" or "not religious" is an error because it pays no heed to secular people's effort to avoid religion while also embracing it. That ongoing labor indexes their need to avoid religion's pollution but also its permanent proximity.

Whether secular people feel the need to reject religion and the extent to which they do depends on what they think religion is. These definitions remain mostly implicit, though the speech and behavior of secular people provide plenty of clues about the kind of religion they see themselves embracing or rejecting. For instance, many nonbelievers hold a belief-centered understanding of religion, so for them, being an atheist means not being religious because being religious means believing in God. Behaviors that can be religious or quasi-religious, such as meditation or yoga, can become taboo for the atheist with a belief-centered approach that relies on a broad conception of religion because affirmation of the supernatural can pollute religious practices and ways of belonging by association.[43]

On the other hand, a belief-centered approach with a narrow conception of religion can allow engagement with religious practices and institutions because they can be separated from beliefs and thus purified of religious error. Nontheistic religious humanists, for instance, disaggregate belief from other aspects of religiosity, embracing religious behavior and belonging without exposing themselves to religious pollution. Others, like secular humanists, also negate religious belief, but they purify religious behavior and belonging through the work of analogy and abstraction. They avoid religious language even when their institutions or practices resemble religious equivalents. Instead of clergy, they have Secular Celebrants; instead of orthodoxy, they have eupraxsophy.[44] Some nonbelievers avoid anything that resembles religious belief, behavior, or belonging—including groups for nonbelievers. Because the work of being secular always depends on what religion means, it takes place at the intersection of two shifting terrains: the things people think and do and the labels that describe them. To really understand what it means to be secular requires navigating both terrains at once, the possibility of which is good evidence that they are not entirely separate.[45]

Defining and delimiting religion is vital work for people who identify strongly as secular, who engage in secular activism, and who shape their identities in face-to-face communities with other nonbelievers. Because being secular is so important to them, they negotiate their ambivalence toward religion more often and more thoroughly than people with weaker secular identities do. This book examines very secular people closely to observe the effects of secularism's ambivalence on their speech, their feelings, their bodily habits, their institutional structures, and their legal strategies. Though I focus specifically on nonbelievers who join groups, all secular people, even those who have no interest in joining a nonbeliever community, struggle with secularism's ambivalence and face decisions about what things are too religious. This is the condition of being secular. Thus, while this book focuses on organized nonbelievers and secular activists, it can provide insight into what it means to be secular in a more general sense in the United States today.

Others who have studied secular people have noticed a similar ambivalence and have struggled to name it.[46] I aim to make a big deal of it because it explains so much and because the causes and effects of this structuring ambivalence have come into increasingly better view with the help a growing body of social scientific and historical research. I argue that being secular is inherently paradoxical; its internal tension defines it. In one of the earliest and best studies of nonbelievers, the sociologist Colin Campbell observed at two extremes the "abolitionists" and the "substitutionists," who seek to abolish or replace religion, respectively.[47] Campbell recognizes that these are not the only ways to be secular but rather the poles of a kind of spectrum. He also observes a fuzzy boundary between the substitutionists who want to replace religion and the traditionally religious.

More recently, sociologists including Jesse Smith, Stephen LeDrew, and Jacqui Frost have studied how nonbelievers emphasize what they share with one another and how they model their communities, at least in part, on religious equivalents.[48] These substitutionists, in Campbell's terms, want to focus on what they affirm rather than what they negate. The Sunday Assembly, a group founded in London in early 2013, and the Oasis Network, founded in Houston in 2012, are examples of affirmative movements that have grown rapidly in the United States since I completed the bulk of my field research. Though these movements aim to build something new on their own terms, a bigger view of organized secularism shows how they fit snugly within its history. If they continue to grow and have staying power, they will represent the latest generation of secular people to organize themselves around their shared beliefs and values, echoing earlier movements like Ethical Culture in the nineteenth century and humanism in the twentieth.

Scholars have identified a similar binary within atheism.[49] Philosopher Antony Flew has described "negative" and "positive" atheism as two ways in which the "a-" can negate "theism."[50] For Smith and for other philosophers such as George H. Smith and Michael Martin who have built on his work, negative atheism is a lack or absence of belief in God.[51] Positive atheism is more than a mere absence; it is an active disavowal. Smith also uses the terms "implicit" and "explicit" to capture this distinction, and a number of social scientists have used the terms "passive" and "active" secularism to describe a similar division between those who are merely indifferent to religion and those who affirm a secular worldview and take on a secular identity.[52] Sociologist and theologian Stephen Bullivant observes an "ambiguity" in atheism, by which he means something more like confusion. His is less a bifurcation and more an entire range of ways in which atheism negates or even affirms.[53] Atheism can negatively target the supernatural, gods, religion, or monotheism, or as for Smith and Martin, it can signal a mere absence of avowed belief. Bullivant's positive atheism can describe a belief system that is atheistic as a consequence rather than its raison d'être, such as existentialist atheism, Soviet scientific atheism, or Ayn Rand's objectivism.

Certain worldviews are more atheistic than others, both in their ontologies and in their historical associations. French historian of atheism Georges Minois has paid close attention to the positive that atheism contains, while also observing what it negates: "Atheism is not merely an attitude of refusal, rejection, or indifference, defined only by its relationship to religion. It is also positive, constructive, and autonomous. Contrary, once again, to the assumptions of religious historians of atheism, the atheist is not merely one who does not believe. Atheists believe—not in God—but in man, in matter, and in reason."[54] The ambiguity that Minois identifies in the history of atheism I encounter as productive ambivalence among secular people in the United States today.[55] Understanding secularism requires that we understand what secular people negate and what they affirm—as well as the tension between.

Misfits of the Secular Paradox

Few secular people can simply reject religion and live in religion's remainder. Their need to affirm what they believe to be true and share in that truth with like-minded others leads secular people to gather together—if not always in nonbeliever communities, then in cities and neighborhoods where they feel at home. The secularism they affirm, however, is not one-size-fits-all. Many secular people—especially people of color—feel out of place in most nonbeliever communities in the United States. Particular ways of being secular arise from myriad small decisions about what parts of culture are too religious and what parts can be affirmed. If a secular community has a culture, whose culture is it?

Over drinks at a bar in Detroit, an ex-Muslim man told me about his double bind: "There's no way to separate Arabic and Islamic culture. There's nothing left. There's no Arabic culture. There's Islamic culture. What's left? The desert?" The man, who was born in the United Arab Emirates, was only half joking. In American secularism, he sees little that resembles his birth culture, so being secular means rejecting much if not all of it. A Latino humanist who used to be a Pentecostal youth minister described the same problem in different terms when speaking to me and a white leader of a local nonbeliever community in Los Angeles: "Religion is a culture as much as being Mexican is. We have to include a lot of culture when we reach out to the Latin community.... White culture is a culture. I respect you and believe what you believe, but this [secular community] isn't my culture. It doesn't feel homey." Being secular requires them to negate too much—"What's left?"—and American secular culture has mostly failed to replace it.

Many women I spoke with have also felt excluded from the culture of organized secularism. In its distrust of emotion, in its confidence that critical thinking can produce ethical outcomes, and in its pattern of supporting men who have sexually harassed and assaulted women, organized secularism in the United States has disappointed many women who are ardently secular. In the backhanded words of one woman, reflecting on why more women are not involved in nonbeliever groups, "Many activist women may prefer to give their support to feminist organizations." Another woman, describing the founding of a prominent nonbeliever organization in the United States, said that she and her co-founders "would not have done so" if they "weren't feminists." For her, there is a strong connection between her secularism and her feminism: "We wanted to keep religion out of laws affecting women and social policy." While some women have tried to reform organized secularism, others have given up on it, founding their own groups that work in parallel or shifting their focus to other causes and making their secular identities secondary or tertiary rather than primary.

Though secularism negates and affirms, it affirms the culture of white men more easily than the cultures of women and people of color. As one Chinese American woman who left the secular movement told me, "I'm an atheist, and my family worships our ancestors. I don't have a problem with that, but these secular people do." The stories of women and people of color are woven throughout every chapter of this book in order to demonstrate that secularism is a racializing and gendering formation that struggles to contain those who are not cisgendered white men. In the double movement of negating religion and affirming what secular people share, some lives mis-fit. At the same time, these misfits are creating new ways of being secular in which their lives can become legible. They are pioneering some of the most interesting forms of secular religiosity in the United States today, and their stories show not only who and what misfits the secular but how and why. They also represent the horizons of what secularism is becoming.

Each chapter of this book examines a different aspect of religion: belief, community, ritual, conversion, and tradition. Because secular people struggle to simply remove all of these religion-like elements from their lives, they affirm them in part or entirely, sometimes uncritically but more often quite carefully and not without reservations. In the chapters on belief and tradition, this book shows that the avowedly secular people I met and interviewed share many strongly held beliefs about reality and the best way to know it. They also share many of the same values, and they largely agree on the terms of their internal debates, if not the conclusions. I found that these fundamentally shared beliefs cut across differences of race and gender and define secular people at least as much as what they refuse. In carefully exploring secular people's ambivalence toward religion, this book thus excavates an epistemological and ontological tradition that binds secular people in religion-like ways that cannot be acknowledged as religious in any simple terms. Their ambiguous religiosity provides ways to think through and beyond outmoded conceptions of religion that have reached their breaking point. America's Christian inheritance—its concepts and its vocabulary—can only capture the lives of secular people as a paradox with mis-fitting remainders. Through an immanent, affectionate critique, I explain why and provide a map for navigating a new and emerging American religious landscape.

1

Belief

The Paradox of Nonbelief

I called Ismail. Meeting was out of the question, and he was hard to get on the phone. The first time I called, he was driving. Right away, he asked if I am Christian because he "refuse[s] to work with Christians." When I told him, "No, I'm not," he told me to call back later. I waited an hour and tried again, this time with better luck. Sitting on a couch in Brooklyn, I wondered about the noises I heard in the background, behind his voice. Where was Ismail? Was he at home in Queens? Or was he out on the street, dodging dog leashes and darting past teenagers walking three abreast? Ismail is full of energy and fiercely intelligent. He speaks loudly and quickly, he repeats himself, and he curses a lot. After talking for about forty-five minutes, he told me abruptly that he does not really know who I am, so I need to text him with some kind of evidence. I hung up and texted him my faculty profile page, and he called me back fifteen minutes later. The interview was full of stops and starts, fervid dissent and adamant agreement. No one I spoke with captured the paradox of a nonbeliever's beliefs better than Ismail.

By the time I interviewed Ismail, I had already conducted years of fieldwork among secular people. I knew that "belief" could be a touchy word. Toward the end of our interview, I asked Ismail a question intended to provoke, and then I rephrased it: "Could you tell me about some of the things that you believe? Or could you tell me about what you think is true or think is real?" "I don't believe anything," he replied immediately. He continued,

> If there's evidence of something, I will accept it or reject it. I don't believe anything, anything. I don't believe in anything that there's no evidence to prove. I think the word "believe" in itself is a stupid word. I don't under-

stand why people consider belief to be a good thing. Belief is the definition of stupid—to accept something without evidence. The definition of belief is to accept something without evidence. Why is that a good thing? . . . I don't have like, "This is my ideology." I don't have an ideology. I'm pragmatic. I see the world for what it is. It's just the product of what we've made it. And we're not perfect, so the world's not perfect, and we just have to work with it the way it is.

He rephrased my language from "believe" and "think is true" or "think is real" to "accept" and to "see the world for what it is." He rejected forcefully and then qualified his refusal: "I don't believe in anything that there's no evidence to prove." Wondering what he accepts and what evidence proves, I followed up with another question, which I knew from experience might resonate: "What about the idea that everything is governed by natural law?" He replied quickly and again searched aloud for a better verb than "believe":

I agree with that. I would say I accept that. I accept that everything is governed by natural law. I think what happened to me that made me an atheist was that I could not reject evolution anymore. The evidence was so clear to me. It was like, there's no way it's not true. And I had to accept it. Because I wanted Islam to be right. I wanted Islam to be right, and I was forced to see that it's not. There's no way that it's right. It's completely wrong. I wanted it to be right, but it wasn't. I was trying to look at it in a way that it was right. It was wrong. I had to accept that. And once I was comfortable with that—"All right, it's wrong!"—I'm gonna just accept that it's wrong and treat it like it's wrong. And I feel that that's what all rational people should do. But I totally understand that not everyone can do that.

In his responses, Ismail alternated quickly between affirmation and refusal. His acceptance that nothing can contravene natural law led the flow of his thoughts to atheism, which is the consequence of his assent to the truth of evolution, which meant, for him, rejecting Islamic practices and a Muslim identity in addition to rejecting belief in God. He does not "have an ideology" because that implies a frame that distorts or gets in the way of his perception of reality.[1] Instead, he "see[s] the world for what it is." Ismail is describing a conversion process in which he cannot separate his rejection of what he once believed from an affirmation of what he now knows is true. If Ismail has converted (or deconverted), then what has he become?

Believing is the fundamental paradox for nonbelievers. Ambivalence like Ismail's was common among secular people I met during my fieldwork, as it is among secular people I meet all the time. Early on in my research, before I had gotten used to the ongoing debate over what secular people should call themselves, a man named Roger corrected my calling him and others "nonbelievers." "We're not nonbelievers," he told me curtly. "We're believers, and we believe in lots of things, like humanism." I met Roger in 2012, in Latham, New York, where I was spending the weekend at the annual conference of the American Ethical Union. I understood later that he corrected me because he wanted me to avoid a misconception that people often have about members of Ethical Culture. Like many others in his movement, Roger identifies as religious. Speaking to a researcher, he wanted to disassociate himself from antireligious "atheists." He even explained this to me in our conversation, but I failed to understand him at the time and was surprised to encounter my confusion in my field notes when looking at them years later to write this book. Though he admitted that there are many atheists who are members of Ethical Culture, the group usually thinks about itself as a religion.[2] Participants in the Ethical Culture movement try to avoid language that frames them in the negative and makes them unlike other religious people. Roger does not believe in God, but perhaps if I had asked him if he were a "nontheist," he would have assented. I discovered later that many in the Ethical Culture movement prefer this term to "atheist" because they consider atheists too negative, too combative, and too certain in their ontological beliefs. Throughout that weekend in upstate New York, I felt a strong push and pull that was new to me but would become familiar.

In many ways, Ismail and Roger are on the same page. They are both naturalists, neither believes in a person-like God, and both are rigorous empiricists who think science is the best way of knowing the world. In a sense, they share "beliefs," or in other terms, they share many ideas about what is real and how to know whether something is true. And yet, if we take their word for it, Ismail is a nonbeliever who does not believe in anything, and Roger is not a nonbeliever at all. Dismissing their claims as merely rhetoric or confusion can seem to settle their ambivalence, but it fails to recognize their struggle with the secular paradox and its generative persistence. A philosopher could hope to resolve their dispute through rational argumentation and then move on,[3] but an empirical scholar must confront their debate ad infinitum because no attempt has succeeded in convincing all nonbelievers to agree.

The organized nonbelievers I spent time with are clever, read a lot, and engage in debate for fun, but their best attempts to convince one another of a particular perspective or to adopt a collective label only lead to more divisions.[4] In short, if we decide, here and now, that Ismail in fact has beliefs or that Roger does not, we only *appear* to have resolved the secular paradox. The aim of this chapter, like the aim of this book, is to describe this paradox and its effects. Though perhaps a deeper understanding of this paradox will change how some of its readers relate to their secular identities and the Christian inheritance in which they emerge, it cannot do much to change their constitutive conditions.[5]

At issue, of course, is what I and others mean by the term "belief" but also what it is to believe. The framework of "belief" assumes a lot about people, their existence as individuals with distinct wills or souls, and the importance of the things their individual minds assert to the people around them. The anthropologist Joel Robbins draws a useful distinction between believing *in* and believing *that*.[6] To believe in something is to trust in it and rely on it. Believing that something is true means asserting that it describes reality accurately, though it also connotes that the belief rests on faith rather than empirical evidence. In Christian cultures, in particular, believing *in* and believing *that* are often conflated, such as in the phrase "I believe in God." The nonbelievers I spent time with usually reserve the preposition "in" for claims about values or ethics, and in general, I found nonbelievers much more willing to announce what they "believe *in*" than what they "believe" is true or real. Roger told me he believes in humanism, and Ismail, still distancing himself from belief, told me what he aspires to believe in:

> I told you I don't believe in anything. I would like to believe in some things. I would like to believe that humans can get over their primitive tribal differences, but they're not ready for that. Not even white people are ready for that right now. Muslims are far, far back. They're not any-

where close. So I feel that there's value of human—I struggle finding the words—human progress on planet Earth. It's always been going up. I'm not a pessimistic person. I see the bigger picture, and the bigger picture is that civilization has always prevailed.

Ismail accepts *that* nothing contravenes natural law, and he believes *that* evolution is true. Ismail's beliefs *in* whiteness and civilization are just as important and revealing. They are also complicated, especially given that Ismail is not white and was born and raised in Egypt. Beliefs in things like secular purity, critical thinking, and the danger of myth inform what it means to be secular, though they do not define it. Those who want to understand secular people must take all of these beliefs seriously, which is what this chapter does.

Accepting claims like Ismail's—that nonbelievers do not believe—is tempting in part because it provides a way to avoid generalizations and false claims to homogeneity. Not all nonbelievers believe in the same things or believe that the same things are true, but this does not mean that they have no beliefs. Thinking about the beliefs of Christians, Muslims, or Buddhists demonstrates this well. Despite efforts like creedal statements, punishments for heresy, and initiatory practices like baptism, there is no one value or proposition that unites all those who claim membership in any of these religions.[7] High-stakes debates about who is in and who is out are common among insiders and outsiders alike.[8] The inability to define a group of people perfectly with an elegant phrase or two about what they believe should not prevent us from trying to understand the beliefs that members of these religions espouse and possess, especially when they are part of communities that regulate true and false beliefs.[9] The same is true for nonbelievers. Their active relationships among one another produce networks, intellectual and material, that studies like this one can identify and map. Nonbelievers unify themselves in their collective efforts to believe correctly, form communities, create rituals, convert the religious, and uphold a tradition.

Secular people's relationship to belief reflects the push and pull of the secular paradox. They must emphasize what they share but also how they differ from religious believers. The Freedom From Religion Foundation, which is one of the most vocally antireligious groups in the United States, has in recent years sponsored several billboard campaigns that include a quote from a secular person, along with a head shot, the person's full name, and their occupation. An aerospace engineer in Ohio named Dave Huntsman appears next to the statement, "I believe in science, reason and secular values." A retired teacher in Chicago named Mary Schulatz declares, "I believe in reason and logic!" Another billboard features three students from the University of Akron next to the words, "We don't believe in any gods," and one featuring two sisters from North Carolina announces, "We put all our faith in science."[10] A billboard from an earlier campaign that emulated the style of illuminated manuscripts took a more antagonistic stance: "Praise Darwin / Evolve beyond belief." Strategic phrases like these are secular people's response to their constitutive paradox. Understanding secular people's ambivalent relationship to belief is key to understanding the work that belief does for and on nonbelievers. Paying attention to what they believe does not assume, however, that they all share the exact same beliefs. It neither invalidates what they consider true and real simply by calling it "belief" nor assumes that the beliefs they hold cohere into a perfectly rational system. There are differences of belief among and within secular people, and attending to these beliefs is crucial for understanding their unique challenges.

Because of the role that belief plays in bounding the identities of secular people and setting the conditions of membership in their communities, beliefs are both hugely important and fervidly disavowed among those who join groups for nonbelievers. Really understanding nonbelievers requires acknowledging their ambivalence and their ambiguity, as well as the work they do to try to resolve it. This chapter looks closely at the range of beliefs that nonbelievers affirm without dismissing their insistence on not believing. Ismail's claim that he does not believe is just as important as Roger's claim to share beliefs with his fellow members of Ethical Culture. What emerges from this investigation is a set of beliefs, affirmative and negative, that hang together in various combinations and establish the boundaries of being secular today.

In the next section, I show that beliefs matter a lot to organized nonbelievers even when they say they do not. The beliefs they share can remain unspoken, but when a group member crosses the line and espouses beliefs the group deems inconsistent with secularism, they are censured in tacit and overt ways. In the next few sections, I show how nonbelievers identify according to a range of belief-centric labels, which when viewed as a constellation, outline the set of beliefs that nonbelievers usually hold. I discuss the most popular labels that secular Americans use to identify themselves to describe what each emphasizes and thus to illuminate the various ways organized nonbelievers rally around what they share. As secular people learn these and other terms, they become experts in a specialized language that helps them refine what they believe and systematize a collectively shared secular worldview.

Beliefs Matter to Nonbelievers

The core belief that matters to nonbelievers is belief in God. Despite the preposition, believing *in* God usually means believing *that* God is real. Nonbelievers are defined by the refusal of this assertion, either actively, as a rejection, or more passively, as the absence of assent.[11] Still, not believing in God is different from identifying as a nonbeliever and quite different from joining groups for nonbelievers. For instance, during the first week of a large, lecture-based course on religion and politics that I teach at the University of California, Santa Barbara, I ask students to complete an anonymous survey, and I present the results of the survey in charts and graphs that compare the students with the rest of California and the whole of the United States. The survey asks follow-up questions to encourage students to clarify what they mean when they say that they believe in God, that they do not, or that they are not sure. In the fall of 2018, more than half of the students who stated that they do not believe in God clarified that they "believe in a higher power or spiritual force, but not God." Though these survey results are not scientifically valid samples of the American public, they provide a useful jumping-off point for more ethnographic inquiry. Conversing with students during and after class, I learned, unsurprisingly, that some of those who responded that they do not believe in God consider themselves "spiritual," and they understand a "higher power" as a real force in the world. Others who affirm a higher power consider themselves secular, and they want some way to explain how little control they feel over their lives and to express that there is meaning in the universe. They might not believe *that* a "higher power" or "spiritual force" is real, but they believe *in* them all the same. I return to this tension between believing *that* and believing *in* later in this chapter by focusing on what nonbelievers say they lose when the empirical validity of truth propositions becomes paramount.

Some of the students who turn to the language of a "higher power" are struggling to describe their thoughts and feelings through the concepts of their Christian-centered cultural inheritance. Their struggles echo the ambivalence of secular people who routinely frame themselves in Christian terms even when refusing Christian answers.[12] For example, about one in five people who identified as atheists in a 2017 survey conducted by Pew Research said they believe in "a higher power or spiritual force in the universe."[13] "Higher power" language can provide nonbelievers who are not strongly secular with a vague but humble response to questions about belief in God and the composition of the universe. I have found this nonliteral use of "higher power" to be common among my students and in my largely secular social milieu. Most organized nonbelievers are averse to "higher power" language, however. This aversion has even spurred the creation of an entire group. James Christopher founded Secular Organizations for Sobriety (SOS) in 1985 as an alternative to Alcoholics Anonymous in order to avoid AA's insistence that recovery requires dependence on a "higher power."[14] For decades, SOS has made its home in the Los Angeles branch of the Center for Inquiry, the largest nonbeliever organization in the country.

Though discussions of a higher power rarely arose during my fieldwork, they usually marked a boundary that nonbelievers refused to cross. For example, a young man named Aditya told me that one of the things he likes about a meditation center he goes to is that they never mention a higher power. Sometimes "higher power" references were more ambivalent, however, like when a man named Hassan told me about the criteria he uses to decide who can join a group for ex-Muslims. Because of concerns about the safety of their members, Hassan and others act as gatekeepers for entry to the group. They want to ensure that everyone involved is sufficiently secular. "Our group is nontheistic," he told me. "So that's the limit. You can believe in a higher power, but if you believe in a religion or a personal God, we're not comfortable with that." Immediately after telling me this, Hassan talked about a man who is a recovering alcoholic with a relationship to a God-like figure he imagines as a higher power. After he attended a meeting, group leaders decided he would not be a good fit and chose to exclude him. Hassan concluded, "We draw the boundary at nontheistic people."

The point of Hassan's story is similar to the lesson I learned from my students: sometimes "higher power" language can map onto a secular ontology or epistemology, but sometimes not. To be acceptable among organized nonbelievers, a higher power needs to be more metaphor than reality. Very secular people know the difference, and they police it by having a coherent, collective understanding of which beliefs are sufficiently secular and which are not. When nonbelievers join groups for secular people, they begin to become more secular. They try, consciously and unconsciously, to refine and systematize their beliefs into a worldview that they share with one another. During conversations, nonbelievers often told me how becoming involved with a secular community or secular activism changed how they think. When I was talking to a woman named Shalette about growing up in a Black nationalist household, she reflected on these changes:

> My mother, who raised me and my brothers to be critical thinkers, told us at one point that if we brought home someone white or if we turned out to be gay, she would disown us. So for a while I thought homosexuality was a sin even though I wasn't Christian. I thought there was something wrong with it. It was against nature, or it was anti-life. It was designed for population control. Me being openly atheist helped me understand that the evidence on homosexuality shows that it's natural, it's innate. It also helped me understand and unlearn a lot of the indoctrination I was taught.

In the larger conversation, Shalette was explaining how grateful she is for her upbringing but also how much she appreciates her Black atheist community. They understand where she comes from, and they can help her think in ways that are more aligned with science and evidence—which in the example she gave meant changing her mind about homosexuality.

Systematizing a worldview is difficult, probably impossible work, and leaders of nonbeliever groups often act as shepherds, helping people become more thorough in their secularism and letting them know when certain beliefs are unacceptable. Hassan made this point during our conversation:

> One thing we try to do, we sort of encourage rationalism. Things you're bringing up should be grounded in reality or scientific fact. But that isn't a requirement. Everybody has a right to believe or live their lives. If you're into alternative healing and crystal healing, we're not thought police or anything like that. We do have people who are into those kinds of things, but the only thing we tell them when they join is that a lot of people are scientifically minded, so if you bring up these ideas that aren't scientifically based, people will point out why they're wrong and have that conversation. So it's up to you if you bring it up. If you don't bring it up, nobody cares. It's not something we enforce one way or the other.

Like many of the group leaders I spoke with, Hassan emphasized that his group has no creed and no strict requirement for entry. They are not the "thought police." In practice, however, they encourage particular ways of thinking, and they repeatedly emphasize evidence, science, and rationality. This need to defend freedom of thought while encouraging secularism arises from secular people's inherently awkward relationship with belief, as well as their aversion to the top-down authority and groupthink they associate with religion.

Over the course of my field research, I got to know a woman named Tanya. She works as both a group leader and a university chaplain, and she identifies as a religious humanist. During one of our conversations, she wanted to emphasize that her group does not make distinctions based on belief:

> I think the beauty of being a nontheistic religion of ethics is that the emphasis is not on belief; the emphasis is on behavior. Now if you were to take a survey, the odds are great that Ethical Culturists would be atheists, humanists, or agnostics. Or if they had a theistic belief, the odds are that it would be more metaphorical and poetic. It would not be literal. Then that's the case of so-called believers in mainline Protestant denominations today. . . . It's interesting to know what people believe, but that's never been our emphasis.

I found the same disavowed exclusivity in practice among members of Tanya's Ethical Culture community. As in Hassan's group, there are subtle and overt ways in which the group creates belief-based barriers to inclusion. For example, a member of her group named Myles considers these barriers the reason for the group's decline in membership: "If they would just accept people [from] other religions, openly accept [them]—believe what you want to believe and come on in; it doesn't matter—I believe they could fill this place up." Myles admires the approach he sees some Unitarian Universalist (UU) churches taking, where belief appears unimportant.[15] He thinks the secularist culture of his group forces people to hide their heterodox beliefs: "There's a lot of hidden religious people in Ethical Culture, I believe. They still have a belief in a higher power, but they do not put it out there for people. And they don't talk about it. Some may say they're 'spiritual.' That's a commonly used word."[16] Group members know when a belief contradicts the accepted secular worldview, and they keep it to themselves.

Though Tanya deemphasizes belief, she disagrees with Myles's prescription for recruitment. Later in the same conversation, we discussed her role as an adviser to a campus student group. I asked her about one of the group's members, a student I spoke with who identifies as spiritual and told me that all paths lead to truth. I wanted to know how Tanya handles students who have unorthodox beliefs. She told me that she allows the students to determine the criteria for membership, but as someone who moderates some of their conversations, she draws a line:

> It's what I call the "woo-woo line." Because there's a lot out there now in terms of science and understanding energy, but I think there's a difference between [that and] understanding energy with evidence, like the recent verification of Einstein's theory of gravity, which is so exciting. So maybe there's a little bit of, "Oh, see, it's not proven! There are these waves! There is this energy." But it's not magic. It's really important not to cross over into woo-woo land. I think that's where my red flag goes up, when I hear something like that. I have both feet firmly planted on the ground.... So if I hear something going off in that direction, I say, no, we're not going down that rabbit hole.

The beliefs of nonbelievers are complex and layered. Even though Tanya identifies as religious, she draws hard lines about the beliefs that group members can espouse. Like most other secular groups, Ethical Culture expressly avoids the affirmation of a creed and prides itself on freethinking. Yet as Myles observes and Tanya demonstrates, their groups depend on belief-based barriers to remain exclusively for nontheistic people. They police the boundaries of a naturalist worldview and shame members who cross the "woo-woo line." Nearly all of the secular people I interviewed remain within these boundaries, but a few, like Myles, told me they have private beliefs that cross them, which they keep to themselves because they know they want to observe their group's norms. This layered heterodoxy demonstrates the limits of believing too much in the analytic efficacy of belief, but it also demonstrates the degree to which belief structures the lives of nonbelievers and remains important to analyze. Though most secular people disavow believing, they subtly reproduce an orthodoxy that they and their communities can never fully enforce.

Labeling a Secular Worldview

Accepting that beliefs matter to nonbelievers, the question then becomes, Which are acceptable, and which are not? Though nonbelievers are an identitarian group that has successfully organized a lobbying outfit, a political action committee, and an international aid organization, they struggle with an unusual amount of semantic ambivalence. The secular paradox creates a situation in which secular people are not religious, but they nonetheless share beliefs about reality and how best to know it. Whether to define themselves in negative or positive terms is an inexorable dispute. Their ambivalence toward belief stems from their need to distance themselves from religion despite recognizing that they largely agree with one another about many fundamental questions. This ambivalence structures the constellation of labels they use to describe their worldviews and, by extension, who they are. Because the labels they use bear the sediment of debates over what beliefs they share and how they differ from religion, a closer look at nonbelievers' most common self-descriptors elaborates their closely related secular worldviews and sheds light on the fault lines that emerge from the generative contradictions inherent to the secular paradox.

Most of the people I spoke with who run organizations for nonbelievers downplay differences among the most common labels. Many have worked for several nonbeliever organizations throughout their careers and participated in coalitions of secular groups. They see more coherence than differences among nonbelievers. When I interviewed a secular activist named Tim who works for a small nonbeliever group with a national presence, he rattled off an impressive synthesis of labels and their meanings:

> All these labels are overlapping. I don't know any secular humanists who aren't also atheists. I don't know any humanists who aren't also freethinkers. I don't know any atheists who don't have some humanist values. I'm an atheist, an agnostic, a humanist, and a freethinker. I'm an atheist because there are no gods. I'm an agnostic because I'm not sure, and no one is. I'm a humanist because my values come from mutual responsibility for others and from recognizing that there's no supernatural power. Freethought means being independent of an organized authority.

Tim's organization encourages nonbelievers to give to charitable organizations and volunteer their time, so he thinks a lot about how to describe the values that secular people share. Before starting his organization, he "repeatedly came across this need of having some sort of systematic, collective way for humanists to express their values. This is something the religious have—a really good thing—to systematically and on a regular basis express their worldviews in a positive way." He sees charitable giving as an active way to express shared values and beliefs—a collective perspective on what they believe *in* and what they believe *is* true. "The cohesion that a group achieves [through charitable work] is incalculable," he told me. "We're making an impact but also providing the freethought community with a way to cohere around positive values." Tim recognizes that nonbelievers can fracture easily by emphasizing only their shared differences from religious people. He used the term "worldview" throughout our conversation, and he switched easily among a wide range of labels when describing himself and the nonbelievers he tries to organize.

An activist named Charles who works for the Secular Student Alliance made a similar case for a shared secular worldview, despite ostensible divisions: "I'm an atheist because there is no God or gods. I'm an agnostic because the question of a transcendental creator can't have a verifiable answer. I'm a humanist in terms of how I live my life and in my basic values. I'm a naturalist in terms of thinking about how to understand the natural world. These are all useful terms, and they describe different things. They're not mutually exclusive." Nonbelievers often have a label they consider primary even if they are comfortable with several others. For instance, Charles told me that despite working for a group with "secular" in its name, he prefers the term "atheist" to describe himself because it makes a stronger impression in public and "it's just better to come out and say it." Though Charles has a term he prefers for practical reasons, in his words, the other terms are "not mutually exclusive."

Chad, who is a prominent donor to secularist causes, echoed other organized nonbelievers I spoke with when he described the relationship among these identities as a developmental process:

> There's an evolution most people go through. You start as a skeptic, asking questions. Then you don't really find those answers. That leads you to agnosticism. "I don't know if there's a God or not." But oftentimes you still believe in one—kind of a theistic agnostic. Then that becomes, "Wait a minute, I don't just not know. I don't actually believe." This leads to atheism and then to humanism, which is a philosophy and life stance beyond lack of belief.

Chad told me that he uses a range of labels to describe himself depending on the context. I found the views of leaders like Tim, Charles, and Chad to be common among everyday members of the groups I visited throughout the country. No one I met was committed exclusively to a single term. The following sections explore the various connotations of each of the major labels that nonbelievers use to describe what they do or do not believe.

Freethinker

"Freethought" is a term that nonbelievers sometimes use to express their opposition to dogmatism and to emphasize their autonomy and rationality. It also identifies a tradition of secular activism and institution building. Those who adopt the term assume that religion constrains freedom of thought, so it should be avoided or eliminated. They also encourage "critical thinking" to emphasize skepticism and empirical testing or falsification. When I attended a symposium on African American humanism at the Borough of Manhattan Community College in 2012, one of the speakers defined "freethought" as "thought free of religious dogma." Tim described freethinking as "being independent of an organized authority," and the executive director of a different organization described his "average member" as "a freethinking person, generally—a nonjoiner, individualist, seeker." Chad, the same prominent donor, told me that "freethinker" is his preferred self-identification, and he joked, "If we have any dogma, it's that there is no dogma." He also warned that "when you have no doubt and don't question, you risk becoming a fundamentalist and blowing up planes." In his worldview, freethought is an antidote to the dangers of religious pollution, such as dogmatism, groupthink, and irrationality. Doubt and freethinking are means of purification.

Freethought first became an intellectual and social movement in the United States in the nineteenth century, when the term had a broader meaning than it does today.[17] Historian of nineteenth-century freethought Susan Jacoby captures the term's breadth in a definition worth quoting at length:

> Often defined as a total absence of faith in God, freethought can better be understood as a phenomenon running the gamut from the truly antireligious—those who regarded all religion as a form of superstition and wished to reduce its influence in every aspect of society—to those who adhered to a private, unconventional faith revering some form of God or Providence but at odds with orthodox religious authority. American freethinkers have included deists, who, like many of the founding fathers, believed in a "watchmaker God" who set the universe in motion but subsequently took no active role in the affairs of men; agnostics; and unabashed atheists.[18]

Another historian of nineteenth-century freethought, Sidney Warren, agrees: "Freethinkers in the United States were hardly a closely knit group in an ideological sense."[19] When Horace Seaver spoke at the Freethinkers' Convention of 1878, held in Watkins, New York, he declared freethought a big tent: "whether the Freethinkers are in western New York or in Massachusetts, they are one family—the whole of us, whether Spiritualists, Infidels, Liberals, Atheists, and (perhaps I might say it) Christians."[20] Seaver was the editor of one of the leading freethought journals in the United States, the *Investigator*. Later at the same convention, he insisted again on unity: "If they are only Liberal, in favor of free thought, free speech, and free press, if they will give you and me equal rights, let us shake hands with all of them, and press forward like a band of brothers and sisters in the maintenance of universal mental liberty."[21] Though inclusive, Seaver's remarks also reveal fault lines among freethinkers. If Spiritualists and Christians were already included in the freethought fold, then Seaver would not have needed to make such an effort to include them. Still, freethought was a broader movement prior to World War I than it is today. Spiritualist mediums are not welcome among twenty-first-century freethinkers.

Though the term "freethinkers" fell out of widespread use by the middle of the twentieth century, it is now commonplace among secular activists and people who join secular communities. One group in particular has laid claim to its contemporary usage: the Freedom From Religion Foundation. When I spoke with one of the group's leaders at its offices in Madison, Wisconsin, she credited FFRF with reviving "freethinker" in the 1970s: "We popularized the term. I think FFRF is responsible for bringing that back into the lexicon." Since 1984, FFRF has published a newsletter titled *Freethought Today*, and the organization's leaders see "freethought" and "freethinking" as central to their mission. One of FFRF's cofounders and its current copresident, Annie Laurie Gaylor, published a volume of writings by "women freethinkers" in 1997, which preceded by several years the publication of Jacoby's more widely read trade-press history of American freethought.[22]

References to freethought and definitions of its cognate terms abound in FFRF's literature. For instance, in the 2011 announcement for its annual scholarship essay contest, FFRF instructed applicants, "Describe a moment that made you proud to be a freethinker (atheist/agnostic/nonbeliever)," and quoted a dictionary definition as "one who forms his or her opinion about religion based on reason rather than faith, tradition or authority."[23] FFRF's Greater Sacramento chapter gives a similar definition on its subpage of the national organization's website: "We are freethinkers: people who form opinions about religion and spirituality independent of tradition, authority or established belief, in favor of rational inquiry."[24] I encountered phrases like these throughout my field research, whether at an atheist convention, a meeting of a campus student group, or a meetup at a bar. They are part of a secular vocabulary that outlines what nonbelievers should avoid or embrace. In FFRF's framework—and in the worldview of organized nonbelievers—faith and established belief are antithetical to autonomy and rationality. Dogma, tradition, and authority are all forms of religious pollution that pose a danger to freethinkers' secular purity.

Because "freethinker" used to have a more capacious meaning, some secular people use it as a polite self-identifier, in sharp contrast to FFRF's antireligious usage. When I asked Jonathon, the head of a major atheist organization, what he thought of the "freethinker" label, he told me that he considers it "a broad term" with a "softer connotation," used by "atheists who don't like the word 'atheist.'" He also told me that his group "has always been the marines of the freethought movement. Not all atheists are marines. Some atheists are accommodationists. Some atheists want to work with religion to defeat hunger or the hypocrisy in the government. That's all good. That's not what we do. We're the hard-asses. We're the edge of the sword." Another activist, Jim, who has worked in various roles at two humanist organizations, expressed a similar opinion over beers one night in Buffalo, New York. He told me that "freethinker" has replaced "agnostic" as the preferred term for atheists trying not to offend believers. Jim is at least partly right. During my field research, I occasionally heard nonbelievers use "freethinker" as a gentler or more polite term. As for FFRF, one of its leaders told me that the group "doesn't care what you call yourself," but she followed up by referencing a survey of FFRF members in which around three-quarters identified as "atheist" and the other quarter "agnostic." "Freethinker" can do a lot of work, but in the twenty-first century, it labels a distinctly secular worldview.

This secular vocabulary and the assumptions that undergird it are just as common among organized nonbelievers who do not self-describe as freethinkers as they are among those who do. According to a prominent leader named Rich who identifies primarily as a secular humanist, "freethinker" is "the old-time term." He told me that his secular humanist organization "believes strongly in individual autonomy," "rejects religious dogma as a source of ethics," and seeks "to remove any influence of dogma or religion on public policy." Greg, a nontheistic religious humanist who is a member of the Unitarian Universalist Association, uses "freethinking" and "freethinker" in unusually inclusive ways. His denomination has strong Christian roots, but it does not require its members to adhere to a Christian creed and openly accepts those who identify with other traditions.[25] Greg is part of a national network of secular activists, and his organization, the UU Humanists, participates with other nontheistic groups in the Secular Coalition for America, a secular lobbying organization founded in 2002. As an avowedly religious humanist, he fits awkwardly at times within an activist movement that opposes religion. In our conversation over lunch at a restaurant below Rockefeller Center, he used a range of phrases that included the term "freethinker" in order to cut across the religious/secular divide, such as "freethinker movement," "local humanist freethought groups," "humanistic freethinking," "freethinking and nonbelief," "freethinking groups, religious or secular," "freethinker atheist groups," and "the secular movement, or the freethinker movement." Greg is well-read and knows how capacious the term "freethinker" was in the nineteenth century, so like Horace Seaver, he uses it to create a big tent that still emphasizes individual autonomy, skepticism, and rationality.

Like Tim, Greg used the term "worldview" throughout our conversation. Curious about the usage, I asked him whether he sees a difference between his worldview, which he considers secular and religious, and other religious worldviews. His response is fascinating:

> I don't think it is [like other religious worldviews]. In fact, I think it's got a dimension to it that other worldviews don't have. The primary defining characteristic of humanism is its monistic approach to reality. We really don't accept anything other than the reality we experience. We may not understand, and maybe some of it we'll never understand; but there's only one reality, and we're an integral part of it. There isn't another reality that created this reality. There isn't some other authority, some other entity, other than—the natural is super enough. We don't need the supernatural. So I think the fundamental thing is not whether you believe in God, because you can define monistically that God is everything there is, then you've got that problem there. What is important is that our life stance says that we are part of, evolutionarily, the last bud on an evolutionary tree. We are responsible for ourselves and what we do, our conditions.

That life stance gives us not only freedom but a complementary sense of responsibility that the other life stances don't have. "God's gonna take care of it"; "we're just pilgrims passing through"—that's an irresponsible way to look at it, and that's why we're destroying the planet, because we don't feel a sense of responsibility for being the universe becoming conscious of itself. Which is what we are. So I think it's a life stance. It has to do with living and not what happens before living or beyond living.

Greg explains his monistic cosmology by saying that there is only one world—the natural one—and he gives a progressive understanding of evolution in which humans are the most developed animals. He says that his worldview differs from other religious worldviews because it is a "life stance," which for him means a focus on the material life of this world. For Greg, other religious worldviews demand obedience to an authority outside the individual self; his worldview emphasizes autonomy but also responsibility. He sees himself as both religious and a freethinker, but he also sees his secular religion as unique and superior to other religions.

Humanist: Religious and Secular

"Humanism" is the most common term that organized nonbelievers use to signal shared values and a shared worldview. Some, like Roger, who choose "humanist" as their primary self-identifier refuse labels like "atheist" and "agnostic," which they see as merely negative. Luis, who organizes a monthly meetup for Hispanic atheists in a city in the Midwest, told me that one of the challenges he faces as an organizer is the wide variety of Hispanic nonbelievers who come to his meetings. He sees potential for humanism to help newcomers understand what they share:

> That's one of the reasons I'm starting to embrace humanism more. Because I think those are things that bring us together. If you just have the one thing that everyone's pretty certain we're all against—you don't like religion and how much it's permeating our political system and affecting policy—we can all talk about that. But beyond that, we've had so many different people come through the group. We've had Satanists come to the group. We've had Republican gun-toting people. We've had people that are very critical of religion, but they're very uncritical about other

things. They're talking about UFOs or about ghosts or "There's gotta be something out there." You realize that there are so many things that can divide you. So I'm always trying to find the thing that could be a glue for everyone that comes in. I think humanism is the way to go.

Another Hispanic humanist, Juan, began our conversation by talking about humanism and its power to affirm:

> We use a lot of words to describe people who are nonreligious, like the "nones," "freethinkers," "atheists," "agnostics," "secular," "humanist." But we use the word "humanist" because we feel that it's not just a rejection of religion. It's not just moving away from something. It's moving towards something. In our movement, we talk about humanism as claiming ownership of the values that religion has claimed [for itself], such as love, charity, and compassion. We believe that the human experience involves dealing with pain, dealing with joy, becoming stronger, learning. Religion is all of those things, plus God. We don't believe in God, but we believe that all the other things are [owned by] humanity. So that's why we use the word "humanism."

Juan used to be a Pentecostal youth minister, and now he wants to be a minister for secular people. He believes strongly in his worldview, including his ethics. He cares deeply about others, and he wants to help them. Like Tim, whose organization encourages nonbelievers to volunteer and donate to charity, Juan wants to show his fellow nonbelievers that they share a worldview and deeply held values that can guide their collective action and be a source of optimism and strength. Juan, however, says that he "can't create a humanism for everybody." Some humanists want to join a community, and others do not. Even among joiners, there are significant differences. Juan finds that most communities for nonbelievers are too culturally white to be welcoming to nonwhite people. I return to Juan in chapter 2, which focuses on community, in order to show how the whiteness of American secularism subtly excludes nonwhite secular people.

Like many other humanists I spoke with, Juan described his first encounter with humanism as a moment of self-discovery.[26] He realized that there is a name for what he already was. A woman named Sarah whom I met at the Secular Student Alliance conference in Columbus, Ohio, in 2012 described a similar self-realization. Two months after the conference, I interviewed her by phone to discuss her work at Camp Quest, a nonprofit that has created more than a dozen summer camps for secular children throughout the United States. Sarah told me that she has considered herself an atheist since she was thirteen, but she was unaware that people organized as atheists until she started graduate school at Ohio State University in 2003:

> I found out there's a whole group of people out there organized around the things I believe. I was amazed to find out that the conclusions I had come to on my own, others had, too. I didn't realize there were other people working on humanism. Humanism is atheism plus living an ethical life based on reason and compassion and being concerned about this world. I thought this was something I'd made up. Then I found out it has a history. There are all these other people who share these values.

"Humanism" provides many organized nonbelievers with a name for the presence they find latent in themselves and others; it labels a worldview that some secular people recognize has already been their own. I discuss this process more in chapter 4, which focuses on conversion. A concealed process of conversion and its later discovery stem from the secular paradox. Juan and Sarah have gone through a process of secular conversion without fully realizing it because they only perceived themselves *de*converting from their previous beliefs. They had acknowledged the negative half of their secularism but not the affirmative. When they first met people who have given names to the secular beliefs they share, they recognized those beliefs as theirs.

Because "humanism" names a worldview and set of values, it appears more religion-like than "atheism," even though both terms work as self-identifiers for nonbelievers who share many of the same beliefs. A conversation I had with a university chaplain named Jack provides a good example of what humanism enables but also the dangers it poses to secular purity. Though Jack is a good fundraiser and institution builder, he faced difficulties in his first few years on the job. He described for me an early breakthrough communicating with students on his campus:

> I put together this flier [on humanism], and I think it said something to the effect of, "It's a form of spirituality for the nonreligious." One of the officers of the [student] group got so angry [about the word "spirituality"] that it caused a rift between me and the first year of students. And yet, that spring, one of the freshmen spoke up at a meeting and said, "Wouldn't it be cool if nonreligious people had some kind of ceremony, like when you were born or maybe when you were thirteen and you were becoming more of a mature person, and it was a ceremony to mark what your values were as a family, but it wasn't religious, and there wasn't praying to God? It'd be interesting." And I pulled her aside afterwards and said, "That's kind of what I work on. A lot of us refer to that as 'humanism.'" She said, "Oh, cool," and I took her out to lunch and talked more. I feel like that was the first really good moment.

Jack reached for the term "spirituality" when making his flier because he wanted to help the students understand the affirmative side of secularism. He now knows that he needs to choose his words carefully because some terms are overdetermined by the secular paradox and they obscure his intentions. Humanism's proximity to religion threatens to pollute it, so Jack and others have to draw sharp lines in order to maintain its purity.

The history of humanism makes religious pollution difficult to avoid.[27] Organized humanism in the United States grew primarily out of the Unitarian Church, through the efforts of nontheistic ministers like John H. Dietrich, Curtis W. Reese, and Charles Francis Potter.[28] Humanist Unitarians wanted to remain within their existing religious framework but remove the supernatural.[29] Dietrich began talking about "humanism" around 1915, shortly before becoming minister of the First Unitarian Society of Minneapolis—a community I introduce in more depth in chapter 5. Dietrich borrowed the term from an article that appeared in the British Ethical Culture journal, *Ethical World*, which derived it from Auguste Comte's nontheistic Religion of Humanity (shortened to "humanism").[30] Unitarians were the first to formally institutionalize humanism, initially within their churches and later outside their denomination. In 1929, Potter broke with his Unitarian congregation and founded the first independent humanist community in the United States: the First Humanist Society of New York.[31] In 1933, Reese,

Dietrich, and Potter were among those who published the first "Humanist Manifesto," which in clear terms describes humanism as "religious."[32] The manifesto declares that the world is "self-existing and not created," denies the existence of the supernatural, and endorses "the scientific spirit and method." It also criticizes the "existing acquisitive and profit-motivated society" and argues that "man . . . alone is responsible for the realization of the world of his dreams, that he has within himself the power for its achievement."[33] Whether religious humanism can be purified of its bad religiosity or whether humanism is sufficiently different from religion to be pure of its pollution is an ongoing debate that continues to divide humanists.

One of the most significant breaks *within* humanism took place in the 1970s and culminated in the founding of the Council for Democratic and Secular Humanism (CODESH) by the SUNY Buffalo philosophy professor Paul Kurtz. Kurtz worked for the American Humanist Association (AHA) for more than a decade as editor of its magazine, the *Humanist*. Facing accusations of financial malfeasance, he parted ways with the group in 1978.[34] According to Glen, a man I interviewed who worked for AHA at the time of Kurtz's departure, many of the group's prominent donors and around half of its membership left to join CODESH, which was the first organization for avowedly *secular* humanists. Prior to CODESH, religious and secular humanists who considered themselves nontheists had been welcome in the same organizations, and like today, many humanists did not qualify their humanism as *religious* or *secular*.[35] Humanists who append the adjective "secular" to describe their humanism do so to emphasize their nonreligiosity and to express a desire to avoid forms of nontheistic humanism that they consider too religious.

Though there is little evidence that very many people called themselves "secular humanists" in the 1970s, the nascent Religious Right made "secular humanism" into a powerful bogeyman.[36] For instance, in 1978, the same year that Kurtz left AHA, John Whitehead and John Conlan published an article in the *Texas Tech Law Review* that argued that secular humanism is a religion and violates the Establishment Clause of the US Constitution.[37] In their view, secular humanism has superseded Protestantism as the de facto established religion in the United States, and the country needs to return to its Christian roots. They blamed the nation's highest court for aiding this new establishment: "The Supreme Court has adopted a concept of religion which is tantamount to Secular Humanism's position of the centrality of man, because the basis of both is the deification of man's reason."[38]

Two years later, the same year that Kurtz founded CODESH, Tim LaHaye published *The Battle for the Mind*, an influential text among politically mobilized evangelicals. LaHaye built on evangelical theologian Francis A. Schaeffer's criticisms of "humanism" to argue that "secular humanism" had nearly been destroyed with the fall of the Roman Empire but was preserved by the transmission of Aristotle through St. Thomas Aquinas.[39] According to a man I interviewed named Dave, who worked with Kurtz for decades, Kurtz founded CODESH to take back the label for those who aver it: "Secular humanism was being widely criticized by people on the Religious Right, and nobody was speaking up for it." In his break from AHA, Kurtz realized an opportunity to unify the relatively few humanists who emphasized the secularity of their humanism with the larger subset of Americans who opposed the Religious Right and its goal of making American government more Christian.

Kurtz and other humanists may have wanted to secularize humanism in part because of AHA's decision to make itself more explicitly religious. In 1968, in the wake of a series of lawsuits in which Ethical Culture societies received recognition as religious groups from state and federal courts, AHA filed to change its nonprofit status with the IRS from an educational 501(c)3 nonprofit to a religious nonprofit.[40] AHA stated that it made the change in order to enable its ordained clergy to legally solemnize weddings. It also benefited by no longer having to file Form 990, a financial-disclosure statement required for all secular tax-exempt nonprofits reporting over an amount of income set by the IRS. Today, far fewer humanists consider themselves religious, and those who do are affiliated primarily with groups like UU Humanists, the Society for Humanistic Judaism, and the American Ethical Union. When I spoke with AHA's leaders at its offices in Washington, DC, they told me that only 2 or 3 percent of their members identify as "religious" according to internal surveys. In 2007, AHA changed its tax status back to an educational organization, and leaders told me that they self-consciously embraced the term "atheism" in more of their publications.[41] An AHA leader named Jill described why the group made the change:

Back in the '60s and '70s, they had no problem calling humanism a religion because back then religion wasn't so extreme. There wasn't this extremist Christian Right and this extremist fundamentalist types of religion that were getting all the media attention. So the word "religion" was comfortable for people. It was just a belief system. Nowadays when you say "religion," you mean a belief in God. That's a requirement when you define religion. For a long time, humanism had passed as this sort of pseudoreligion: "We're not atheist, but we're not Christian. We're not these hard-core religious people." We needed to be really clear about our beliefs. We don't believe in God. We don't believe in supernaturalism. But we do believe in good, and we believe in ethics. One of the things that we had to do to fix that was change our tax-exempt status.

Because "humanism" remains a name for the worldview and values that many secular people share and want to affirm, it is more proximate to religion than "freethought," which indexes fierce independence, and "atheism," a more clearly negative appellation. Humanism's proximity to religion and its attendant ambiguity make it a persistent and generative site of conflict among secular people.

Atheist

If humanism affirms but also negates, then atheism negates but also affirms. Among organized nonbelievers, the difference between these isms is more a matter of emphasis than sharp distinction. I met many secular people who identify as both humanist and atheist, and like humanists, atheists can be more and less averse to religious pollution. As Jonathon told me when describing his group's role in the freethought movement, not all atheists "like the word 'atheist.'" Some are the "marines," and some "are accommodationists." Organized nonbelievers are acutely aware that "atheism" and "atheist" can do different types of work in different contexts, and they often reach for one label or another as a means to an end. Chad is a prominent donor I introduced earlier who is thoughtful about labels and what they mean in particular situations. He used a wide range of terms to describe himself in our conversation: "A lot of times I refer to myself as an atheist, but sometimes I refer to myself as a humanist, too. But people don't know what you mean, which is a challenge. Frankly, I'm an agnostic atheist humanist skeptic. I'm a freethinker." He defended atheism, in particular: "It's important to get out there and be the militant atheist. It's important for someone to get out there and say the things that might piss people off and be the truth."

With an array of terms available, Chad reaches for the term "atheist" to describe the activist work of confronting people with what he believes to be true, even if it makes them angry. Atheists, so named, have an antagonistic relationship with theists by expressly disavowing perhaps the most important aspect of a theistic ontology. Inherently, atheism dissents.[42] Especially when unqualified by the term "secular," humanism does not disagree with anyone in particular, so it can do different work. Chad and other secular people use "atheist" and "atheism" strategically. It helps them claim a long-disparaged identity and state directly how they differ from those who believe in a personal deity.[43]

Atheism does not negate the same way for everyone. For those who live among many secular people, atheism can seem banal in its lack of particularity. Several times throughout my research, I heard nonbelievers use the phrase, "Everyone is an atheist to someone else's gods," to demonstrate the limits of "atheism" as a descriptor for what they share with other secular people. Atheism, for them, merely negates a set of beliefs that few around them seem to hold. For other secular people, atheism indexes heresy and apostasy, so it possesses unique power. Using the term can announce a break that exceeds the imaginations of friends and family. A woman named Jacqueline told me that the two nonbeliever organizations that are most important to her focus expressly on atheism and have the term "atheists" in their names. Like other Black atheists I spoke with, Jacqueline said that many times in her life people have simply denied her existence: "People will say to me, 'You're Black. You can't be atheist.'" Her illegibility makes it important for her to announce in the clearest terms possible that she embodies what for some people is a contradiction.[44]

Shalette, whom I introduced earlier, told me a similar story when describing how important it is to build communities for Black nonbelievers: "Recently there was a Black woman at a conference where I was speaking in Atlanta who actually yelled at me in my face that she couldn't believe that as a Black woman, I would identify as an atheist.

[She said] I had a slave mentality, and I was a traitor to the community." Throughout several years of interviews and participant observation among secular people, I heard no stories like this from white nonbelievers. The experiences of Jacqueline and Shalette are part of a long history of assuming that Black people are innately religious.[45] Their rejection of religiosity is also part of this history and structured by the contradictions of the secular paradox.[46]

White Americans, and white men in particular, can more safely declare themselves atheists, which in a Christian-centered culture can have seriously negative social consequences. Sociologists Penny Edgell, Jacqui Frost, and Evan Stewart show that nonreligion is stigmatized in many contexts in the United States and that women and other marginalized groups are less likely to identify as atheists because they face greater risk of experiencing social stigma.[47] In the term's first usage in ancient Greece and for much of its history, "atheist" was a synonym for "heretic" rather than a neutral descriptor of someone who does not affirm the reality of a Christian-like god.[48] The early Christians called the Romans "atheists" for denying their God, and Romans called Christians "atheists" for denying their pantheon. In the wake of the Protestant Reformation, "atheist" was a common epithet for Lutherans and Catholics alike. Until the late eighteenth century, it was not a term that anyone used as a self-descriptor.[49] The white, well-to-do European men who first declared themselves "atheists" appropriated it as a flippant badge of honor.[50] Men like Baron d'Holbach and Denis Diderot are better known in the history of philosophy as the French materialists, a name that describes the ontology they affirm. "Atheism" continues to bear the ambiguity of epithet and coherent worldview. Though not everyone is willing to identify with terms that the prevailing culture has used to brand its bogeymen, when Jacqueline and Shalette reach for the term "atheist," they drag forth the sediment of this history and wield it like a weapon against a Christian-centered culture they want to reject. Embracing the social abrasiveness of the term "atheist" helps them be seen and heard.

The appropriation of the term "queer" in the 1980s is another largely successful attempt to take control of an epithet, though like "atheist," the term bears the traces of its older usage more obviously in some contexts than in others.[51] Degan Loren and Carol Rambo suggest understanding atheism's relationship to religion as a kind of queerness because religion is a normalizing discourse that structures atheism into a form of resistance.[52] Surely, there is something queer about a paradox. On the one hand, the history of atheism is very white and male because it is in part the history of the privilege to sarcastically embrace the persecutor's perspective and call oneself a heretic. Jacqueline knows she faces extra social stigma, but through sarcasm and irony, she blasphemes the Christian frame: "I'm out. I'm loud. I'm proud. I'm evangelical. In fact, I do use that word to describe myself. I'm an evangelical atheist."

On the other hand, women and nonwhite people have made important contributions to this history.[53] Observing how women and people of color face different struggles than white men who declare themselves secular helps explain why secularism has been so eminently white and male. In 2016, I attended a conference on women and secularism in Arlington, Virginia. The majority of the presentations focused on religion's reinforcement of patriarchy and its harmful effects on women, but some presenters turned their attention to the failings of the nonbeliever community. For instance, one of the presenters discussed the stereotype that "women are more naturally religious." She acknowledged that women are more religious, statistically, but debunked any natural origin by enumerating social causes like the patriarchal assumption that women are responsible for domestic morality, so they bear the burden of taking the family to church.[54] As a Black woman, Shalette combats secularist assumptions on at least two fronts. "Atheism is still seen as a white thing," she told me, "so it becomes important for the representation of this community to be shown. There are Blacks who are atheists and Blacks who are nonbelievers." To conceive secularism as inherently male or white erases the work that Black women like Shalette have dedicated their lives to—and have accomplished.

Understanding Black atheism sheds light on atheism in the broadest sense of the term. Assuming that atheism is distinctively white or male participates in a long refusal to recognize Black and other nonwhite forms of secularism. Throughout this book, I insist on calling attention to this diversity within secularism—racial, gender, and also religious—which undermines any attempt to reduce secularism to Protestantism, colonialism, imperialism, or whiteness. Doing so offers a more complete and thus better understanding of nonbelief, and it acknowledges the efforts of people like Shalette and Jacqueline who have fought for legibility and recognition. It is impossible to understand secularism without recognizing the unique experiences of atheists who are women and people of color—without including secularism's misfits.

Agnostic

Part of what makes atheism such a sharp barb to people who are not secular is its ontological certainty. In its everyday use, "atheism" is not merely an absence of evidence for theism. Calling oneself an "atheist" in the United States expressly denies the reality of a personal deity and makes that denial into a religion-related identity.[55] And yet the epistemological beliefs of most nonbelievers I met belie this ontological certainty. Over and over, I heard people identify as agnostics, sometimes as their primary identity and sometimes alongside a range of other labels, including "atheist." "Agnostic" can be a precise description of the limits of empiricism, or it can be a polite alternative to "atheist," like the way some people use "freethinker." I met with John, a now-former leader of a national organization, at his home in Altadena, California. A clear thinker who has written several books, John captured both senses of "agnostic" with a flip sarcasm typical of many people in the secular movement:

> I'm an atheist. I don't believe in God. The simplest distinction I make now, ontologically speaking, I'm an agnostic. As Huxley meant, it's unknowable. There's no experiment we're going to run to resolve the question. But no one's an agnostic behaviorally. You act as if there is or is not a God, or you act as if you do or don't belong to a religion. So to that extent, I'm an atheist. [It's] pretty straightforward actually, and people misinterpret it all the time. I always liked Stephen Colbert's comment: "Agnostics are just atheists without balls." Or my other favorite one is a bumper sticker I saw: "Militant agnostic. I don't know, and you don't either."

John is saying that in strict terms, he is an agnostic, though he lives like an atheist, as if there is no God. Because he is an empiricist committed to the scientific method, he relies on sense data as the epistemological ground for his worldview. Science can falsify a hypothesis when it finds empirical evidence to the contrary, but it cannot assert that something is universally true or real in the way that one can logically deduce a conclusion from its premises or that God can ground a universal truth. Though the outspoken atheism of Jacqueline and Shalette makes Colbert's testicle joke flop, John is trying to express the idea that agnostics are hedging against the bolder claim of atheism. John sees this hedge in probabilistic terms because strict empiricism and application of the scientific method foreclose the possibility of knowing for certain that anything, including God, does or does not exist. Other agnostics are the type that Colbert's joke satirically derides. Their epistemological humility enables them to avoid direct disagreement with those who believe in a personal God, which in turn lowers their exposure to the risk of social stigma. In short, agnosticism can be a measured epistemological position or a polite and cautious way to signal nonbelief.

For John and other strict empiricists, claims to ontological reality are always a matter of faith. The Huxley John references is Thomas, the grandfather of the more famous Aldous. Thomas Huxley was a zoologist and fierce advocate for Darwin's theory of evolution, a subject he debated with Samuel Wilberforce at Oxford University in 1860. The elder Huxley coined the term "agnosticism" in 1869, though he did not elaborate its meaning in writing until twenty years later, in 1889.[56] He did so to contribute to the nascent discourse about labels among nonbelievers, which continues today. Huxley reflects on his original coinage: "When I reached intellectual maturity and began to ask myself whether I was an atheist, a theist, or a pantheist; a materialist or an idealist; Christian or a freethinker; I found that the more I learned and reflected, the less ready was the answer; until, at last, I came to the conclusion that I had neither art nor part with any of these denominations, except the last."[57] Huxley argues that all actions and ontological assertions rest on faith, though like John, he does not think this means that faith is sufficient for knowledge.

When pressed, nonbelievers who identify primarily as humanists, secular humanists, atheists, or freethinkers frequently told me they are also agnostics because they believe, along with John and Huxley, that ontological certainty is beyond the limits of empirical science. Frank, a longtime leader of a group in California, told me that his atheism entails agnosticism: "I don't think most atheists deny the existence of God. There's a little bit of difference in my mind from absolutely not believing in something and denying that that thing exists. The difference is that I'm not omniscient, and in order to deny that something exists, I think you have to be omniscient." Frank's observation about omniscience is subtle. Because evidence for any claim is limited to data from the senses, whether collected by the naked eye or the Hadron Collider, one can only form a partial picture of reality. Frank is acknowledging that he could only know for certain that something exists if he had a perfect data set, which is all possible sense data. In its absence, he is an agnostic atheist.

Less Common Identifiers

Few of the secular people I spent time with have read Huxley, but they talk about these ideas with one another at their local meetings and national conferences. When they reach for a term like "humanist" or "atheist" as their primary identifier, they grab it from a constellation of labels that hang together. Each term in the constellation emphasizes a different aspect of their similar worldviews, and in a particular social context, it accomplishes a specific end. Other labels like "rationalist," "naturalist," and "materialist" came up frequently in conversations I had with secular people. Though like "agnostic," these terms are not in the names of the biggest national groups that organize nonbelievers, they sometimes appear in the names of local secular groups throughout the United States.[58] Because these lesser-known terms are more precise, they make it possible for nonbelievers to emphasize certain beliefs over others and to strive for coherence around particular principles. And because they are more esoteric, they are not as good for organizing secular people who are uninitiated in this specialized jargon or for convincing them to make their secular identities more primary.[59]

Specialized terms and concepts help organized nonbelievers systematize their beliefs in conversation with one another. Defining and using these terms is part of the work of becoming very secular. I had to learn this vocabulary to be a participant observer in nonbeliever groups. When I turned to scholarly books to help me understand this vocabulary better, I realized that their academic usage can differ somewhat from their everyday use among organized nonbelievers. For instance, even though many nonbelievers identify with the term "rationalist," they are not rationalists like philosophers René Descartes or Baruch Spinoza.

They do not try to logically deduce the nature of reality from axioms like self-existence or the unity of substance.[60] Frank thinks this kind of rational deduction would only be possible if he were omniscient because he is primarily an empiricist, like David Hume or like Huxley. I discuss these epistemological distinctions in greater depth in chapter 4 to explain who nonbelievers become when they deconvert to secularism. Discrepancies in how terms are used show that organized nonbelief in the United States is a distinct discursive field, with its own vocabulary and norms, that reshapes those who engage it.[61]

The term "skeptic" also arises frequently when talking with organized nonbelievers, but everyone I spoke with distinguished the secular movement from the skeptic movement. This is in part because skepticism is open to those who are traditionally religious and believe in the supernatural so long as they advocate for science and critical thinking. In October 2012, I saw how "skepticism" and "secularism" can overlap or be distinct when I attended a congressional briefing organized by the secular lobby.[62] A question-and-answer period followed a set of presentations from a panel of experts, including a law professor and two leaders of the secular movement. A young staff member of Republican US representative Michelle Bachmann asked the first question, which he directed toward Greg Epstein, the Humanist chaplain at Harvard. The young man identified as an evangelical Christian and asked "what the Harvard Community is doing to promote the fight against pseudoscience." He clarified that he meant the growth of alternative healing practices like Reiki, which have become more common in hospitals throughout the United States.[63] Epstein and the other panelists recognized his concern as one that secularists share with born-again Christians, and they responded sympathetically. The skeptic movement is not necessarily a bigger tent but one with a different focus. Because those with whom I spoke repeatedly established a boundary between the secular and skeptic movements, I adopted the limit in my field research, conducting only a handful of interviews and site visits with people and groups that identify primarily with skepticism.

I heard organized nonbelievers use the terms "spiritual" and "spirituality" more frequently in recent years than when I first began my ethnographic research. This shift is in part thanks to Sam Harris, one of the so-called New Atheists, whose *End of Faith* and *Letter to a Chris-*

tian Nation helped propel a public resurgence of atheism. According to leaders of nonbeliever organizations I spoke with, he and other New Atheist authors helped spur an influx of members and money to their groups.[64] In 2014, Harris published *Waking Up: A Guide to Spirituality without Religion*, in which he argues for the importance of an empirical study of human experience. Harris looks to Buddhism, in particular, as a storehouse of knowledge and practice. Though he does not discuss phenomenology or acknowledge its difference from empiricism, he in effect advocates for a phenomenological approach to the aspects of human experience that are not testable through experimentation.[65] Harris reaches for the term "spirituality" to describe that which is not empirically falsifiable by science but is still empirically available, if only through individual consciousness and experience. In so doing, he participates in a long history of inquiry into human experience as a secular and spiritual endeavor.[66] Harris acknowledges that "many nonbelievers now consider all things 'spiritual' to be contaminated by medieval superstition," but he continues, "I do not share their semantic concerns."[67] During the period of my field research, from 2010 through 2018, practices like meditation and mindfulness became much more acceptable among organized nonbelievers. Like Harris, some people I spoke with described their engagement with these practices in the language of spirituality. Harris and others have in effect expanded the limits of empiricism for organized nonbelievers, providing new ground for a secular worldview.

Committed to Ambivalence

Is Ismail wrong? Do nonbelievers in fact have beliefs? As this chapter has shown, a proper answer to this question is complicated. If by "belief" one means assumptions that guide everyday actions, then Huxley and many other agnostics would agree with Roger that nonbelievers in God are believers in other things. However, if by "believing" one means relying on faith alone, then few nonbelievers would assent to having beliefs about the world. Concepts like belief straddle two sides of the secular paradox because they are both taboo and indispensable. Most very secular people try to be purely secular, so they depend on working definitions of "religion" and its related terms to avoid religious pollution. Like Harris, in his attention to the semantic, many of the ardently secular people I met are hyperaware of the constructedness of the terms they use to describe their secular identities and worldviews because they face their limits and contradictions frequently. Their debates and conversations among one another help them systematize or rationalize the worldviews they largely share. Differences within and among secular worldviews can be subtle or significant, and though important, they should not distract scholars from recognizing the frequently shared terms and sticking points of nonbelievers' debates. Very secular people navigate the multiple meanings of the terms they use with care, and in debating their various uses, they refine the specificity of their field and create knowledge barriers for full participation. Not everyone participates in these conversations equally, but as a framework, they dominate the discussions I listened to and participated in at local meetings and national conferences throughout the country.

Siding with Ismail or Roger forecloses the arguments that this chapter makes about secular people's ambivalence toward belief. It is precisely the openness of the secular paradox, its irresolution, that fuels debates among nonbelievers over terms and their meanings and drives their factionalism into groups and subgroups that are more and less secular or religious. Settling the question of the beliefs of nonbelievers one way or the other would attempt, yet again, to suture a conceptual wound. It would pretend, on finishing the final stitch, that the wound has already scarred over. This book approaches this wound as a site of conceptual trauma to which nonbelievers and others who are invested in suturing it return again and again.[68] The paradox is a contradiction buried in the sediment of a Christian-centered inheritance, which overdetermines all religion-related questions. Throughout this book, I observe the repeated return of secular people to the unresolvable question of the secular and its proper relationship to religion. I do this to try to understand the reasons for its irresolution and the consequences of attempts to resolve it. Paying so much attention to the secular paradox provides a better understanding of secularism—both its effects on secular people and the conditions that make its inherent contradictions so inexorable.

2

Community

Believing in Belonging

All nonbelievers are ambivalent about belief, but organized nonbelievers are also ambivalent about belonging. On June 30, 2013, I attended the first meeting of the Sunday Assembly in the United States. It was held in a dirty little room in the back of a New York City bar called Tobacco Road, on Forty-First Street between Eighth and Ninth Avenues. The Sunday Assembly was founded in London in January of the same year by Sanderson Jones and Pippa Evans. The two are comedians with a background in marketing who set out to found church-like communities for nonreligious people. Evans was unable to attend the first US Sunday Assembly, but Jones was there and stole the show. He is tall and handsome, with a huge beard, quirky clothes, and lots of charisma. He announced their intention to plant fifty "churches" all over the world by the end of 2013, including one in New York by October. He talked about "joy" throughout the raucous first meeting, in which attendees were encouraged to clap and sing along to songs backed by a live band. Jones emphasized that for him, "atheism isn't a denial." Rather, it is an assertion about this life, how limited it is, and how it should be appreciated. This tension between the denial of God and the way of life that atheists affirm stems from the secular paradox. In this founding moment, the paradox proved once again to be a generative fault line among secular people.

Within months of the New York group's first meeting, it divided in two: Sunday Assembly (SA) NYC and the Godless Revival.[1] Neither group lasted long. SA NYC announced its hiatus on its website—a subsite of the international organization—in January 2016.[2] The Godless Revival, which billed itself as the first atheist variety show, confirmed its demise in September 2018 with a blunt post to its Facebook page: "This is a dead page for a dead project. Screw organized atheism."[3] Seeing this first US outpost as an important step in the growth of the Sunday Assembly movement, Jones was directly involved with SA NYC's organizers. He told them he favored more openness, which meant less talk of atheism and a more inclusive venue than the bar in which they were meeting. Some members of SA NYC's board agreed with Jones. They felt they should avoid talking about atheism and should not invite speakers from the United States' existing secular movement. Board members also disagreed about how family-friendly the group should be and whether a bar was the right place to hold its meetings. Those who broke away to found the Godless Revival considered Jones's hands-on approach too authoritarian and not godless enough—in short, too much like religion. Sunday Assembly's founders had encountered a problem that has challenged very secular people for centuries: where to draw the line between too secular and too religious.

Organizers of the New York branch of the Sunday Assembly started a Google Group to discuss the practical details of getting the community off the ground. Knowing some of the early organizers, I joined the group and followed their efforts. In August 2013, one of the group's conversation threads caught my attention. It focused on the Sunday Assembly's use of the terms "atheist" and "atheism." The organizer who started the thread advocated a big-tent approach that would separate Sunday Assembly NYC from the many other groups that had come before: "I think we can agree that when we primarily invite the folks who attend atheist meetups already, we're not reaching the vast untapped market of people who don't believe in god but don't consider themselves atheist. That group doesn't go to atheist meetups. That's the group Sunday Assembly is uniquely positioned to reach out to—if we focus on them." Most of those who responded agreed, including some who would go on to found the Godless Revival. Jones replied to the thread with official branding documents from the Sunday Assembly in London, which encourage the phrase "godless congregation" and use the phrase "part-atheist church." Jones responded again later in the thread, acknowledging that terms like "atheist" and "godless" might have different connotations in the US than they do in England. He suggested a phrase he was workshopping: "All the best bits about church, except with no religion, and better songs."

A negative question loomed throughout the group's conversation about inclusivity: Who is not welcome? One of the organizers drew clear lines:

Here's what I don't what [sic] to see. I don't want SA to be hijacked by any weird kinds of theism, new-ageyness, or pseudo-spiritualism. I think the advantage of the word "atheist" is that it suggests very firmly that we're are [sic] *not* going to buy into any practice that doesn't have strong, tangible evidence of its efficacy that everyone in the group can plainly see, that's generally accepted as invalid by academic scientific consensus, or that fails a reasonable person's critical thinking. Poetry is OK, but "the Word of God" is not. Bringing someone chicken soup when they are sick is OK, but crystal healing stones are not—at least not in the name of Sunday Assembly. Talking compassionately to each other about our lives is OK, but talking to an undetectable deity is not. Beer is OK, but Scientology stress-machines are not. Etc. So "atheism" is very much part of our theoretical basis, but not a full description of who we are. Do I make any sense?[4]

Those who replied debated the value of other terms from a marketing perspective. Trying to avoid expressly negative language, one person suggested the term "secular," while "admit[ting] that for some this just means separation of church and state."[5] Several acknowledged that part of their motivation in creating a big tent was to get people in the door and to convince them that being secular is a better way to live. The organizers were having a practical conversation about whether halfway measures are acceptable and, ultimately, whether being part of a secular community means not believing in God or believing in a consistently naturalistic worldview. How much to focus on beliefs is a persistent, strategic consideration for anyone trying to engage in the paradoxical work of organizing nonbelievers. Disagreements over where to draw the line between secular and religious can lead easily to factionalism and to new groups bearing new names—as it did in the case of Sunday Assembly New York and the Godless Revival. The former was founded by those who wanted a more religion-like community for nonbelievers and the latter by those who thought they had gone too far. Both groups are products of the secular paradox.

Organized nonbelievers care about more than just beliefs. The groups they form range from small local communities to national organizations with tens of thousands of members. They meet in churches and synagogues but also in bars and restaurants, and they get together for lectures, film screenings, volunteer days, and boozy brunches. Some of these communities consider themselves religious and have IRS-recognized status as religious nonprofits, but most do not. National nonbeliever organizations are usually led by paid, full-time employees, many of whom have experience working for other nonprofit groups or engaging in grassroots organizing. A few dozen local communities are led by clergy trained in seminaries or by Humanist Celebrants trained in workshops held throughout the country. The vast majority of local groups are led by volunteers with the time and energy to do the day-in, day-out work of organization. Many of the leaders I spoke with described secular people as "nonjoiners," and I often heard that getting them together is like "herding cats." Unsurprisingly, doing religious or religion-like things can be a tough sell for secular people.

This chapter looks at some of the reasons that secular people get together in communities with others who share their beliefs, and it explores why doing so can feel too religious. It also examines the different kinds of groups that secular people form. In a variety of ways, these groups blend opposition to religion with an embrace of particular religion-like activities. When nonbelievers do not recognize themselves among the existing ways of being secular, some start new groups and invent new ways to be secular. Women, people of color, and people converting to secularism from religions outside mainstream Christianity have to find ways of being secular that feel right for them while working from within a cultural inheritance that often marks them as more or inherently religious. Though Christmas is often unmarked or perceived as generic cultural heritage in the United States, celebrations like Passover and Eid are usually religious or culturally specific. Secular people need to decide how to draw the line in order to maintain their secular purity. This chapter examines the diversity of secular communities to show how the secular paradox generates a variety of ways of being secular.

Playing the Protestant Game

In 2012, I attended the annual conference of the American Humanist Association (AHA) in New Orleans, Louisiana. While there, I participated in a training for Humanist Celebrants. I was surprised to learn that the hour-and-fifteen-minute workshop gave me all the training I needed to become officially certified as Humanist clergy. At the time, the certification process also required a several-page application, a fee, at least one year of prior membership in AHA, and four letters of recommendation, including one from an AHA member. I did not meet the other requirements. In 2018, I tried to attend another training to become a "Secular Celebrant" through the Center for Inquiry (CFI), which offers a less rigorous process for certification. I failed when the workshop was canceled because I was the only person who signed up. In June 2019, I made a third attempt, attending a daylong training at the University of Southern California. Though I am now officially trained as a Humanist Celebrant through the American Humanist Association, I still have not pursued certification. My ordainment by the Universal Life Church enables me to solemnize weddings legally in most of the United States, but I remain among the secular laity.[6]

Oliver, the man who ran the Celebrant training workshop in New Orleans in 2012, is an experienced Celebrant who served on AHA's board of directors. He began the session by providing an overview of who Celebrants are, what they do, and the history of their role in humanism. He told us that AHA wants its Celebrants "to promote the humanist movement" as "ambassadors." Oliver always wears a humanist lapel pin and carries a card in his wallet with the Humanist Manifesto, though he did not specify which version: 1933, 1973, 2000, or 2003.[7] Celebrants are like clergy, and they can perform life-cycle rituals like weddings, memorial services, and naming ceremonies. In Oliver's words, "People can come to you and get a ceremony crafted that's free of theism." A seven-member committee "from a very diverse background" reviews all applications to become a Celebrant through AHA, though Oliver stressed that not all applications are certified. Maude, who chaired the committee in 2012 and was present in the room, chimed in to tell us she discovered that one of the members of the committee "was collaborating on a book with her dead son, who was talking to her from the beyond." Oliver and Maude said that they and the other committee members "had to ask her to step down" because she was "not really stable." From the context of the conversation, it was clear that they found her insufficiently secular to be in a leadership role at a humanist organization.

Some attendees were like me and fairly new to the idea of humanist clergy, but many of those present had been Celebrants for years and asked technical questions about legal jurisdiction. They also offered strong opinions about AHA and the role a Celebrant should play in the lives of humanists. About halfway through the workshop, a debate erupted over nomenclature and the legal status of AHA's Celebrant program. The group's Humanist Celebrants are recognized as religious clergy throughout the United States, though their ability to solemnize weddings varies by state law. In order to possess the authority to endow this recognition, AHA maintains a subgroup called the Humanist Society that retains its legal status as a religious nonprofit, even though AHA has been federally recognized as an educational organization since 2007. The Humanist Society was called the Humanist Society of Friends when it was founded in Los Angeles in 1939, two years before AHA.[8] Now it exists primarily to endorse Celebrants, chaplains, and military lay leaders, which are all categories recognized in US statutes as having special rights. Eric, an army veteran who has dedicated years of his life to getting the military to recognize humanist chaplains, explained their significance to workshop attendees: "Chaplains in the military get clergy confidentiality because they're allowed to wander around and be friends with people. If you have a mental issue with a psychologist or psychiatrist, that goes on the record and can damage your ability to get a promotion." The Humanist Society's religious status with the IRS is crucial for achieving legal recognition in other parts of the federal government, like the military and the Federal Bureau of Prisons, so AHA has important reasons for keeping it.[9]

A man from the New Orleans Secular Humanist Association (NOSHA) spoke up to say that he had a problem with AHA's religious tax status and a phrase that Oliver and Eric had used: "atheist chaplain." Their brief exchange captures organized nonbelievers' ambivalence toward religion, especially as it relates to the law:

MAN FROM NOSHA: We can't redefine words!
SECOND MAN: The hell we can't!
ERIC: We've already redefined religious words, but it's fine if nonbelievers want to choose a different word to describe it [outside the legal context].
OLIVER: We have to use their legal word if we want access to solemnizing weddings and becoming chaplains.

ERIC: If it's the Chaplain and Counselor Corps [instead of the Chaplain Corps, as it is today], that's fine.
OLIVER: This is the game we play.

If this is the game that Oliver and other humanists play, what kind of game is it? Nonbelievers and other non-Christians must engage in mimetic play in order to be recognized alongside established religious groups in the United States.[10] Until recently, Protestantism has been the religion of more than half of Americans.[11] Though not the sole influence on US law, Protestant prevalence has established its assumptions about who can play and on what terms.[12] Accepting that play can be serious, the metaphor of a game describes well how organized nonbelievers have no choice but to express their non-Christian beliefs and values in the language and concepts of Christianity—especially Protestantism.

The need for mimetic play stems in part from the social and legal structures in which nonbelievers find themselves.[13] In the United States, one of the rules of the game is that religion is special, which means that the law treats religious people, groups, and claims differently. Protestants' belief that there is a legitimate authority beyond the state has justified the carving out of significant exceptions to governmental authority, which have raised the game's stakes. The game becomes especially serious when it is the sole means of accessing privileges like wedding solemnization and exceptions like lucrative tax breaks.[14] The demand to mimic Christianity runs deeper than the law, to the forces that have shaped the everyday concepts and speech of all Americans, including nonbelievers. Speaking and thinking in English, it is difficult to escape Christian-centric categories and frameworks.[15] Christianity is the prism through which "religion," in its European specificity, became "religions," a concept that unifies cross-cultural analogues. European merchants and missionaries understood those whom they traded with, converted, and subjugated through the lens of their own understanding. Religion and concepts like the secular, spirituality, superstition, magic, and science are interdependent, and they delimit important boundaries.[16] It is a very big game that many people all over the world must play.[17]

Understanding the efforts of Humanist Celebrants as semantic gamesmanship runs the risk of reducing their religiosity to an insincere expedient. Deciding they are disingenuous tells only half the story of their ambivalence and misses how Celebrants' work exceeds the mere semblance of religion. Oliver and others who attended the workshop are very serious about being Celebrants. Jerome, who described himself as a member of the certification committee and the Humanist Society's board, said he might be the only Celebrant in Missouri. He considers his work important not only for secular people but also for interfaith couples. Jerome told a story about a couple he married, one of whom was Catholic and the other Muslim. They wanted a wedding "as church-like as possible," so he wore a stole with the humanist logo, which is sometimes called the "happy human." (Oliver said he refuses to wear the stole because it feels too religious.) Jerome tries to cater to what the couples want when designing a ceremony, and though he does not use "anti-God language," he tries to "leave God out of it." Sometimes, he admits, he toes the line: "If some imagery reminds people of God, and that keeps the families happy, that's OK with me." When a workshop attendee challenged Jerome by asking, "How far would you go? Would you read Psalms?" he replied, "Nope, I won't do it. I'll refer them to one of the local pastors." Another man described his own compromise: "I will not say those words [that reference God] or put them in the ceremony, but if they have a father who's deeply embedded in religion and wants to say some words, why shouldn't he be allowed to do that?" For Humanist Celebrants, the dangers of religious pollution are real, even if the work of religion is too important to leave solely to the religious.

Nonbelievers can play the game in several different ways. Some refuse to abide by the usual rules, so they play with a handicap. When I visited the headquarters of the Freedom From Religion Foundation in Madison, Wisconsin, in 2012, I asked Phillip, one of its attorneys, about whether US courts consider nonbelievers religious or secular. He responded by explaining that nonbelievers have options:

> The law will assume that nonbelievers are a religion for certain inquiries and not for others, and it's completely unresolved which go for which. There's no rhyme or reason to it yet. It obviously puts us in a strange position because you have more power arguing before a court that you're a religion in some respects, whereas really we're not. That's one of our main things. We are not a religion! It's a doctrine of our faith. The Supreme

Court has said time and time again that the Establishment Clause, in addition to preventing the government preferring one religion over another, also prevents it from preferring religion over nonreligion. So that's what we [at FFRF] try to rely on, but in Indiana, the Center for Inquiry is suing to get officiants [i.e., Secular Celebrants] recognized. They ran into this conundrum because they were arguing, "We're religious for these purposes," but in their depositions they're saying, "We're not religious." And the court said, "Well, you can't have it both ways," kind of. So that is an area that I can't give you a definitive answer, but it's going to be an interesting and probably evolving area of law.

Phillip and FFRF play the same game as Eric and Oliver, but they play it differently, by persistently attacking one of its fundamental rules: the specialness of religion. They want the courts and the rest of the US government to treat religious groups like any other nonprofit; they want them to grant all nonprofits the special rights of religions or remove those special rights. That FFRF refuses to identify as religious puts it at a disadvantage in many ways because Phillip is correct that religious organizations have more rights under the law. Organizations like AHA play along with the rule of religion's specialness, identifying as religious when needed in order to gain special rights. CFI has adopted a different strategy and succeeded in having its cake and eating it too. The case that Phillip raised about Secular Celebrants in Indiana was decided in CFI's favor in a federal appeals court in 2014, and the group can now solemnize weddings as nonreligious clergy in the state of Indiana.[18] The United States' Protestant game is evolving and can be played in many ways, by Protestants and non-Protestants alike.

Most scholars of religion and secularism do not play directly in the game of American law, but they do play in the larger game, structured by Christianity's language and religion-related concepts.[19] In this very big game, scholars have tried to explain the significance of Protestantism's influence on secularism, arriving at a set of options similar to those faced by organized nonbelievers. Is secularism distinct from Protestantism because it rejects religion, makes universally true claims based in science, and grows from roots that antedate Protestantism and even Christianity?[20] Is secularism a new kind of Protestantism that results from another Reformation, this one secular but still reactionary, a mere antithesis?[21] Or is secularism part of Protestantism, shaped by its assumptions, entangled in its logics, even mirroring its structures, so as not to be distinguishable despite its ostensible differences?[22] As I argue in chapter 5, it would be an error to mistake that which is influenced by Protestantism for the thing itself, but it would also be an error to overlook secularism's similarities to Protestantism, Christianity, and religion more broadly.[23] They are imbricated and similar but not identical. The one does not spring wholly from the other because their roots are varied and tangled and their descent is convoluted. Secularism's ambiguity and the concomitant ambivalence of secular people make questions of identity impossible to settle conclusively. Paradoxically, that ambiguity raises questions that sometimes need settlement, such as in court cases like that which CFI won in Indiana. The secular paradox is so generative because it resists resolution even as it demands it.

This Is Not a Church

In 2012, sociologist Alfredo García and I created a database of all of the local nonbeliever communities in the continental United States.[24] We found exactly 1,400. When I revalidated the database in 2017, I identified 1,359 local groups. Though this decrease in the number of groups seems small, it conceals a much larger turnover. Only 942 of the groups that we identified in 2012 were still active in 2017, which means that during 2012 and 2017, 458 groups—nearly a third—either formally disbanded or ceased being active, and 417 new groups were formed. This churn makes sense when viewed through the lens of secular people's ambivalence toward religion.

Many groups are averse to aspects of institutionalization because it would make them too religious. Communities vary widely in size, structure, goals, and strength. They are often loose formations, ad hoc, and organized around one or two leaders who show up to all events and do the difficult, everyday work of organizing. Their collective activities can include everything from attending a lecture by a scientist to cleaning up a local beach or participating ironically in a Satanic ritual. Some groups focus primarily on the negative side of nonbelief, getting together weekly or monthly to vent about religion's harms. Others focus more on affirmative beliefs or values that they share with one another, like humanism.[25] Nonbeliever communities can be church-like, and some communities even gather in churches, like nearly all Humanist Unitarian Universalists. But most communities I spent time in do not invest in physical infrastructure, have not registered with the IRS as 501(c)3 nonprofits, do not train or pay their leaders, and avoid assigning formal hierarchical roles.

One of the impediments to institution building among secular people is their distrust of giving donations to their local communities. Few people I spoke with have a habit of donating to their local group, even if they attend regularly and even if they donate to national secular groups and other charitable organizations. I learned a lot about the donation habits of nonbelievers from Danny, a former Protestant minister who now makes his living in the secular movement and speaks at secular communities throughout the United States. Danny and I met at a conference he spoke at, and we agreed to have a longer conversation by phone about a month later. I caught him in July 2012, while he was driving across the state of North Carolina to get from one secular community to another. Until the year before, Danny had been a successful evangelical minister who supported himself and his family on donations received from his congregation. After experiencing deep doubts, he left his church, as well as Christianity. He was helped through the process of deconversion by the Clergy Project, a nonprofit founded in March 2011, around the same time that Danny experienced his crisis of faith. Cofounders of the Clergy Project include Dan Barker, codirector of FFRF, and two prominent New Atheist authors, Richard Dawkins and Daniel Dennett. Throughout our conversation, Danny credited the Clergy Project and another organization, Recovering From Religion, with helping him through the difficult process of rebuilding his life. Danny lost a lot when he left Christianity. He and his wife separated, and she moved out of state. When I interviewed him over the phone, he told me that earlier in the day he had spoken with an attorney to begin the process of declaring bankruptcy. His house had undergone foreclosure, and he said "it would go to auction in twenty-nine days." He told me the "poor little PT Cruiser" he was driving while we talked was also his home.

Despite Danny's hardships, he was upbeat both times we spoke, and he remains one of the most joyful people I met during my research. When I jokingly called him "an atheist circuit rider," he chuckled and began telling me stories about the nice people he had stayed with and their generous hospitality. He also gave me a breakdown of the economics of being a secular itinerant preacher. They are bleak: "I had the hope that I could travel and speak to [nonbelievers] and maintain a livelihood, but people don't give in the atheist community the way they give in the religious community." He finds that when he asks groups of nonbelievers for money directly, he gets very little. He receives a little more money when a facilitator puts a can in the back and lets people know that donations go directly to him. Without my asking, Danny ventured a theory for why getting donations from secular people is so difficult:

> What's happened is financing of organizations has been lumped into religion. Financing an organization is seen as part of religion. We make exceptions for giving to political causes because none of us feel like we're giving to a preacher when we give to a political candidate. But what we call religion is just what happens naturally when organizations continue to progress. That's how religion developed traditions and codified documents: a little bit at a time. Within the atheist movement, there are obvious denominations. These organizations will develop in time, and you don't need supernaturalism for religion to develop. Fundraising is a part of that.

Danny's assessment is consistent with what I learned talking with other leaders of secular groups, as well as with everyday members. Money is usually tight for these organizations, and most donations come from a small number of major donors. Groups that own their buildings, like some Ethical Culture societies and Humanist UU churches, passed collection plates at the meetings I attended. I never heard a request for donations when attending less religion-like local groups, which usually fund events more directly by charging one-time fees. I spoke with a few first-time attendees when I visited Ethical Culture and UU services, and I found that some were uncomfortable with these monetary requests because they associated the requests with the religious experiences they hoped to leave behind. Secular people struggle to justify giving money to their communities because donating feels too much like tithing. Supporting clergy and buildings feels too much like religion. Secular people's ambivalence toward religion has a big impact on the forms their groups take and the potential for a group's growth as a religious or religion-like movement.

When I visited the offices of the Freedom From Religion Foundation, I spoke with several of the group's leaders. Though FFRF's stated mission is "to promote the constitutional principle of separation of state and church, and to educate the public on matters relating to nontheism," as of 2019, the group had twenty-three local chapters, which function as communities for members of the national organization.[26] These chapters are located in cities like Grand Rapids, Louisville, and Colorado Springs, and some are also affiliated with other national organizations like the American Humanist Association and the Center for Inquiry. Among the national nonbeliever organizations, FFRF is the only one that requires all members of local chapters to pay national dues, so it has a precise head count when assessing its national membership. In December 2012, one of FFRF's leaders told me it was "the largest expressly atheist and agnostic organization in the country," with more than nineteen thousand total members—nearly four times the five thousand members it had in 2004.

FFRF's growing number of local communities, organized under a dues-collecting umbrella organization, makes the group's leaders both proud and uncomfortable. During an interview over lunch near the organization's offices, a leader named Bill wanted to clarify how FFRF understands itself and its relationship to its local chapters:

> We don't view ourselves like religions view themselves, as trying to convert the world or make the world in our image. We're there for people who already don't believe—not like a religious movement who's trying to proselytize and gain converts and set up churches and dioceses all over the world, although we are getting more requests for chapters, which is interesting. We've never been big on chapters, but we have it in our bylaws, and we have some wonderful chapters. Our attitude toward the chapters is that they should be as autonomous as possible and as local as possible, with a minimum amount of us, partly because we don't have the time, really. The only chapters that should exist are the ones that can't help it. It's a local group of people that just spontaneously, organically, just can't help forming a group. And that's cool. It's not like we're making it happen. They'll come to us and say, "How can we be a chapter?" ... It's

a movement, but it's a bottom-up movement. "It's a movement with no followers" is what I like to say. Every person in it is a leader. There's no hierarchy, no clergy. Everyone is the same. . . . There's no "I'm the bishop, and you're the parishioner."

Bill, a former born-again Protestant minister, associates belonging with religion, and he worries about authority. The chain of Bill's thoughts shows how, as he was talking, he recognized that FFRF's hierarchy resembles a religious hierarchy. He disassociated his movement from "high church" structures, in particular: "churches and dioceses" and "bishop and . . . parishioner." To make it clear to me that his organization's activities are wholly secular, Bill insisted that FFRF's chapters organize "spontaneously, organically," and they approach the national organization with the idea of forming a group and not the other way around. There are no "followers" in the freethought movement: "Every person in it is a leader," and "There's no hierarchy, no clergy." Phrases like "autonomous," "local," and "bottom-up" minimize FFRF's role and distance it from Bill's understanding of clerical authority. These communities, which in some ways mediate between FFRF's members and the national organization, are hybrid forms of secular religion that bear a close-enough resemblance to religious congregations. They require purification to make them secular, at least for someone as allergic to religion as Bill is. He wants to emphasize that every individual in his movement remains autonomous and in possession of their independent authority.

Despite this aversion, and though FFRF is the organization that has done the most to popularize the term "freethinker" in the twentieth and twenty-first centuries, Bill does not believe that nonbelievers should avoid organizing into communities or that doing so is a contradiction. He worries that gathering together encourages people to submit to "dogmas" and to religious authority, but these concerns are not specific to Bill or to FRFF. They are common among very secular people in the Anglophone world, who understand religion, by definition, to require submission to authority and the sacrifice of critical rationality. Writing in support of humanism and against religion, British philosopher A. C. Grayling echoes this view: "There are very few sources of conflict and mental enslavement as bad as an ideology which demands self-abnegation by submission to its dogmas and to the self-appointed interpreters of its dogmas. Religion is the paradigm of this."[27] Grayling's language depicts a battle for the mind in which religious authority and groupthink pose serious dangers to individual autonomy. These are the dangers to secular purity that Bill and other organized nonbelievers want to avoid, despite forming communities.[28] Secular people's ambivalence toward religion hinders their commitment to building and maintaining robust institutions. It is no surprise that nearly a third of the local nonbeliever communities in the United States foundered between 2012 and 2017, nor is it surprising that nearly as many groups were established during the same period. The movement to resolve the secular paradox—toward religion's negation but also its affirmation—perpetuates a cycle of dissolution and reinvention among secular people.

Secularism's Misfits

From the perspective of a Christian-centered culture that takes seriously the boundary between secular and religious, organized nonbelievers are misfits. Inasmuch as "secularism" has become a name for the separation of secular and religious and the formation of both, these nonbelievers mis-fit secularism because they occupy its excess.[29] Calling the process of separating secular from religious by the name of one of the separated terms—"secularism"—sows confusion and too easily conceals Christianity's role in establishing the boundary between secular and religious. Secular people, in their ambiguity, are also religion's misfits. Among secular people who mis-fit, there are nonbelievers who make even less sense, which is to say, who accord less to the everyday, inherited sense of where they belong, religious or secular. Hispanic freethinkers, Black atheists, and secular Jews and Muslims are all betwixt and between, and their irresolution is both difficult for them and telling of the discourses that structure them and render their secularity illegible, despite its avowal. Though they face unique challenges, their mis-fit creates new and important ways of being secular.

The process that pluralized Christian-based "religion" by extrapolating it into cross-cultural analogues, "religions," found little if any secularism at the colonial periphery and located it mostly in the white, colonial centers of Europe and the United States.[30] This uneven distribution of secularity, religiosity, spirituality, magic, and superstition has enabled regimes that privilege colonizers and postcolonial extractors by affording the most rights and recognition to those who are Euro-American or sufficiently similar.[31] Christian-centered cultures can secularize without disrupting many of their fundamental assumptions about religion because the secular is an ambiguous simulacrum of Christianity; it is both its inverse and its doppelgänger, though it is important not to conflate the two.[32]

On the one hand, if being secular means negating religion, then negating the most Christian-like religion will produce the least amount of religious remainder. For instance, deconverting from Judaism does not simply unmark a person as Jewish.[33] "Jewish" remains a cultural or ethnic marker even after the rejection of Judaism—to the frustration of one of the secular people I met who identifies as formerly Jewish and believes that being "Jewish-atheist is completely oxymoronic." The negative half of the secular is a Christian-shaped hole.

On the other hand, if being secular means affirming a tradition that antedates Christianity, variously named Epicurean, atheist, materialist, or immanentist,[34] then it requires the affirmation of a distinctly European tradition—albeit one with analogues in other times and places where an empiricist epistemology developed, such as in South Asian Carvaka.[35] The positive half of the secular is highly specific, as secular communities demonstrate when they exclude, for instance, those who believe in Tarot, astrology, and other forms of "woo-woo" that are "spiritual," and not "religious," but are not part of the secular tradition. The less Christian-like a secular negation and the less a secular affirmation resembles the secular tradition of Europe, the greater the excess of its fit.[36] In secularism's double move of negation and affirmation, some secular people are too religious to pass through the Christian-shaped hole and insufficiently secular to fill it. These excesses are the misfits of the secular paradox, and they leave us at a loss for words because they exceed not only the language of our cultural inheritance but often the limits of its imagination.

The secular people who join local nonbeliever groups in the United States participate in larger networks. They talk with one another in person, they are often members of national nonbeliever organizations, and they consume a lot of the same media. Through these interactions, they come to a share a set of related secular worldviews, even as they disagree on certain questions or on what to call themselves. During my field research, I found that secular beliefs are largely shared across differences in race, ethnicity, and cultural background. Chapter 1 tries to capture these similarities across difference by synthesizing a wide range of voices. In other aspects of being secular, differences are more pronounced. The culture in which secular people are raised influences the types of groups they join, the activities they engage in, and their group's aesthetics or style. Secular people have created groups specifically for Jews, for people of Latin descent, and for African Americans, as well as for ex-Muslims and for people who have deconverted from tight-knit religious groups, like Jehovah's Witnesses or the Church of Jesus Christ of Latter-day Saints. Each is a different way of being secular.

Because secular people often imagine their worldviews and ways of living to be universal and because emphasizing the negative half of the secular can make secularism feel unmarked or lacking in particularity, some nonbelievers have opposed the creation of subgroups based on other identities. Older white men occasionally expressed to me or in groups when I was present that they find identity-based subgroups unnecessary and divisive. Black and brown nonbelievers, especially, told me that they hear these criticisms often from white or mainstream secularism. In the following sections, I take a closer at identity-specific communities. I consider why they are important for those who join them and how they differ from other secular communities, which usually go racially and ethnically unmarked even as they are largely composed of white people over the age of fifty. Looking at communities for secular Jews, Hispanics, Blacks, and Muslims highlights assumptions that misfit them. It also shows how these nonbelievers are developing new ways of being secular together and changing what secularism is in the United States today. In chapter 5, I return to secularism's misfits with a focus on how they rework the secular tradition in which they struggle to find themselves represented.

Humanistic Jews

I visited the Birmingham Temple in the suburbs of Detroit, Michigan, on a gorgeous day in September 2016. I flew out from California for the research trip, so I rented a small room with an adjoining bathroom in a mansion in Detroit's Boston Edison neighborhood. Though the area is full of large, beautiful homes, most are now in disrepair, and some have been condemned or razed completely. On my way to the Temple, I drove up Woodward Avenue because I needed to make a stop in downtown Birmingham. As I passed 8 Mile Road, Detroit's northern city limit, I saw the grass on the boulevards change from brown to green and the faces around me from Black to white. The transformation was immediate. Though Detroit's economic inequality is also obvious within its city limits, the drive was my first trip to the city's suburbs and a stark introduction to the geography of the area's brutal structural racism.[37]

The Birmingham Temple is actually in Farmington, to the southwest of Birmingham, on a large lot across the road from a cemetery. The Temple was founded by Rabbi Sherwin T. Wine in 1963, with just eight families. By 1965, it had grown to more than 140. In 1969, Wine created the Society for Humanistic Judaism (SHJ) to provide a national umbrella organization for ten local groups throughout the country.[38] As of 2019, SHJ has nearly thirty local affiliates, down from its peak of over forty.[39] Wine's influence today extends well beyond Humanistic Judaism and into the broader humanist and secular movements. Near the end of his life, Wine trained Rabbi Greg Epstein, Harvard's humanist chaplain and the founder of the Humanist Hub. Epstein was ordained as a rabbi by Wine's International Institute of Humanistic Judaism, and he dedicated his book to Wine, titled *Good without God*. Along with his former collaborator James Croft, Epstein has built on Wine's work among secular Jews, outlining a broader strategic vision for the growth of what they call "congregational humanism."[40] Formerly known as the Humanist Community at Harvard, Epstein's Hub has become recognized as a model of community building for nonbelievers and employed several humanists who have gone on to become chaplains or professional leaders in other communities. The Birmingham Temple is not only the starting point for Humanistic Judaism but also a distinct way of being secular that has influenced how secular people negotiate their ambivalence toward religion.

Because there were no services the day I visited the Temple, I did not walk through the main entrance or see the space fully lit. I entered, instead, around the side, through SHJ's national office, where I met with a rabbi who helps run the organization. Later, I received a tour of the synagogue from another leader, Alan, who described to me his first experience of the Birmingham Temple and how it differs, in his words, "from the *traditional*, or the *conventional* synagogues, as I prefer to call them":

> When I got here, it didn't seem like any synagogue I'd ever been to. First of all, we don't call it a "sanctuary." I didn't know that at the time. We call it a "meeting room." And I walk into this room, and there's a sculpture that serves as the backdrop. It's hideous, but I understand what they were getting at. It says in Hebrew *adam*, which means "humanity." At the time, I was taken aback. If you go into a standard sanctuary at any conventional synagogue—if you're Orthodox, Reform, or anything in between—there's a big holy ark where they keep the Torah scrolls. There's an eternal light. There's usually a ton of other kinds of things, like Hebrew Bible passages on stained-glass windows. But there ain't none of this stuff. There ain't none of it! It's just a room for gathering. I actually like this. They have candles. There's not a menorah, but there are seven of them. I guess they're a kind of modern menorah. The next day, I walked into the library that's right behind us and saw that there was a Torah scroll. But it was in the library, and I thought to myself, "You know, that makes a lot of sense. It's a book."

Alan's description captures well how the Temple navigates its ambivalence toward religion. Some elements of what Alan would call a "conventional sanctuary" are removed, some are preserved, and some are translated from their original meaning. The congregation avoids the religious language of "sanctuary" by abstracting it to "meeting room" and calling it "a room for gathering." The bronze sculpture, mounted on a wood-paneled wall, represents humanism literally, albeit in Hebrew, by consolidating the letters of *adam* into a massive, logo-like emblem. Seven brass candleholders sit before it, atop a short brick wall, but contrary to my initial impression, they are not a Brancusi-inspired menorah. The ceilings are low compared to most religious spaces, and the room feels spare and minimalist in the midcentury modern style of the 1960s, which has made its return among millennials in the 2010s. As Alan said I would, I found the Temple's two Torah scrolls in the library, resting on a custom shelf amid a wall of other books, below a plaque honoring Rabbi Sherwin T. Wine.

In Wine's writings and lectures, he situates Humanistic Judaism at the foundations of Jewish history by finding humanism in the Torah and in the books of the Prophets.[41] This is the relationship to the Jewish "tradition" that Alan wants to preserve when he calls other synagogues "conventional," rather than "traditional," thus refusing to separate Humanistic Judaism from the Jewish tradition. As an ism, humanism is a nineteenth-century category, first used to describe Renaissance humanists and then, a few decades later, to describe the beliefs of nonbelievers.[42] Despite the anachronism of ancient humanism, I discuss in chapter 5 why Wine is right to find that the Jewish and secular traditions interweave. Even the Rabbinic Hebrew word for "atheist," *apikoros*, is helpful for understanding the ambiguity of secularism, as it comes from the word "Epicurean," which is the ancient school of empiricism that has shaped secular thought more than any other.[43] Jewish thinkers like Baruch Spinoza, Karl Marx, and Sigmund Freud are seminal figures in the secular tradition that is sometimes called "immanentist," "monist," or "materialist."[44]

As I discussed in the introduction, Felix Adler's Ethical Culture movement, which he founded in the 1870s and which lives on today, is effectively a secular offshoot of the Reform Judaism of his father, Samuel Adler, who was rabbi of New York City's Temple Emanu-El.[45] The Jewish freethinker Emma Goldman was a contemporary of Adler's and an outspoken atheist, anarchist, and labor activist in New York.[46] Though she emigrated to the United States in 1885, Goldman was born in the Russian Empire, in the Pale of Settlement, which is the set of territories where Jews were allowed to reside and where the social and intellectual movement that historian Eliyahu Stern has called "Jewish materialism" first developed.[47] This is also the area in which Joseph Sossnitz began work on a rapprochement between science and kabbalah that privileged the former and where Sossnitz's most well-known student, Mordecai Kaplan, was born.[48] Working within Conservative Judaism and eventually breaking from it, Kaplan pioneered a "Jewish naturalism" in the decades between the world wars, which later became Reconstructionist Judaism.[49] Kaplan wanted to hang onto "religion" and even a notion of "God" but do away with literal belief in the supernatural. Though Wine was not the first to develop a distinctively secular way of being Jewish, he was the first to create an institution that is both Jewish and expressly "humanistic." Today, SHJ works with the Congress of Secular Jewish Organizations, a group founded in the 1970s, to train rabbis and help organize secular Jewish congregations, but SHJ remains the most established institution in secular or Humanistic Jewish life.[50]

"Jewish" and "secular" fit together differently and in some ways more comfortably than "Christian" and "secular." For example, it was worthy of a BBC headline when Richard Dawkins described himself as a "cultural Christian." To help make the idea more comprehensible, he likened it to being a "cultural Jew" or "cultural Muslim" because he assumed his audience would recognize that those traditions leave a cultural remainder that cannot be scrubbed off.[51] Though Dawkins is perhaps the most prominent atheist in the Anglophone world, he believes Christianity has a special place in British and US culture: "So, yes, I like singing carols along with everybody else. I'm not one of those who wants to purge our society of our Christian history."[52] Dawkins's mis-fit in the eyes of most Brits and North Americans is secular Jews' gain but also their loss. As Jewish studies scholar Laura Levitt has rightly observed, an overemphasis on the Protestantism of the secular and the Protestant influence on religion constricts too narrowly what "religion" can usefully describe. Jewishness exceeds religion—and by extension the secular—because, in Levitt's words, "Jewishness is both more and less than a form of faith."[53] Elsewhere, she writes, "American Jews . . . are both too religious and not religious enough."[54] Jewishness persists even if a Jewish American becomes secular, which forecloses Jews' full assimilation into the norms of American pluralism and public life.[55] Suspicion of Jewish conversion and the danger of a Jewish remainder date at least to the Spanish Inquisition and, as Gil Anidjar has shown, have their origins in Christianity's powerful blood-based kinship.[56] Depending on the context and perspective, however—which is to say, depending on asymmetries in power—a religious remainder can mean different things. Being Jewish, in its mis-fit of an analogy to Christianity, can be a life-threatening identity that is impossible to change or an opportunity to live beyond inherited assumptions about the purity of the secular and the danger of religious pollution.

Humanistic Jews described to me their risks and possibilities in the US today. In 2012, on the last day of a conference for secular students held in Columbus, Ohio, I met Janet, one of the leaders of the Society for Humanistic Judaism. Neither of us had time for a long conversation that day, so a little over a month later, I reached her by phone at her SHJ office in Birmingham. After I reintroduced myself and explained my research—but before I could ask my first question—Janet told me, "The starting point for understanding Humanistic Judaism is that we straddle two worlds." She elaborated:

> We're not necessarily viewed by some in each world as part of their world. In the Jewish world, we're not quite Jewish enough. In the secular, humanist, the atheist, the nontheistic world, we're just a little too religious for a lot of people. The world reacts to us in different ways. Your view depends on whatever world you're a part of. Humanistic Judaism is both humanistic and Jewish, so it combines the elements of cultural Judaism—a strong attachment to Jewish identity, the literature, the history, the customs that we identify as Jewish—with the values that are identified as humanism.

For Janet, Humanistic Judaism is for people who are sufficiently secular but also distinctively Jewish. Describing her fellow congregants, she told me, "Some believe in something greater than themselves, but the line gets drawn if you have a belief in an intervening God. If you do, you're not going to be comfortable in Humanistic Judaism." About a minute later, she said, "You're not going to find stuff that isn't Jewish." Even though some members who are part of interfaith families might have other religious elements at home, Janet said, "We're not going to do anything to promote Christmas or Easter or anything else of that sort." Humanistic Judaism is distinctively Jewish and sufficiently secular; there are lines it does not cross.[57]

Janet understands Christianity's influence on the prevailing definition of religion, even as she embraces Jewish religiosity and rejects Christianity. She attended carefully to perspective and to language when she explained to me how her organization plays the Protestant game:

> In the eyes of the IRS, the Society is a "church." The Society is the mother church, and virtually all the local communities are organized as churches. I'm adept at speaking the language of the "church" because it's the language of the IRS. At that level, what, really, is a religious organization? It's a community that provides everything a church would provide: life-cycle

rituals to education to counseling to community to support. Whether it's joy or sorrow, we're there. We're a church.

She knows that whether something is religious or secular is not arbitrary, even though it is in the eye of the beholder. During our conversation, she explained to me that SHJ and its local communities deserve the same tax exemptions that a Christian church receives. The rabbis they ordain should also benefit from the ministerial housing allowance—sometimes called the "parsonage allowance"—which is a substantial tax break on housing for clergy members.[58] When Janet rattled off to me the qualities that her communities share with churches, she was listing high-stakes criteria for governmental recognition. This is why she has become so adept at speaking the language of the "church." Living in the United States and communicating primarily in English, Janet operates within path-dependent institutions and concepts that pattern what religion is. And she navigates them with finesse.

Later in our conversation, Janet again saw herself and Humanistic Judaism from the perspective of an authority, but this time through the eyes of a social scientist:

> Put me in a survey, and how I answer depends on who's doing the survey and whether I want to be considered part of the Jewish community.... If they ask questions about God, I'm not going to say, "No, I don't believe in God," but I'm going to fall somewhere in that secular outlook because God is irrelevant to how I live my life. If you're a secularist trying to determine how secular the country is, I may give you very different answers. At some level, my responses are based on who's doing the survey and asking the question.

Janet and other Humanistic Jews whom I spoke with think a lot about boundaries—what makes a person Jewish or secular—and they negotiate them ad hoc. Perhaps recalling the mental preparation she did before our interview, Janet told me how she responds strategically to social scientific questions about her Jewishness and her humanism. Listening to a social scientist asking her questions, she assesses the narrative in which she is being made a character, and she presents herself as who she would like to be in a story like the one I now tell.

Bob, a humanistic rabbi I spoke with, also found new possibilities in the ambiguity of Humanistic Judaism: "Instead of trying to find out the boundaries of being Jewish, we'll find out that there are no boundaries." He went on: "[My Jewishness] is a toy box, and I pull out the things that work for me. It's a heritage toy box—a cultural toy box." He grabs from a set of "toys" and uses them to create rituals, to write lectures for Friday gatherings, and to counsel members of his congregation. How Bob uses and combines these "toys" or "tools" is up to him. Lorraine, another humanistic rabbi, told me something similar when describing how she comes up with new rituals: "You have to open yourself up to possibilities. It's one of the things that's really easy for me to do." She went on to describe what she calls "a process for innovation" that she developed. Lorraine gives a packet of materials to couples who want to get married or to parents and young people thinking about a bar or bat mitzvah. They look over those materials together, and using them as a guide, they develop rituals to suit their beliefs and their specific family needs. In Lorraine's words, "I get into innovation."[59] Owing to the excess of Jewishness, Humanistic Jews in the United States can be both secular and religious. Though this ambiguity can lead to exclusion, in the right situation, it can also be an advantage.

Hispanic Nonbelievers

Though "Hispanic" is not a religious adjective in the way "Jewish" is, Hispanic nonbelievers negotiate a similar ambivalence toward religion. They need to identify the parts of their culture that they want to preserve and the parts that are too religious. Leaders of Hispanic and Latinx secular communities recognize the challenge of this task and its importance for a population that first achieved an organizational presence at the national level in 2010, with the founding of Hispanic American Freethinkers. In February 2018, I drove from Santa Barbara down to Los Angeles to see Juan, a former Pentecostal preacher whom I introduced in chapter 1, give a lecture to a group of mostly white secular humanists. Juan is comfortable speaking to large groups, and one-on-one, he is immediately engaging. After the lecture, I stood in line to introduce myself and to ask Juan some questions. As I waited, I heard a white man in his sixties named Michael ask why groups like his have a hard time attracting

Hispanic nonbelievers. Michael leads a secular humanist community in the LA area, and he recognizes that his membership looks mostly like him: white and near or past retirement. Juan got right to the point:

> Religion is a culture as much as being Mexican is. We have to include a lot of culture when we reach out to the Latin community. We need people who communicate with culture. This culture in here looks a certain way. It's the culture of white older people. It won't feel like a cultural home to Hispanic people. There needs to be music, people handing over knowledge from old to young, color. You have to create a cultural environment. What elements would have to be included to provide a culture? You can't just have jalapeños painted on the wall. There needs to be music, more color, an emotional connection. There needs to be a reading, some poetry, some homemade food—and not pizza like this. Kids need to be involved.

Juan had just explained, gently and in few words, something I had observed but struggled to fully understand, much less articulate. I told him as much after he saw me standing nearby, writing frantically, and invited me into the conversation. The rest of Juan's response to Michael is just as insightful:

> In religion, we [Hispanics] liked the community. This event is announcements and a speaker. This doesn't feel like community. . . . In minority culture, we have parents and grandparents, someone who has knowledge, passing it on. We have activities for kids and teenagers. White culture is a culture. Older male culture is a culture. I respect you and believe what you believe, but this isn't my culture. It doesn't feel homey. Minorities will have art and color and will think this room is gray and sterile. Culture is also the color of the room. Think about this question: "How can we create a culture?" Atheism is a majority white people. They look like this, here in this room—great people, but there's a reason why it hasn't clicked for people of color. A lot of people would gather if we made an emotional connection, but emotion is weird to them [i.e., white atheists], and they're threatened by it. Anything that makes it sound churchy, they're afraid of. I embrace it and take it in. I understand you want to run away from church, but there's the humanist experience. I talk about humanism now and the human connection.

Juan's first phrase in response to Michael is loaded: "Religion is a culture as much as being Mexican is." Not only do many secular people throw out the culture of religion with the religious bathwater, but in the process, they foreclose the possibility of embracing Hispanic culture because—as Juan sagely implies—older white nonbelievers associate the aesthetics and affect of Hispanic culture with religion. This is why Juan starts by urging Michael to recognize that religion is a culture and concludes by observing how allergic white atheists are to it. Abstracting to "culture" allows him to argue that removing religious beliefs does not require the elimination of the other parts of the "religious." Aesthetics and communal rituals can be made "cultural," as opposed to "religious," and thus purified of their religious pollution. They can then be preserved and repurposed.

Juan recognizes that when nonbelievers avoid anything that "sounds churchy" and "run away from church," they handicap their efforts to welcome new members and unify them into a community. Older white atheists prefer minimalism and iconoclasm, and "emotion is weird to them." Even the modernist sculpture and candles in the minimalist "meeting room" of the Birmingham Temple would be too religious for most of the organized nonbelievers I met during my research. In their ambivalence toward religion, secular people share beliefs and form communities; but they get uncomfortable when things are too religious, and they often "run away from"—to use Juan's phrase—things they associate with religion, like color and emotion. Because Americans' assumptions about religion are shaped by Protestantism and older European understandings of what parts of culture are similar to Christianity and thus religious, avoiding religion often means avoiding the colonial periphery and colonialism's domestic others.[60] Alfredo, the leader of a group for Hispanic freethinkers, told me, "A lot of the mainstream nonbeliever groups would rather ignore the Hispanic community because they don't know how to talk to them." For Juan, humanism provides the answer to Michael's question because it is the most religious form of nontheism available to nonbelievers in the United States. As a secular analogue, humanism can bear an association with religion and provide a wedge for preserving and reintroducing elements of Hispanic culture that Juan knows will feel too religious to many white nonbelievers. Juan's ongoing work is to create a kind of humanism that is not so averse to religious culture and thus also to the culture of nonwhite people—"minority culture," as Juan puts it—but still palatable to white humanists and other kinds of nonbelievers.

Several nonbelievers of Mexican descent described to me the challenge of disentangling Mexican culture from religion because they have to choose what to exclude and what to embrace. They have to ask themselves what aspects of their culture they can retain as they become more secular and what parts they must leave behind because those parts are too religious. For instance, a man named Luis, who was raised Catholic, told me how much he loves the symbol of the cross for its aesthetics, rather than its religious significance: "Before, when I was in high school [and had become an atheist], I loved the symbol of the cross—not necessarily the Roman Catholic but the Celtic gothic cross. I had pens. I had shirts. Then when I became Pentecostal [in college], it was like the best of both worlds again. Artistically, I loved it." Because Luis likes how the cross looks, he enjoyed wearing it more when it also had religious meaning for him. Now that he has become an atheist again in his thirties, Luis said he would never wear the cross, but he was sad to give it up: "It was painful. I couldn't wear it because it was now a symbol of a prison." Another Hispanic nonbeliever, José, told me, "[Crosses] should be easy to take on, but as someone growing up [Catholic], what the symbol is intended to mean, I can't do it." He said that he has seen other "Hispanic atheists use [the cross] in ways that take away its religious significance" because "some say it's just fashion." He told me that he, however, cannot. When he receives a necklace with the cross as a gift from a relative, he puts it in his jewelry drawer.

Though Hispanic nonbelievers' stories can sound similar to those of any secular person with religious family, they also reflect a distinctly Hispanic secularism. A woman I spoke with named Sandra told me that she avoids anything she finds too religious, but when she visits her extended family for the holidays, she faces difficult choices. Some decisions are obvious: "If my grandma tells me to do something, if she says, 'Get on your knees and pray this rosary,' I will do it. My grandma is getting old, and I just want to make her happy—even if it is a waste of time." Other decisions are more complicated. Sandra might participate but feel uncomfortable, or she might decide that parts are fine and refuse others. When she visits family over Christmas in Palm Springs, in California, she and her relatives "go house to house singing songs, kind of like caroling, but kind of in a parade. They call it 'Las Posadas.'" When they reach the final house, they share tamales and Ponche Navideño, a Christmas punch with tea and fresh fruit. Sandra participates for the most part, but sometimes she draws a line: "They'll have the *nacimiento* [a statue of the baby Jesus], and they'll pass it around, and everyone kisses it, and then it disappears somewhere. So now, I'm not kissing the baby Jesus!" She also told me that her sister, who is a Jehovah's Witness, participates even less in the family's religious activities. Because her sister converted as a teenager, she inadvertently paved the way for Sandra to refuse certain activities without causing a scene.

Sandra also emphasized the importance of family and recognized how coming out as secular or refusing to participate in family traditions can strain family bonds. Several Hispanic nonbelievers told me that family is extremely important in their culture and that making their families happy is often a higher priority than avoiding religious celebrations or rituals. According to Alfredo, "The difference with Hispanic deconversions, they're not afraid for themselves, but they don't want to hurt people's feelings. I haven't told my parents I'm an atheist because they'll feel like they failed." Other Hispanic nonbelievers told me they are more reluctant than white nonbelievers they know to tell their grandparents or other relatives that they no longer believe. In their descriptions of family gatherings, they emphasize practical social relations and say that there is little point in conversing about their secular beliefs because they are more likely to lead to conflict than to secular conversion. This does not mean that they never get into arguments with their relatives, but no one I spoke with described a big argument like the sort I heard about more frequently when speaking with white nonbelievers about the effects of their becoming secular. And importantly, none of the Hispanic nonbelievers I spoke with grew up with secular parents. Hispanic secularism is not new, but in the United States, it is emerging on a smaller scale and on a different timeline from white secularism.[61] As a subculture, it is nascent.

The close affinity between Catholicism and Hispanic culture inflects Hispanic secularism in complex ways. In the words of Alfredo, "A lot of [Hispanic] people see that Catholic Church as my family, my culture, my heritage." Sandra told me a story about visiting her family in Mexico in 2017: "We went to this big church for the Virgen de Guadalupe, and I was present there for everything. I wasn't thinking, 'I'm not going to be there because I'm an atheist'!" The church was a stop on a pilgrimage, and surrounded by pilgrims eating meals the church provided, Sandra felt uncomfortable: "I went in there, but I felt bad because I wasn't a pilgrim. My mom wanted to eat with them. I felt fake."

The reason that Sandra felt "fake" is important to consider. Anthropologists Webb Keane and Mayanthi Fernando have observed that Protestants tend to think of ritual as representing belief, thus making rituals into sincere manifestations of an interior state.[62] For Sandra's sister, a Jehovah's Witness, participating in a Catholic ritual is an outward betrayal of her interior religiosity; it goes against her religious beliefs because the sign does not align with what it should represent. In her story, Sandra was concerned more with being impolite than with betraying her secular beliefs. She was not worried about her inauthenticity but, rather, that she was an interloper. She felt guilty not about her lack of religious conviction but about not being who the other pilgrims presumed she was. Sandra's fakeness was performative rather than representative. She understood intuitively that being in the church and eating with the pilgrims would perform her into a social role that she did not want to occupy. She felt anxious because the pilgrims who were eating had tithed and had participated in their home religious communities, and she had not. She felt that she did not have the right to be there. Whereas her Protestant sister betrays herself and her religion when she participates in Catholic rituals, Sandra betrays her family and other Catholics. Though Sandra's anxiety about being "fake" describes an interior state that implies a lack of sincerity, she did not understand herself in a way that anthropologists like Keane and Fernando would consider Protestant or post-Protestant.

Sandra's secularism is better understood as post-Catholic. Though it would be wrong to describe all Hispanic nonbelievers this way, all of those I spoke with grew up in majority-Catholic communities even if their families were Protestant. Juan is right when he describes what white nonbeliever communities lack. Sandra and other Hispanic nonbelievers tend to feel more comfortable with ritual, iconography, and emotion than white nonbelievers do, though Humanistic Jews are a notable exception. The Hispanic nonbelievers I met are more able to go through the motions of religious practices even if they find them inefficacious or, in Sandra's words, "a waste of time." This is especially true if participation maintains good relations with their relatives.

For most nonbelievers who grew up Protestant, the sights and smells of a Catholic Church and its rituals can feel strange and baroque—unfamiliar and distinctively religious. For Sandra, they are familiar and feel like home. As with Jewishness, Sandra's Catholicism exceeds the religious and becomes what Dawkins described as "cultural." In a very real sense, if being secular in the United States means converting to the secularism of white former Protestants, then it requires a far-greater sacrifice for Hispanic nonbelievers like Juan, Luis, José, and Sandra than it does for most white Americans. The cultural excess of white religiosity—Dawkins's Christmas carols, a Christmas tree, Santa's elves—can more easily go unmarked in American culture and avoid the stigma of religious pollution. For Hispanic nonbelievers living in the United States, a strong commitment to secularism demands tough decisions about what parts of their culture can be preserved from the erasure of secular purification. To be secular without losing too much of themselves, they need to create new kinds of secularism—and form their own communities.

Black Atheists

In the United States, Humanistic Jews and Hispanic nonbelievers share with Black atheists an excess of "religiosity" that mis-fits most existing forms of secularism. The origin of this excess is unique for each group, as is how they create new ways of being secular that are free from religion but not merely copies of the white, post-Protestant culture that prevails among secular people in the United States. Centuries of racism have forced Black Americans, in particular, to bear the burden of religion on their bodies and institutions, and today, they remain overwhelmingly religious. Black Americans believe, pray, and attend religious services at the highest rates of any racial or ethnic group in the United States, and Protestant churches remain at the center of many Black Americans' lives.[63] According to a 2014 study by Pew Research, 94 percent of Black people in the United States are absolutely or fairly certain that they believe in God, which is nearly 10 percent more than the next-closest group, Hispanics. High rates of religiosity do not, however, mean that all

Black Americans are religious or believe in God. As of 2014, 18 percent claim no religious affiliation, including nearly a third (29 percent) of those between the ages of eighteen and twenty-nine. The percentage of Black people who are nonbelievers has also grown in recent years, as has the number of local communities in which they can meet face-to-face. Though Black nonbelievers remain a minority of a minority, there are more of them than ever before in the United States.

I was living in Brooklyn in 2013, and on a Saturday in July, I took the 7 train out to Flushing Meadows Park to attend the BLACKOUT: Secular Rally, billed as "the first outdoor rally/celebration that will predominately feature nontheists of color." Those who attended told me that the event was the first of its kind in the New York area for at least a generation. I arrived early, before noon, to watch the organizers set up tables, audio equipment, and a small stage on a patch of parking-lot blacktop. Feeling more like an outsider than usual, I mostly observed and kept to myself. The rally's speakers addressed a range of issues that nonbelievers of color face, but one that came up again and again—and that arises in every interview I have conducted with a Black nonbeliever—is legibility. I saw several veterans of the secular movement there, including people I had met and interviewed, but the event was clearly a coming-out party for many who had never been to a nonbeliever event before. Nearly five years later, I was at a nonbeliever conference in Washington, DC, when I overhead two men talking about the BLACKOUT rally. One man told the other that when they met on that July day in Queens, it was the first time he had ever met another Black nonbeliever in person. As the examples of Jacqueline and Shalette showed in chapter 1, people sometimes deny that Black people can be atheist and consider their very existence a contradiction. Coming out as atheist—or holding a rally for atheists to meet each other in public—can help those who feel like a sort of glitch in the system to realize that they are neither aberrant nor alone.

Observing that Black Americans are very religious and that Black nonbelievers are hard to find can shift easily into claims about the innateness of Black religiosity, which risks erasing the identity that Jacqueline and Shalette work so hard to project. In 2012, I spoke with a man named Vince who has been organizing for Black humanism since 1989. Vince's humanist résumé is long, and over the past three decades, he has probably done more than anyone to promote nonbelief among Black people in the United States and Africa. When I asked him to describe his most successful efforts, he told me that while he sees strong growth in Africa, he remains frustrated by the small numbers of Black nonbelievers in the United States: "I don't know what it would take to get more African Americans to come out [as nonbelievers]. It might have a lot to do with their history. Historically speaking, African Americans have been pathologically dependent on religion. They have been a religious people. I don't know how to break through, but I want to. They need to." Vince does not believe that Black people are innately religious. He is African American, and his decades-long efforts to deconvert Black people—to convert them to humanism—testifies to his belief that secular conversion is possible. Nonetheless, when describing Black religiosity, Vince shifted from an analysis of a historical trend to the medical language of pathology, which essentializes religiosity as a Black bodily condition. In so doing, Vince echoed claims about the innateness of Black religiosity, invoking, perhaps intentionally, their contradictions.

Historian Curtis J. Evans has shown that although the notion that Black people are innately religious is centuries old, its meaning and significance has changed over time, and its assertion has always been ambiguous.[64] Slave owners worried about enslaved people converting to Christianity because it could establish them as spiritual equals and threaten the moral legitimacy of slavery as an institution. With the help of missionaries, they also justified enslavement as a path to conversion and used Christianity for surveillance and control. Enslaved converts integrated elements of African culture into their new Christian faith, making their Christianity uniquely African American. But this synthesis also fueled white Christian doubts about the sincerity of their conversions.[65] In the nineteenth century, pseudoscientific ideas about the inferiority of Black people's intellectual abilities complemented equally racist Romantic notions of Black people's superior capacity for "feeling" and "moral sense," and thus religiosity. At the turn of the twentieth century, "Black religion," in the form of indigenous African influence, became a pathology that enabled immorality, even as the "Negro Church"—later the "Black Church"—was heralded as the most important Black institution.[66] In the middle of the twentieth century, sociologists like E. Franklin Frazier and Melville Herskovits debated whether African influence survived in African American culture. Herskovits redeployed tropes of innate Black religiosity that Frazier and

Arthur Fauset rightly countered, but Herskovits also saw "retentions" from African culture that Frazier and Fauset overlooked.[67] In the wake of their debate, scholars and activists transformed innate Black religiosity into the aesthetic and spiritual uniqueness of Black culture in order to establish an identity with continuous historical roots that antecedes slavery and possesses value apart from white culture and Christianity. Despite attempts to settle the question of Black religion, it remains generative.[68]

Black nonbelievers form their own communities in acknowledgment of their unique experience and not in rejection of what they share with other nonbelievers and certainly not out of their shared innate religiosity. I first met Luke, a research scientist at a historically Black university, in Amherst, New York, just outside Buffalo, where we were attending a conference for secular students. During an interview later, over the phone, Luke told me a story about cofounding a secular student group at his university in 2010. At the time, there was a strong taboo against discussing secularism in his Black community: "There's an inherent religiosity among Black people. Being on a Black campus and talking about anything that's nonreligious, specifically secular, specifically atheist, it's unheard of. You just don't talk about that." Though Luke, like Vince, is Black and secular, and though he believes secular conversion is possible, he still reaches for the word "inherent" to describe Black religiosity. It misunderstands Vince and Luke to take them literally, but that they reach for language like "pathologically dependent" and "inherent" to describe Black religion captures well their frustration with the history in which they find themselves inscribed.

Luke and his cofounders strategically called their group "secular" instead of "atheist" to minimize confrontation. He explained that they sought out partnerships with religious groups on campus for the same reason:

> We were easing our way in, before we started pissing people off, which was part of the plan.... We were cosponsoring programs with other religious groups and doing community-service programs, outreach programs, stuff like that. And we were just reaching out to our own community and saying, "Hey, we know there's a lot of secular people out there that need some place to go and somebody to talk to." Because you can't talk to your family. You can't talk to your friends.

Like Janet's careful parsing of her Humanistic Judaism, Luke announces his identities strategically, though for different reasons. Because atheism is so rarely discussed or accepted among Black Americans, Luke and his cofounders began by framing themselves as religion-like—one among "other religious groups"—and emphasized their morality. Though Jacqueline and Shalette expect to face harsh reactions, they take a more aggressive approach because they want to blaze a trail for other Black nonbelievers. Their strategies differ, but their actions respond to a shared condition.

Black nonbelievers experience their burden as a double negation.[69] They bear the burden of religion in the eyes of the religious and the burden of Blackness in the eyes of the secular. Shalette, Luke, and others who organize groups expressly for Black nonbelievers receive criticism from secular people who refuse the particularity of their Blackness. As Shalette told me, "[Some organized nonbelievers] viewed our groups as being racist. 'Why is there a Black group? You're being separatist. You're being divisive.' We've been told that we're racist even before they find out more information. Some of the comments have been really ugly."

Shalette also told me stories about white men commenting on the tightness of her clothes after she speaks at atheist events. Unfortunately, I was not surprised to hear that white men in the secular community have tried to make her feel uncomfortable; she is certainly a threat to their feelings of superiority. Shalette is a powerful speaker. She has great points, and she makes no apologies for who she is. I saw older white men push social boundaries at nearly every nonbeliever event I attended, usually in the name of free thought and free speech, which provide a smoke screen for avoiding the difficult work of questioning assumptions about race and gender. Secular activists who are committed to social justice have argued that "critical thinking" demands the interrogation of racism and misogyny, but some white male atheists have advocated "critical thinking" in support of the scientific racism of people like Charles Murray.[70] The experiences Shalette described are entirely consistent with what I witnessed from these men.

Atheist activist and scholar Sikivu Hutchinson has dealt with the same racism and sexism that Shalette faces. Hutchinson is especially critical of Richard Dawkins and those who valorize him: "In Dawkins's world, straight white male experience is the universal template for scientific inquiry, rationality, aesthetics, morality, and ethics; anything that doesn't conform to that is framed as other."[71] Hutchinson is critiquing the embodied self-superiority of positivist science and the mostly white men who consider themselves its inheritors. By claiming the universal truth of scientific inquiry, very secular people risk denying the difference of the Black American experience and the importance of communities that focus specifically on the needs of Black atheists. By trying to unify everyone in secularism, they devalue the important differences among secular people. Jacqueline and Shalette mis-fit the double movement of the secular paradox. They reject the religious communities in which they were raised, which also reject them to the point of denying their existence. And they mis-fit the secular communities unified by the denial of religion and the affirmation of abstract philosophical principles. The double negative of Black atheism is a rejection of secularism by Black America and a rejection of Blackness by the secular movement.[72]

In 2016, I spoke with a humanist activist named Justice at his office in Washington, DC. Though we did not know each other then, Justice was also at the BLACKOUT rally in Queens in 2013. I wanted to learn more about his efforts to promote antiracism in the secular movement, so I asked him about some of the essays he has written. He described at length the barriers he faces to being heard. He finds that white nonbelievers have a hard time understanding intersectionality, or the ways in which multiple forms of discrimination can overlap, producing unique experiences of prejudice:

> In the atheist community, I meet a lot of people who see the atheist identity as an undifferentiated category. It's hard for them to tease out the differences and acknowledge that we have different identities. I'm atheist, and I'm Black, so there are issues I deal with that you don't have to deal with. The mainstream narratives that are being sold [in this movement] are being sold by white males. And anything that diverges from what they're selling, that's less important or not important at all.

Justice engages in public debates on social media and responds to those who comment on the essays he publishes online. He told me that secular people he engages with are often repeating what they read or hear from prominent white atheists who argue against Black difference and do not believe that humanism entails a commitment to fighting inequality.

Justice told me a story to show me how some white atheists dismiss the importance of race and antiracism because they are too focused on religion as the root cause of social problems:

> This goes back to the "religion poisons everything" concept [that Christopher Hitchens promoted], which is erroneous for more than one reason. I've met people with the most absurd logic. I had this conversation with this one guy who was all gung-ho atheism. But then when I would talk about racism and how that impacts our society, this guy would get so upset. And he said, "Well, I don't understand why you feel you need to say these things when if we just dismantle religious ideology or Christian hegemony in our society, then that would erase racism"— somehow, because of magic. I thought we didn't believe in magic! But this guy did.[73]

Though Justice has little love for his Pentecostal upbringing, he disagrees with atheists who blame all social ills on religion. With his tongue in his cheek, he flips the atheist script by calling this way of thinking absurd, illogical, and magical. "In general in society," he told me, "you meet a lot of willful ignorance," but there is an arrogance that he finds among atheists, in particular:

> Those who benefit from the status quo don't want to deviate from it. In the secular community, you have that, but then on top of that, you have this tradition that says, "We don't believe in God because we're smarter." So you have a lot of people who think they've arrived at a certain intellectual level where they're beyond certain mistaken beliefs and cultural prejudices. Some seriously think that since they no longer believe in God, they're not affected by the same type of conditioning that everyone else is when it comes to racism and how they view certain groups of people. That's obviously not the case. The double whammy is that I have to speak to both issues, to both religion and race.

The arrogance he encounters among white atheists is consistent with what I witnessed at secular events. Justice's "double whammy" is the same double negative that Jacqueline and Shalette experience. Religion is the default in his Black community, and white is the default in his secular community; he has to combat discrimination that stems from both. Like Humanistic Jews and Hispanic nonbelievers, Black nonbelievers are betwixt and between.

Writing on the challenges that Black nonbelievers face in the United States, William Hart describes the "social pressures within black communities where religion, especially Christianity, is regarded as a constitutive element of authentic black identity."[74] Josef Sorett makes a similar claim about the prevalence of Protestantism among African Americans. In *Spirit in the Dark: A Religious History of Racial Aesthetics*, Sorett finds a pervasive Protestant influence on even the most secular aspects of Black life, including the art and literature of avowed nonbelievers. The Protestant and the secular exist in tension, resisting attempts to resolve the one into the other through a process of secularization.[75] Ashon T. Crawley finds within the Black Pentecostal tradition an aesthetics that exceeds Christianity and operates as its immanent critique. Blackpentecostalism, for Crawley, is a performance against racial distinction but also against the distinctions between religious and secular, spiritual and aesthetic. Its excess resists reduction and thus tidy categorization, which makes it a fertile site of resistance.[76]

Some Black nonbelievers told me how much they miss the aesthetics and social life of the Black church now that they have become secular. In the years since I first met Luke in New York, he has become much less involved in secular activism. He told me that he now distinguishes between extreme, conservative religion and liberal religion that engages in humanitarian work. He even goes to church sometimes: "I will go to church, and I will go for the community. In the Black culture, the church is one of the only places you can go for community because historically, it was that way for so long. It was the only place you could go to be safe. But there's still a massive community—and still a massive entertainment aspect." Luke grew up Catholic, but he appreciates Protestant churches and feels comfortable in them: "As far as I'm concerned, African American Protestant music is the best in the world. It's just simply, absolutely amazing. It's why you hear a Black choir in everything from rap to country to rock. It is a great place if you take all the God stuff out. If you take all that stuff out, it's a great place to be." Luke wants to cut God out of religion, but if Luke were to cut religion from his life completely, as he used to do, he would lose things he continues to value even as an atheist.

Not everyone agrees with Luke. Shalette grew up in a Black nationalist home, and her mother was deeply critical of all religion, including the Black church. Though she loves singing and is classically trained, she does not associate it with the church or find it necessary to go to church services to enjoy it. Justice shares Shalette's view. Raised Pentecostal, partly in the Holiness tradition, he echoes Sorett's scholarship and acknowledges the Black church's historical importance: "The Black church evolved from slavery and became a hub for community. It's the only Black-owned community and fellowship, where you can come together. So much art and culture, so many social movements go through it." Though he respects the Black church, Justice feels no nostalgia for it, nor does he long for something lost.

Part of the mis-fit for Black nonbelievers in predominantly white secular communities is cultural, in the narrow sense of aesthetic, but it is also cultural in a broader sense of the experience of particular bodies in a particular time and place. Shalette, Luke, and Justice cannot feel at home among people who do not acknowledge the pervasiveness of racism in the United States and its myriad effects on Black and brown Americans. Justice has made it his vocation, at least at this stage of his life, to educate secular white people on the importance of intersectionality and the need for racial justice. He and many other Black nonbelievers refuse to participate in secular communities that fail to recognize the unique lived experience of Black Americans and the ongoing effects of racism.[77]

Secular Muslims

In September 2016, I met up with a man named Hisham at a coffee shop about twenty minutes outside Detroit. Though he lives in Dearborn, a suburb of Detroit with the largest Muslim population in the United states, Hisham wanted to meet in Allen Park, an adjacent suburb that is more than 90 percent white. Hisham is stout and jovial, with an almost cherubic face. He speaks carefully, with a gentle intensity that signals he can defend himself in an argument when he needs to. Hisham was born in the United Arab Emirates and came to the United States when he was fourteen, after spending two years in Lebanon. While living in Lebanon, he discovered that during his family's time in the UAE, they hid—even from Hisham—that they are Shi'ites of Lebanese descent. He attended an American university and afterward became an engineer, though throughout his youth, he was deeply committed to Islamic scholarship and trained to be an imam, or Muslim teacher and worship leader. Because of his deep knowledge of the Sunni and Shi'ite traditions, some Muslims and ex-Muslims still address him as "Imam Hisham" when seeking his advice.

Hisham's worldview began to unravel in his midthirties, when he was conducting background research for an article against evolution. He consulted Muslim scholars he trusted, but he was unsatisfied with their knowledge of science. To better understand evolution, he read a few popular science books, including Dawkins's *The Selfish Gene*. As he struggled to articulate an argument against evolution from an Islamic perspective, he started to become depressed and reached out to a friend in Ottawa with whom he used to study Islam. After listening to Hisham's questions, the friend traveled to Dearborn and stayed with him for several days. In conversations that lasted late into the night, Hisham learned that his friend had become an atheist, and together, they "deconstructed [Hisham's] twenty-five years of religious structure." Today, Hisham is an avowed atheist who speaks and writes publicly as a lay scholar of both Islam and atheism. He told me twice that he finds himself defending Islam to atheists and atheism to the religious.

After talking at the coffee shop for almost two hours, Hisham invited me to get a drink where some of his friends might be: a bar in Detroit called Mudgie's. He insisted on driving, and on the way, we talked about how much Detroit has changed since he first moved to its suburbs. I noticed him limping on the way to his car, and he told me that he walked too much on a recent trip to San Francisco. His feet were still sore. It was his first visit to the city, and he was shocked by its strong support for its LGBTQ community. Though he made it clear he approved, he also seemed a little scandalized, which I understood as him adjusting to his secular conversion. Hisham then quizzed me, gently, about my research, about my personal life, and finally, about my worldview. When I told him I consider myself secular, he grabbed his phone and began texting with one eye on the road. I had a hunch about the sudden pause in our conversation, but it took me a few hours to confirm that I was right:

Hisham's friends wanted to know if I was religious. If I had been, two of them told me later they would have left the bar to avoid me.

Safety is a big concern for ex-Muslims, so they often filter whom they meet and who can attend their events. For instance, Ex-Muslims of North America (EXMNA), a national organization with more than two dozen local chapters throughout Canada and the United States, screens new members with a series of interviews, usually over phone and video chat. Sometimes they hold events to which they invite people whom they are "unsure about" so they can "see how it goes," according to Hassan, one of EXMNA's leaders whom I introduced in chapter 1. After these events, leaders consult with veteran members, who judge the prospective member's level of comfort with rejecting Islam. Hassan estimates that they reject 20 to 25 percent of those who apply, and he was careful during our interview to protect the criteria for membership, lest I publish information that would aid someone wanting to infiltrate. Even among full members, some events remain off-limits to certain people. Hassan gave me an example of an exclusive event and explained why the group is so careful:

> You're coming from such a repressed culture. People want to rebel, want to do outrageous things that push those boundaries. We had a Halloween party, and it was titled "Mullahween." *Mullah* means "priest." So you have to dress up as some sort of Islamic religious figure. There were lots of very interesting takes on it, and if I was public about the specifics, people would try to kill us. But people had a lot of fun at that. They came up with lots of interesting costumes and ideas, drinks even. We came up with religious-themed drinks. People had a lot of fun with that.

The event that Hassan describes is not a good fit for all ex-Muslims because while some find release in the blasphemous subversion of Mullahween, others take offense, sometimes viscerally, despite their rational rejection of Islamic teachings. The anxiety of breaking the physical, sensory discipline of belonging to a cultural group can be distressing or exciting—or sometimes both.[78]

When Hisham and I got to Mudgie's, he introduced me to his friends, Mo, Rami, and Jenny. Mo is tall, with a beer gut and a scraggly beard, and he was wearing hip glasses and a T-shirt. He is infectiously fun. Rami is short, with a shaved head. He is quiet and reserved, though friendly and very kind once he opens up. Mo was born in Saudi Arabia and first came to Michigan as a graduate student, and Rami was born in Lebanon. Like Hisham, both speak Arabic. Jenny was tending bar, so I spoke with her less, but I learned that she was born and raised in Dearborn and identifies as Arab. Like many children of immigrants, she does not speak her parents' native Arabic, but when Hisham, Mo, and Rami would talk to each other in Arabic, she gave no sign that she felt excluded. After a few hours and some prying, I discovered that Hisham often makes clever jokes in Arabic that play on blasphemous senses of words or pun with English idioms. His jokes had Mo laughing all night, and I was sorry to miss them.

Close attention to language and a love for blasphemy is common among the ex-Muslims I interviewed and spent time with. Ismail, the Egyptian man I introduced in chapter 1, told me he wants to purify his Arabic speech of all references to God:

> A lot of the [Arabic] language has God in it. I think that for Muslims that's the most obvious thing [that changes when you become an atheist] because everything's "insha'allah"—God's willing—"insha'allah" or "thank God": "Hamdullah." "Thank you" is "thank God." "I will do this if God's willing." The language itself is so—the religious language is so deep in it. It's very hard to actually pull it out. . . . I'm determined enough to remove these words from my vocabulary, and I'm aware of it. I'm trying to intentionally change my language and create my own language. But not everyone can do that! Not everybody's interested in doing that!

Ismail's attempt to purify his language is not unusual among nonbelievers, though his intensity is. Ismail never compromises. To help me understand his willingness to fight even the smallest battles, he told me a story about his daily visits to his local deli:

> "Alhamdulillah" is "thank God." Everybody says that. I don't say "Alhamdulillah." Like the guy who works in the deli that I get my sandwich from, he's Muslim. I always get a ham sandwich. He knows I'm Arab. I go, "I want a ham sandwich." Then he says in Arabic, "And how is your health?" And I say, "I am good!" The answer to his question is, "Thank God." When someone asks you, "How's your health?" you have to say,

"Thank God." You don't say, "I am good." You can't say that. It's almost blasphemous. And I tell him, "I'm good," and he looks at me, and he says, "Thank God," because he's saying the right answer for me. And it's been like that for two or three years. I go there, and he says, "How are you?" and I say, "I'm good," and he's like, "Thank God."

Like Ismail's everyday blasphemy, Hisham's jokes signal that he is no longer a practicing Muslim but also that he is still part of Muslim culture. He is a secular Muslim.

Mudgie's closed at 10 p.m. that night, so around 9:30 we moved to another bar located in an alley in downtown Detroit, near the Quicken Loans headquarters. The area was being redeveloped—a boon for Quicken Loans founder Dan Gilbert, who by no accident owns much of it. As is often the case when I visit a trendy neighborhood in a new city, I felt transported to a simulacrum of cool, surrounded by murals of "graffiti" and Banksy-inspired pop art.[79] Mo tends bar at a brewery, so he recommended a delicious beer he saw on tap. After helping me, he asked the bartender for "the sweetest drink on the menu," which he wanted to order for Hisham. He settled on an Irish coffee and ordered himself one too. Rami had to get up very early for a class the next the morning, so he drank water. None of the men seemed to enjoy the taste of alcohol, though their delight in drinking was palpable.

Shortly after we sat down, Mo and Rami started talking about how when they left Islam, they went through a total conversion, and they felt like they "lost everything."[80] After listening for a while, Hisham chimed in with a joke I shared in this book's introduction. It was so interesting I had to pull out my phone and write it down: "There's no way to separate Arabic and Islamic culture. There's nothing left. There's no Arabic culture. There's Islamic culture. What's left? The desert?" Hisham captured wryly the loss they feel and the work it takes for them to remake themselves. Ismail told me something similar: "I think it's easier for me because I'm Egyptian. I have something that is not Islamic. It's so diluted with Islam. Islam has been in charge of that part of the world for a very long time. Everything has an Islamic flavor to it. It was hard to try to separate what's Egyptian for me or what I like." When these Muslim men became secular, they had to rethink the miracles that happened in their families and retell stories that depend on the supernatural. They changed how they interpreted their dreams, and words they had long spoken felt strange as they left their mouths, as if they had betrayed them. This process of self-translation into the secular is ongoing for all three men and, at times, still very challenging.

Being a secular Muslim is on its face a contradiction, exacerbated by the fact that in the United States, Islam has become synonymous with "bad" religion and a frequent target of atheist diatribes. New Atheist authors Sam Harris, Christopher Hitchens, and Richard Dawkins have all attacked Islam and received criticism for being Islamophobic.[81] In *The End of Faith*, for instance, Harris spends dozens of pages criticizing the Qur'an and, in other chapters, identifies with and defends Buddhism.[82] Scholars Amarnath Amarasingam and Melanie Brewster argue that while some organized nonbelievers have espoused Islamophobic rhetoric, others within the secular movement have opposed it and continue to defend "multiculturalism."[83] I found the same divide in my research. For instance, at a conference I attended in Minneapolis that focused on secular women and social justice, two panelists spoke about their frustration with atheists who use criticism of religion as an excuse to be Islamophobic:

> DEBBIE GODDARD: I get frustrated by the online dialogue in the secular movement around Islam and Muslims, especially white men who use ex-Muslims and women in Muslim countries to say, "I care about this, and that's why I'm such a raging Islamophobe."
>
> SAM FAROOQUI: I refer to that as scapegoating because you're using the plight of a specific group to go on raging with your biases and ignorance.
>
> GODDARD: They use it to attack Western feminists too: "Why are you concerned with [sexual harassment] in an elevator when there's female genital mutilation?"

Sam Farooqui was especially frustrated that her criticisms of the Muslim culture in which she was raised are sometimes appropriated by white atheists who claim to be allies but who really just want to legitimize their own attacks. The two women are on one side of an internal debate that continues to be waged.

Hisham and Mo told me that they find it hard to walk the line between Islamophobia and criticizing Islam because in different contexts, their comments are perceived differently. Some members of EXMNA talk about "attacking Allah" or "attacking Islam" and "defending Muslims" to describe the balance they aim to strike.[84] Ultimately, Mo feels like anything critical he says "ends up sounding Islamophobic." Though I felt that the men were open with me about their criticisms, they told me that they sometimes hold back. Mo related a story about a class he took in graduate school on women and Islam, which he described as "very pro-Islam." The professor invited women to class who wear headscarves so that they could talk about and normalize their experience, but Mo wanted to oppose their view. Instead of doing so head-on, and without announcing himself as an ex-Muslim, he asked why no ex-Muslims were invited.

Criticizing Islam without being Islamophobic is the paradoxical inverse of being a secular Muslim. In our conversations, the topic of Islamophobia often tracked closely with discussions of the challenge of separating Muslim culture from Islam. The secular Muslims I spent time with were raised and continue to participate in cultures that are difficult, if not impossible, to separate from Islam, but they have also converted to a way of understanding the world that alienates them from their upbringing and sometimes fundamentally opposes their previous way of life. They are at once both self-critical and critical of an other. They live the contradiction of being both secular and Muslim, and like all secular people, though in their own way, they have to negotiate the secular paradox.

Feeling like a Herd of Cats

The local communities that nonbelievers form can provide respite from discrimination and fellowship to ease loneliness, but they can also feel too religious and cause discomfort. For some secular people, the very idea of organized nonbelievers is paradoxical enough to be an oxymoron. Secular groups like the Sunday Assembly resemble religious congregations in their structure and activities, and others try to avoid anything that seems religious, even if it means disavowing ways of getting together that could draw in more members or create stronger bonds between them. Sometimes these are rational, deliberate decisions that nonbelievers debate among one another, and sometimes they are affective responses to a particular way of being secular, felt as anxiety or revulsion, cozy familiarity or laughter. Because the secular culture of a group can be felt so viscerally, where a group meets, the activities they engage in, and even the colors and smells they encounter at gatherings can influence whether a nonbeliever feels comfortable in a particular secular community.[85] To capture the affective dimension of the secular paradox, I have used a lot of emotional language to describe how nonbelievers feel about their communities and their particular way of being secular, despite some nonbelievers' discomfort with emotion and aesthetics.[86]

This chapter has demonstrated the consequences of American secularism's Christian-centrism by focusing mostly on Humanistic Jews, Hispanic nonbelievers, Black atheists, and secular Muslims. In their struggles to become legible and to carve out new ways of being secular, they are the exceptions that prove the rule. Humanistic Jews have developed an especially religious form of secularism that allows them to embrace their Jewishness while remaining faithful to their secular worldview. Hispanic nonbelievers are often uncomfortable with the iconoclasm and minimalism of secular culture, which feels specifically white. Black atheists bear the burden of Black religion on their bodies and institutions, combating the assumptions that Black people are inherently religious and that secularism is universal and thus colorblind. Secular Muslims struggle with the both/and of their secular religiosity, needing to make hard choices about which parts of their culture can be purified of religious pollution and preserved and which remain too polluted, even after being cleansed by the inverting power of blasphemy. These secular subgroups are inventing new ways of being secular that are literally changing what secularism is and can be.

As I noted before, many times during my research, I heard leaders who organize nonbelievers describe their work as "herding cats." Like so much I encountered in the culture of avowedly secular people, the phrase winks at the secular paradox without seeming to acknowledge it. Though cats are usually solitary, when they form into groups, they are called a "clowder" or a "glaring." "Herd of cats" is awkward and a little wrong, but it is useful and more recognizable than "clowder." It captures well the challenge of organizing "freethinkers" who are "nonjoiners" and averse to the dangers of religious "dogma," "authority," and "groupthink."

"Organized nonbelief" is also an awkward term, but so are alternatives like "secular religion" and "atheist church," which demand explanation too. Awkward ways of being secular that openly embrace aspects of religion, analogize or invert religion, or feel religious despite their best efforts to be secular demonstrate the power of the secular paradox and especially its irresolution.

Scholars of Black American life like Sorett and Crawley find religion operating through the secular, in excess of the religious, but also find the secular suffusing religion, at times as its immanent critique. The perspective they offer, indebted to Evans, is capable of holding a contradiction in tension and tracing its effects. It offers a way of seeing secularism that can capture the perpetual movement of its Sisyphean effort to resolve its paradox. As it swings back and forth, resisting resolution, the paradox generates new ways of being secular and, indeed, new ways of being religious, which can seem peculiar and contradictory if understood as only one or the other. Real but rare and awkward to name, "organized nonbelief" is a bit like a herd of cats.[87]

3

Ritual

Secular but Human

The master of ceremonies lit the wick of a skull-shaped candle and held it up before the audience. When she told us she was burning it in honor of John Lennon, the opening chords of "Imagine" began to play. Several people crowded the front of the stage and urged us all to stand and sing along. I took off my participant hat and just observed, as about half the room stood up. To my left, on the other side of the table, I heard Colin, a man I had met a few hours earlier, announce loudly and to no one in particular, "I hate the Beatles." The song's opening lines—"Imagine there's no heaven / It's easy if you try"—drew whoops and applause, and Colin repeated himself, with emphasis: "I *hate* the Beatles." I stifled a smile, and he and I both stayed sitting. "Imagine" is a staple at events for organized nonbelievers, and the next few verses are favorites of the very secular: "No hell below us / Above us only sky / Imagine all the people / Living for today." Lennon's most popular hit as a solo artist will almost surely be played at a conference for freethinkers, a cocktail hour for atheists, or a death-themed dinner for humanists. Unlike Colin, I have no problem with the Beatles, but after years of fieldwork among organized nonbelievers, I hate "Imagine."

The song was an awkward end to a series of rituals celebrating El Día de los Muertos, the Mexican Day of the Dead. On November 1, 2018, I spent an evening with around seventy nonbelievers at La Fonda, a Los Angeles restaurant opened in 1969 by Grammy-winning pioneer of mariachi music Natividad Cano.[1] Wanting to elevate mariachi, Cano maintained a strict rehearsal schedule for his group, Los Camperos, and refused to play standards that the audience expected, like Ritchie Valens's "La Bamba." He made the band the genre's star by removing solo vocal performances and putting the musicians in flashy matching costumes. At La Fonda, Cano elevated mariachi literally, taking the band off the floor of the restaurant, where it usually played among the diners, and putting it on a stage. The restaurant is Spanish revival, inside and out—carved wood, wrought iron, and stucco—and mariachi outfits are on display in glass cases along the walls.[2] On Fridays and Saturdays, La Fonda hosts two mariachi performances a night. November 1 fell on a Thursday in 2018, so the restaurant added an extra night of shows for the days-long holiday.[3] The secular Día de los Muertos event that I attended started at 6:00 p.m. to give us time to mingle and have a drink before the early show started at 7:00. An all-female mariachi band and two young dancers wearing skull face paint performed several songs, separated by costume changes. La Fonda oozes LA kitsch, and the food is unlikely to win awards, but it was a great show.

The avowedly secular part of the event kicked off a little after 8:00, once the show finished and the restaurant staff had cleared most of the plates. The MC was a white woman in her thirties who captured the secular's ambivalence perfectly. "More and more people are secular," she told us, "but we're still humans who need each other and mark time in our lives with rituals. We have none of the superstition and religion that normally go with this day." In these loaded sentences, she conveyed an entire theory of religion and secularism: Secular people are not religious, but community and ritual, which our culture associates with religion, are fundamental human needs. Secular people need ritual, in particular, to mark major life events and give life a temporal structure. El Día de los Muertos is normally religious and superstitious—Catholic and indigenous—but this version has removed those elements so that it can become secular.[4] In the MC's theory, living merely in religion's remainder requires secular people to sacrifice too much. To save community and ritual from religion's domain, they must be made pure. Community and ritual are in fact ways to become more secular.

After the MC's opening remarks, the organizers lit four candles for four "freethinkers": "St. Frida Kahlo," Charles Darwin, Carl Sagan, and Christopher Hitchens. The man who lit Darwin's candle said that when he and his wife were last in England, they went on a "pilgrimage" to Darwin's house, about an hour outside London. A young woman then played two songs on her guitar, each followed by a short speech. The first was about Christopher Hitchens and the second about her late grandmother, to whom she had given a written version of her eulogy before her death. A series of speakers followed. Each person brought to the stage with them a photo of the dead loved one they wanted to honor, which they retrieved from an *ofrenda*, or altar table, that was placed nearby.

After one woman grabbed a photo of her father, she told us, "I've been in Mexico several times over this day. It's a celebration I really love. I have an altar-ish thing in my house." Most speakers talked about their fathers, whom several credited for their atheism. The last woman to speak told an especially moving story about her mother, who was a midwife, and the gallows humor they shared on her mother's deathbed. I did my best to be discreet when my eyes filled with tears, and I welcomed the dull feeling of annoyance that numbed me when "Imagine" started playing. After the sing-along finished, we were encouraged to leave in a hurry because we had run over time and the room had to be cleared for the second and final mariachi performance.

Throughout the night, I found myself confused by the blurry boundaries between secular, not secular, and antireligious. When finding a seat for dinner, I struck up a conversation with a woman from Inglewood named Angie. I tried making the small talk common among organized nonbelievers—"Have you been to an event like this before? What group are you part of?"—but I quickly realized that Angie was there for other reasons. She had come to meet up with some friends from high school, one of whom had invited her to reconnect now that they had retired. From what she told me, Angie was probably not secular, and she avoided the topic tactfully. I suspect that her friend had invited people from her broader network, trying to attract newcomers to nonbelief. Angie had not seen the friend in so long that she was unsure what she looked like, and when she was swept up in conversation by another older woman, I was out of earshot.

After talking with Angie, I looked around, trying to figure out who had bought a ticket for a secular event, who came for a spooky mariachi show, and who simply walked in for dinner on a Thursday night. Though most of the main dining room applauded the first couple of speakers, some tables paid far less attention as the night wore on. When nonbelievers made antireligious remarks, laughter came only from people near the stage. There were just three people who appeared to be of

Hispanic descent who were definitely among the nonbelievers, though many other Hispanic people were in the restaurant, including the staff. I tried to imagine the memorial speeches from Angie's perspective and through the eyes and ears of the Hispanic families in the balcony who seemed to have come for a normal dinner. These were not their rituals.

My life experience makes me a poor judge of the authenticity of a Día de los Muertos celebration, but surely, this event at La Fonda was not authentic. Living in Southern California, I often feel strangely at home, but the strangeness is more comfortable than uncanny—more *heimelig* than *unheimlich*.[5] My mother married my stepfather, a meatpacker from Michoacán, when I was seven, and I grew up in Minnesota in a bicultural white-American and Mexican home. Though my parents mostly spoke to each other in Spanish when I was a young child, my verbal Spanish as an adult is transactional, and I am more likely to turn bright red than impress anyone with my Mexican accent. As a child and a young teenager, I spent time with my stepfather's family outside of Los Angeles, and the Mexicanness of Southern California's culture sets me at ease in a way that only familiarity can. I grew up eating Mexican food most nights of the week, and I spent countless hours among Mexican and Mexican American families, but I have limited experience with traditional Mexican holidays or rituals. Generations of poverty and migration within and beyond Mexico have left my stepfather's family without a strong sense of cultural heritage, and neither of my parents thinks much about that disconnection. Poverty, migration, and intermarriage did the same to my mother's side of the family, which talks vaguely about Norway, Sweden, and Ireland but knows well that those are mere fractions of a motley mixture. Sitting in La Fonda, with its show-business blend of artifice and authenticity, among a mostly white group of nonbelievers, I felt how my family feels about Cinco de Mayo celebrations in Minnesota. This is not our ritual.

Why did a group of mostly white secular people living in the Los Angeles area want to celebrate the Day of the Dead? What were they trying to accomplish? Part of the answer lies in the conversation between Juan and Michael I discussed in chapter 2, which I listened in on after Juan's lecture in Los Angeles several months before. Juan made a strong impression on the nearly all-white nonbeliever communities he met with, and they sought to heed his advice by embracing color, music, and emotion. Though the four local groups that worked together to create the event did so in part to try to attract Hispanic nonbelievers, the celebration's demographics showed that their efforts failed. When the only Black speaker took the stage to talk about his nephew, who was killed on the north side of St. Louis, he opened with a joke that called attention to the obvious absence of people of color: "Can I get a round of applause from the Black people in the room?" The crowd laughed, and he exchanged a wave with the only two Black members of the audience, including Angie. Near the end of his speech, he chastised the secular community for not having more African Americans onstage and told them they "need to work on that." He did not try to speak for the Mexican Americans who were not present for this secular Día de los Muertos.

The event's organizers had other goals too. As the MC told us at the outset, they wanted to give nonbelievers' lives temporal structure by observing a seasonal holiday that asks them to confront their inevitable deaths. Other speakers talked about how they wanted to honor the dead and create closure for the living. Conversing with some of the organizers before and after the event, I learned that they wanted to strengthen their community by sharing food and deep emotional experiences. Leaders from Sunday Assembly Los Angeles have tried various rituals to fortify the bonds among their members, and they considered this event another experiment they could learn from.

The secular Día de los Muertos was definitely problematic, and no one whooped or applauded for Lennon's verses on capitalism—"Imagine no possessions / I wonder if you can"—but as a symptom of the secular paradox, the ritual is revealing. In the organizers' attempts to affirm the religion-like parts of the secular and to remove from a ritual what is too religious, they displayed their assumptions about the religious excess of non-Christian cultures and their willingness to appropriate that excess for their own ritual ends. Nonbelievers are secular but human, religion-like but not religious, and mostly white.

Making Ritual Nonreligious

The aim of this chapter is to describe how nonbelievers approach ritual and to capture their paradoxical engagement with it, which rejects religion but grabs hold of it too, while affirming a secular way of life. This chapter also treats their ambivalence as an ambiguity, which disturbs the boundary between the secular and the religious. I observed this duality firsthand in June 2019 when I attended a training for Humanist Celebrants held at the University of Southern California's Office of Religious Life. The all-day workshop was organized by the American Humanist Association's religious subsidiary, the Humanist Society, and cost $85, including lunch. Only two of the five other participants lived in California, and one came all the way from Houston, Texas.

The two-hour morning session focused on weddings, and the three-hour afternoon session on memorial services, naming ceremonies, and invocations. Organized nonbelievers commonly refer to naming ceremonies, weddings, and memorial services as "life-cycle rituals."[6] Naming ceremonies are the secular analogue of a Christian baptism, and invocations are analogous to an opening prayer at a meeting or event. Celebrants usually prefer the term "memorial service" to "funeral" because technically the latter refers only to services at which the corpse is present, which is not usually the case at humanist services in the United States.[7] The people attending the workshop were most interested in weddings because all except one have side businesses working as wedding officiants. Mark, the man who does not, has a full-time job as executive director of a large nonbeliever community in the Southwest. He hopes that performing weddings and naming ceremonies can raise some revenue for his group and provide a needed service. Given the age of many of his members, he knows he will have to perform some memorial services too.

The Humanist Society does not require Celebrants to attend a training in order to endorse them, so attendees were there to become better at creating rituals and running a business doing it. Topics included a mix of business advice ("use spreadsheets for accounting; have a lawyer look over your contract template") and ritual advice ("practice the ceremony in front of a mirror at home; if you're scattering ashes, know which way the wind is blowing"). A woman in her fifties named Cindy flew in from Minnesota to run the workshop, which she has led before in other parts of the country. Over the course of a decade as a Humanist Celebrant, Cindy has performed more than three hundred ceremonies. Most were weddings she performed through her officiant business, though she has also conducted memorial services and naming ceremonies. The vast majority of the couples she marries do not hire a wedding planner, so she told those of us attending the workshop that she helps them organize their ceremony with an eighty-item checklist that includes tasks like getting a marriage license and deciding where to stand. She ran our training with the same meticulousness.

After telling us how our day would be structured, Cindy directed our attention to the third and fourth pages of the Humanist Celebrant training manual that we all received by email a few days before. There we found several dozen questions that Celebrants should ask themselves before they start working with clients. Most were practical: "Will I run rehearsals? Will I provide sample vows? How far will I travel to meet with potential clients? Will my fees be set or variable?" One of the questions on the list caught my eye because it encourages Celebrants to decide whether they will provide services to "religious couples" or "couples wanting to include religious content in their ceremonies." After reading through the list, Mark asked Cindy what I was also wondering: "What should we do when clients want something religious?" Cindy answered carefully. The Humanist Society, she told us, expects its Celebrants "to be professional and to be consistent with a humanist life stance," but it has "a code of ethics" that allows Celebrants to decide on their own whether and how much religion to include. "Informally, I would discourage you from including too much religion," she said, "but as long as you're not standing up there espousing religious beliefs, the individual Celebrant decides."

Those in the room who had already performed weddings in their local area said it was common for couples they worked with to ask for ceremonial elements that they considered too religious. They have to draw a personal line that makes them feel comfortable but also gives the couple the ceremony they want and keeps them in business. Cindy gave some examples that capture well the paradoxical tension between the secular's two sides: the absence of religion, sometimes called "neutrality" or "nonsectarianism," and the affirmation of a secular worldview, which Cindy calls "humanism." Cindy occasionally marries "interfaith couples" who are both religious because "they see humanism as a common ground." They want to remove any religious elements to avoid upsetting family members, "which is great," Cindy told us. Put differently, these interfaith couples see Cindy's humanism in purely negative terms, which unmarks it as a presence and thus renders it religiously neutral.

Cindy accepts that her humanism can be a negation or an affirmation because it is both. In some cases, interfaith couples want to include religious elements, which Cindy deals with in different ways, usually by distancing herself from them. She will not offer a religious reading during the ceremony, but she will allow someone in the family to do so. In one instance, Cindy married a Catholic couple who could not get married in the church because one of them had been divorced. They wanted to include a lot of Catholic elements, so she used phrases like "per the Catholic tradition in which they were raised," in order to signal that the religiosity was theirs and not hers.[8]

Cindy also captured well the freethinker's ambivalence toward tradition, or that which is received and not created individually. "Once you get out of the requirements of a religion," she told us, "you can organize a ceremony however you want. But there are some ways that are better than others." Being free from a tradition is creatively liberating, but there is no need to reinvent the wheel every time, and some rituals are more effective than others. A successful ritual, Cindy explained, must "create an emotional arc" and must "feel authentic." Over the course of the day, I learned that sincere feeling and authenticity are ways of measuring whether a secular ritual works. The ritual must be authentic to the individual rather than a tradition, and personal feeling provides the test of its authenticity. Cindy advised us "to speak from your own essence as a human" and "to speak in your authentic voice." I thought about the secular Día de los Muertos event several times while listening to Cindy talk about ritual authenticity. I wondered if other people who were at La Fonda that night found the event "authentic," and if so, was it authentic for them or authentically "Mexican"?[9]

Rituals, in Cindy's theory, are ways of evoking and harnessing emotions for the purpose of the occasion. In the case of a wedding, the goal of the ritual is to bring the couple being married into a feeling of union and to bring the people observing the ceremony into communion with them, as affirming witnesses to their love and as a lifelong community of support. For instance, Cindy told us about a ceremony in which the couple adds two different colors of sand to a jar or vase, which they can shake up or leave layered. For blended families in which the couple has children from previous relationships, this can be a powerful metaphor, she told us. One variation on this ritual is to create a ceremony in which everyone present, including the audience, adds a layer of sand, one person at a time. Cindy warned us, however, that "candle and sand ceremonies are the most overused and least significant." Though she encouraged us to begin with templates because they have been shown to work, she also encouraged us to personalize the ritual, which makes it feel authentic. A ritual that is too common, in her view, risks feeling rote or trite. If it feels inauthentic, it will fail to signify the importance of the moment; it will lose its significance. She also spoke often about what a particular ritual element "represents" or "symbolizes." "Candles are terrible for outdoor weddings," she advised. "When the wind blows the candle out, the whole symbolism is lost." She told us to remove the religious symbols that some funeral homes have in place, such as the cross, because they will bother the nonreligious family of the deceased. "Leave the stage blank," she advised. Emptiness can signal the secular's negative half.

Cindy would reject any aspect of a ceremony that felt overtly Protestant, but her theory of ritual is in some ways "post-Protestant." It emphasizes authenticity and sincerity, it sees ritual in symbolic terms, and it seeks to remove symbols like the cross that Protestants have sometimes perceived as distinctly Catholic. Cindy's approach to ritual, however, is an odd amalgam that is true to its secularity. Her goals are functional; she wants to use symbols to achieve the concrete social and psychological ends that functionalist anthropologists have long seen as the purpose of ritual. Her theory is as performative as it is symbolic and as dedicated to the body and to feeling as it is to rational assent and authentic representation. Organized nonbelievers' secular rituals are fittingly paradoxical.

Secular people depend on an abstract concept of ritual that has been shaped by Protestants and by secular scholars of religion. To be available for secular people to appropriate, "ritual" needed to become a distinct thing that people do, which happened through Protestant criticisms of Catholic practices. It then needed to become something that all humans do, including secular people, which happened when scholars started looking at other cultures and finding ritual everywhere. In *Genealogies of Religion*, Talal Asad criticizes fellow anthropologist Clifford Geertz for adopting a post-Protestant and post-Enlightenment understanding of religion that reduces it to meanings or, in Geertz's language, "a system of symbols," at the expense of bodily practices, disciplines, and feelings.[10] Rather than propose a new understanding of "religion" or "ritual" that incorporates the body, Asad's goal is to show how theorists who use these categories recapitulate Christian understandings that they have dragged forth in their intellectual inheritance. They universalize and secularize "religion" and "ritual" by assuming that they are not particularly European and Christian concepts and by applying them to all times and places.[11] Scholars of religion Jonathan Z. Smith and Kathryn Lofton have shown how Protestant polemics against Catholic ritual and intra-Protestant debates have persisted in secular academic theories of religion, as well as in popular ritual discourse.[12] For anti-Catholic Protestants who privilege "faith" over "works," sincerity and authenticity are opposed to ritual's thoughtless repetition.[13]

In *Ritual: Perspectives and Dimensions*, scholar of religion Catherine Bell acknowledges the validity of Asad's criticisms, but like Smith and Lofton, she argues for ritual's analytic recuperation. In her approach, a focus on contextualized ritual activity, or "ritualization," enables scholars to sidestep some of the problems created by abstracting ritual. Bell finds, however, that in recent years, ritual practitioners have confounded the active and the abstract:

> For modern ritualists devising ecological liturgies, crafting new age harmonies, or drumming up a fire in the belly, the taken-for-granted authority to do these things and the accompanying conviction about their efficacy lie in the abstraction "ritual" that scholars have done so much to construct. We are seeing a new "paradigm" for ritualization. Belief in ritual as a central dynamic in human affairs—as opposed to belief in a particular Christian liturgical tradition or the historical practice of Jewish law—gives ritualists the authority to ritualize creatively and even idiosyncratically. Ritual is approached as a means to create and renew community, transform human identity, and remake our most existential sense of being in the cosmos.[14]

Though Cindy gave no indication that she is familiar with nineteenth-century Protestant debates about ritual or twentieth-century scholars' ritual theories, she is one of Bell's "modern ritualists." Like other Celebrants and ritual creators, she depends on a scholarly tradition that abstracts "ritual" into a universal category of human behavior.[15] Bell is probably right when she speculates, "We may well be in the very process of actually creating ritual as the universal phenomenon we have long taken it to be."[16] By abstracting ritual and putting it to work, organized nonbelievers are post-Protestant and post-Enlightenment, which is to say, Christian and secular. They embrace a Protestant-influenced concept but do so ambivalently, against the grain of Protestantism's antiritual polemics and in rejection of Protestantism and other forms of religion. They also embrace a secular tradition, as I discuss in chapter 5.

Secular people engage in ritual self-consciously, for this-worldly ends.[17] Cindy told us that Celebrants have four goals when conducting a memorial service: (1) "celebrate the life of the person who's died"; (2) "help people offer support to one another, especially those closest to the person"; (3) "help people support themselves"; and (4) "set people on a path to healing." Like the MC of the secular Día de los Muertos event, Cindy believes that she and her fellow nonbelievers are secular but human. They need "life-cycle" and other rituals to mark life's major moments, create community, and heal the trauma of loss. Ritual is goal-directed for Cindy. She wants Celebrants to use rituals to achieve the social ends of the community and the emotional and psychological ends of the individual. By emphasizing ritual's social and individual functions, she and other secular "ritualists" remove ritual from the exclusive domain of religion. They abstract, secularize, and universalize it, as scholars before them have done. This abstraction and universalization enables them to borrow ritual templates from other religions and cultures, which through various means they purify of religious pollution. Their strategies of purification—avoidance, blasphemy, abstraction, and translation—render ritual safe for secular use but also transform it. In what remains of this chapter, I examine these strategies more closely and show how they produce distinct forms of the secular.

Modes of Secular Purification

During the several years I conducted research among organized nonbelievers, I observed four modes through which secular people purify the secular of religious pollution. Though these modes of secular purification can make religious rituals acceptable for nonbelievers without compromising their secularity, they are not inherently secular. They negate in some ways and affirm in others, so they can be used by anyone who wants to negate or affirm any religious or religion-like tradition. In the hands of secular people, they can negate all religion and affirm a secular way of life.

1. *Avoidance* is the most straightforward strategy, and at its extreme, it means avoiding everything that feels religious. Avoidance can also mean *excision*, as when Sanderson Jones, one of the cofounders of the Sunday Assembly, described his group as "all the good bits of religion." Standing on a stage in 2013, at the New York Society for Ethical Culture in Manhattan, he told a group of about a hundred of us, "If you have a rock in your shoe, you don't throw out the shoe. You take out the rock." You excise what is too religious. Avoidance can also take stronger forms, like visceral aversion or antireligious antagonism.
2. *Blasphemy* embraces an aspect of religion but profanes it, often in a provocative way. Acts of blasphemy that I witnessed or discussed with secular people usually accompanied strong emotions like anger or joy, though some organized nonbelievers utter antireligious remarks seemingly out of habit. Ex-Muslims organizing Mullahween is blasphemous, and so are the offhand jokes I heard at nonbeliever conferences about Catholic priests being pedophiles. Blasphemy is both derision and preservation, which can, ironically, be quite loving.
3. *Abstraction* is a way to remove religion's particularity, and it suffuses the language of organized nonbelievers. When Humanistic Jews refuse to call where they gather a "sanctuary" and instead call it a "meeting room," they are not just avoiding religious language. They are filtering it through a cipher and replacing it with a term that can contain both religion and the secular. A "church" can become a "house of worship" in order to remove Christian particularity and include other religions. It can also become a "gathering place" to include secular people.
4. *Translation* is the most complex mode of purification. It requires recognizing or establishing an analogy between the religious and the secular and then translating the former into the latter. Un-

like abstraction, which removes particularity, translation affirms a secular worldview in all its particulars. An example is when atheists like Sam Harris explain the cognitive benefits of meditation in order to reposition the practice within a secular ontology and discourse.[18] Focusing solely on meditation's material benefits extracts the practice from the cosmic temporality of karma and reincarnation and places it firmly within the homogeneous time of the natural world.[19]

The modes of secular purification often depend on one another in order to work effectively, but they are all distinct in their operation. For example, avoiding religion—not being religious—is the goal of all secular purification, but living in religion's remainder is difficult, especially if religion is defined broadly. To embrace aspects of religion without being polluted by its religiosity requires religion to change; this is the work of blasphemy, abstraction, and translation. Blasphemy profanes the religious but retains some of its particularity. Blasphemy's profanation removes religion's polluting power by rendering it ridiculous and making it unnecessary to avoid. Blasphemy does not, however, fully translate religion into a secular ontology and discourse. Abstraction removes religion's particularity to a level at which it can be grouped with the secular under a single concept. It does not excise religion's pollution so much as filter it through interpretation and then dilute it by making it more capacious. Translation translates the religious into the secular by remapping it ontologically and discursively. Translation into the secular can only take place because the secular is a discursive tradition, including an epistemology and assumptions about ontology but also practices and sensibilities. Translation is thus more totalizing than blasphemy and an affirmative corollary of abstraction's negation of particularity.

Modes of the Secular

Each mode of secular purification produces distinct modes of the secular. Avoidance produces the absence of religion, sometimes experienced as indifference, but it can also negate more actively when secular people are antireligious. Antireligiosity is usually hostile, so it has a distinct feel. It is different from the affect of indifference, which is a subtler form of avoidance that can feel passive and go unnoticed. The Freedom From Religion Foundation provides good examples of antireligiosity, which can include blasphemy. In its very name, the group seeks to avoid religion, and in practice, its avoidance is often antagonistic. In June 2018, FFRF paid for an antireligious billboard to go up in Atlanta that read, "Supernatural belief—the enemy of humanity."[20] This enemy ought to be avoided but also destroyed.

When FFRF relies on blasphemy to produce its secularity, it leaves a residue of the religiosity it subverts. This residual religion can become a problem for very secular people, as it did in 2013, when federal attorneys argued that Dan Barker, one of FFRF's codirectors, could be considered a "minister" by the IRS. In the attorneys' legal brief, they wrote that Barker "has been 'in demand' for 'de-baptisms' and has been sought out by atheists for counseling and other services, given his special qualification as former theistic clergy."[21] Barker's blasphemous inversions of baptism rituals and his personal history of being a minister pollutes him with the religious, which compromises, according to these attorneys, his secular purity in the eyes of the law. A federal judge ruled against Barker and FFRF but left it to the IRS to decide on his secularity.[22] In a surprisingly literal way, blasphemy can be dirty business.

Abstraction produces other forms of the secular—the neutral, the empty, and the universal—by filtering the religious through a cipher, or zero, which removes its specificity or dilutes it by grouping it with secular particulars. An abstract category like "community" is not specifically religious and can contain both nonbeliever groups and religious congregations. Abstraction is thus useful in attempts to create the secular neutral, though abstract categories always bear the specificity of their source, despite abstraction's claim to universality and the nonspecific.[23]

Translation, like translation from one language into another, depends on abstract concepts like belief, ritual, and prayer to provide referents for comparison across ontologies, even as those categories come from a particular discursive tradition, such as Christianity. Because these categories continue to bear particularity, they remake the subset of elements they abstract and create in the image of their source. As I described earlier, "ritual" arises from a particular history of debates between Catholics and Protestants before becoming a secular category of cross-cultural comparison. Ritual in the abstract does not, however, free itself completely from ritual in its Christian particularity, so it is not a fully neutral referent for comparison.[24]

Once rendered fungible through abstract ciphers, religion can be translated into a naturalist discourse. Translation depends on and produces a religion-like form of the secular, which is not usually acknowledged as such on account of the negative half of the secular paradox. Secular translation, that is, translation into the secular, is often misrecognized as what Charles Taylor has called a "subtraction story" of secularization, which describes the production of the secular as the removal of religion.[25] Unlike avoidance or excision, however, translation is constructive; it remaps the phenomenon into a new world, if always with a haunting remainder. Acts of translation are necessarily incomplete; they leave parts untranslated, mistranslated, or obscured.

For secular translation to work, there must be a secular discourse into which religious and spiritual discourses are translated. A man named Frank, whom I introduced briefly in chapter 1, helped me understand this better and provided strong evidence that the secular is not merely a negation. When I interviewed him at his office in Los Angeles in 2012, Frank told me about an organization he participates in called the Independent Investigations Group (IIG). Founded in 2000, IIG investigates claims of the paranormal in order to explain them within a naturalist discourse. In negative terms, this work could be called debunking, though framing it this way ignores the affirmative half of the secular paradox and misses the fact that Frank and his fellow investigators do not merely excise the supernatural but translate a phenomenon from one ontology into another. He told me a story that explains how it works:

> There was an actress in West Hollywood who moved into a new apartment and experienced three weird things in quick succession. She asked us to come and check it out because she didn't want to turn around and move a week later. People just call us and say, "This weird thing is happening. Can you come and look at it?" We don't charge them. We actually—we're curious ourselves as to what happened. We do it for our entertainment too, for our own gain. We don't charge them for anything, but sometimes we really get to educate someone and say, "Here's what happened." This woman, for instance, had a light diffuser fall in her kitchen for no reason. She had a puddle of liquid form in the center of her

kitchen with nothing dripping on it, for no reason. And then these odd odors were wafting through her house for no reason. So we showed up, and we checked out the diffuser. And the frame was a millimeter smaller than the diffuser itself, so any draft would make this thing fall out. We traced the liquid to coming from behind her refrigerator. We just answered all these questions, and this woman was greatly relieved to have us come and say, "You're not living in a haunted house. You're just having some weird shit happen."

The actress called Frank's group because she attributed these strange events to her apartment being haunted, which made her want to move out. Frank erases her attribution of the supernatural in his retelling by saying that the events all happened "for no reason." They are zeroed out in the abstract cipher. He then explains that the events all have material causes and can be understood through empirical inquiry and reason. Frank's investigation translates the woman's apartment from a world in which the supernatural is real and also frightening to one in which strange events have natural causes and are thus not frightening. She is "not living in a haunted house." Ghosts are merely "weird shit" and are difficult, though possible, to explain naturally. Inasmuch as the woman is one of the people Frank "educates," she is also translated or converted into a naturalist ontology. Frank and IIG are quite literally making the world a more secular place.

Up to now, I have mostly avoided using religion as an analytic category.[26] I have observed instead how my secular interlocutors engage religion and its related concepts, like belief, community, and ritual. Rather than give these concepts fixed meanings, I have attended to the work they accomplish in their shifting signification.[27] I have approached religion as a "field," in the way sociologist Pierre Bourdieu means it, as a social system with a constitutive logic that delimits its own boundaries, outside of which most secular people attempt to stand.[28] In chapters 1 and 2, I approached "belief" and "community" through nonbelievers' usually tacit definitions of religion, which are available indirectly, through their feelings and sensibilities. Secular people's desires and anxieties coalesce around an ambivalence that stems from a paradox. This paradox is the secular's simultaneous claim to universality, by way of emptiness or nonspecificity, and its nonetheless contingent presence within a discursive tradition.

Secular people live with the tension of being both religion-like and by definition not religious. In a field approach, they are "religion-related."[29] This approach also follows philosopher Friedrich Nietzsche's perspectivism: "There is *only* a perspective seeing, *only* a perspective 'knowing'; and the *more* affects we allow to speak about one thing, the *more* eyes, different eyes, we can use to observe one thing, the more complete will our 'concept' of this thing, our 'objectivity,' be."[30] For Nietzsche, there is no external ground on which to stand because observing and knowing always take place from perspectives that are themselves embedded within a conceptual and material inheritance. No third term can mediate the engagement between researchers and their subjects; no cipher can encode them equally. The best a researcher can do is aggregate perspectives, though this process also binds researchers to their subjects. These ties grow tighter when two sides like the secular and the religious imagine and engage each other.[31]

Secular purification can make religious rituals acceptable for people who want to avoid religion, but I am not arguing for their actual efficacy or asserting that they are essentially secular or religious. The modes of secular purification are processes that I observed again and again among secular people, for whom the distinction between secular and religious is meaningful and important. These are ways that secular people produce and maintain a distinction that is constitutive of their identity. These modes are efficacious within the secular discursive tradition, though the effects of this tradition extend well beyond those who participate in it consciously or willingly.[32]

I adopt the idiom of "secular purification" to provide a way to recognize these secular modes in the abstract, as purification rituals in the religion of secularism. With the language of "purity" and "pollution," I blaspheme the secular by translating it partially into ostensibly religious particulars. The effect of this blasphemy is a doubling of what "religion" and "ritual" can mean, and it is no coincidence that I announce my blasphemy in the very middle of this book. My work to invert secular blasphemy and unmoor the secular by way of the religious is in the long tradition of Émile Durkheim.[33] It also marks an empiricist approach to the a/theological tradition, which has up to this point followed Hegelian idealism to trace Christianity's haunting of the secular.[34] By remaking the secular rather than the secularized, I also work in the tradition of anthropologist Saba Mahmood, who as a graduate student at Stanford debated cultural theorist Stuart Hall over whether the colonized or colonizer should be translated.[35] Flipped and blasphemed, the secular becomes religious and vice versa. As religious, the secular has a theology, or logic of operation, though operations like blasphemy and translation are not essentially anything. They are actions capable of making things appear one way or another—secular or religious—from a particular perspective. They are rituals for secular people trying to purify themselves of religious pollution.

Avoidance

The different ways of avoiding religion produce subtly different modes of the secular. Observing this subtlety requires attending to absence, as well as presence—to what secular people do *not* say or do, as well as what they expressly disavow. It also requires attending to feelings, which can be difficult to interpret, even if they are my own. Secular aversion manifests most clearly when someone fails to avoid religion. My failures, in particular, gave me the opportunity to observe, however imperfectly, what this failure feels like. Several times throughout my research, I was the exception that proved the rule when secular people felt they had to correct me for being insufficiently secular. This kind of social regulation is one of the ways that secular people maintain a rigorously secular sensibility. The first time I realized I was being censored was in June 2012. I was sitting in a dark lecture hall, listening to a panel of speakers at the headquarters of the Center for Inquiry in Amherst, New York, just outside Buffalo. When someone near me sneezed, without thinking, I said, "Bless you." A gray-haired man to my left laughed at me and shook his head. Before I had time to reflect and realize what I had done, I experienced a strong feeling of shame. I had failed to avoid religion.

The next morning, I received a follow-up lesson in appropriate secular behavior. The conference was mainly for student leaders who run campus groups throughout the country, but older donors and mentors also attended and, like me, paid their own expenses. The conference organizers encouraged us to stay at a motel nearby, so we usually ran into each other in the mornings on our way to CFI's headquarters, where the conference was being held. This particular morning, a man offered to give a few of us a ride the half mile or so down the road. I was sitting in the backseat, between two people, when the woman to my left sneezed. Having been chastised the day before, I remained silent, but the two men riding in front responded in unison with "Gesundheit." After a long pause, the man on my right asked what "Gesundheit" means and explained that he was worried that the term has religious connotations in German. He implied two concerns at once: that he might repeat the phrase and spread its religious pollution and that the two men in front had already done so.

The precise nature of the pollution is ambiguous from a secular perspective. Invoking a phrase that indexes, however indirectly, the existence of a supernatural being perpetuates the myth of that being. It also perpetuates the myth that someone who sneezes requires a blessing in order to secure their health. The absent God in "[God] bless you" remains dangerous. I have found that very secular people often want to erase religion from speech for more visceral reasons. They want to live as if religion does not exist. This is more instinctive than the execution of a thoughtful linguistic strategy to avoid the perpetuation of unconscious assumptions about the existence of unreal beings. The two men in the car's front seat assured the man next to me that "Gesundheit" comes from the German for "health" and is purely secular. He was clearly relieved. Wanting to be helpful, I offered "salud" as a Spanish alternative that my family often uses. The others in the car with me nodded their approval. I was learning how difficult it is to avoid religion. From then on, every sneeze I heard made it into my field notes. Later the same day, for instance, a man sneezed twice during a workshop. No one responded, including me—not in English or any other language.

To be purely secular requires practice and attention. A surprising moment like a sneeze can demand an improvised response. Bodies and their habits can betray secular people like me who are not properly trained. Late one evening at the same conference in Amherst, I spent a couple of hours at a bar with the conference organizers and some of the older student leaders who were also graduate students. We had drunk enough that we were in our feelings, so to speak, and we were talking about the experience of being an outsider, which all of us shared. A secular humanist conference in a suburb of Buffalo is, after all, probably not where people who grew up fitting in are likely to find themselves.

Dan, a former Christian and a leader of a secular student group in Illinois, tried to express to us how fortunate he felt to have a college degree and be in graduate school despite having grown up very poor. He stumbled over his words on his first attempt, and then he did so again. Watching his mouth pantomime a word, I suddenly realized what Dan was avoiding: he wanted to tell us that he felt "blessed." I spoke up and said that it can be hard to find secular words for how we feel when we speak a language and live in a culture that are so thoroughly organized around Christianity. Everyone agreed. But when I suggested that this Christian saturation makes it acceptable to use Christian language sometimes, my sense was that no one else felt comfortable using the b-word.

Secular people avoid religious pollution in different ways and with different degrees of purity. For some, rituals are inherently religious and need to be avoided altogether. For others, only some rituals or some parts of a ritual are essentially religious; those parts can be excised. Sometimes religiosity is incidental or trivial, so it can be allowed to remain. Nonbelievers I interviewed were always thoughtful about their relationship to religion when I raised it to the level of consciousness, but it was also clear from their responses that they have trained their bodies to be habitually secular and sensible of religious pollution.

Greg, the monist I introduced in chapter 1, helped me understand this dynamic. For many years, Greg has been active among Unitarian Universalists who consider themselves humanists, and he explained how they manage their relationship with religion:

> The point is that when something good has been created or pioneered or developed under the banner of religion, we adopt it or adapt it. When something has come along through the filter of religion or through a religious community that is no longer helpful to humans or to us, . . . then we just get rid of it. So, sure, we adopt a lot of things from religion: the community structures, certain ways of conceiving of ourselves as a community, some rituals—not many but some—some leadership structures, etcetera. But it's almost like the stopped clock being right twice a day

kind of thing. Religion was bound to get some things right, and I think more importantly than that, religion was the only thing that people had to answer questions and to structure society for so long.

Greg distances himself from religion by denigrating it, but he is not a secular purist. He embraces religion in particular ways. When an aspect of religion is good, right, or helpful, it can be removed from its religious context, or its religious excess can be excised. Religiosity that secular people like Greg find acceptable is incidentally religious rather than essentially so, and Greg emphasizes that he and other humanists adopt or adapt religious structures but not religious substance. The strength of Greg's avoidance and the specifics of what he avoids determine the form that his secularism takes. In Greg's case, this is a hybrid form of secular religiosity that embraces congregation-like community, clergy-like leadership, and "not many but some" rituals.

Other very secular people avoid ritual completely. John—a former leader I introduced in chapter 1—has a personal aversion to the kind of secular religion that Greg embraces:

> I've spoken to a lot of humanist groups and UU churches, and they're sort of secularized religions. I don't personally need that. I just don't care. I don't miss it in the least. But a lot of people do. Our lectures are on Sundays, but that's as close as we get to a pseudoreligion or faux religion. There's just so many other outlets like the Unitarian Universalists and maybe humanists that do something pretty close to like a religion. That's great. Go for it. But we don't do that. I have plenty of friends and family and my cycling friends. Sundays I'd rather go for a mountain bike or a hike than go to some pretend religion group.

John sees his group as part of a landscape of alternatives for nonbelievers of various levels of secular purity. His organization is for people who are more averse to religion. He makes this clear by explicitly comparing his organization to UU churches, but he also denigrates religion more than Greg does because he considers it more polluting and thus a greater danger to his secular purity.

Mark, who is a humanist chaplain at a research university, expressed a similar disinterest in rituals, despite his clergy-like office: "I'm just not comfortable with the ritual aspect of humanism. It's great to do weddings and funerals, but I'm not interested in the ritual side. It's just not how I want to spend my weekend." Mark expresses his aversion in both emotional and intellectual terms—as both discomfort and disinterest. Ritual is religious pollution, and though he is fine with others embracing it, he wants none of it. Phil, a lawyer and secular legal activist who lives in Virginia, is not as antiritual as John and Mark are, but he is still averse: "I just didn't need the ritualistic thing that I'd already experienced in a Catholic Church. Some have this need for spirituality, and there's certainly some need for fellowship. Song does have a lot of good qualities. I just don't need that stuff." Phil provides a nuanced breakdown of how he understands religion by disaggregating it into ritual, spirituality, fellowship, and aesthetics. He rejects all of it.

For some secular people, their aversion to ritual, in particular, is not intentional but a consequence of their larger aversion to religion. Though they are not specifically opposed to ritual or other religion-like practices, they are so far removed from institutional religious life and religious people that they do not encounter religiosity. They are sufficiently buffered from religion so as to become indifferent. Luis, whom I introduced in chapter 2, is a leader of a local community for Latinx atheists in Chicago. He describes his incidental aversion:

> If there was an Easter egg hunt, I'd let [my daughter] participate in it, and we could discuss later if she had any questions about it. I'm not at all opposed to her participating in any of those things. That's more of a fault on my part. Because they're not central things in our lives, and we're not part of that community, just to be very honest with you, we just kind of let those things fly right by on the calendar, and we don't give them much notice when they're around. I wouldn't be opposed to it. We just do our normal thing—the normal things we do on the weekends. Quite frankly, I wish in the secular community that we'd have more traditions or more rites of passage or something that we can all come together as a community and celebrate milestones or things like that. I don't think I'm the person to put something like that together, and I certainly don't feel bad about it given that the Catholic Church and a lot of the older religions have a two-thousand-plus-year head start on us. It'll take some time, I guess.

Luis is more open to embracing ritual than John, Mark, and Phil are. Though he "wouldn't be opposed to it," it is not a "normal thing" that he and his family do on the weekends. Unlike Mark, the chaplain, he wishes it were, but he recognizes that creating secular religiosity requires more work than he is willing to do.

Though John, Mark, and Phil have little interest in joining religion-like communities and engaging in religion-like rituals, they still celebrate holidays like Christmas, which they inherit from their Christian-centric culture. A man I spoke with named William, who lives in St. Paul, Minnesota, has thought a lot about whether and how to celebrate holidays now that he is an atheist. Raised a Jehovah's Witness, he never celebrated them growing up because Witnesses prohibit the celebration of holidays and birthdays, which they consider pagan corruptions of Christianity. Their avoidance also helps them distinguish themselves from the "World," which is their term for non-Witnesses.[36] William feels that being a secular person means that he can now celebrate any holiday he wants:

> I notice that a lot of atheists won't do Christmas because Christmas is Christian, and we should say bah-humbug to that. We shouldn't celebrate it, and we should take a stand. Maybe we should just have a solstice celebration that fall or something like that. But I think, you know, I spent so long being told what I could or couldn't do. I'm going to celebrate Christmas, and I'm going to go hang out with my wife's family. . . . I still get the good parts of it. I didn't have to go to church with them in the morning, so I didn't get the bad part, but I still got the good part, which was a great meal, fun time with the family, and a fun gift exchange that we did. And my kids got to be with their cousins.

William's secularity enables rather than prevents him from celebrating Christmas; being secular means he can engage in holiday rituals if they are not substantively religious, and he can excise the parts he dislikes. He does not have to avoid them completely.

Thoughtful and introspective, William recognizes that he is becoming more secular, but he continues to bear a Jehovah's Witness sensibility: "There's a certain part of me that always wonders, 'Am I just behaving this way because I used to be a Witness, or have I really assessed it for myself? Or have Witnesses brainwashed me so much that I still agree with them even though I vehemently say that I don't agree with them?'" This self-questioning acknowledges the stubborn persistence of a self he has mostly left behind. It also finds a similarity between the disenchanting impulse of Protestantism, especially in its extreme forms, and the disenchanting impulse of secularism.[37] Self-reflection is a critical practice that helps William remove his old sensibility and replace it with new, secular feelings.

William is a misfit in the sense that I described in chapter 2, despite his attempts to translate himself into the purely secular. He does not always fit in with other secular people because he does not negate a mainstream form of Christianity. He retains too much from his Witness past and does not inherit enough of the Christianity that has already been abstracted into "culture" or nonspecificity:

> A lot of [secular] people have nostalgic feelings and fond memories [of Christian holidays]. They'll hang up a Christmas ornament and say, "This was given to me by Great Grandma so-and-so when I was five years old, and it's been hanging on my tree for forty years since then." I don't have that. Or they'll say, "When I was three years old, I was Batman for Halloween, and now that my son's three years old, he's gonna be Batman for Halloween." But obviously we don't have that history, so there's not really that pull. But that has a certain advantage too, because you can just take the celebrations people do and decide if you want to participate in them or not. . . . So when it comes to something like Christmas, I'll pick and choose. I'm not going to go to a morning Mass. I'm not gonna pray before the meal. I'm not gonna put plastic Jesus in my yard. But yeah, the tree is really beautiful, and putting up fun ornaments, and giving my kids gifts—that stuff seems good, so we'll do that part.

As a misfit, William can reflect more critically about how his inheritance differs from that of other secular people. His mis-fit produces a distinct way of being secular. Like all secular people, however, he lives with the secular paradox and feels like religion is important both to avoid and, in its secular modes, to embrace. He can embrace it if it is good or helpful or if its religiosity is trivial or incidental. He excises the rest. Though these conscious and unconscious modes of avoidance produce distinct forms of the secular, all secular people share an ambivalence toward religion that structures their attempts to avoid it.

Blasphemy

Blaspheming—committing blasphemy—is a religious act, in the sense that the concept and term derive from Christianity and index its negation.[38] Freethinkers who are blasphemers are not on their own terms; like the atheist, they are, paradoxically, both their own way of life and a negative of what they negate. Secular people who engage self-consciously in blasphemy are half serious. Their halfness, or ambiguity, is the key to understanding blasphemy's unique mode of secular purification and the distinctive mode of the secular it produces. Secular blasphemers' self-conscious blasphemy—secular blasphemy—is a mode of secular purification that transposes an element of religion into a secular context.[39] Unlike avoidance, blasphemy embraces religion and its pollution, which can get messy. Unlike abstraction, which filters religion through an abstract, secular cipher, blasphemy lets religion through, unfiltered but reframed. And unlike translation, which fully rearticulates religion into the secular, blasphemy only recontextualizes the religious. Blasphemy makes religious pollution safe for secular consumption by dropping it, untethered and unaided, into secularity. Out of place and no longer on its own terms, the religious becomes absurd and often comical. The blasphemed is a fish out of water.

William used to be a Jehovah's Witness, but he identifies mostly as an atheist and participates in groups for atheists and humanists. If he were to identify more as an "ex-Jehovah's Witness" and attend groups exclusively for "ex-Witnesses," it would reflect that he feels more comfortable among people who mis-fit the secular in the same ways he does. Ex-Mormons and ex-Muslims, like ex-Witnesses, are in this sense half secular.[40] The people I spoke with who identify as ex- recognize that their thoughts, feelings, and behaviors are still deeply shaped by their religious past, despite their conversion to—translation into—secularism. Their bodies are blasphemous toward the secular because they are excessively religious. Blasphemy provides a way to purify this excess by polluting their residual religiosity.

William recognizes his affective difference from other secular people when he sees them excited for a holiday they have known since childhood. Because the secular usually occupies the empty shape of mainstream Protestantism in the United States, for most secular Americans,

Christmas feels more cultural than religious. William mistrusts his feelings of aversion and indifference to Christmas because, ironically, they might reflect the persistent excess of his religious past as a Jehovah's Witness. Embracing Christmas by experiencing his children's joy for the holiday is one way for William to retrain his body; it is, for him, blasphemous. Rami and Hashim drinking alcohol despite its awful taste is another form of blasphemy, which imposes self-discipline.[41] Irish coffee, fruited beers, and syrupy stouts help Rami and Hashim blaspheme their excessively religious bodies without wincing. They become more secular by polluting their felt religiosity.

Blasphemy provides secular people a way to quarantine and purify the religiosity they cannot avoid, abstract, or translate. It also provides a way to hang onto parts of themselves that they do not want to lose. As Hashim joked over drinks, if he takes away his Muslim past, what remains? Blasphemy is an alternative to excising this religious remainder or abstracting it away through explanation. William can avoid religious pollution by transposing it piecemeal into his newly secular self. Like some bodies and like the English language, some rituals cannot be fully abstracted or translated, though they remain a part of life.[42] Nonbelievers are secular but human. For most secular Americans, the religiosity of Christmas can be ignored or overlooked, but its potential for pollution persists and can appear again if looked at directly or from another perspective. Blasphemy is one way of dealing with persistent or inevitable religious remainders. All the modes of secular purification are responses to the secular's need to be not religious and to the diverse, capacious forms that religion can take.

Hassan, who helps run Ex-Muslims of North America and whom I introduced in chapter 2, told me that he and other ex-Muslims "tend to bring a hint of blasphemy in everything" they do. To help me understand blasphemy's power, he told me about some of the rituals that ex-Muslims create:

> I think that language is the main thing [that's changed when becoming secular]. We also, with the Qur'an, we change the words a bit. Like, there's a member who memorized the whole Qur'an as a young kid. He memorized the whole thing. Everyone has memorized two or three verses, and we'll take it, and we'll change it, and we'll make it something funny. And

it's empowering! But it's, like, very blasphemous. And we don't do that publicly. We just do it around ourselves: eating pork together, having beer together. During Ramadan, we have a Haramadan party. Haram is, like, not kosher. Every Ramadan, we have a Haramadan party where you do everything you're not supposed to do on Ramadan. We'll have a barbecue. We'll have pork. We'll have beer. And we'll have a big party! 'Cause it's, you know, Haramadan. And it's just funny! And it makes us feel better, I guess. It's our way of fighting.

Many now-ex-Muslims learned to be good Muslims through memorization and the repetition of bodily practices. These practices have made the Qur'an a part of them.[43] Passages and in some cases the entire text are inscribed in their memories, and religious movements and gestures, like those of prayer, are bodily habits they may never forget. Hashim and other ex-Muslims blaspheme their minds and bodies to make themselves secular without losing or denying who they are. Like how Rami and Hashim made blasphemous puns in Arabic when we were at Mudgie's, ex-Muslims recontextualize polluted parts of themselves by transposing them into secularity. These transpositions are "just funny" in part because they are absurd juxtapositions of the sacred and the profane, which is to say, of the symbolically disparate.[44]

Ex-Muslims who participate in Haramadan blaspheme their bodies by blaspheming religious ritual and its sensuous experience. Eid al-Fatr is the celebration that marks the end of Ramadan. Consuming pork and beer purifies participants of the religiosity that would normally pollute them by forcing Eid out of its Islamic context and into secularity. These ex-Muslims do not do away with Eid completely. Haramadan's blasphemy makes it safe for them to hang onto a part of their lives that would otherwise be too religious. In the process, it produces a distinctive mode of the secular, which is inverted or decontextualized religion. This inverted religion is inherently ambiguous, and what it means is a question of perspective. The devoutly religious feel blasphemy viscerally, as an attack on them and their beliefs. For the very secular, blasphemy is a kind of sublimation that preserves the religious safely.[45] Surely Hassan is right when he sees Haramadan as a way of fighting religious authority, but this tells only half the story. His blasphemy, in the form of an ironic embrace, is also an act of love for the parts of himself that remain too religious to be secular.

Blasphemy helps secular people perform their autonomy but typically does so in negative ways. Every year on September 30, organized nonbelievers around the world celebrate Blasphemy Day. The Center for Inquiry created the event in 2009 and selected the date to commemorate the publication of several editorial cartoons depicting the Prophet Mohammed in the Danish newspaper *Jyllands-Posten* in 2005. By transposing Muhammad into visual media, the cartoons violate prohibitions that many Muslims maintain against visual representation of the Prophet. Their publication led to complaints from Muslim groups and diplomats and, eventually, protests and violent reprisals around the world.[46] The cartoons remain a catalyst in narratives that lend legitimacy to violence between Muslims and Europeans.

One of CFI's leaders told me a college student first suggested that the organization create Blasphemy Day and that it did so only after a fractious internal debate over whether the event would do more to affirm secular values or negatively target religious people. CFI's descriptions of Blasphemy Day acknowledge this tension but disavow it, declaring the event's aim to promote the liberal value of free speech:

> While many perceive "blasphemy" as offensive, this event is not intended to ridicule and insult others. Rather, it was created as a reaction against those who would seek to take away the right to satirize and criticize a particular set of beliefs given a privileged status over other beliefs. Observing International Blasphemy Rights Day is a way of showing opposition to any resolutions or laws, binding or otherwise, which discourage or inhibit freedom of speech of any kind.

CFI's claim that the event "is not intended to ridicule and insult" is only half true. Secular student groups celebrating Blasphemy Day on college campuses will sometimes create a "Wall of Blasphemy" on which students write inflammatory slogans and draw obscene images that primarily target Christianity and Islam. Their aim is to ridicule and insult the religious *and* to perform their government-protected right to do so. The positive expression of their secular values demands, in their very secular view, negative opposition to an imagined religious interlocutor.[47]

Campus student groups and others celebrating Blasphemy Day sometimes perform de-baptisms, which demonstrate blasphemy's power to purify through inversion and transposition. These deconversion rituals parody the form and structure of a baptism and are especially fun for students who were baptized into Christianity but no longer consider themselves Christians. Even though de-baptisms are blasphemous rituals that affirm secular subjectivity, they risk religious pollution by transposing religious ritual rather than simply avoiding it. This is the danger Dan Barker encountered when federal attorneys suggested that his performance of de-baptisms was evidence that he could be recognized by the IRS as a minister of the gospel of atheism.[48]

Antireligious jokes like those made by leaders onstage at the secular Día de los Muertos celebration also signal self-awareness about the awkwardness of participating in religious ritual and make it clear that, despite appearances, they are not religious. When I attended a wedding officiated by a longtime, self-avowed humanist, the man peppered the ceremony with jokes about the Christian ritual he was emulating and assured the audience of its secularity. His ironic performance interfered with my enjoyment of the ritual by shaking me out of my immersion, though he probably intended this alienation, which prevented me from submitting to "groupthink." It was also clear from his nervous laughter that his jokes broke the tension of his felt ambivalence. Ritual leaders' irony and sarcasm distances very secular ritual participants from religious pollution and the anxiety it provokes. Blasphemy preserves religion by purifying it for secular consumption.

Abstraction

Abstraction can produce different forms of the secular by abstracting to different degrees. It can purify religion by making it less particular, but it can also neutralize it by making it plural and treating religions as comparable. The former mode produces the purely secular and the latter mode the secular neutral. For example, "churches" can become religious (but not specifically Christian) when they become "houses of worship." These in turn can become secular as "gathering places." The first abstraction creates an ostensibly neutral secular by making religions and their sacred communal spaces comparable to one another. Christianity, however, and its particular uses of space remain the basic referent and thus belie abstraction's neutrality.[49] Not every religion has a "house of worship" in the way Christian English means it, so presuming that all do makes Christianity the abstract category's normative baseline.

The second abstraction, to "gathering places," goes even further by removing anything particularly religious about a church; it includes nonreligious communal spaces and anywhere else people get together intentionally. "Happy holidays" provides another example. The phrase abstracts from "Christmas" to include other religious holy days, like Hanukkah and Kwanza. "Have a good break," a phrase common among academics, does away with religion altogether by abstracting beyond the holiness of particular days to a span of time that law and convention have set aside for many people as free of labor. Religion in the very abstract, shorn of what makes it special, becomes innocuous and safe for secular consumption.

Abstraction that pluralizes religion and makes religions comparable neutralizes religious substance but nonetheless preserves it, producing the secular neutral. Abstraction that purifies religion and makes it equivalent to the secular preserves its structure but evacuates its substance, creating a lacuna, or the empty secular. A "house of worship" is generic until certain people "worship" there; a "gathering place" is empty until certain people fill it. Because of abstraction's power to neutralize and purify the religious, it remains a ubiquitous strategy among very secular people, as well as among scholars of religion. By moving from the particular to the generic, abstraction creates the nonsectarian and the "objective." By reifying genera as the real, abstraction also creates universals, which are conditions for universal knowledge and truth.[50]

Organized nonbelievers, of course, are not the only people to claim objective knowledge about reality, nor are they the only people to use abstraction. Abstraction is not inherently secular. Ancient Pythagoreans built a religion from the belief that the abstract rationality of numbers is the basis of reality, and some transhumanists have done the same today. These groups show that abstraction is not an inherently secular mode.[51] Indeed, a simple shift in perspective can render the secular religious and vice versa; it is impossible for a basic mode of reasoning to be inherently either. The secular *qua* secular is always locked into a relationship with religion. Abstraction produces the distinctively secular only when it abstracts from religion enough to create the neutral or when it goes further and creates the empty.

Abstraction works through a cipher—literally a "zero"—which paradoxically encodes as well as erases religious particularity. Sometimes this encoding is obvious, as when the US tax code uses the term "churches" to include "cathedrals," "synagogues," and "mosques" or uses "ministers" to include "priests," "rabbis," and "imams." Abstraction from "church" to "mosque" is connoted in the tax code rather than explicitly denoted, such as in "house of worship," which would be a more neutral term. "Gathering place" would be too abstract for the purposes of the US tax code, which makes religion special by giving religious leaders and organizations special exemptions to taxation and other governmental authority. The tax code seeks enough abstraction to be neutral but not so much that it becomes empty and no longer recognizes religion as special. It makes religions comparable and thus ostensibly equal to one another, but it maintains a distinction between the religious and the secular. Abstraction can remove what makes religion special by making it a subset of "culture" or by making religions into belief-centered "worldviews," as European governments sometimes do in attempt to make the religious and the secular comparable.[52] A number of legal scholars have also argued against religion's specialness by demonstrating the superfluity of distinctively religious rights. They lose their legal necessity when they become guaranteed by other rights that abstract elements of religion, like freedom of speech and freedom of conscience.[53]

A recent controversy over government-endorsed prayer demonstrates how different levels of abstraction produce different forms of the secular. In February 2016, the City Council of Phoenix, Arizona, voted to end its practice of beginning meetings with a prayer after receiving pressure from groups like FFRF and local Satanists who are avowedly nontheistic.[54] The City Council made the decision in order to preempt an "invocation" that members of the Satanic Temple planned to give at the start of the meeting later the same month. The controversy stems from the US Supreme Court's 2014 decision in *Town of Greece v. Galloway*, which declared that prayer before council meetings does not violate the US Constitution.[55] "Invocation" is an abstraction from "prayer" that expands the religiously specific to include secular alternatives, which the courts recognize as equivalent. Its abstraction erases the particularity of religion in the name of neutrality, though it does not empty its contents fully because it preserves space for any prayer-like act. Through this dilution by abstraction, secular people such as Satanists can participate alongside the traditionally religious, though in order to participate, they must acknowledge that they are analogous to religious people.

To preserve the ritual but at the same time prevent Satanists from giving invocations, Phoenix's City Council opted to change its opening prayer to a "moment of silence." This action produced the empty secular, or a lacuna, beyond neutrality. The absence of religious substance preserved an evacuated religious structure that could only point back to a now-concealed religious origin even as it foreclosed prayer-like acts. A moment of silence makes no sense without being haunted by the ghost of Christian prayer. This absent religious referent makes the product of its abstraction distinctively secular.

In March 2016, under pressure from local conservatives who considered this substantial absence a ban on prayer, the City Council reinstated the "invocation" but restricted who can give it to specific roles like police and fire department chaplains. The council thus shifted the criterion for inclusion to a group with more specific conditions for entry: the chaplaincy. This in effect excludes secular equivalents because there are no Satanist chaplains, and humanist chaplains have only achieved government recognition in rare circumstances. The council figured out a way to return to substantial variety and ostensible neutrality while restricting participation to the traditionally religious.

Abstraction from "prayer" to the more generic "invocation" initially allowed nonbelievers and Satanists to participate as religion-like. Further abstraction reduced the moment to literally nothing, in which no one specific could participate: an absence within a religious structure—silence within allotted time previously reserved for prayer. This empty secular does not even demand that secular people occupy a religion-like identity, so it makes indifference possible, in the sense that it does not require "secular" people to acknowledge the specificity of their difference from the religious in order to be included. The empty secular is beyond neutral; its indifference recognizes no distinctions among a variety. It sets the stage for moving beyond the plural to the universal. Like the secular neutral, however, the empty secular privileges tacitly, by maintaining structural asymmetry.

The City Council's return to the language of "invocation" moved back to a more particularistic framework that recognizes religious and religion-like equivalents. "Invocation" is an abstraction of "prayer," so it carries with it assumptions from Christianity, even as it ostensibly includes Christian analogues like Jewish and Muslim. The council's strategy to frame equivalence through the figure of the chaplain was savvy. "Chaplain" is a Christian-specific term that has been abstracted to include other "faiths," though it effectively excludes secular people like Satanists because they have not been fully admitted to the chaplaincy. "Chaplain" is a precisely calculated abstraction that balances the council's competing pressures of inclusion and exclusion at the expense of groups like FFRF and the Satanic Temple. The Phoenix City Council abstracted religiosity to the secular neutral, then abstracted to the empty secular, before returning to a more restricted neutrality, which is a lower, adjacent level of abstraction.

During the ritual workshop I attended in 2019, Cindy explained that groups like the Humanist Society have begun training nonbelievers to do invocations as a way to push back against the Supreme Court's decision in *Town of Greece v. Galloway*. The Humanist Society and its parent organization, the American Humanist Association, are ambivalent about invocations, and so is Cindy. She told those of us who participated in the workshop that AHA discourages us from doing invocations at school board meetings because the group "wants to keep religion, worldview, and philosophy stuff out of government." It wants to avoid religion and avoid becoming particularized as the religion-like secular, which abstraction to the secular neutral encourages.

Because *Greece v. Galloway* has already affirmed the legality of prayer at county board and city council meetings, invocations in those spaces "are OK," according to Cindy. She explained AHA's concern: "there are children who might have to attend the school board meetings, and we don't want to have them indoctrinated." Indoctrination is only possible when there is something specific to convert into or become. On this model, one cannot become indoctrinated into indifference, or an empty secular, but one can be indoctrinated into a secular discursive tradition, or a religion-like secular, that secular neutrality implies. A secular tradition can depend on concepts that have been secularized by abstracting from religious concepts, but indoctrination and conversion depend on these concepts being organized into a secular system and way of life.[56]

AHA and Cindy want to avoid enabling religion and the religion-like secular to pollute public schools, so they want to avoid the nonspecific secular abstraction of "invocation" because it violates their value of an empty secular, which is the absence of religion and a condition of universality. They would much prefer a moment of silence because they are secular purists and secular universalists, which is to say, they believe theirs is the one true worldview. Where religion is already allowed, such as in county board and city council meetings, they advocate for a compromise: an abstract secular like "invocation," which dilutes religion's specificity so that the religion-like secular can be included. Prayer should be avoided, but where it cannot, it should be abstracted to the neutral "invocation." A moment of silence abstracts it further, nearly to the point of erasure; it avoids the substance of religion but preserves its generic structure.

Extreme purification of the secular would do away with a moment of silence; it would erase religion's ghost and universalize secularism. Though a moment of silence is an abstraction, it is haunted by the structure of its source, Christian prayer. A more complete erasure creates the condition of indifference because it allows secular people to avoid contact with religion that might point back to their constitutive paradox. But because extreme purification demands that secular people live in religion's remainder and because religion can be such a capacious and thus pervasive category, extreme purification can lead to a countermovement in which secular people argue that they are, after all, human and that moments of commemoration are more fundamental than religion. The indifferent, in other words, can realize that they long for something that in their cultural inheritance they lack nonreligious language to name. This movement toward purification and countermovement back toward religion is the generative vacillation of the secular paradox, which structures the range of ways in which people are secular in the United States today.

Engaged in fieldwork among very secular people, I learned to feel the effects of abstraction viscerally, as a kind of generic presence or as an uncanny absence. In chapter 2, I quoted Juan, who described the minimalism of secular aesthetics as "white" and "older male" culture. He contrasted it with Hispanic culture, which he considers family-oriented and colorful. To Juan's description, I would add that there is something especially abstract and distinctively secular about the aesthetics of organized nonbelievers, which grows from their aversion to religion and its particularity.

This secular abstraction made itself plain when I attended a humanistic bat mitzvah in Plymouth, Minnesota, in August 2016. The event was held on a Sunday afternoon in the event space of a local community center, which overlooks a beautiful garden and grass-covered hills. The muted grays of commercial carpet, plastic dining tables, and sound-absorbing padded walls make the room a blank slate for the weddings and other events it holds. When I arrived early, I had a hard time locating the event space because the bat mitzvah's organizers added few signs or decorations that would distinguish it from an empty room. Even on the stage, where the ritual took place, there were almost no embellishments.

I was welcomed warmly by everyone I met, including Tova, the precocious thirteen-year-old girl becoming a bat mitzvah—literally, "daughter subject to the law." Her parents, Rachel and Mark, were especially kind and told me that they were glad to have a researcher present, which was a relief under the circumstances. Despite this effusive warmth, the event was less festive than I had expected, having attended the far more raucous bar mitzvah of a friend's little brother a few years earlier.

The ritual centered primarily on Tova's ancestry and on Jewish history—in particular, the Holocaust, which came up several times throughout the ritual, as well as in conversations I had before and after with the people attending. The ceremony's core was an essay that Tova had written about her grandparents and great-grandparents, who had immigrated to the United States from the Soviet Union. A table in the back of the room held neatly organized family heirlooms that Tova connected to her family's history and that she referred to as "artifacts." During the ritual, Tova and her family and friends lit candles, each of which represented a word that Tova associated with the person. Though the ritual's mood was sometimes somber, it was also very joyful, as when Tova's Hebrew teacher cried after hearing her recite a passage in Hebrew. Unlike at most bat and bar mitzvahs, however, the passage was from a secular text and not from the Torah. By the end of the ritual, the stage was full of people standing behind Tova, representing the community that will support her throughout her life.

During the ritual and conversations after, participants expressed anxieties and ambivalence about being Jewish and the criteria for inclusion. Remembrance of the Holocaust provided a consistent nonreligious focal point for Jewish identity, which the secularity and universality of humanism simultaneously disavows. A man named John told me that he is not very Jewish even though he was born Jewish. When another man, Burt, overheard John, he teased him repeatedly, saying that he "doesn't count" as Jewish and was thus in a "mixed marriage" with his Jewish wife. Ironically, Burt is a convert to Humanistic Judaism whom I interviewed earlier in the week. Later, in a separate conversation, Burt's wife told me that she is not only atheist but antireligion and does not understand how anyone can believe in God. She said that her parents were the same and that for her father, "It came down to the Holocaust." He would ask, she told me, "How could a God do that?" She made it clear that the question is also hers.

In one of my two brief conversations with Rachel, Tova's mother, she told me that she likes Humanistic Judaism because "you get all the good stuff without the bad." Avoiding the bad appears to mean avoiding the physical presence of the Torah and its recitation, as well as ceremonial attire and kippahs. By emphasizing ancestry and history, the bat mitzvah ceremony abstracted from the specificity of Jewish law and tradition to the more generic categories of Jewish ethnicity and culture. By centering Jewish identity on the Holocaust, the Jewish people who were present grounded what they share in a secular event and a genocidal interpellation rather than an essentially religious substance like Jewishness. The result was minimalist, austere, and in a scholarly sort of way, explicative. That Rachel and Mark would welcome an academic studying the ritual makes sense because my participation supports the event's objectivity, which is to say, my presence validated a way of relating to religion as an object of study rather than a site of immersion. This distancing move, by way of abstraction, is familiar to anyone who has studied or worked in a secular department of religious studies. In uncanny symmetry, the family welcomed me, and I felt at home.

Translation

Translation from one discourse to another takes place through an abstract referent that brings them into analogical relation.[57] Secular discourse often assumes a materialist ontology as a working model if not hard fact, so secular discursive translation usually entails rearticulation into a naturalist monism or, at very least, an empirically falsifiable ontology. Secular translation is thus a change in what something actually *is* or at least is perceived to *be*. This change depends on abstraction to create a cipher through which particulars can become equivalent and fungible with one another. As described in the previous section, "religion," "belief," and "ritual" are all abstract ciphers for religious equivalence. Abstracting further, "tradition," "life stance," "worldview," and "practice" enable comparisons beyond religion by including secular ways of life. Structuring this book's chapters using abstractions from the level of both the secular neutral ("belief," "conversion," "ritual,") and the empty secular ("community," "tradition"), I have tried to demonstrate how these abstractions can be remade, or translated, by shifting discursive perspective. I have also tried to show how they can be made universal when signs of alternatives are erased.

Categories like "prayer," "prophet," and "scripture" operate with a double sense because they are explicitly Christian but also secular and generic. To say that there are prophets in the Hebrew Bible and in the Qur'an is to adopt a Christian frame of comparison at the level of the Christian-derived word "prophet" but also a secular frame, on another, more abstract level that makes no judgment as to whether they are truly prophets of God. Who counts as a prophet depends on what one means by "prophet." In Christian and secular frames, Daniel and Muhammad are both prophets, though not in the same sense. In Muslim and secular frames, Muhammad and Jesus are both prophets, though again, not in the same sense. "Prophet" is a divisive category in that Jesus is God in one discourse, a prophet of God in another, and in a third, a prophet simply because people claimed him to be. Literally, Christianity's God-Jesus is one thing, Islam's prophet-Jesus is another, and secularism's prophet-Jesus is yet another. We could thus say that there is a Christian Jesus, a Muslim Jesus, and a secular Jesus, all of which exist on their own terms. Moving from one discourse to another, Jesus is translated.⁵⁸ Dropping a Jesus into a discourse that is not his own—as Kevin Smith does with Buddy Christ in his 1999 film *Dogma*—is blasphemous. Publishing an image of Muhammad in a Dutch newspaper is also blasphemous. Both take sacred figures out of context, thus threatening the power they possess in their respective ontologies.

During an interview I conducted by phone in 2012, a lawyer named Mark begrudgingly discussed with me his meditation practice, which he purified of religious pollution by articulating in secular terms. Mark is worth quoting at length because he is self-conscious about the need for secular purification and its significance:

> That part of my life [meditation] is not really relevant to my claims to the nonexistence of God. I have a tough-enough time getting my atheist arguments out there. So unlike Sam [Harris], it's not my thing to explain to people whatever possible benefits there might be to a naturalistic form of meditation. There's nothing wrong with nonbelievers maintaining the outward forms of certain rituals, like Christmas or Hanukkah. These ritualistic connections with heritage are not the problem. The problem is believing the underlying myths. These practices can have a benefit for the nonbeliever if the nonbeliever stops at the core, where the supernatural or paranormal begins. They're valuable up to a point, but I'll get off the train sooner than others.

Mark was probably right to be anxious, though much has changed since 2012. Mark's friend Sam Harris has appropriated the term "spirituality" to describe his exploration of a phenomenological approach to experience through Buddhist meditation.⁵⁹ A decade ago, many very secular people would have considered meditation practice too religious for a purely secular person. Mark did not want to raise the issue and have to defend himself, so he was reluctant to discuss it during our interview until he got a better sense of who I am and how I understand the secular. I became used to apprehension like Mark's during interviews. Many organized nonbelievers worried that because I was a PhD student in a religion department and, later, a professor of religious studies, the goal of my research was to cast them as religious. As it turns out, their suspicions were half right.⁶⁰

Mark stressed to me that although the "outward forms" or structures of rituals like Christmas and Hanukkah are acceptable, religious substance, or "believing the underlying myths," is not. If nonbelievers excise or avoid "the core, where the supernatural or paranormal begins," then they can successfully translate a religious structure, like meditation or Christmas, and fill it with secular substance. The secular Día de los Muertos event translated a nonwhite religious ritual into a white secular one. We as participants did not avoid religion; we embraced it. To do so, we relied on a two-step process of ritual purification: first abstraction and then translation. As with the secular bat mitzvah I attended in Minnesota, the organizers preserved the ritual's structure and did away with its religious substance by interpreting its social function in the abstract. Día de los Muertos is, in secular social scientific terms, a "life-cycle ritual" that depends on an abstract concept, "ritual," and the belief that as humans we need rituals because, in the words of the event's MC, we need to "mark time in our lives." At the end of the event, the same woman told us that the ritual's purpose was "to help us reflect on how precious life really is."

Those who took the stage throughout the event asserted that secular people have a privileged relationship with reality that allows them to appreciate life more.[61] They affirmed truths about the world and the best way to know it, literally rearticulating what the Day of the Dead can mean. A man who is a professional comedian tried to reassure us: "We don't believe in the afterlife and all that nonsense, so all we have is our legacy. Knowledge and science can help us heal." A woman speaking in honor of Stephen Hawking told us, "We shouldn't be afraid of death because we're just matter and energy." And another woman lamented, "I feel bad for people who believe because they can't appreciate that this is our only time. We're all gonna die." The two women agreed on what reality is, which one expressed in affirmative terms and the other negative. From the second woman's perspective, nonbelievers are the only people who really understand the meaning of death and the value of life because they accept our ontological finitude.[62] By translating Día de los Muertos into the secular—by translating it into secular discourse—the ritual's participants rearticulated it within a new world, reinscribed what it means, and made it safe for secular consumption by purifying it of its religious pollution. They were building and maintaining secular ways of life.

Religion's Ghosts

In July 2016, on Manhattan's Upper West Side, I attended the second in a series of private workshops on atheism that happened to overlap with my short stay in New York City. The woman who ran the workshop is a brilliant author with a PhD who identifies as secular. At several points during the session, she tried to balance the positive and negative halves of the secular paradox, though she never named it directly and did not seem to recognize it as a distinctively secular condition. "We all know that atheism has negative connotations," she said to about a dozen of us. "I believe in recuperating it. I call myself an atheist." She further established her secular bona fides by telling us, "In my house, we literally say 'Einstein' instead of 'bless you.'"[63]

The author's declarations of secular faith prepared us to hear other views she holds that many secular people would consider blasphemous: "We who've left religion share a lot of beliefs. A lot of those beliefs have rituals [that go with them]. I don't want us to be stuck saying no to religion forever." Like the MC of the secular Día de los Muertos event, the author reminded us that we are secular but human, so we need to mark time in our lives and should not contain ourselves to the small space of religion's remainder. She then told us about the secular religions that citizens of the early French Republic attempted to found in the wake of the Revolution, all of which eventually failed.[64] "Rituals are hard things to propagate," she warned. Secular religion-making is tough work, especially because it is so paradoxical. There was no public secular Día de los Muertos event in Los Angeles the following year.

Secular purification rituals make it possible for secular people to participate in religion without compromising their secularity. Avoiding, blaspheming, abstracting, and translating are all modes of purification that help secular people deal with religion as they get close to it or, more disturbingly, find it already within themselves. These modes are, in a sense, the basics of secular ethics concerning religion. Engaging in them produces different forms of the secular, such as the antireligious secular, the blasphemous secular, the secular neutral, the empty secular, and the secular way of life. The need to purify the secular of religious pollution arises from the secular paradox because secular people need to strike a balance between not being religious and not living in religion's lacuna, its mere absence.

Not all ways of being secular feel right to all secular people. Though the secular Día de los Muertos event resonated with some secular participants, it felt awkward to others, including me. Secular people pursue purity as much by feel as by reason. For some nonbelievers I met, Christmas bears too much of a religious stain, so they celebrate the winter solstice instead. For a former Jehovah's Witness like William, celebrating Christmas is a blasphemous way to leave his religious self behind. Secular people's different ways of being secular remain marked by particular forms of religion. They are haunted by religion's ghosts.[65]

4

Conversion

Accepting Atheist Reality

On a hot July day in 2016, I visited the Fairfax Public Access television station, about fifteen miles due west of Washington, DC. I was there to observe a taping of *Road to Reason*, a weekly television show that airs live on the station and streams online. Alfredo, the man who invited me, met me in the lobby and took me to a boardroom in the back of the building. Alfredo is the founder of an organization for Hispanic nonbelievers. When he realized I would be in the DC area on the day he was scheduled to be a guest on the show, he invited me to tag along. Soft-spoken and soft-featured, Alfredo was in his fifties at the time we met and has had a successful career working in the defense industry. When we arrived at the boardroom, he introduced me to the three people running the show. Rick, the show's producer, was a big man in his forties who identified himself as a libertarian within a few minutes of meeting me. Aaron, the show's host, was in his late twenties and wore skinny jeans and hip glasses. I noticed a red "A" hanging from his necklace, which is the logo of the atheist Out Campaign.[1] Dan, who looked to be about twenty, managed the technical side of the show and suggested ideas for content. He wore a "Live Free or Die" T-shirt and told us that he was a communist. I took a seat on the far side of the room and explained my research and who I am. Thankfully, the men agreed to let me take notes; their conversation was fascinating.

They began by telling each other jokes about religion, looking for one that Aaron could use at the start of the show. Alfredo suggested a joke about Muhammad being a pedophile, which is a genre I encountered often among atheist men who are antireligious nonbelievers. Eventually, they settled on a less inflammatory barb that relies on abstraction more than blasphemy. Aaron asked us, "What do you a call a Christian who goes to church?" His answer—"A pokémon trainer"—implied that religion is on the decline, and it mocks Christian hypocrisy about church attendance.[2] It also plays with the idea of a "church" abstracting to a "gathering place"—in this case, for pokémon.

The men then discussed recent news articles they planned to announce. The first was an annual report that found an increase in the number of women murdered in "honor killings" in Pakistan.[3] The men were appalled. Aaron suggested a second item about the Yale University employee, Corey Menafee, who smashed a stained-glass window that depicted slaves carrying bales of cotton, which was in the school's Calhoun College residence hall. Menafee, a Black man who was thirty-eight at the time, told the *New Haven Independent* that he was tired of looking at the "racist, very degrading" image.[4] The university fired him, and he was charged with a felony. After the event made national headlines, the state dropped the charges, and the school rehired Menafee on the condition that he no longer speak publicly about the stand he took against injustice.[5]

The showrunners accepted Aaron's item about Menafee without discussion, but it reminded Alfredo of a tough decision he faced. Recently, he told us, a very wealthy atheist contacted him about giving a large donation to his organization for Hispanic nonbelievers. The man wanted Alfredo's group to register as a lobbying outfit so they could lobby the Organization of American States (OAS) to prevent missionaries from proselytizing to indigenous people in Latin America.[6] The donation made Alfredo uncomfortable for two reasons. The first is practical because lobbying has not been part of the group's mission, which is twofold: to support Hispanic nonbelievers and to promote science and critical thinking. The second reason is moral: the donor is openly racist. Alfredo gave no specifics about the man's racism, but he told us twice that he is sure the donor is racist. He said the man wants to give the money because he finds it amusing to make Hispanic atheists interfere with Christian missionaries in the name of indigenous people. In other words, the donor does not support the goals of any of these groups; he just wants to use Hispanic atheists and indigenous people as props to provoke Christians.

When telling the story, Alfredo did not seem offended, and his description of the man's racism was more like a statement of fact than moral disgust. Rick, the libertarian producer, responded first, urging Alfredo to take the money because the act's morality should be judged by its positive effects for the secular cause rather than for its giver's intent or moral character. "Nazis can do good things sometimes," he said. Dan asked how big the donation was because it would be easier to accept a large sum. Alfredo said that for the group, it was substantial, but it was a small amount for the racist donor. The men then discussed how being secular does not require opposition to racism. Antiracism, they argued, is not a necessary logical conclusion from the assumptions of atheism, which in affirmative terms, are generally materialism and empiricism. In the end, the men agreed that Alfredo could take the money without contradicting his secular values because the donor's personal beliefs are irrelevant and because secularism is not inherently antiracist. Despite their consensus, Alfredo did not say he would take the money, and I have found no evidence that his group accepted the donation or agreed to engage in lobbying the OAS.[7]

The men then discussed questions to ask Greta Christina, the prominent atheist activist who was the show's guest that day. Dan suggested prompting Christina to discuss an idea he had been struggling with lately, that "atheism is not a choice." The way Dan framed his suggestion implied that he did not choose to be an atheist. He simply discovered the truth. Alfredo agreed: "I didn't pick atheism. It picked me. I was forty-two and a die-hard Catholic, and I didn't want to become an atheist." I found out later when interviewing Alfredo that becoming a Freemason played a big role in his eventual atheism. After a decade of trying to reconcile his masonry and his Catholicism, and under threat of excommunication from his priest, he gave up on both. He has since found a Masonic lodge that accepts atheists, so he is again a Freemason, though still not a Catholic.

Rick teased Alfredo for not choosing his atheism—"That's such a religious answer!"—but Alfredo stood his ground. Dan and Alfredo identified a paradox that stems from secularism's emphasis on both autonomy and reason. Though critical thinking is essential for a secular, autonomous individual, reason leads inevitably to logical truth, which includes atheism. Alfredo did not convert to atheism, in the sense of making a conscious choice; like Dan, he discovered its truth, which became increasingly undeniable. This makes Alfredo awkwardly ambiguous, as

Rick pointed out with his teasing. For men like Dan and Alfredo, the only alternative to atheism is refusing to accept reality, which for them, is hardly a choice.[8]

Aaron then raised a topic that prods secular ambivalence toward community and ritual. He told us, "[Atheist activist] Matt Dillahunty says about religion, 'We don't need a replacement for cancer.'" Aaron suggested that the men "ask Greta what she thinks about that."[9] Aaron knows that this will be an interesting choice because it points to a common problem that very secular people face: if many parts of life are religion-like or religion-related, avoiding them can be costly. Rick resisted the cancer analogy and the avoidance it demands: "When we lose religion, we lose community," he said. "We lose volunteering. It's false to equate religion and cancer." Rick abstracted from "church" and "charity" to assert that religion meets fundamental human needs. He argued tacitly that some amount of religion must be accepted, even by those who are very secular.

Alfredo pushed back against Rick's argument that all humans need the religious or religion-like parts of life: "It's condescending to think some people need something. They don't." But Rick did not back down: "Where do you do your volunteer work when you lose your religion?" Rick was saying that religion is an important source of moral behavior in American life, and it meets fundamental human needs. It is not a cancer and should not just be cut out. Alfredo was saying that not everyone needs community or volunteering, so their avoidance is an acceptable cost of no longer being religious. Aaron's provocation worked perfectly. He had polarized Rick and Alfredo around a thorny paradox: if being secular means not being religious, and if a broad definition of religion means that a lot of parts of life are at least a little religious, then being secular means avoiding a lot of things—perhaps too many.

The four men are sharp and clearly enjoyed probing these paradoxes, which all stem from the secular paradox. The intractable questions that the paradox leads to provide an endless source of disagreement for secular people who like to debate. Though I never heard very secular people name the secular paradox, their humor often reveals its open secret. As the pressure for coherence builds, secular jokes and laughter release it, like steam from a valve. I learned to listen to my own laughter as it guided me to the sutured gaps in a systematic secular worldview. I collected many jokes in my field notes during my years of research, and I still ask myself sometimes after I laugh, "Why did you find that funny?"

As the four men and I were walking from the boardroom to the studio where they were about to go live on the air, Rick told a joke to break the nervous tension. It made me chuckle, and I wrote it down as quickly as I could: "What do a right-wing former marine, a Latino CIO, a college communist, and a CPA have in common?" After a pause, he told us: "Atheism!" Reflecting later, I recognized our laughter in the face of absurdity. The men had gathered in that studio to share in what they do not share, which is itself ambiguous: religion or belief in God. The absent affirmative—the secular presence that is more than negation—is a funny thing to be.[10]

This chapter examines secular conversion—self-translation into the secular—by looking closely at some of the tough questions that polarized Alfredo, Rick, Aaron, and Dan on a hot July afternoon in Virginia. It also examines secular ethics, which I found inseparable from the question of conversion in my many conversations with very secular people. Is becoming secular a choice, or is it something that happens to a person, sometimes against their will? Does becoming secular mean adopting an ethical code, or is it amoral? Is it ethical for secular people to proselytize, or is trying to convert people too religious? Is deconverting from religion de facto converting to secularism, or does becoming secular require something more? These questions are difficult, perhaps impossible, to settle because they stem from secularism's ambiguity and secular people's ambivalence toward religion. Conversion both is and is not a secular problem.

Not Skeptical of Empiricism

To understand secular people, it helps to understand the skeptic movement, which overlaps with the secular movement but is distinct from it. Many of the nonbelievers I spent time with identify as skeptics, but some of the skeptics I met are Christians or told me that they believe in a spiritual higher power. At the Drinking Skeptically meetups I attended, almost everyone was a nonbeliever, but the meetings felt different from explicitly secular events. Attendees meet once a month, in bars, to drink with one another and discuss issues they find important.

Particular members manage the logistics of convening the meetings, such as maintaining the group's event page on Meetup. When I attended in New York, no one managed the group in a leader-like way, and conversations took place in small groups rather than all together.[11] We were not congregation-like, and religion was not a prominent topic. Attendees discussed subjects like genetically modified foods, chemtrails, and the antivaccine (or "antivaxxer") movement.[12] Social interactions with avowed skeptics were usually more contrarian than those I had with organized nonbelievers. When a participant observer, I tend to seek consensus and affirm what people tell me. At Drinking Skeptically, my nods and affirmations were met with disagreement and nit-picking correction. Skepticism, I learned, is an attitude as much as an identity; it is distinct from secularism but works well with it.[13]

The modern skeptic movement took shape in the nineteenth century, with the popularization of science.[14] Skepticism, in this sense of the term, is the persistent demand for empirical evidence for any claim. In practice, skeptics tend to focus on particular types of claims, such as ghost sightings, telepathy, miracle healing, dowsing, séances, and other forms of "pseudoscience," broadly construed. Some skeptics refer to their movement as "scientific skepticism" to signal its reliance on science as the method for empirical validation, and those involved in the skeptic movement have long been public advocates for science.

Institutionally, in North America, the modern skeptic movement began with the creation of the Committee for the Scientific Investigation of Claims of the Paranormal (CSICOP) in 1976. The group was founded by Paul Kurtz and a few others while Kurtz was the editor of the *Humanist* magazine, prior to his break with the American Humanist Association. Kurtz founded his own group for humanists, the Council for Democratic and Secular Humanism, in 1980. Both groups were later renamed—the Committee for Skeptical Inquiry and the Council for Secular Humanism, respectively—and brought under Kurtz's organizational umbrella group, the Center for Inquiry. The skeptic and secular movements are thus institutionally adjacent, and at times overlapping, despite the distinctness of their participants.[15]

As identities, "skeptic" and "nonbeliever" are two ways of negotiating the secular paradox. They are both mostly negative in their self-understanding. Skeptics are opposed to pseudoscience and often target groups and individuals who participate in the metaphysical tradition.[16] Nonbelievers are those who do not believe in God. Skeptics affirm empirical science as their epistemology and value "critical thinking." Nonbelievers share those values, and they add an ontological claim, the absence of "God," a being with no place in their working ontology. Skepticism is an epistemological mirror image of atheism's ontological paradox. Just as atheists have a negative identity (no God) that also affirms (a working model of materialism), skeptics emphasize vigilant doubting (critical thinking) and an affirmative way of knowing (science). The resemblance between skepticism and secularism makes it tempting to call skepticism's generative tension the "skeptical paradox," but doing so plays down its overlap with secularism and belies the ways in which skeptics also avoid religion. In part because skeptics can be religious, they are less likely to engage in religion-like behavior when getting together as skeptics because doing so would conflict with a religious or religion-like identity.

Skepticism's avoidance of religion can be quite literal, such as when skeptics who meet up avoid talking about religion to prevent conflicts between attendees who are antireligious and those who are religious or spiritual. If they maintain their distance from religion, in the abstract, skeptics can produce the ostensible neutrality of indifference. Skepticism can stand apart from religion, but it combines easily with an ontological identity because it restricts itself to epistemology. It complements religion or secularism by avoiding ontological conflict with both. When skepticism combines with a worldview's ontological claims, it can support a particular religion-like position against others. Skepticism's neutrality breaks down when secular skeptics talk about critical thinking as a means to oppose religion or when Christian skeptics marshal scientific evidence to oppose New Age healing practices in hospitals and schools. Like the way everyone is an atheist to someone's gods, anyone can be skeptical of someone else's beliefs, especially those that are not empirically grounded.

Skepticism, like secularism, is overdetermined and deeply polysemous. Also like secularism, its various and sometimes contradictory meanings hang together and influence one another.[17] Thus far, I have used "skepticism" to refer to the modern skeptic movement, which adopts an empiricist epistemology, aided by the scientific method. The older, ancient tradition of skepticism is more radically skeptical and was revitalized in Europe in the sixteenth century with the republication of the Hellenistic skeptic Sextus Empiricus. Ancient skeptics question epistemology itself, or the foundations of any knowledge.[18] The tension between the modern skeptic movement and ancient skepticism mirrors the tension within secular conversion. Modern scientific skepticism assails nonempirical knowledge from the position of empiricism. It negates from an affirmative epistemological stance but refuses to acknowledge this stance as an assumed ground, instead considering it universal truth. Ancient skepticism assails all knowledge, including empiricism. It negates without an affirmative stance.

Scholar Olav Hammer articulates the difference between these skepticisms in his description of modern scientific skeptics: they are "thoroughly un-sceptical of the foundations of the modern, scientific worldview, and accept a plethora of methods of empirical investigation as valid."[19] Modern scientific skeptics accomplish an important rhetorical act of legitimation when they elide the difference between modern and ancient skepticisms. By imagining that they are skeptical of all knowledge, even though they accept the first premises of empiricism, they make empiricism into a universal ground for truth and erase its contingency as a worldview and a tradition.[20]

Philosopher Peter Boghossian's 2013 book *A Manual for Creating Atheists* is paradigmatic of the paradox of secular conversion. Boghossian invents the figure of the "Street Epistemologist," who is armed with the tools of modern skepticism and can undermine the beliefs of any person of faith. His book is a training manual for Street Epistemologists, who will in turn "create" atheists. In practice, Boghossian's "Street Epistemologist" is really a "Street Empiricist." He recounts a conversation with a colleague who asks him, "If faith doesn't have the earmarks of an epistemology, why call it an epistemology? For an epistemology to be an epistemology, must empirical evidence play a significant role?" Boghossian answers his colleague by distinguishing among empiricist, rationalist, and fallibilist (i.e., pragmatist) epistemologies. Contrary to his colleague's implication, he also includes faith as an epistemology, albeit one that is inherently nonempirical.[21] Even though Boghossian argues—rightly—that there are multiple epistemologies, the "Street Epistemologist" relies only on "reason and evidence," by which he means empirical evidence elaborated with the aid of deductive reasoning. Tacitly, Boghossian is telling us that empiricism is the only true epistemology. The Street Epistemologist is always right because he is an empiricist.

For Boghossian, atheism and empiricism are so right that the Street Epistemologist is guaranteed success. The apparent failure of translating someone into secularism has just two causes: "(1) an interlocutor's brain is neurologically damaged, or (2) you're actually succeeding."[22] Boghossian assumes that the built-in faculty of human reason will lead anyone who encounters empirical truth to deduce a secular worldview in which God does not exist. Only those whose reason is impaired will not be swayed in their beliefs. Writing in a foreword to the book, Michael Shermer, founding publisher of *Skeptic* magazine, asserts the same. He describes *A Manual for Creating Atheists* as "the perfect companion to Richard Dawkins' *The God Delusion*. They should be bundled like an atheist software package to reprogram minds into employing reason instead of faith, science instead of superstition."[23] Shermer's metaphor generates again the challenge that Dan and Alfredo faced. Does a person choose to be an atheist? Or have they simply discovered the truth and allowed themselves to accept it? Is acceptance the only "choice" an atheist has?

Boghossian's book is condescending and raises serious red flags for anyone who has followed closely the arguments of scholars critiquing secularism. Like the New Atheists before him, Boghossian finds in "religion" and "faith" the red thread that unites most of what ails the world. And like the New Atheists, he ignores the empirically grounded research demonstrating that religion and faith are historically contingent concepts and tools for governance that developed in the service of nation-state-based European empires. In scientific terms, "religion" and whatever we rely on "religion" to explain are confounded variables because "religion" and "faith" are as much products of the Euro-American culture that produced them as they are concepts that Euro-American discourse relies on to explain its superiority. An empirical inquiry that does not attempt to understand and control for the factors that shape and bias its perspective is doomed to discover only what it expects to find. By refusing to investigate their own confirmation biases, Boghossian and the New Atheists have predetermined their conclusions. When "religion" is a flexible container for everything bad, then of course a proposal to improve the world by eliminating religion will make sense. It is tautological.

Scholars who are engaged in the critique of the secular have redefined "secularism" from its more popular meanings, such as the separation of church and state and the beliefs of nonbelievers. In their lexicon, "secularism" is a name for the process through which "religion" has become a crucial category for governance around the world. It remains strange to me that the scholars who pioneered the critique of "secularism" did not name their object after what it reifies; "religionism" would certainly be easier for me to explain to my students than "secularism." It is, after all, Christians and the empires they administer that have done the most to propagate religious regulation as a mode of governance. These critics' important work has nonetheless called attention to the violence and oppression to which the ism they critique has led. In secularism's ambiguous discursive regime, "religion" receives special protections and exceptions to the law that things and people deemed "superstitious" or "secular" do not. At the same time, religions have become collective identities, both for supremacist majorities and for minority groups that states attempt to control—or eliminate. The systematic internment and killing of Uighur Muslims by the Chinese government is one of the latest and most horrifying examples of an empire adopting the European category of religion to regulate a population, though there are other examples throughout Asia and around the world.

The global spread of the discourse of secularism has made attacking and preserving religion a logical choice within a limited frame of options. Scholars critiquing secularism have shown that this limited frame grows from deeply held assumptions that are not universal. Fracturing and fragmenting "religion" and its related concepts, they argue, is the best way forward, but doing so requires disorienting self-inquiry into that which we take for granted as true.[24] This self-inquiry is not unlike what Boghossian sets out to inflict on others: "Street Epistemologists should set the realistic goal of helping the faithful become more doxastically open. Sow the seeds of doubt. Help people to become less confident in what they claim to know, and help them to stop pretending to know things they don't know."[25] Scholars who are engaged in the critique of secularism are no less brutal in their attack on inherited assumptions, though they ask us to be skeptical of ourselves first and foremost.[26]

Like Boghossian's *Manual*, the tough question that Dan raised on that July afternoon in Virginia—Did he and Alfredo choose to be atheists?—points back to the rhetoric that conceals the paradox of the nonbeliever's epistemological leap into empiricism. Without realizing that they have become empiricists, Dan and Alfredo feel as if logic itself, against their will, has pulled them toward atheism. They have accepted science as the best, perhaps only way of knowing, and they have affirmed accordingly what they find true. If like ancient skeptics they were to be skeptical of empiricism, they might not feel so intensely the pull to atheism and its attendant secular worldview. (And if governments throughout the world were to be skeptical of the category of religion, they might not feel so intensely the desire to regulate it.) As Hammer puts it, "Sceptics in the classical philosophical sense would, if consistent in their scepticism, be equally suspicious of all empirical propositions. This broad, philosophical scepticism is rejected outright by the modern sceptics."[27]

The nonbeliever's dilemma is one I share. I have argued empirically throughout this book, as its many quotes and notes attest, and hopefully my arguments are well reasoned. As I am a doctor of religion and a professor in a department of religious studies, no amount of knowing self-reflection can purify me of my material dependence on a category that all of us inherit by way of Christianity and colonialism. My aim here is merely to make sense of the paradox to which our shared dilemma points back. Other scholars who have critiqued the secular discursive tradition face a similar problem. Talal Asad's most recent book, *Secular Translations*, relies no less on reason and evidence than Boghossian's does. Dedicated to self-inquiry, my critique can only be immanent and affectionate.[28]

Secularism's Ethical Dilemma

After spending several years among secular activists and organized nonbelievers, I was not surprised that Alfredo, Rick, Aaron, and Dan decided that atheism is not antiracist. There are two ways of understanding their conclusion. One relies on a narrow conception of atheism, in which it is only an assertion about the existence of God, as if that assertion does not rest on other premises. On this view, atheism is a very limited claim and makes no others, such as ethical claims. The other view recognizes that for the same reasons secular people assert there is no God, many do not find meaning inherent in the world.

The second, more systematic view raises one of the fundamental questions that secular people face: Is there moral truth? If so, what is it, and how is it known? And if not, how can a person tell the difference between right and wrong? In a Christian-centered context like the United States, God and religion are default sources of truth and morality. Removing them appears to create a vacuum that must be filled. For several centuries in Europe, atheism was synonymous with immorality, and the so-called practical atheist was a person of low morals rather than an avowed nonbeliever.[29] Atheists remain one of the least trusted groups in the United States.[30] The defensive title of humanist chaplain Greg Epstein's 2009 book *Good without God* captures well the persistent burden of ethics on secular people.

Despite finding widespread interest in ethics among very secular people who participate in the American secular movement, I also found a robust debate over whether atheism, in particular, entails ethics. As I discussed in chapter 1, because of atheism's negative framing of what secular people believe, there is always debate among nonbelievers about whether it is a worldview. The terms that nonbelievers use to describe themselves—"humanist," "atheist," "agnostic," "freethinker," and so on—hang together in a constellation. These self-identifiers do not describe a single secular worldview so much as a related variety of worldviews, systematized, that is, rationalized, to varying degrees. More importantly, the variety of nonbelievers' self-identifiers arises from the persistent debates that are constitutive of being secular. In those debates, humanists usually argue that being secular entails ethics because secular people share many beliefs about the world. This is why nonbelievers like Juan and Sarah, whom I introduced in chapter 1, felt like they had discovered who they already are when they first encountered humanism. It names all of what they believe in, rather than just what they believe is real or the best way to know reality. As a woman named Dorothy put it during an interview in Minneapolis, "To me, humanism is a naturalist worldview, one that you juxtapose against supernaturalism, plus a global ethics, concern for well-being of all and sustainability of the planet." Humanism is the addition of an ethical dimension to a secular worldview that humanists believe lacks it.

Humanism is not the only secular ideology that has attempted to bind ethics to secularism—indeed, this was George Jacob Holyoake's intent when he coined the term "secularism"—but it is one of the most longstanding.[31] In chapter 1, I looked closely at the humanist movement's origin in the middle of the nineteenth century. It grew from a combination of August Comte's Religion of Humanity, Felix Adler's Ethical Culture, and attempts by Unitarian Universalist ministers like John Dietrich to subtract the supernatural from Christianity. Ethical Culture, as one would expect given its name, has placed a strong emphasis on ethics since its founding in 1876 and has influenced humanism to consider ethics more explicitly. In 1952, at the Amsterdam Congress of Humanists, organizations from the United States, Europe, and India established the International Humanist and Ethical Union and created "Ethical Humanist" as an officially recognized term.[32] Ethical Culture and humanism did not merge in this moment so much as Ethical Culture embraced humanism after decades of distancing itself. Today, most people in the Ethical Culture movement consider themselves "Ethical Humanists," and I met many who are also members of humanist organizations. After 1952, "Ethical" became an adjective that qualifies humanism, able to represent both an affiliation with Ethical Culture and a more general orientation toward ethics among humanists.

I discovered the productive ambiguity of "ethical" during a visit to the New York Society for Ethical Culture in the summer of 2013. After the Sunday Platform, Ethical Culture's term for a sermon-like speech at its Sunday meetings, I was talking with a man named Peter, who told me about a conversation he had overheard recently between his son and a few other children at a playground in Manhattan. The topic of religion had somehow come up among the children, and they were identifying as either Christian or Jewish. To Peter's great pride, his son told them, "I'm Ethical." The other children responded by saying that they, too, were ethical. Peter and I were impressed that they knew the term's vernacular definition, but for Peter and his son, the term meant much more. The doubleness of "Ethical" and "ethical" helps Peter see his religious affiliation with Ethical Culture as both a religion and a way of life. In the context of our conversation, Peter was using the anecdote to describe for me the complicated relationship he has with Ethical Culture; it is, paradoxically, both less and more than a religion.

The Amsterdam Declaration of 1952 uses the ambiguity of "ethical" to offer humanism "as an alternative to the religions which claim to be based on revelation on the one hand, and totalitarian systems on the other." The declaration's list of the "fundamentals of modern, ethical humanism" includes a statement on ethics:

> 3. Humanism is ethical. It affirms the dignity of man and the right of the individual to the greatest possible freedom of development compatible with the right of others. There is a danger that in seeking to utilise scientific knowledge in a complex society individual freedom may be threatened by the very impersonal machine that has been created to save it. Ethical humanism, therefore, rejects totalitarian attempts to perfect the machine in order to obtain immediate gains at the cost of human values.[33]

The postwar context of the declaration is clear, as "ethical" defines a limit to the pursuit of scientific knowledge. The declaration contains no reference to Ethical Culture, despite its marking a merger of the two movements. "Ethical" bears a tacit double sense throughout.

In 2002, for the organization's fiftieth anniversary, the International Humanist and Ethical Union issued an updated declaration in which "ethical" makes a more vernacular reference to morality: "1. Humanism is ethical. It affirms the worth, dignity and autonomy of the individual and the right of every human being to the greatest possible freedom compatible with the rights of others. Humanists have a duty of care to all of humanity including future generations. Humanists believe that morality is an intrinsic part of human nature based on understanding and a concern for others, needing no external sanction."[34] Though neither declaration refers to Ethical Culture directly, the organized humanists who wrote them were well aware of the movement's shared history with humanism. The ambiguity of "ethical" works subtly to create links across organizations and blur the boundary between religion and secular categories like philosophy and culture.

Writing in a note to *A Manual for Creating Atheists*, Boghossian disagrees with those who try to link atheism and ethics, arguing that ethics has no inherent place in a secular worldview:

> Whether a person is an atheist or a believer is immaterial with respect to morality, and yet, moral ascriptions are frequently made to atheists and to the faithful. For example, currently there's a (hopefully) short-lived movement called Atheism+. Among Atheism+'s tenets are social justice, support for women's rights, protesting against racism, fighting homophobia and transphobia, critical thinking, and skepticism. . . . Many people try to make atheism into something it's not. Atheism is not about racism, homophobia, or not practicing tai chi; it's simply about not having enough evidence to warrant a belief in God. Atheism is about epistemology, evidence, honesty, sincerity, reason, and inquiry.[35]

Alfredo, Rick, Aaron, and Dan agree with Boghossian about atheism and racism. Their debate at the TV studio in Virginia remaps the contours of a larger debate that has been taking place for centuries.

The Atheism+ (pronounced "atheism-plus") movement that Boghossian refers to started on the internet rather than in real life (IRL). Atheism+ was an attempt to rally nonbelievers who want to emphasize social justice and, specifically, issues concerning misogyny and sexism. The term was coined in 2012 by blogger Jennifer McCreight, a secular activist whose "Boobquake" meme catalyzed conversations about feminism in the secular and skeptic communities.[36] While many online activists were quick to support Atheism+, most of those I spoke with who work primarily IRL considered the term yet another division in an already factious movement. As a humanist leader named Justin told me, "We have been talking about these ideas for a very long time." Another leader, named Chad, a major donor to secular activism, expressed his frustration more bluntly: "This whole Atheism+ thing is just the latest example of 'Let's come up with this new label and intentionally try to be divisive about it.' All these people online are saying, 'You're either with us or against us,' but how is [Atheism+] in any way different from humanism?"[37] Though Justin and Chad do not recognize the generative role of the secular paradox and the way it creates a persistent ethical dilemma for nonbelievers in a Christian-centered culture, they are right that Atheism+ wades into a very old debate about atheism and ethics. It is yet another fracture on an old fault line.[38]

Some of the pushback that Atheism+ received after it appeared in 2012 mirrors a larger debate that has emerged in American culture between traditional and progressive liberals. In July 2020, *Harper's Magazine* published "A Letter on Justice and Open Debate," criticizing what it called "an intolerance of opposing views, a vogue for public shaming and ostracism, and the tendency to dissolve complex policy issues in a blinding moral certainty." Others have called what the letter describes "cancel culture."[39] The letter was signed by 153 scholars, writers, and other intellectuals, including leading figures of the Left, like Noam Chomsky and Malcolm Gladwell. It was also signed by secular movement activists like Sarah Haider, who cofounded Ex-Muslims of North America, and Wendy Kaminer, who along with two other signatories, Steven Pinker and Salman Rushdie, has served on the advisory board of the Secular Coalition for America. The *Harper's* letter responded to what the signatories consider an overreaction on the part of those who, like the supporters of Atheism+ and the #MeToo movement, have sought extralegal consequences for the actions of public figures. The letter's narrow focus on public speech surely helped it gather signatures from a broad range of intellectuals, but the debate it tried to catalyze is being waged over many issues, including racism and sexual assault and harassment.[40]

The conflict between traditional and progressive liberals has led to increasingly sharp divides in the American secular movement. In recent years, I have spoken with secular activists who refuse to work with Michael Shermer or publish in his *Skeptic* magazine because he has advocated strong protections for free speech, resisted cultural critiques of science, and taken conservative positions in debates about sexual assault and trans rights. In March 2017, two weeks after a lecture by controversial race scientist—and scientific racist—Charles Murray was disrupted by students at Middlebury College, Shermer tweeted, "Science is universal, international, inclusive, nonpartisan, a-political, a-gender, a-race, & a-ideological. Don't inject identity politics." A month later, in April 2017, New Atheist Sam Harris had a conversation with Murray on his podcast, *Making Sense*, intensifying the disagreement and drawing more secular activists into the dispute.[41] The debate among very secular people over whether science entails ethics or is merely a method of empirical inquiry is complex enough that it will never be settled. Even Harris, who argued for a scientific morality in his book *The Moral Landscape*, considers the question open. It continues to divide those who consider atheism a restricted, scientific claim about the hypothesis that a Christian-like God exists and those who consider atheism a logical outcome of a worldview or set of worldviews that make no place for a Christian-like God.

Skeptical of Authority

Secular people's moral challenge stems in part from their skepticism of authority. As I described in chapter 2, the secular people I spent time with during my field research are very concerned with freedom from authority. Because organized nonbelievers define themselves against religious groupthink or dogma, they often structure their communities in ways that are skeptical of authority—sometimes to the point of hindering their ability to act collectively or form groups at all. In many nonsecular traditions, God or the gods provide the source of authority. They give meaning and purpose, and they ground truth and value. They also determine the boundary between right and wrong. This is the nature of authority and what contrasts it from power; authority authorizes what power does.[42] In the secular tradition, which lacks a God or gods, authority is a persistent problem. Where to locate authority and how to determine what it authorizes are persistent anxieties for nonbelievers and spur frequent debates. This is partly by Christian design. Beginning in the Renaissance, Christian theologians drew from ancient skeptics and Epicureans, among others, to create an atheism sufficient to be their own God's antithesis.[43] Ancient Epicureans were agnostic about the gods and believed that if they did exist, they were uninterested in human affairs. Epicureans grounded their ethics in sensory experience, so like ancient skeptics, they did not affirm a transcendent authority. This made their philosophy useful to the Christian theologians who played a big role in shaping the secular tradition into the one we inherit today. Debating the problem of authority in the absence of transcendence is constitutive of the secular discursive tradition.

Aristotelian materialism offers a solution to the problem of authority by finding teleology inherent to ontology and offering "virtue" as a ground for ethics. All beings have a purpose, which it is the meaning of life to pursue. This poses its own challenge, however. A tradition holds the inherited wisdom to define the roles of those who live within it. Who, then, gets to decide a person's true purpose or value? Either Aristotle's model is inherently conservative, taking the world that is for what it ought to be, or it kicks the problem of authority farther down the road, making it a question of interpretation.[44] Myriad other efforts to address this problem have been debated for centuries. Baruch Spinoza's *Ethics* is a rationalist description of a monist ontology that advocates for the intellectual freedom to accept one's fate. Spinoza's ethics are a way to live in response to the reality that *Ethics* describes. Through a synthesis of rationalist and empiricist epistemologies, Immanuel Kant articulates the categorical imperative, a procedure that can authorize morality that is universally true.[45] Existentialists like Albert Camus describe the meaninglessness of life without transcendental ground. Rather than critique the need for universal meaning, Camus accepts the absurdity of life and argues that a person should persist nonetheless. The anxiety of deciding what to do in the absence of universal authority is the existential condition.[46] John Stuart Mill's utilitarianism echoes Epicureanism in its focus on sensation, grounding morality in empirical science as a guide for maximizing units of pleasure and minimizing units of pain.[47] The New Atheist Sam Harris has tried to do the same with his fMRI-based research into the brain's moral activity, arguing that humans are hardwired with a universal morality.[48]

Locating authority in scientific empiricism poses its own challenge, however, because as Max Weber argues in "Science as a Vocation," science cannot establish a goal or judge a value but only aid their more effective achievement.[49] Pragmatists like George Herbert Mead and Richard Rorty have tried to ground authority in the social and in tradition.[50] Saba Mahmood, in part by recovering Aristotle, argues that authority's ground does not lie in the self or its resistance to authority that restricts it. Her critique of Western feminism in *Politics of Piety* challenges the tradition of autonomy pioneered by Friedrich Nietzsche and complicated by Michel Foucault and Judith Butler.[51]

Secular people have been convinced by these efforts to widely varying degrees. What matters here is the persistence of the challenge they face and their debates in response to it. Without God or something like him, authority is a problem to address and an open question to answer—and thus so are meaning, purpose, value, truth, and morality. Relativism, both moral and cultural, is a logical outcome of the absence of universal authority and an unsettling dilemma.[52] Wrestling with these questions is by definition what secular people do.

In April 2013, I attended the Northeast Conference on Science and Skepticism (NECSS; pronounced "nexus") on the campus of the Fashion Institute of Technology in Manhattan. Unfortunately, I was only able to make it for the second of "three fun-, fact-, and science-filled days." While there, I watched a live podcast recording of a debate between Massimo Pigliucci and Shermer. Pigliucci is also a leading thinker in the skeptic and nonbeliever movements. To frame the debate, Shermer and Pigliucci gave brief lectures on morality, which is a frequent topic at nonbeliever events.[53] During Pigliucci's lecture, he echoed Weber, pace Harris: "Neurobiology tells us what's going on inside the brain, though not what we should do." Shermer, in line with Mill and to an extent Harris, proposed "a science of morality," grounded primarily in empirical observation. Pigliucci countered with a more socially grounded proposal, relying on John Rawls's notion of "reflective equilibrium," which is a deliberative process of making judgments coherent.[54]

Both Shermer's and Pigliucci's proposals compensate for secularism's persistent lack of a clear moral authority by combining empirical evidence and logical reasoning to discover provisional, context-based moral truths. Both use the liberal ideals of happiness and freedom as guiding norms. Like Boghossian, the worldviews of Shermer and Pigliucci are grounded in reason and evidence, with Pigliucci adding debate, or the collective reasoning of individuals. These are bricolage approaches, assembling various aspects of the prevailing moral theories in the Enlightenment branch of the secular discursive tradition. By focusing on ethics as a process instead of a set of propositions, they avoid religious "beliefs," in the sense of doctrines. By emphasizing the reasoning faculties of individuals, they avoid religious "belonging" and the dangers of authority and groupthink, remaining consistent with the natural rights tradition that underpins modern liberalism. Their engagement with the problem of authority situates them in a broad secular tradition, and their proposed solutions to it align them within a narrower, distinctively liberal branch. Their efforts, in all their ambivalence, are eminently secular.

Secular Social Justice

In April 2018, I attended the third annual Secular Social Justice conference, a daylong event held at All Souls Unitarian Church in Washington,

DC. The auditorium in the far back of the church holds about 220 people, and it was near capacity by late morning. The event was, without a doubt, the most diverse secular gathering I attended during my several years of fieldwork. There were many women and people of color, and there was more diversity among nonwhite attendees than I have seen at a secular event before or since. The conference also differed in tone and feel. Jessica Xiao, the event's MC, began with a land acknowledgment that she "prepared in consultation and labor with Desiree Kane, a Miwok woman who was involved in protesting the Dakota Access Pipeline." The conference was held on Nacotchtank land, she told us. Xiao also encouraged us "to make new friends," and tongue in cheek, she suggested a series of politically loaded icebreakers: "Who did you vote for in 2016? What are your thoughts on abortion? Tell me your life story from the moment you were born in as much detail as possible?" Later, she defined a "question" and then a "statement." "They're not the same thing," she warned. "Q&A is for asking questions, not making statements." Her disciplinary charm had me and many others laughing.

The conference's opening remarks were given by atheist activist and scholar Sikivu Hutchinson. I have seen her speak several times, including when she presented on a panel on Black atheism that I helped organize at UC–Santa Barbara.[55] She is always direct and forceful. Hutchinson addressed "so-called white humanist allies" and asked of social justice, "Is it a secular issue? Is it a humanist issue?" As a veteran of the secular movement, she knows well the liberal Enlightenment ground on which very secular people claim to stand, and she criticized it candidly. "As atheists and humanists of color," she told the audience, "we're asked to justify and soft-pedal our anger over the human rights crime scene that is American public education, while the lives of white children—their heritage, their identities—are taught as social gospel in our miseducation system."

Like Boghossian, many very secular people believe that education, and "critical thinking," in particular, is the panacea for correcting not only the ills of religion but society in general. As one prominent donor to secular causes told me during a phone interview in August 2016, "The best way to solve problems is to prevent them. If we can graduate caring students who are ready to look at life maturely, we won't have our prisons jammed up like they are. People are wasting their time on religion.

Superstition is counterproductive. Let's face it." Against this perspective, Hutchinson told those of us gathered at All Souls that education is not enough. Teaching students the histories of people of color and white supremacy helps, but actions help more.

Hutchinson called out the "leadership vacuum in the upper echelon of white-dominated organizations, AHA [the American Humanist Association] and SSA [the Secular Student Alliance] among them." There are "no people of color" in executive management positions.[56] "We know that it's precisely because of anti-atheist religious bigotry—white atheist and humanist racism—and [because of] this leadership vacuum that people of color are not going to step out and openly identify as secular, as atheist, as humanist." Racism in the secular movement, in other words, is the reason more people of color do not make their secular identities public or primary. This is the double negative of Black atheism that several Black atheists described to me in interviews and that I discussed at greater length in chapter 2. Their atheism makes them illegible in Black communities, and their Blackness makes them outsiders in secular communities.

Hutchinson connected this double negative to concrete harms: "Until this shifts, queer Black children will continue to be more likely to be policed, incarcerated, become homeless, and be victimized by oppressive religious idolatry and conversion quackery." Most nonbelievers I met are like the donor I spoke with on the phone. They believe that if they make the United States more secular, it will become more ethical. Hutchinson does not share their optimism: "This talk about the rise of the religious 'nones,' the cultural propaganda about how this is going to be a paradigm shift—it's just going to be a footnote for segregated communities of color." Promoting secularism and advocating for secular people are powerful ways to combat conservative beliefs about gender and sexuality, she told us, but they will not lead to racial equality.

After the conference, I went to dinner with a few of the organizers and several other leaders and activists. Some were people I had known for years, and others I met for the first time that evening. We gathered at a dive bar called Red Derby and sat shoulder to shoulder at a couple of tables near the door. As always at these gatherings, it was an eclectic group spanning decades in age. And as usual, there was a lot of cursing and a lot of beer. Within about ten minutes, the organizers began to debrief the day's events. My nebulous reflections were catalyzed by a Black woman, Joann, whom I have known since 2012, who is now in a prominent but not executive leadership position at a large secular organization. She and I have run into each other often at conferences and workshops, and we usually have long conversations about the state of the secular movement. She is always full of insights, some of which have shaped this book deeply.

I watched Joann observe the conversation, and I wondered what she would say. She soon asked the group whether they thought there was a connection between secularism and social justice. After a couple of the young activists responded by thinking aloud about a difficult question, she shared her own view. The conference gathered a lot of secular activists who are also activists for causes like antiracism, she told us. It provided an opportunity to get the secular community to think more about the importance of social justice. Throughout the day, however, speakers and participants struggled to make connections between secular views and social justice activism. According to Joann, this is because becoming secular will not in itself make a person less racist. There is no inherent link between secularism and ethics.

Black atheist and scholar William Hart agrees: "I reiterate an earlier claim: atheism, secular humanism, and naturalism are not an ethics or a politics. The connection between one's identity as a [Black atheist] and a specific ethical-political orientation must be an intentional act. This orientation is forged through the life you live, the choices you make, the associations you maintain or abandon, and the allies and the enemies that you cultivate. There are many choices."[57] Activists suture the gap between secularism and ethics in the way they live their lives, but atheism and other secular worldviews do not lead inevitably to justice.

The group as a whole discussed Joann's point for a couple of minutes before breaking naturally into smaller conversations. I was sitting next to a youth leader and podcaster named Brian, whom I had met earlier in the day. He and I began chatting, and we realized at once that Joann had named a question that we had seen through a glass darkly while talking on our walk to the bar. We returned to the topic of a book Brian is writing on materialism and its relationship to humanism, wrestling with the challenge that Joann's observation posed. He associates materialism with science and was articulating the relationship between the two. As I listened to him, it was clear to me that he recognized that materialism is an ontology that science, as an epistemological method, often leads to, though he did not use these philosophical terms. Humanism, for him, is a worldview that contains materialism but also includes ethics.

Recently, Brian told me, he had been reading Max Horkheimer and Theodor Adorno's *Dialectic of Enlightenment*, which, he found difficult to read but productive to think with, especially on the harms of faith in the salvific potential of science. I told him I felt the same about both the text's difficulty and its productivity. We talked for a while about the Frankfurt School's challenge to the Enlightenment atheism that prevails among New Atheists like Richard Dawkins and Sam Harris, of whom he is critical. But both of us felt like we were talking in an abstract way about Joann's more mundane provocation, and neither of us felt like we had a good answer. Humanism, Brian thinks, connects secularism or materialism and social justice. I have argued in this book that humanism certainly tries but that the persistence of Joann's question among secular people proves the stubbornness of secularism's ethical dilemma.

The Ethics of Secular Conversion

Whether it is ethical for secular people to proselytize is unsurprisingly a source of conflict among secular activists and organized nonbelievers. Boghossian advocates for spreading atheism, but even he considers this activity in solely negative terms. The Street Epistemologist debunks religious worldviews, leading people to the truth revealed when illusion is stripped away. Boghossian does not advocate for religion's replacement; he believes that people will become secular when you show them the flaws in their religious thinking. He does not see becoming atheist as an act of secular conversion or translation; it is merely deconversion.

The secular paradox structures the tension between the negative effort of debunking and the positive effort of replacement or translation. Secular is *both* not religious *and* religion-like or religious. By tracking concrete organizational ties and broader public and private conversations, I have shown that very secular people do not share a single worldview, but they do share a related set of worldviews organized around persistent questions and debates. Becoming secular means leaving traditional religion, but it also means becoming part of the secular, religion-like discursive tradition. Becoming secular means deconverting from religion *and* converting to secularism.

Very secular people speak carefully about conversion and what types of outreach activities are acceptable. Some atheists I met with are committed to converting the faithful. For instance, I mentioned in chapter 1 that a woman I interviewed named Jacqueline describes herself as an "evangelical atheist." She told me that she tries to proselytize whenever she can. Converting people to secularism is too religious for many secular people, however. It violates their secular values, which in the United States typically include individual autonomy and skepticism of authority.

When I asked a popular humanist author about what he hoped his recently published book would accomplish, he told me, "I didn't intend it as a vehicle for converting believers to nonbelievers. The arguments I put forward are in favor of the secular worldview, but most of us find it inappropriate and bad strategy to convert people from their views. [The book] is not intended to deconvert people." Julian, one of the leaders at the Center for Inquiry, told me something similar: "Some organizations are interested in converting to atheism, but CFI is not, principally. In its education mission, CFI discusses religion from a critical view. We're nonbelievers because that's the correct view of the universe." Both men see their work as education, as Boghossian does. They believe that they are doing good by inviting believers into the truth of secularism, which is the truth of scientific inquiry.

Frank is a secular activist whom I discussed in chapter 3, who participates in a group that debunks paranormal phenomena. He also helps run a nonbeliever organization in Los Angeles. During our conversation at his office, Frank and I talked about his organization's efforts at outreach and education. He described his visits to a Christian high school east of Los Angeles:

> I go to a high school called Ontario Christian High School twice a year to give a lecture to their comparative religion class about our side: atheism, agnosticism, secular humanism. I think I've snagged a couple of converts over the years. There's a teacher who brings me in every time. I give him a lot of credit because I don't pull any punches with these kids. I try to do it in a way that's not adversarial, but I really challenge them. I'm amazed at how little they know about their own religion, and I'm

amazed by how little they know about how the universe works. . . . A lot of these kids barely know that the Earth floats around the sun every year. They're Young Earth creationists. Pretty hardcore. They're biblical literalists. That's a tough position to defend.

Secular conversions are for Frank a fortunate collateral benefit of visiting Ontario Christian, but he and the teacher who invites him believe that educating young people is the primary reason for his biannual trips.

Sometimes, Frank told me, he receives invitations to speak at churches, and he takes the same approach. Conversion is not his aim, but he hopes he can at least change how evangelical Christians view atheists. He described to me an event he participated in at Moment Church in Tustin, California, which is in the heart of Orange County, one of California's most conservative regions:

> I said, "OK, well, the worst thing I could be is the angry guy and the bitter atheist." I was relaxed and happy and unabashed about my positions, tried to be engaging and pleasant. That's it. There was nothing for them to dislike about the way I was. They're still not going to agree with me, but at least they're not going to pin "He's an evil person" on me. It was a discussion onstage in the middle of the sermon. We talked about death, good and evil, and a lot of different things. I was looking hard for some ulterior motive, but they seemed pretty sincere, and ostensibly [the pastor who invited us] was trying to build bridges between communities. I think the most cynical thing I could say about it is they understand that they have a PR problem with being intolerant. And they do.

For Frank, outreach work is not about conversion, primarily, even if making secular converts is a desirable outcome. Outreach is about education and improving perceptions of nonbelievers.

Secular parents face the ambiguity of secular advocacy in their own home. The vast majority of the secular people I spoke with about parenting told me that they want to leave the choice of being secular up to their children. Though they would prefer their children not become religious, many teach them about different religious traditions and want their children to make their own choices about what to believe and how to live. Sarah, a woman I met in Columbus, Ohio, and later interviewed over the phone, helps run Camp Quest, a network of "humanist residential summer camps." I introduced Sarah's path to humanism in chapter 1, but her thoughts on conversion are also fascinating. Camp Quest's website describes the camps as an "educational adventure shaped by fun, friends and freethought, featuring science, natural wonder and humanist values."[58] Sarah said that even very secular people have misperceptions about the camps: "They tell me, 'That's just as bad as Jesus camp'—just as bad, indoctrinating their children. That was really frustrating, to see it coming from people within our community who share our worldview." When Sarah gives interviews in the media or speaks at conferences, she is "very careful to emphasize that it's not a camp for atheist kids but a camp for freethinking families." The camp's goal is to help children "know there's nothing wrong with being an atheist." She told me, "We want them to develop critical thinking skills, to be unafraid to ask questions. We also want them to have fun and make friends at the same time." Sarah needs to walk the line between education and acceptance, on the one hand, and advocacy and conversion, or indoctrination, on the other.

Christel Manning has studied nonreligious parenting extensively, and she found similar opinions among a much larger sample of secular parents. She identified four distinct worldviews held by nonreligious parents, of which secular is just one. The others are spiritual, unchurched belief, and religious indifference.[59] Manning describes secular people in much the same way that I have described the people I spent time with. The secular are those who identify with terms like "atheist," "agnostic," "humanist," and "freethinker." The indifferent are a difficult group to categorize, though she is right to separate them, even as they, too, are part of a secular discursive tradition. In Manning's taxonomy, the indifferent avoid religious practices and groups, do not consider themselves spiritual, and do not believe in God or the supernatural. By emphasizing the negative half of the secular paradox, the indifferent are less systematic in their secularism, which is not "substantive," in her terms. They do not think about religion-related questions very often.[60] This less engaged form of secularism—indifference—is important to recognize when thinking about secular conversion because the indifferent are the primary group that secular activists and those who run nonbeliever organizations try to reach. People who are indifferent to religion but do not identify with spirituality and avoid religious practices are already translated into the secular discursive tradition. The question for organizers is how to get them to understand themselves as part of a secular minority in the United States.

In the next three subsections, I describe in greater detail the strategies that organized nonbelievers and secular activists use to grow their movement. They resemble proselytizing, but they usually stop short of trying to make converts. One strategy is getting secular people to "come out," or identify publicly in the religion-related terms they use in private. Some of the organizers I spoke with couched this strategy in the sociological language of identity and described it as making one's secular identity primary. A second strategy is advertising or outreach to raise awareness of nonbelievers. Organized nonbelievers want to normalize their presence in American culture and improve their reputation among the religious; they also want to make secular people aware that groups for people like them exist. One part of this strategy is offering a range of ways to be secular so that there is a group for every kind of nonbeliever. A third strategy responds to the latter effort by trying to unify the various kinds of nonbelievers under a single umbrella. Because nonbelievers describe themselves using so many different terms, they do not always see themselves as like one another and part of a unified minority, despite their participation in a shared discursive tradition.

Making Secular Identity Primary

Sociologists who focus on very secular people have made identity one of their early and long-standing areas of inquiry. This is in part because identity is a concept that organized nonbeliever groups use in their activist work. Identity is both emic and etic, both insider language and the language of researchers. Identity-related questions that secular activists try to answer translate easily into the concerns of sociologists who study them. Researchers like Richard Cimino, Christopher Smith, Stephen LeDrew, and Steven Kettell have taken interest in many of the same questions that activists ask themselves. What would make the secular movement more successful? Why has it achieved so much success in the first decades of the twenty-first century? What impedes the movement's continued success? For some sociologists, their interest is both academic and more personal because they are very secular or have leadership roles in nonbeliever organizations in the United States.⁶¹ Shared interests between social movements and those who study them are common in the history of the sociology of religion, and I find no reason to believe that they have compromised the integrity of the research on nonbelievers.⁶² To the contrary, I have tried in writing this book to make my own secularism an object of inquiry, as doing so has guided me to many of its insights. These shared interests do, however, help explain some of the questions that researchers have asked about secular people, especially concerning identity and social movements.⁶³

In 2006, in one of the first volumes to focus on the contemporary secular movement, psychologists Bruce E. Hunsberger and Bob Altemeyer published the results of a study they conducted among organized nonbelievers, with the aim of describing all American atheists. Avowedly exploratory, they focused on differentiating types of nonbelievers and explaining why certain people become atheists.⁶⁴ Phil Zuckerman, the most recognized sociologist of nonbelief and the founder of a secular studies program at Pitzer College, published two large-scale studies of nonbelievers in 2008 and 2012 and has published several more since. The first, based in Denmark and Sweden, "analyze[s] the unique contours of the worldviews" of the "nonreligious, irreligious, [and] religiously indifferent" and explains why some countries are more religious than others. Zuckerman argues that nonreligious people are just as happy as the religious, if not happier.⁶⁵ His second study focuses on nonbelievers in the United States and explores how and why people become nonreligious by describing the personality traits and life experiences that these individuals often share.⁶⁶

In 2007, Richard Cimino and Christopher Smith published an article in *Sociology of Religion* that opened the floodgates for the contemporary study of organized nonbelievers. The pair has since contributed several more articles relating to similar themes of collective identity formation and social movement mobilization.⁶⁷ In 2014, they repackaged several of those papers into a volume, *Atheist Awakening: Secular Activism and Community in America*, which is the first nationwide social scientific study of organized nonbelief in the United States. Focusing on the local level, Jesse M. Smith has published several essays on atheist groups, describing their process of collective identity formation. He has more recently turned his attention to the Sunday Assembly, a group that I discussed at the beginning of chapter 2, which is one of the most religion-like organizations for secular people. Stephen LeDrew published an indirect response to Smith in *Sociology of Religion*, which is sensitive to the blurry boundary between secular and religious among organized nonbelievers and seeks to nuance the multiple ways in which individuals arrive at an atheist identity.[68] Katja Guenther, Kerry Mulligan, and Cameron Papp have also published on the subject of atheist identity formation while linking those local groups to a national social movement. Stephen Kettell has argued directly for the existence of a secular movement and speculated about its future and effectiveness.[69]

These researchers agree with what many leaders of secular organizations told me: the publications and lectures of the New Atheists—Sam Harris, Richard Dawkins, Christopher Hitchens, and Daniel Dennett—sparked a resurgence in interest in organized nonbelief and increased their membership and donations.[70] In interviews with organized nonbelievers who "self-identify as atheists and were involved in the organized secularist movement," Richard Cimino and Christopher Smith found that nearly all of their research participants had read at least one book by the New Atheists.[71] They also found that the New Atheists weakened the taboo against atheism in the United States and provided nonbelievers with a way to imagine themselves as a community and a social movement.[72] Guenther, Mulligan, and Papp assert the importance of the New Atheists for organized atheism in their analysis of atheist collective identity and boundary work.[73]

Most of the very secular people I spoke with during my fieldwork told me that the New Atheists were a catalyst in their lives—whether for leaving religion, "coming out" as a nonbeliever, joining a nonbeliever community, or becoming involved in secular activism. One leader who founded a humanist group in New York City in the 1990s described Hitchens as his hero, and a young woman I met at a student leadership conference half jokingly revealed that she wanted to find out where Harris lives so that she could knock on his door and profess her love. Other leaders reflected on the impact of the New Atheism for nonbelievers and their organizations. Though one prominent atheist told me that he does not like using the "New Atheist" label "because there's nothing new about them," he also told me that their books "really got people reading" and that there used to be "a dearth of books on atheism." Another leader observed that the New Atheists "made atheism more visible" and inspired her humanist organization to start using "atheism" and "atheist" more frequently in its publications and press releases. A growing subset of the secular movement rejects the New Atheists because of their conservative approaches to social justice, though their influence continues to loom large even among their critics.

In response to the widespread interest in nonbelief that the New Atheists helped to spur, nonbeliever organizations in the United States strengthened their efforts to encourage nonbelievers to "come out" and openly embrace atheist, humanist, secular, and other nontheistic identities. For instance, every major nonbeliever organization in the United States joined the Openly Secular Coalition within a few months of its founding in May 2014.[74] Secular activists have self-consciously modeled their "out of the closet" strategy on the gay-rights movement, and lawyers for the major nonbeliever organizations have also looked to gay-rights activists for new legal strategies. David Niose, former president of the American Humanist Association and the Secular Coalition for America, pioneered this strategy in a case that challenged the inclusion of "under God" in the Pledge of Allegiance in Massachusetts.[75] Niose found inspiration in *Goodridge v. Department of Health*, the 2003 decision that made Massachusetts the first state to legalize gay marriage.[76] He outlines his strategy and the debt it owes to the gay-rights movement in his 2012 book *Nonbeliever Nation: The Rise of Secular Americans*.[77] The thrust of the book is that nonbelievers should "come out" as "secular" in order to combat the Religious Right, even referring to nonbelievers en masse as capital-*S* "Seculars."[78] For Niose, Seculars are a minority facing discrimination, and they need to consciously embrace contemporary identitarian politics by making their "Secular" identity primary. Niose argues that secular people accepting themselves as a religious minority provides them better protection under the law and more recognition alongside other religious minorities.

Though Niose writes that he "would be pleased to see humanist centers springing up across the country," he remains apprehensive because "the reality is that many no longer find the traditional benefits of religious communities relevant in modern society."[79] Several leaders I interviewed disagree. Two leaders I spoke with at the Humanist Community at Harvard (HCH) quoted Robert Putnam and David Campbell's 2010 book *American Grace* to frame the opportunity they want to seize. One of the leaders is worth quoting at length because he describes well the entanglements of secular activists and scholars who study them:[80]

> Very influential in my thinking has been Robert Putnam and his sociological work on social capital. . . . He's rather conservative in his views, frankly, but I started reading his work, particularly his big work studying American religious life, called *American Grace*, and basically, I was convinced by his argument. He found—and this really stuck with me—that people who are religious give more of their money to charity, they volunteer more of their time, they give their organs and blood more frequently, they vote more frequently, they run for office more frequently, they're generally more engaged, civically speaking, and also, according to him, they're just nicer to people in the sense that they're more willing to help someone with their groceries, they're more willing to help someone cross the road, this sort of thing. And I read that, I was like, hmm. Then he breaks down the data, and he says, but this isn't correlated with intensity of religious belief. It's not about their faith belief. He found that if people were less religious but for whatever reason they went frequently to religious communities, they displayed the same civic benefits that very religious people did. If people were really religious but they were basically a hermit, they didn't. And so he said this doesn't seem to be about religious belief, but it seems to be about moral communities. And he says, and this is a direct quote, I think, "Morally intense, nonreligious social networks could have a similarly powerful effect."[81] I think that's the quote. But, he goes on to say, there are too few of them to study. And I read that, and I thought, that's the problem with the humanist movement. We don't have morally intense, nonreligious social networks. . . . This is a decades-long process. This is not going to happen until I'm an old man. If people really take this seriously and start building these communities, what we're looking at in maybe thirty or forty years, we'll have a network of thriving humanist community centers in major cities across America, which have some political clout because they have large memberships.

The leaders of HCH understand that the percentage of Americans who have no religious affiliation and the percentage who consider themselves atheist or agnostic are both on the rise. They recognize this growth as an opportunity, albeit one they might miss.

Like other nonbeliever organizations, HCH is caught within the secular paradox. Leaders I spoke with both claim and disavow credit for the growing number of secular people who join their groups. Some leaders consider their group's growth a product of secularization, of a process beyond their control. During interviews, their anxieties about proselytizing were palpable, and they were adamant that they only try to recruit those who are already secular. Other leaders see themselves as agents of secularization, either by making more secular converts from the religious or by organizing secular people who are indifferent and convincing them to profess their nonbelief in public. Some clearly enjoy toeing the line, and their tone sounded disingenuous to me when they said that they were uninterested in converting theists. These activists know the right thing to say in public, but in private they will admit that they want everyone to become secular. Despite the diversity of individuals' attitudes to proselytizing for nonbelief, the public rhetoric of the national nonbeliever organizations is uniform, and they draw a sharp distinction between advocacy and evangelizing. The ethics of secular conversion stem from anxiety about religious pollution, and they structure the choices nonbelievers make.

Advertising for Nonbelief

One of the first nonbeliever groups to launch a major billboard campaign in the United States was the United Coalition of Reason, or UnitedCoR. In July 2012, I interviewed Glen, one of the group's leaders, in Washington, DC. He described for me the group's history and strategy. UnitedCoR began in 2008 when businessman Steve Rade approached the Philadelphia chapter of the American Humanist Association with the idea of creating the Philadelphia Coalition of Reason (PhillyCoR) to unite the local Philadelphia nonbeliever groups. Rade also wanted to fund a billboard to promote the coalition. The billboard's design was borrowed from one created by FreeThought*Action*, which advertised on I-95 in Ridgefield, New Jersey, earlier the same year. In white lettering across the top of the billboard, against a backdrop of blue sky and clouds, was written the question, "Don't believe in God?"

Assuming a dialogue, it responded in the bottom right corner: "You are not alone." In black writing at the bottom, it also included a URL for the group's website and a toll-free number. The PhillyCoR billboard ran on I-95 near the Philadelphia International Airport through the summer of 2008. With more of Rade's support, PhillyCoR evolved into a national organization, UnitedCoR, which was incorporated in February 2009 and hired a full-time executive director the following month.

In addition to billboards, UnitedCoR began funding advertisements that ran on public transit, inspired by the atheist advertising campaign launched on British buses in the fall of 2008.[82] UnitedCoR's advertising campaigns do more than just promote nonbelief; they make a shared endeavor an opportunity for cooperation among local groups. The coalition's bigger goal is to build a national grassroots network of nontheistic communities. Leaders at UnitedCoR create local coalitions by contacting the heads of local groups and gathering them for a meeting, usually over dinner, with the lure of funding for an advertising campaign. Local groups work together to decide the wording and style of their advertisements. Though they do not have to become a UnitedCoR affiliate, most do.[83] Once the groups are organized as a coalition, UnitedCoR suggests that they cooperate to organize other events, like a celebration of Darwin Day, the National Day of Reason, the winter solstice, or Banned Books Week. In almost all cases, UnitedCoR offers money for an ad campaign only once, at the time of the coalition's founding. UnitedCoR now has several dozen local coalitions in its network, including in Canada.[84]

With roughly fourteen hundred local nonbeliever organizations in the United States,[85] most metropolitan areas have a range of groups. UnitedCoR has designed its website as a clearinghouse for nonbelievers interested in joining one of these communities. The ads that groups run avoid specific language like "humanist" and "atheist," which can fuel sectarianism among nonbelievers. UnitedCoR hopes that those who see the ads will seek more information and realize that there are many types of groups they can join. In Glen's words, "Not everybody wants an edgy atheist group, but they learn that there are choices. Part of my job is helping people learn that there are choices at the local level. We link to Ethical Culture societies and humanist groups and atheist groups and skeptic groups and all different types so that people will have a choice." One of UnitedCoR's larger aims is to reduce tensions that are common among local and national organizations. To build trust and prove that the groups do not fundraise from the same donors, UnitedCoR relies on its own small group of backers and gives all the donations it receives from advertisements to the local groups. UnitedCoR has the endorsement of the major nonbeliever organizations in the United States and has expanded its initiatives to include conferences, training workshops, events that highlight discrimination against nonbelievers, and ads on satellite radio. More recently, activists have told me that the coalition has lost some of its funding and decreased its activity.

Local groups choose their billboards from a limited set of options. In addition to the background with a blue sky and clouds, they can also choose images of a mountain sunrise or the Earth's horizon from space. Two of the three options ask the original billboard's question: "Don't believe in God?" Coalitions can choose to respond, "You are not alone" or, more sarcastic and literal, "Join the club." They can also choose a third billboard that asks, "Are you good without God?" which responds, "Millions are." Glen speculated that coalitions with more religious humanists might favor "Are you good without God?" because "it somehow seems softer, less abstract, not to overfocus on the God issue but focus on something else." He told me, "Sometimes they even ask, 'Why do we have to mention God at all?'" He tells them what he has learned from experience: "Because it doesn't get any attention if you don't."

Glen and UnitedCoR need to strike a careful balance between promotion and provocation, and Glen speaks carefully when describing the goals of the advertising campaigns:

> These billboards shouldn't be controversial because they're not even talking to religious people. None of them actually address religious people and say, "Give up your religion" or "Why do you believe in God? That's a dumb idea." We don't say that. They're not focused on provoking that audience. We know they have that effect. I mean, we're not blind to that. But they shouldn't have that effect because we're not even talking to them. We're talking to our own audience, saying, "Are you one of those people who, like us, doesn't believe in a god and is moral without that belief? Well, here's where to find us. We're over here." That's the message. And that ought not to bother anybody. . . . If you're not one of those people who wants what we have to offer, then look away. It has nothing to do with you.

Glen knows that the line between advocating and proselytizing is thin, and he and other leaders debate where to draw it. Glen told me that humanists, especially religious humanists, want to avoid antagonizing the religious and are wary of seeming to want to convert them. UnitedCoR's goal has been to create a big tent under which all nonbelievers can gather, so it, too, has been averse to conversion.

My interviews and participant observation affirm Glen's view that religious humanists are generally wary of recruitment and fundraising. When I attended the 2012 annual conference of the American Ethical Union, the umbrella organization for American Ethical Culture societies, I was surprised how little they discussed strategies for recruiting new members. At the conferences of organizations like the American Humanist Association and the Secular Student Alliance, I found strategies for recruitment common. Workshops at the Ethical conference covered more pastoral topics like financial management, creating a warm community, and recruiting and coordinating volunteers. In general, Ethical Culture's leadership emphasizes the health of an individual society more than its growth. While recruitment was not taboo and even loomed as a concern, it was not a topic of frequent or serious discussion. Even when the leaders at the conference were thinking about their social media presence, they asked whether an Ethical Culture society should start a Facebook page—not whether it should take out ads on Facebook. During interviews and casual conversations, leaders and members of Ethical Culture societies repeatedly emphasized that they want to avoid anything like evangelism, even as they lamented the challenge of finding new members without proselytizing. Though Ethical Culture is the most avowedly religious subset of the US secular movement, its members are also the most wary of conversion.

Consolidating Secular Identities

Secular activists struggle in their outreach to the indifferent for various reasons, including branding. Though the variety of labels that nonbelievers use to identify themselves can be helpful because it provides more options for potential members, secular activists find it difficult to unify nonbelievers and get them to see themselves as a single minority. As I discussed at the end of chapter 2, leaders told me many times that they feel like they are herding cats when trying to rally secular people. In response to the problem, activists have reached for a number of different labels to unify the disparate ways of identifying as a nonbeliever. Though "secular" and "humanist" are probably the most popular for nonbeliever groups' outreach efforts, I met many strong advocates for the term "atheist" who argue that it does more to normalize nonbelievers because it is more direct and provocative. As I described in chapters 1 and 2, the secular paradox is the generative source of this variety, as nonbelievers vacillate between identities that are too religious and not religious enough.

In the summer of 2012, I encountered an innovative solution to label proliferation while attending a student leadership conference at the Center for Inquiry's headquarters in Amherst, New York. The conference organizers invited me warmly when I asked to attend as a researcher, so I made the long bus trip up from Manhattan. CFI's headquarters is a modest gray building that contains in its basement one of the best freethought libraries in the world. When I arrived, I picked up a binder with my name on it, which also bore the conference's striking logo. On the left side were the words "ATHEISM, HUMANISM, REASON, INQUIRY, SCIENCE, SECULARISM, FREETHOUGHT, AND SKEPTICISM" in all-caps, arranged vertically. From top to bottom, red to blue, they were colored with the visible spectrum of light: a rainbow. Colored lines leading out from the words, from left to right, unified into a single beam of white light, which led to the right side of the logo, where it met CFI's name and the title of the event: "CENTER FOR INQUIRY | LEADERSHIP CONFERENCE 2012." The symbolism was clever, and its meaning was clear: CFI was claiming to unify nonbelief's diversity. On the final day of the conference, all the participants were given T-shirts bearing the conference logo, which we were encouraged to wear on a trip to Niagara Falls. Before handing out the T-shirts, one of the conference organizers explained the logo as "full spectrum enlightenment." "We're not going to solve these problems with any one aspect of strong, positive, reality-based thinking," she told us. "We need to come together to create this white light, this enlightenment of thought."

The organizers' attempt to unify the various strands of organized nonbelief is a long-standing ecumenical project among nonbelievers and one that varies in its motivations. Some groups, like the Secular

Student Alliance (SSA), find a range of labels acceptable. SSA encourages students to label their groups as they see fit and then affiliate with the national organization. Other groups seek a single label that can unite their factions, such as when humanists argue for dropping "religious" and "secular" adjectives.[86] Leaders at the Freedom From Religion Foundation told me that they had similar motivations for recovering the nineteenth-century term "freethought," since it had once rallied disparate groups to a shared cause. CFI's conference logo is ambiguous in that it could represent an effort like SSA's to join existing groups into a neutral umbrella category, or it could represent an attempt to speak for all nonbelievers, however they self-identify. If the latter, CFI's unification of the spectrum of "enlightenment" is consistent with the decades-long efforts of its founder, Paul Kurtz, to annex other groups and remain the dominant voice in secular activism. CFI's merger with the Richard Dawkins Foundation in 2016 is the latest example.

The Secular Coalition for America (SCA) is a lobbying organization, which like UnitedCoR, has successfully unified many of the disparate organizations in the US secular movement. Like SSA, the group chose "secular" as its big-tent term. SCA and the secular movement as a whole use the ambiguity of "secular" to align its various meanings when consensus is required and to distinguish among them when targeting specific subgroups with narrower interests.[87] When SCA is unifying its member organizations, it understands "secular" as an umbrella category for all nontheists. When SCA is lobbying alongside the Baptist Joint Committee for Religious Liberty, "secularism" is the separation of church and state. And when SCA's president and other secular activists want to mobilize as many Americans as possible, "secular" can refer to spiritual or theistic Americans with no religious affiliation. Like SSA, SCA uses the ambiguity of the secular to its advantage.[88]

SCA's founders wanted to establish a strong lobbying presence for secular people in Washington, DC, and in states throughout the country, but they also wanted to unite the national nonbeliever organizations. Conflicts among groups can be fierce, and some groups are effectively sects of one another, having arisen from disputes among leadership. Despite fighting for many years over members and donors, SCA's member organizations now share the financial burden of supporting SCA, and they send their leaders to an annual meeting of the board, which they call "the meeting of the heads." Though an ambiguous "secular" helps SCA create a big tent, drawing distinctions at key moments is necessary for working with allies who might agree with only part of its mission. Recruiting member organizations, seeking allied and endorsing organizations, and presenting itself in coalitions alongside other lobbying groups all require different combinations of the secular. For instance, three of SCA's member groups—the American Ethical Union, the Society for Humanistic Judaism, and the Unitarian Universalist Humanists—are registered with the federal government as religious nonprofits.[89] They see no contradiction in being both religious and nontheistic, and many of their members prefer to call themselves "religious humanists." All three groups are religious members of the Secular Coalition for America.

When the American Ethical Union was deciding whether to join SCA, its name, mission, vision, and issues were all important considerations. Two Ethical Culture leaders I interviewed told me that members of the Ethical Culture movement were hesitant to ally themselves with an organization that considers itself "secular" given the wide range of connotations that the term carries. For a time, Ethical Culture's leaders were stuck on the wording of SCA's name and felt they could join only if SCA changed its name to the Coalition for a Secular America. This would allow Ethical Culture to be a member of a coalition that supports secular values but is not itself secular. SCA refused the change, and in 2008, the American Ethical Union set aside its concerns and became a member group. Ultimately, the American Ethical Union felt that it could agree with SCA's mission, as the majority of its members consider themselves nontheists who support the separation of church and state.

While many of SCA's coalition partners support separation, its advocacy for America's nontheists is what makes SCA distinct and able to attract the nonbeliever organizations from which it draws its support. Many very secular people, especially those who organize as such, are concerned with discrimination against secular Americans. According to a study published in 2006, Americans are less accepting of atheists than of any other group, including gays, Muslims, and Jews.[90] In a follow-up to the study published in 2016, researchers found that Muslims had passed atheists, who are now the second-least-trusted minority in the United States.[91] Speaking to a group of student leaders at a conference

I attended in Columbus, Ohio, the former executive director of SCA Edwina Rogers told the audience that SCA's "mission is to increase the visibility of nonbelievers and to fight for equal rights." Having advocates communicate their interests to state and national governments appeals to nontheists for the same reason a secular identity does: it normalizes their beliefs by officializing them and brings their voices into the public sphere. For member organizations like American Atheists, which have a reputation for taking iconoclastic and confrontational positions, SCA also provides access to government officials who would otherwise probably spurn them. The many meanings of "secular" accomplish a great deal of work.

SCA's leaders are conscious of the secular's ambiguity and navigate it carefully in their outreach. In the "Vision" statement of its Secular Decade plan, SCA describes the United States of America that it would like to see: "An America that has returned to its secular roots and where secularism is an influential, respected force in American civic life, and in which there are numerous openly nontheistic elected officials."[92] In this one sentence fragment, SCA creates a bridge between the two sides of its mission: the separation of church and state and advocating for nonbelievers. The phrase "secular roots" implies an American tradition of separation, and "nontheists" refers specifically to nonbelievers. "Secularism" is ambiguous in the sentence because it could imply either separation or nonbelief.

At the Secular Women Work conference I attended in Minneapolis in 2018, I watched a presentation by Sarah Levin and Sarah Frey, who were there speaking on behalf of SCA. The pair made the case for "secular values" as a strategic talking point because it has broad appeal. "Not all Americans are secular, but all Americans can adopt secular values," they told us. Levin explained the strategy:

> When Pew says "religiously unaffiliated," we borrow that term from them. It's important to understand what they mean. Only about a third of Americans says they don't believe in God. The other two-thirds are everything from "I do believe" to "I sort of believe," "I am spiritual," or "I don't care." That might seem problematic because we don't agree on our identity, but if you look at the same bloc of people and how they respond to really important issues like abortion, same-sex marriage, evolution taught

in schools, this group agrees as a group more than evangelicals do. As a bloc, 73 percent of the religiously unaffiliated support safe and legal access to abortion, and only 63 percent of evangelicals oppose it. The numbers for same-sex marriage are similar.

SCA's political strategy and its very existence hinge on the secular's ambiguity. There are secular values that follow from nontheism, and there are secular values that undergird secular government. SCA links the two when it benefits the organization and separates them when it does not. If SCA focuses on "secular values," its leaders can partner with religious people more easily in their lobbying efforts and count more religious and nonreligious people among their ranks. The ambiguity of "secular" allows the group to consolidate a broad range of Americans, including many who would not consider themselves secular.

Nonproselytizing Nonbelief

At the start of this chapter, I suggested that conversion both is and is not a secular problem. For atheists like Peter Boghossian, it is important to try to convince people to become atheists, but doing so only disabuses them of their misconceptions; it does not convert them to a new worldview because that would be too religious. For some secular activists, making more people secular will make the world a better place—for example, the prominent donor I spoke with on the phone who told me that education is the way to create more secular humanists, which in turn will reduce mass incarceration. For other activists, there is no inherent connection between secularism and social justice; making more people secular will not solve all the world's problems. Secular activists like Joann work for both secular and social justice causes, but they do not believe that secularism and social justice are inherently linked.

When very secular people are advocating for nonbelievers and doing outreach work for their organizations, they usually stop short of trying to make converts, even as they are glad if it just so happens that they do. Organizational leaders emphasize that they are advertising to the already converted despite many telling me that it was reading the New Atheists or debating a friend that led them to lose their religion and become secular. The fundamental question of secular conversion is whether a person becomes secular merely by leaving religion or whether they must also translate themselves into a new discourse, adopting a secular worldview and way of life. This tension exists within secular people and across their organizations. Secular people are at once both not at all religious and very religion-like. This is their paradox, and being secular means struggling with its contradictions.

Throughout this chapter, I have also tried to show how closely linked the question of conversion is to secular people's ethical dilemma. Skepticism of empiricism, or a lack of it, determines whether secular people understand themselves to be taking a leap of faith into a new way of life when they adopt it as their epistemology—or whether they are just accepting reality for what it really is. The worldviews that secular people arrive at when they become empiricists who rely solely on reason and evidence usually exclude other epistemologies that see scripture and revelation as sources of truth. These worldviews usually lack a transcendent authority to authorize a universal ethical ground, and they raise the specters of cultural and moral relativism. This lack of authority, made profound in Christian-centered cultures that frame its absence more starkly, is a persistent source of secular people's defensiveness of their morality. Theirs is a problem that demands solving, as centuries of philosophical treatises, late-night arguments, and lectures at conferences attest.

Alfredo, Rick, Aaron, and Dan are in a sense aware of these challenges, inasmuch as they understand intuitively how discussing them makes good television for very secular people. In another sense, they remain unaware of the ways in which the secular paradox has structured their concerns and created contradictions that make certain subjects the source of debate ad infinitum. Keeping track of the questions that get secular people to tune in—and that keep them up at night—is a good way to identify who participates in the secular discursive tradition.

5

Tradition

An Absent Presence in Common

On November 1, 2016, the First Unitarian Society of Minneapolis celebrated a hundred years of religious humanism, commemorating the arrival of John Dietrich as the church's pastor in 1916. As I mentioned in chapter 1's brief history of organized humanism, Dietrich is one of the movement's founders, having borrowed the term "humanist" from the self-appellation of followers of Auguste Comte's Religion of Humanity. Dietrich created within Unitarianism a space for nontheistic religion, which later evolved into a separate movement with independent institutions.[1] First Unitarian has a special place in the history of US nonbelief, and its centennial celebration was sure to be a fascinating event for an ethnographer of secular people. Unfortunately, by the time I found out about the event, I had already scheduled my research trip for late August, a month too early. On the day of the centennial, I was back in Santa Barbara, proctoring a midterm for a new course on religion and politics.

My visit to First Unitarian was nonetheless one of many revelations I experienced during my field research. The church is in a beautiful historic neighborhood of Minneapolis and sits on a hillside overlooking the city's modern art museum, the Walker Art Center, and its sprawling outdoor sculpture garden. Built in 1951, the Society's exterior looks more like a high school than a church, and the same is true of most of its interior rooms. Its Upper Assembly Hall is a dramatic exception, with rows of wooden pews and a full wall of windows facing the northeast. The hall's design is midcentury modern and minimal, with tall ceilings and elegant wood paneling. The building had no air conditioning at the time of my visit, and I was told the congregation usually meets downstairs in the summer because the Lower Assembly Hall provides a cool escape from Minnesota's sweltering humidity. To the left of what would traditionally be the altar—a stage—was a large, beautiful organ that went unused during the service. Some of the wood panels on the back wall had been replaced by blown-up photographs of nature scenes, and on the stage stood a lectern, a few chairs, and a bronze sculpture of a flaming chalice, the symbol of Unitarian Universalism.[2]

As I walked into the Upper Assembly Hall, a welcomer handed me a fan to keep myself cool, which bore the words, "I'm a fan of social justice." The service that day centered on "the last lay sermon of the summer," which I later learned is "a way to keep the platform open to members of the congregation." The senior minister, Rev. Dr. David Breeden, presided over the service, which he began by addressing the congregation with an inclusive list of religion-related labels: "Theists, atheists, apatheists, agnostics." He followed with a promotion of the Society's capital campaign ("Building Humanism Inside Out") to raise $4 million for renovations, including air conditioning. Next, a Cat Stevens song played over the room's speakers: "Oh Very Young," from an album called *Buddha and the Chocolate Box*. Then Rev. Breeden invited us to open our hymnals for the collective singing of "Amazing Grace." The Unitarian Universalist hymn book has undergone several revisions to keep up with the denomination's changing doctrine.[3] Despite the updates, the hymn's fourth verse—"When we've been there ten thousand years, bright shining as the sun, / we've no less days to sing God's praise than when we'd first begun"—remains too religious for many humanists, so the congregation only sang the first three verses.

Given the words on my fan, I was not surprised that the layperson's talk addressed race, though I was surprised by its message. Referring to the hymn we had just sung, she told us, "I used to have problems with the words, 'Amazing Grace saved a wretch like me,' that Christian bullying. Engaging with the bully who wants a fight is not my way." She then explained that the man who wrote the poem on which "Amazing Grace" is based "was a cruel slave trader, the cruelest." Abruptly, she pivoted to recent protests in response to Minneapolis police murdering Philando Castile, which shut down the Twin Cities' major east-west corridor, I-94.[4] She described it as an event in which "young Black people threw boulders at passive white officers." She then told us that we need to "rise from the dark depth of racism into the height of understanding." Though I had a hard time following the thread of her sermon, she seemed to be saying that those of us in the hall that day should forgive Black protestors and show them kindness.

Later in the sermon, the woman told a cryptic anecdote about her husband protecting her from an alligator on a trip to Florida and her yelling, "Why are we here?!" "The alligator is transformed by kindness," she explained. In the analogy, it was unclear whether the alligator represented a Black protestor or police. After her sermon, the congregation was invited to sing "the African American national anthem," a song included in the UU hymnal called "Lift Every Voice and Sing." As with "Amazing Grace," the congregation omitted the final verses because they mention "God." Though the sermon does not reflect the views of everyone who listened, Joann was certainly right when she reminded us at the Red Derby that more secularism does not mean less racism.

The Sunday service at First Unitarian displayed many of the ambiguities I have come to associate with secularism, not only concerning ethics. Near the beginning of the service, the senior minister told the congregation, "We are joining together not in common beliefs but in common values." This disavowal of shared beliefs is inclusive, and accurate, but it does not tell the whole story. Interviewing the Society's leaders, I learned that the last survey they conducted found that more than 80 percent of the Society's members are atheists or agnostics. From the stage, in interviews, and on its website, First Unitarian proclaims, "a humanist worldview is at the center of what we do."[5] Like the Secular Coalition for America, which uses the ambiguity of "secular values" as a way to include theists in its lobbying efforts, the Society defines humanism more according to values than to nontheistic ontological claims. "Atheists have spouses," one leader told me, explaining that some religious people attend because their secular partners do. The Society takes pride in its long humanist tradition, and its members distinguish themselves from another UU church in Minneapolis that is more inclusive of people with supernatural beliefs. Like other very secular people, they affirm what they share, sometimes with strategic vagueness, and they draw lines to exclude what they do not.

The First Unitarian Society emphasizes its place in the humanist tradition in part because it can trace it for more than a century. Though its members are surely participants in this tradition, it is important to recognize that many who have participated do not agree with all of the ontological claims of a humanist worldview. Uniform agreement on all aspects of a worldview—"common beliefs" or shared doctrine—is not necessary for a belief-based tradition. I have found that humanists, in general, are more likely than other kinds of nonbelievers to aver their participation in a secular tradition. The boundary they maintain with religion is more porous, and their identity is more hybrid. They are less anxious about religious pollution compared with those who identify primarily with atheism. This intimacy with the religious makes humanists more comfortable with belief, community, ritual, and tradition—even as most avoid proselytizing and continue to distance themselves from religion. In the words of one of the Society's leaders, "I avoid the term 'religious' as much as possible."

In what remains of this chapter, I explore the possibility that humanists are right, that there is a secular tradition. In the next section, I look at how humanists have defined their tradition and consider why they include some people and ideas and not others. In the section after, I consider what a tradition is and why defining one poses many challenges. Building on the work of humanists, I argue for a secular discursive tradition that is defined more by its paradoxes than by a shared worldview. This tradition includes practices and bodily dispositions, as well as beliefs. I conclude with a discussion of the efficacy of identifying this tradition, as well as its ongoing challenges.

The Humanist Tradition

In the opening pages of Mason Olds's history of organized religious humanism in the United States, he identifies five types of humanism because "a kind of ambiguity surrounds the subject."[6] The five types are Greek, Renaissance, Literary, Nietzschean, and Naturalistic. Though Olds describes how religious humanism relates to all five, he considers the "Naturalistic" strain its parent and closest relative. Olds's typology provides an outline of humanism's historical self-reference, though it does not settle its ambiguity. The periods and people he includes reveal how one of the few historians of nontheistic humanism—himself a practicing religious humanist—imagines the humanist tradition. Because he delimits the tradition in conversation with other humanists who have tried to do the same, his history synthesizes broader trends in humanist discourse. To further broaden the sketch he provides, I supplement Olds with the perspectives of other humanists, including those who have tried to construct a more diverse tradition. Some of these humanists have redefined humanism to expand its tradition beyond just nonbelievers, though always as a way to make contemporary nontheistic humanists the inheritors of the humanist legacy. I also include the work of historians who do not write self-consciously as humanists but who nonetheless illuminate its contours. Though brief, this sketch shows how secular people who consider themselves humanist embrace tradition with ambivalence and to various ends.

The first type of humanism that Olds identifies is ancient Greek. Olds recognizes that many humanists trace "their spiritual ancestry" to pre-Socratic Greek philosophy, but he disagrees with strong claims of continuity made by influential humanists like Charles Francis Potter and Corliss Lamont.[7] Potter is one of the founders of organized humanism and the author of *Humanism: A New Religion*, one of its important early texts. For Potter, "It is from the Greek Humanists . . . and through the Renaissance, that modern western Humanism derives."[8] At times, Potter is careful to distinguish ancient Greek philosophers as "forerunners" of later humanism, implying that they are not humanists in the modern sense but still concretely linked.[9] Elsewhere, Potter is unequivocal: "In Protagoras we discover a real Humanist. His famous sentence, 'Man is the measure of all things,' was the Emancipation Proclamation of the human race."[10] For Olds, philosophers like Anaxagoras, Protagoras, Democritus, and Epicurus only espouse the "embryonic" form of modern humanists' commitment to science, skepticism, and human-centered ethics.[11] To explain why humanists like Potter have seen themselves in ancient Greeks, Olds argues that they "were not seeking a new orthodoxy in Greek humanism; rather, they saw the Greeks as having had the questioning, adventurous spirit they exemplified in their own age."[12] Similar to the senior minister of the First Unitarian Society of Minneapolis, they recognize the continuity of the humanist tradition in values rather than beliefs.

The second type that Olds identifies is Renaissance Humanism. For Potter, some Renaissance humanists were only humanist "in the sense of being passionately devoted to the new learning, . . . interested more in collecting manuscripts of the Greek and Latin classics than in contributing to the thought of their time." He contrasts them with men like Lorenzo Valla and Pomponazzi, whom he describes variously as "rationalist," "somewhat of a freethinker," or "unbeliever."[13] Dietrich is more boldly inclusive and considers humanism "a lineal descendant of Renaissance Humanism."[14] According to scholar of the Renaissance Paul Oskar Kristeller, the "-ism" of "humanism" was introduced in the early nineteenth century as a variant of the term "humanist," which was coined during the Renaissance "to designate a teacher and student of the 'humanities' or *studia humanitatis*."[15] This humanism describes "devotion to the literatures of ancient Greece and Rome, and the humane values that may be derived from them."[16] Potter and Dietrich believe they have received their ideas from ancient Greece by way of Renaissance humanists' rediscovery and translation of texts. They imply a chain of transmission, though they do not trace every link.[17]

Writing in *The New Encyclopedia of Unbelief*, Vern L. Bullough calls Renaissance humanism "the new humanism," giving credit for the "old humanism" to ancient Greece and Rome: "In this context [in the fourteenth and fifteenth centuries], humanism emphasized what we now call the humanities, but also included elements of the earlier humanism, including a sort of skepticism that promoted a willingness to challenge church doctrine."[18] Bullough is a former president of the International Humanist and Ethical Union and one of the founders of the Council for Secular Humanism. The *Encyclopedia* in which Bullough's entry appears is edited by Tom Flynn, executive director of the Council for Secular Humanism and editor of *Free Inquiry* magazine. The *Encyclopedia*, now in its second edition, is published by Prometheus Books, a publishing house founded by Paul Kurtz, the SUNY Buffalo philosophy professor who first institutionalized secular humanism by spearheading the creation of the Council for Democratic and Secular Humanism in 1980.[19] The volume's list of contributors is a who's who of prominent organized nonbelievers active in the late twentieth and early twenty-first centuries. The authority of the *Encyclopedia* and Bullough's institutional credentials give weight to his efforts to argue the humanist tradition's ancient birth, its revivification in the Renaissance, and its nurture in the Enlightenment.

The third type that Olds identifies is Literary Humanism, an early twentieth-century movement associated with the intellectuals Norman

Foerster, Paul Elmer More, and Irving Babbitt.[20] Because this movement developed contemporaneously with religious humanism, Potter and others sought to clarify their differences.[21] Babbitt's "humanism," often called "the new humanism" by literary scholars, is concerned with the humanities and the kind of character their study imparts. The humanist is a "gentleman" who values "poised and proportionate living." The "humanistic virtues" are "moderation, common sense, and common decency." The "higher will" can and should keep the "natural man" in check.[22] Babbitt also criticizes the modern valorization of the "original genius" and the priority that modern culture places on uniqueness and novelty. He associates this idea with the philosopher Jean-Jacques Rousseau and contrasts what he calls "Rousseauism" with his "humanism." The latter emphasizes the study of the humanities as a way to maintain a "humane standard," which should be the benchmark for judging all other culture.[23] The new humanism harbors an ethos that goes beyond merely recovering and studying the "humanities," but it differs too much from the humanism pioneered by Potter, Dietrich, and others for Olds to include it in the humanist tradition. Humanism's ambiguity can be its strength when connecting it to other movements that bear the same name, but that ambiguity requires clarification when unwanted associations grow too strong.

The fourth type that Olds identifies is Nietzschean Humanism. His short section casts the philosopher Friedrich Nietzsche as a radical atheist who considers religion, and in particular theism, to be a manipulative delusion.[24] He also explains Nietzsche's influence on the founders of religious humanism, such as Potter, who adopted the term "Superman," the English translation of Nietzsche's *Übermensch*.[25] Olds's Nietzsche is eminently concerned with the role of the human after the death of God; inasmuch as the *Übermensch* is the destroyer of God and creator of his own good, the individual human is at the center of Nietzsche's "humanist" philosophy. In *An Atheism That Is Not Humanist Emerges in French Thought*, intellectual historian Stefanos Geroulanos observes that while many people have adopted this reading of Nietzsche, others, such as philosopher Maurice Blanchot, thoroughly reject it.[26] For Blanchot, Nietzsche's *Übermensch* is like the gods, yet another empty, insufficient theory.[27] The human does not merely replace God as the new foundation and the measure of meaning, as in the anthropotheism of philosophers

Ludwig Feuerbach and Auguste Comte. The human can and does negate itself, providing no foundation but always possessing the limitless power to negate.[28] Blanchot and his Nietzsche participate in what philosopher Emmanuel Levinas calls "an atheism that is not humanist."[29] During my field research, Nietzsche's philosophy only came up in informal conversations at conferences and workshops I attended. He seemed to stand in for a kind of nihilism, closely associated with cultural relativism, as a foil for attempts to make humanism the ethical complement to mere atheism. Blanchot's Nietzsche is no humanist and fits awkwardly in the far more positivist tradition of nonbelief that predominates in Britain and the United States.[30]

The French philosopher Jean-Paul Sartre came up more often than Nietzsche during my field research, though still mostly in casual conversations, as I did not include questions about philosophy in my interview schedule. In "Existentialism," a relatively accessible essay that many people have treated as the definitive statement on existentialism, Sartre argues that the existential condition is humanist: "This is humanism, because we remind man that there is no legislator but himself; that he himself, thus abandoned, must decide for himself; also because we show that it is not by turning back upon himself, but always by seeking, beyond himself, an aim which is one of liberation or of some particular realisation, that man can realize himself as truly human." For Sartre, "Existentialism is nothing else but an attempt to draw the full conclusions from a consistently atheistic position."[31]

German philosopher Martin Heidegger criticizes Sartre for being still too metaphysical, which is to say, "determined with regard to an already established interpretation of nature, history, world, and the ground of the world, that is, of beings as a whole." In "A Letter on Humanism," Heidegger compares the humanisms of Marx and Sartre to Christianity, which he considers no less humanistic and thus metaphysical. Every humanism "presupposes an interpretation of beings without asking about the truth of Being. . . . Accordingly, every humanism remains metaphysical."[32] For Heidegger, metaphysics describe what a human is rather than how a human exists. Heidegger is acknowledging the criticisms asserted by ancient skeptics to any metaphysical system or worldview. He responds to them with the phenomenology that he articulates in *Being and Time*, in which he argues that the truth of a human's being is their unique way of being in the world, a human's mode, which cannot be captured by a metaphysical description, including a materialist or scientific worldview.[33] Heidegger's goal is hypersecular in the negative sense of not religious. He seeks a philosophy free of metaphysics, which are not only Christian but precede Christianity. It is, after all, from a more ancient metaphysics that Christianity draws its own.

Olds's fifth and final humanism is Naturalistic, and he identifies it closely with the religious humanism he practices and studies. Olds describes Naturalistic humanists as "monists" because they "maintain that the world of nature is the sum total of reality."[34] In the words of humanist philosopher Corliss Lamont, "The whole of existence is equivalent to Nature and outside of Nature nothing exists."[35] Naturalistic monists disagree with dualists, who maintain that there is another kind of reality that exists in addition to the natural world, such as the supernatural realm of God or the immaterial realm of the mind or soul. Philosophically, naturalism is related to and compatible with materialism, though both terms can vary in their precise meaning depending on the context to which one applies them and the extremity of their application.[36] Olds contrasts the "new naturalism" of the twentieth century with what he calls the "mechanical naturalism" of the nineteenth.[37] Whereas the mechanistic approach reduces the complexity of human living to the laws of the physical world, the new naturalism applies the scientific method to questions of experience and how one ought to live.[38] Rather than reducing ethics and religion to epiphenomena, the new naturalism evaluates religion "critically" and, where appropriate, seeks to reform it "on the basis of its social usefulness."[39] Olds's new naturalism names another solution to secular people's problem with authority, and it preserves "religion" even as it secularizes it.

Expanding Humanism

Olds's humanist tradition, like every version of the tradition with which I am familiar, is very white and male. This makes its inheritance especially challenging for nontheistic women and people of color, who do not see themselves represented in its lineage. To address this problem, some humanists have tried to broaden the tradition, or they have made contributions of their own. A powerful example of the latter is theologian

William R. Jones's critique of Black liberation theology, *Is God a White Racist? A Preamble to Black Theology*. Jones focuses mostly on the theodicies of liberation theologians, but he grounds his critique in a secular humanist worldview, which he poses as an alternative. Writing in 1973, he was thus among the first to adopt an expressly "secular" humanism to describe his beliefs. Though Jones does not aim to provide a history of Black nonbelief, he cites "the humanist existentialism of de Beauvoir, Camus, Fanon, and Sartre" as a key influence in his own formation as a nonbeliever. Jones was a professor of religion, first at Yale Divinity School and later at Florida State University. He was also ordained as a Unitarian minister, and *Is God a White Racist?* was published by Beacon Press, the publishing arm of the Unitarian Universalist Association.

Critical theorist of religion William Hart considers theologian Anthony Pinn the inheritor of Jones's legacy, arguing that Pinn tends to overemphasize their differences.[40] Pinn is a prominent humanist theologian whom I saw speak at several humanist events during my field research. He is also a scholar of African American religion in the United States who has made significant contributions to its study.[41] Over the past two decades, Pinn has expanded the humanist tradition to include more women and people of color, especially African Americans. There is no other text like the volume he edited, *By These Hands: A Documentary History of African American Humanism*, which has provided me with valuable source material for a course I teach on atheism.[42] Along with Pinn, Hart rightly includes Sikivu Hutchinson in the tradition of Black nonbelief, and Hart and humanist scholar of religion Monica Miller should also be included.[43]

Because so few African Americans have publicly espoused nonbelief, a narrow definition of humanism as a nontheistic worldview poses a challenge for Pinn and others who have tried to expand the tradition. I discussed a number of reasons for the whiteness of nonbelief in chapter 2, including people of color wanting to avoid additional discrimination and the historical importance of Black churches as centers of Black social and political life. One way to expand the tradition is to expand humanism. Hart observes that Pinn wrote "the first systematic nontheistic African American theology," though he is also correct that Pinn sometimes defines humanism obliquely, in ways that can include religious African Americans in the humanist community. In Hart's view, this strategy comes at the cost of watering down humanism to the point of making it "ineffable."[44]

In an essay in a volume Pinn edited in 2013, he articulates a version of humanism that he considers a revision after long reflection. Pinn draws on the philosopher Corliss Lamont to describe humanism as a life orientation, "a non-supernatural means by which to assess life options and perspectives on proper actions and thought."[45] In so doing, he joins many other humanists who have tried to articulate an affirmative way of life that they feel is too often expressed in solely negative terms. By emphasizing an orientation of the human, as opposed to a representation or worldview, Pinn also echoes Heidegger to an extent. Though Pinn could hardly be described as Heideggerian, his vision of humanism also resembles the avowedly Heideggerian philosophy of Martin Hägglund, who argues for a minimalist understanding of secular life as oriented toward this world, as opposed to another. Hägglund's treatise on finitude and the secular life assumes that there is no afterlife and argues that those who live toward one are lying to themselves.[46] From the perspective of the secular paradox, Pinn and Hägglund attempt to shake off the negative baggage of the secular in a Christian-centered culture by focusing on how secular people live, but in order to take epistemological and ontological questions off the table, they must assume their answers in advance.

In the same volume that Pinn articulates his new version of humanism, humanist philosopher and historian Howard Radest offers his own account. In a subsection titled "*Mythos* and Tradition," Radest navigates the secular paradox with apt ambivalence. He suggests that "stories might serve as building blocks of humanism's *mythos*, freeing the celebration of its values from reliance only on the abstractions of rationalism, the charisma of this or that personality, or the *word*." The *mythos* he wants to recuperate "is the seed and nourishment of tradition, connecting humanist stories across time and paradigm and connecting humanists to each other over time and space."[47] He acknowledges that like other religious pollution, tradition is dangerous. It need not be avoided, however. Along with *mythos*, it can be embraced and translated:

> Of course, tradition has its risk as it does its promise. It can lead to blind loyalties, authoritarian powers, and alienation from those with other

stories and connections, with other traditions. It can become the mere appearance of accessibility without its reality, setting humanism on a sectarian course while dogmatically announcing itself as anti-dogma, for example. Without tradition and without *mythos*, however, humanism is fated to convey a shallow and narrow reality, one that does not effectively house the passions and emotions of the persons who live in it. Tradition reminds us that others came before, without which criticism and analysis lose their depth and deteriorate into the humanism of the *word*.[48]

Radest's apprehension about tradition is shared by scholars who study traditions and try to discuss them in meaningful ways. Very secular people share his apprehension too. Most consider the idea of a secular tradition too religious—just like beliefs, communities, rituals, and proselytizing. In the next section, I take up the meaning of tradition and the challenges it faces. In the section after, I sketch a secular discursive tradition that is broader than the humanist tradition and defined by its persistent questions and disagreements rather than a single worldview or even orientation. Heeding Radest's warnings—as well as those of historian Michel Foucault and anthropologist Talal Asad—this discursive tradition includes practices and feelings, in addition to beliefs and words.

Invented Tradition

Humanism is not only a tradition but also a break—from the Unitarian Church, from nineteenth-century nonbeliever movements, from Reform Judaism, and from the *bad* kind of religion. It breaks with the authority of the institutions from which it springs at the same time that it reaches backward into the recent and ancient past to strengthen its own authority. It shares its suspicions of inherited practice with deism and atheism but also with the sects that sprang from the Lutheran and English Reformations, including Congregationalism and Unitarianism.[49] It borrows from these traditions and modifies their practices to make them new. It discourages some forms of belief and practice altogether. Humanism responds to the secular's paradox by rejecting and embracing traditional religion. It is, in many ways, what the historian Eric Hobsbawm calls an "invented tradition": "a set of practices, normally governed by overtly or tacitly accepted rules and of a ritual or symbolic nature, which seek to inculcate certain values and norms of behavior by repetition, which automatically implies continuity with the past. In fact, where possible, they normally attempt to establish continuity with a suitable historic past."[50]

For Hobsbawm, the past two centuries have been especially ripe for the invention of traditions because the Industrial Revolution reshaped material conditions such that "old traditions and their institutional carriers and promulgators no longer prove sufficiently adaptable and flexible, or are otherwise eliminated."[51] His modernization narrative resembles that of humanism's founders, who argued that early twentieth-century religious institutions and beliefs had fallen out of step with the demands of modern life. Hobsbawm writes, "It seems clear that, in spite of much invention, new traditions have not filled more than a small part of the space left by the secular decline of both old tradition and custom; as might indeed be expected in societies in which the past becomes increasingly less relevant as a model or precedent for most forms of human behavior."[52] Hobsbawm's secularization story is one of loss and "subtraction," in the terms that the philosopher Charles Taylor uses in *A Secular Age*. In this story, religious traditions fail to adapt and fall away. Secular equivalents replace some of what was lost. Demand—a space—remains.[53]

Humanism, like all forms of secularism, encourages the affirmation of certain ontologies and epistemologies rather than others. Those who live in its tradition make choices, conscious and unconscious, everyday and momentous, against the background of its related set of worldviews, or what Taylor calls "social imaginaries."[54] The space left by the ostensible loss of religion is never empty.[55] I did not attend a secular memorial service during my field research, but the anthropologist Matthew Engelke has studied the death practices of secular people in Britain and observed that the body of the deceased is not usually present because the body's presence perpetuates the illusion that the person persists.[56] I heard the same observation about secular people in the United States from the Secular Celebrant who ran a workshop I attended on creating rituals, which I discussed in chapter 3. The anthropologists Jacob Copeman and Johannes Quack have found that many nonbelievers in India donate their bodies to science, and I found the same intention widespread among the very secular people I spent time with.[57] These secular approaches to death are no less concrete than were the rituals I participated in, the communities I visited, and the basement libraries I browsed during my field research, but they are especially telling of how worldviews influence practices, sensibilities, and dispositions. They also show how secular people reinvent rituals independently, in the absence of a legible tradition, the presence of which is foreclosed by the secular paradox.[58]

No one has illuminated the secular tradition's engagement with death better than anthropologist Abou Farman. His ethnography *On Not Dying* is a study of "immortalists," or people who try to live indefinitely with the help of science. Farman describes the anxieties that structure the lives of secular people who fear finitude, whom he considers participants in a secular discursive tradition, even if some do not consider themselves secular.[59] As Farman shows, secularism and what we mean by it are flexible, and its influence is pervasive.[60] Though the anxieties of secular immortalists are distinctively secular, they are not shared by all secular people. Among my research participants, I rarely encountered anxiety about death. To the contrary, several people I interviewed cited the death of a loved one as a catalyst for their secular conversion. One young man told me that his Catholic grandmother's death and the suffering she experienced drove him to read more about dying and the afterlife, which in turn led him to secularism. A famous author of books on atheism told me a similar story, and a woman who works at an organization for atheists even suggested in an offhand joke that her eventual death would be a welcome respite from the pain of life. Secular approaches to death vary, and some secular people feel far less anxiety about dying than others do.

Because Hobsbawm's notion of an invented tradition depends on a narrow understanding of what tradition is—a siloed project with robust institutions—it fails to recognize secularism's pervasive influence, including its role in shaping the conditions that produced the secularization narrative. Since the early 1990s, a large body of scholarly literature has reconsidered secularization theory to account for the so-called return or resurgence of religion.[61] Though sociologists like David Martin have long questioned the theory's assertion that modernization would remove religion from public life, separate it from other "value spheres," and diminish its overall prevalence, the theory's revision has been slow. Only in the past few years has secularization become apparent as a product of its own invention.[62] A wide range of scholars have studied how the narrative took hold, identified the assumptions on which it depends, and offered new ways of understanding the secular that do not consider it the absence of religion but a presence of its own.[63]

Discursive Tradition

Talal Asad provides the best tools for understanding the immersive haunting of the secular tradition. Asad narrates a partial genealogy of the secular, secularism, and secularization as normative logics that structure the modern world and create subjectivities suited for life in European and American empires. For Asad, the secular and secularism are not coterminous with "modernity," but they are constitutive of it and vice versa. The secular and its related terms presuppose and regulate individuals who can act freely in the pursuit of pleasure and the avoidance of pain, who practice their religion privately, and who cede control of violence to the secular state. Rewriting the narrative of secularization theory, "secularism" becomes a name for the production of secular modernity, which translates everyone into secular subjectivity. Secularization is the historical process through which that production has occurred.[64]

I engage with Asad in what remains of this section because his approach explains well what I have learned about secular people and because no one has done more to shake secular people loose from the assumptions that have blinded them to their assumptions. Asad develops the notion of a discursive tradition in an essay he published in 1986, to provide an alternative to approaches that consider Islam a monolithic religion:

> A tradition consists essentially of discourses that seek to instruct practitioners regarding the correct form and purpose of a given practice that, precisely because it is established, has a history. These discourses relate conceptually to a past (when the practice was instituted, and from which the knowledge of its point and proper performance has been transmitted) and a future (how the point of that practice can best be secured in

the short or long term, or why it should be modified or abandoned), through a present (how it is linked to other practices, institutions, and social conditions).⁶⁵

Nearly thirty years after introducing the idea of a discursive tradition, Asad published *Secular Translations*, a thoroughgoing critique of the secular, from which I have borrowed the notion of translation that I identify in chapter 3 as one of the four modes, or rituals, of secular purification. Asad again outlines why discourse and tradition are the strongest concepts for linking the disparate ways of life called "Muslim" into a singular object of study. When he turns his attention to the secular and its discourse, like Hobsbawm, he considers it in negative terms, as threatening and breaking tradition: "When the particular materiality of the body is treated as accidental to its life—a 'natural' life that is born, that learns, succeeds and fails, shares a form of life with others, feels pain, and dies; a life whose trace moves through generations of subsequent living beings—then the very sense of a discursive tradition is undermined."⁶⁶ This approach to the secular indulges the negative half of the secular paradox.

As Engelke, Copeman and Quack, and Farman have shown, however, treating the body as an accident of evolution and a material object of scientific inquiry is a tradition of its own, which includes distinctive rituals for memorialization and disposition of the deceased. For Asad, secularism is antithetical to tradition; and it is. But it is also not. The notion of a discursive tradition applies just as well to the affirmative half of the secular as it does to Islam. I adapt Asad's notion slightly by thinking about secularism as a religion-like or religious tradition. Asad is reasonable in wanting to avoid "religion" in framing Islam because it is a Christian category with a colonialist history, making it untenable for cross-cultural comparison. Avoiding the secular's paradoxical identity with the religious, however, would only repress its religiosity and stage the latter's inevitable return.⁶⁷

Secular people's engagements with death are various, and they have a long history. Still, they are distinctively secular and grounded in secular beliefs about the world and how best to know it. Asad's discursive tradition is useful for stitching this variety together and demonstrating the impact of ideas on practices and bodily dispositions. By emphasizing disagreement rather than doctrinal unity in constituting a tradition,

Asad's approach helps make sense of secular people's frequent debates among one another and their aversion to a unified doctrine or even a single shared worldview. For Asad, a tradition grows from disagreements among interlocutors about what is essential to it, what goods constitute it, and how a person should live according to it: "The 'essence' [of a tradition] is not neutrally determinable because it is subject to argument. A living tradition is not merely capable of containing conflict and disagreement; the search for what is essential itself provokes argument. A concern with 'essence' is therefore not quite the same as a concern with authenticity."[68]

Conflict is inherent to a tradition. Conflicts among a tradition's participants and those who break from it or oppose it can be key moments in its constitution. These conflicts are also embodied. By focusing on discourse—a notion he borrows from Michel Foucault—Asad includes in his analysis not just words but bodily comportments, sensibilities, and dispositions. And he rightly insists on attending to the role of power, which grounds abstract disagreements in material conditions, including the body.[69] A nonbeliever's everyday acts of secular purification, like saying "Gesundheit" or keeping a cross necklace that will never be worn, are just as much part of the secular tradition as is the National Day of Reason or a book by Richard Dawkins. Secular norms grounded in secular beliefs regulate the bodies of secular people just as much as any religious discourse regulates the religious.[70]

Asad is also right that scholars who identify and research a tradition play a role in shaping it. They become participants, at least of a sort:

> To write about a tradition is to be in a certain narrative relation to it, a relation that will vary according to whether one supports or opposes the tradition, or regards it as morally neutral. The coherence that each party finds, or fails to find, in that tradition will depend on their particular historical position. In other words, there clearly is not, nor can there be, such a thing as a universally acceptable account of a living tradition. Any representation of tradition is contestable. What shape that contestation takes, if it occurs, will be determined not only by the powers and knowledges each side deploys, but by the collective life to which they aspire or to whose survival they are quite indifferent. Declarations of moral neutrality, here as always, are no guarantee of political innocence.[71]

In the next section, I sketch the outline of a secular discursive tradition. I do so as both a secular person who is a part of that tradition and as a scholar of the secular attempting to delimit it, who relies on secular scholarly norms of reason and evidence. It is from this doubled secularism that I offer an immanent, affectionate critique.

The Secular Discursive Tradition

If there is a secular discursive tradition, what does it look like? What unifies it, and who participates in it? What are the ways in which the tradition regulates the bodies of those who participate? And what role do embodied practices play in its reproduction? In previous chapters, I have described the distinctiveness of secular people's ways of life. I have observed their agreements and disagreements about what they believe to be true and real. I have spent time in the communities they form and learned about the ways of gathering they refuse. I have participated in rituals they create but also learned which ones they avoid. And I have analyzed their efforts, which they often limit, to proselytize their worldviews and ways of life to others. In so doing, I have described some of the secular people who inherit and reproduce the secular discursive tradition. By focusing on organized nonbelief in the United States, which is overwhelmingly liberal and positivist, I have sketched only a piece of a much larger whole. In what remains of this section, I expand on the sketch thus far provided and add to it ways in which secular discourse extends beyond liberal, positivist secularism and even permeates parts of life that are typically considered religious.

The secular paradox unifies the secular tradition, though it also makes it strange. On the one hand, as Asad argues in *Secular Translations* and as philosopher Alasdair MacIntyre argued before him, the secular tradition that extends from the Enlightenment imagines itself breaking with tradition. It tries to avoid it.[72] On the other hand, humanism is a branch of the secular tradition that considers itself both a break from tradition and a tradition of its own. It abstracts an idea of tradition and translates its contents into a secular worldview.

Recognition of the secular paradox demands suspicion of secular people's avoidance of tradition, even as their traditional translation demands skepticism. Though an individual secular person might not share the identical beliefs of another secular person, many people who are secular find common cause in communities and activism *qua* secular people. To acknowledge their differences, they have come up with a range of labels, which they sometimes represent under a single umbrella identity, like secular, or sometimes as a long list: atheist, agnostic, freethinker, secular humanist, religious humanist, rationalist, naturalist, materialist. The nonbelievers who debate a particular label's efficacy or try to subsume all labels under one are participating in the secular discursive tradition by arguing over what defines it and who belongs. The same is true of secular people who want nothing to do with nonbelievers who form communities because they consider them too religious. Both those who refuse and those who join are participating in a shared tradition in which shared ideas of what is true—which many secular people would never call shared beliefs—can form only a fraught basis for communion. The ongoing debates over what is secular and what is too religious are keys to understanding what the secular tradition is and what makes it distinctive.

Both the affirmative and negative halves of the secular tradition bind secular people together, which is to say, nonbelievers are unified in what they share as much as in what they do not. This ambiguity has made it difficult for historians to write the history of secular people and ideas because it is unclear whether they are looking for anyone who denies a Christian God or only those who espouse a version of modern atheism.[73] The secular paradox structures histories of nonbelief just as it structures the lives of secular people.

The Swerve, by literary historian Stephen Greenblatt, became a sensation when it was published in 2011, receiving both the Pulitzer Prize and the National Book Award. Agreeing with nontheistic humanists, Greenblatt argues for continuity between ancient Greek philosophy and modern atheism. He also frames the Renaissance popularization of certain ancient thinkers as a break between medieval Christianity and the secular thought that led to the Enlightenment and modernity. Papal secretary Poggio Bracciolini is the hero of Greenblatt's story for having rediscovered the last surviving copy of *De Rerum Natura*, an Epicurean poem written in Latin in the first century by the Roman poet Lucretius. The poem remains one of the best sources of Epicureanism, most of which have been lost to the *The Swerve*'s antagonists: mold, bookworms, and disinterest on the part of monastics to retranscribe rotting manuscripts.

Critics have challenged Greenblatt's antireligious narrative and the historical accuracy of his periodization, in which ancient thought's rediscovery carries the seeds of modern liberalism out from the dark ages of Christianity.[74] They are right that Greenblatt reproduces twentieth-century myths about the origins of modernity that were popularized by influential humanists like Potter, Dietrich, and Lamont and by secular liberal historians like Peter Gay.[75] Greenblatt's story is antireligious to a fault because it buries the importance of a chain of Epicurean transmission and influence within a simplistic story about secular modernity's sharp break from Christianity. The secular paradox tempts secular people to cast this narrative in anti-Christian terms and tempts critics of Enlightenment discourse to dismiss the influence of Epicureanism on the development of secular thought. The truth lies somewhere in between. *The Swerve* is a contribution to both halves of the secular tradition.

A more careful approach than Greenblatt's can acknowledge continuity and influence without asserting a break with Christianity or a commitment to the truth of a lost-found ancient inheritance.[76] Intellectual historians Ada Palmer and Alan Charles Kors have done the difficult work of identifying the elements of modern atheism and tracking their development from ancient, especially Epicurean sources recovered by Renaissance humanists. Palmer's study of the Renaissance reception of Lucretius is lucid and convincing, and Kors's work on the modern period is also invaluable.[77] Palmer identifies six ideas in Lucretius that she considers "proto-atheist":

> These are, first, creation from chaos, or emergent order, the idea that the cosmos, Earth, nature, life, and human civilization developed gradually from an unplanned and chaotic system. This is closely related to the second thesis, denial of Providence or any kind of design or purpose in nature or human life, history, or experience. The third thesis, denial of divine participation in the everyday functioning of the natural world, is closely related to the fourth, denial of miraculous intervention or any other action by the gods affecting the natural world or human experience, and to the fifth, the argument that the gods do not hear human prayer and never act upon it. The last of the six is the denial of the immortality of the soul and the rejection of any afterlife.[78]

Palmer traces the influence of these ideas among a set of writers who are mostly Christian and who are not secular people in the sense of adhering to a recognizably modern secular worldview.

By disaggregating atheism's history, Palmer renders it contingent, threatening its claims to universal truth and ontological and epistemological supremacy.[79] She does not assert that the Christians and Jews influenced by these ideas are "secret atheists" who adopted duplicitous strategies to survive.[80] Her approach is presentist inasmuch as it recognizes "modern atheism" as a name for a set of secular worldviews that are common today, but she does not see the development of modern atheism as inevitable. Nor does she claim, as Greenblatt does, that modern atheism is a truth discovered by ancient thinkers, recovered and revealed by Renaissance humanists, and realized in its full form by Enlightenment philosophers like Baron d'Holbach. Epicureans, after all, were not even atheists, though their atomic gods were neither creators nor interveners.

Palmer's middle path recognizes what many people before her have seen: there are Epicurean influences on modern atheism that belie a sui generis story of the modern discovery of scientific truth.[81] Tracing these influences sketches a much broader secular tradition that interweaves with Christianity, Judaism, and other religious traditions. It eventually stands independently, such as in August Comte's Religion of Humanity and the humanist institutions created in the twentieth century. As I have shown, however, atheism and secularism are always in a paradoxical relationship of identity with religion because in Christian-centered cultures Christianity's strong gravity determines the orbit of all other traditions.

During my second wave of field research, after I had already completed my PhD and started working at UC–Santa Barbara, I interviewed Abraham, a real-life Epicurean. Our conversation was illuminating, and it proved that the Epicurean tradition is alive and well, if changed. Abraham was raised Catholic in Puerto Rico and told me that he "deconverted" when he was about fifteen. When I asked what drove him away from religion, he described strong feelings of "disgust" toward the Catholic Church and "anger, especially after 9/11." He meets regularly with other Epicureans who are part of a Society of Friends of Epicurus, and he interacts with a global network of Epicureans online. He is also active in atheist organizations, including one in Puerto Rico. He made it clear that his atheism and his Epicureanism are related but different—a distinction with which historians like Palmer would agree.

Abraham has published a book on Epicureanism, and throughout the interview, he grounded his life choices in Epicurean teachings. He does not celebrate holidays or drink alcohol, and he tries to live an austere, "anticonsumerist" life. He explained, "In Epicurean philosophy, the ultimate goal is to live a life filled with pleasure, but that has to be measured against your pains, and sometimes you choose pains or sacrifices for the sake of a greater pleasure." He then told me that I could find evidence for this approach to life in Epicurus's "Letter to Menoeceus."

Abraham's path to atheism and Epicureanism was circuitous. After some time in the "angry atheist phase," he "settled back into the New Agey thing." He first encountered Epicureanism through memes on the internet, though he said, "I didn't think you could be an Epicurean, like actually practice that philosophy." It was only after picking up *The Portable Atheist*, a reader of primary sources edited by Christopher Hitchens, that Abraham took Epicureanism seriously. The first essay in the volume is an excerpt from Lucretius's ancient poem *De Rerum Natura*. "That's when it clicked for me," he told me. "This is a philosophy that's very aligned with my values. This is a philosophy that's comprehensive and complete. It had a complete cosmology, and you could make sense of the world." He said that one reason Epicureanism appealed to him so much "is that atheism doesn't really offer a positive belief system." He continued, "I think that's also what I'm noticing with some of the people that are coming into the study of Epicurus now. A lot of people are just rejecting nihilism. They've studied Nietzsche and Sartre and [Ayn Rand's] objectivism, and they're just looking for something positive to believe in. I know that was the case for me. You get tired of the jokes and the bashing on religion, and you want more depth." Like others who see in atheism only the negative half of the secular paradox, Abraham was looking for something more affirmative. By joining "the Epicurean tradition," as he calls it, in a sense, he came full circle.

Inclusions and Misfits

The histories of Epicureanism and nonbelief that Palmer, Kors, and others have written have implications for the study of secular people. One is that the secular discursive tradition is not settled and includes secular people who are not humanists or liberals. That there is no singular modern atheism is the clearest evidence that Palmer is right to avoid arguing that Epicureanism leads inevitably to a single worldview that we can identify today. Many of the robust debates over secular worldviews have taken place outside the tradition of secular liberalism, which remains dominant in the United States and among the very secular people I spent time with. The clearest example is Marxism. Karl Marx, who wrote his dissertation on the ancient atomists Democritus and Epicurus, identified explicitly as an atheist in an English-language interview in 1871.[82] Through the Soviet and Chinese revolutions, Marx's atheist ideas have spread throughout the world and produced complex hybrids in every culture in which they have taken hold. They have also produced a wide array of practices and forms of embodiment that are distinctive to these cultures.[83]

In a manuscript published posthumously, the Marxist philosopher Louis Althusser outlines a nonteleological materialism by tracing the influence of Lucretius—*un courant souterrain du matérialisme du rencontre*—through a disparate array of philosophers including Machiavelli, Hobbes, Spinoza, Rousseau, Marx, Heidegger, Nietzsche, Deleuze, and Derrida.[84] It is telling that Althusser considers the connections he makes among many of the major contributors to critical theory a subterranean tradition in need of being brought to light. His claims are supported by historians like Kors, Palmer, and Geroulanos, who come after him. The significant point here is that Martin Heidegger, Gilles Deleuze, and Jacques Derrida are just as much theologians of the secular as Anthony Pinn is, even though William Hart is probably the only person to have put them all in conversation.[85] Critical theory—an adequate name for my own subterranean creed—is no less a part of the secular tradition than secular humanism is. The same is true of the secular subjects it produces, who are as diverse as the tradition in which they participate.

Including critical theory in the secular tradition paves the way for other significant inclusions. The acceptance of finitude imbues Afro-pessimism with cynicism and Black optimism with hope.[86] The posthumanism of theorist Karen Barad's performative materialism and anthropologist Donna Haraway's notion of the cyborg have contributed to feminism in ways that are not easily reduced to liberalism.[87] Historians Karen and Barbara Fields and theorist Sylvia Wynter have critiqued and imagined alternatives to deeply ingrained colonialist racism by developing secular perspectives that make major contributions to the secular philosophical tradition.[88] Octavia Butler's prescient science fiction is a secular Afro-futurism, and Mary Shelley's *Frankenstein* is just as secular and imaginative in its sage warnings about the dangers of positivist science.[89] Frantz Fanon's psychoanalytic critiques of colonialism and racism constitute a liberation a/theology, and Viet Thanh Nguyen's novel *The Sympathizer* is no less a contribution to literary a/theology than is the novel to which it pays homage, Ralph Ellison's *Invisible Man*.[90] An understanding of the secular paradox frees these too-long-excluded additions to the secular discursive tradition from the need to be opposed to religion, though writers like Butler never drew a sharp distinction between secularism and religion in the first place.[91] Framed within a much larger tradition, humanists' struggle to include women and people of color appears to be more a limitation of their liberalism than of their secularism.[92]

Another important implication of careful histories of nonbelief is that the secular tradition extends beyond the obviously secular because elements of the tradition have influenced Christianity. A/theological philosophers have long argued that atheism emerges from out of Christianity, which shapes atheism profoundly even as it departs from it.[93] Philosopher Mark C. Taylor has worked to make sense of the sameness and difference of the ostensibly religious and secular by recognizing no methodological distinction between philosophy and theology; both provide his source material. Taylor observes the persistence of questions and limiting paradoxes in a wide range of philosophers and theologians but also in parts of life as diverse as complexity theory, Las Vegas, the art of Matthew Barney, and the novels of Paul Auster.[94] Philosopher Thomas Carlson's most recent book, *With the World at Heart*, offers a compelling philosophy of love and finitude, read through and beyond a number of religious and secular sources, including Augustine, Heidegger's interpretations of Augustine, and Heidegger's love letters to political theorist

Hannah Arendt.[95] Philosopher Mary-Jane Rubenstein has also explored "the historical identity, persistent entanglement, and productive crossings" of the secular and the religious by identifying the anxieties that structure the speculative cosmologies of scientists and a seeking public.[96] The multiverse, for instance, provides a theoretically viable but often nonempiricist outlet for persistent anxieties about the coherence and stability of the universe.[97] Like Farman, Rubenstein observes how debates among secular people are structured by a long history of theological inquiry and the gendered, racialized norms of colonial and postcolonial states. By recognizing theological influences in the secular and vice versa, a/theology performs the work of moving past the distinction between religious and secular.[98] As a social scientist rather than a philosopher, I have tried to do the same.

That secular and theological traditions have long interwoven helps account for some of the similarities that historians of the United States, among others, have observed between secularism and Protestantism.[99] The notion of a Protestant-secular helps explain why some secular people mis-fit the secular tradition, which I discuss in chapter 2 and later in this chapter. Protestants have borrowed arguments from ancient disenchanters of religion like Plutarch to debunk Catholicism and Hinduism.[100] Protestant distinctions between religion and superstition have influenced how secular governments decide which practices and ideas to protect and which to stamp out.[101] Protestants have appealed to the ideal of secular-neutral education to unmark the Protestant specificity of reading the King James Bible in public schools and to oppose public support for Catholic schools.[102] Christian and secular liberals have promoted individualist ideals and patriarchal gender norms to reinforce ways of being that are conducive to the interests of the nation-state.[103] And as the history of religious humanism shows, secular people within Christianity and Judaism played strong roles in shaping the religious liberalism that developed in the late nineteenth century.[104] These entanglements are complex, but understanding the concrete historical influence of a long secular tradition on Christianity, in addition to Protestant and other Christian influences on the secular, will surely help in explaining their imbrication. Epicurus, after all, antedates Christ.

The task going forward is to figure out what to do with a secular discursive tradition. Understanding the tradition as weirdly religion-like helps identify assumptions and practices that shape the everyday lives of secular people in all their variety. By acknowledging the tradition, scholars in particular gain a better understanding of their own participation. Many can fairly situate themselves within a tradition that they rightly critique. A secular discursive tradition provides a useful heuristic, as does any tradition, which is of course a social construct. The contingency of a social construct only renders it meaningless against a demand for the universal, as I tried to make clear in my discussion in chapter 4 of secular people's incessant problem with authority. It would be a shame if secular fear of religious pollution were to blind secular people to their own historical formation because it threatens the narrative that secularism and atheism are the shining truth revealed after religion is removed. And it would be a shame if latent Christian priority of the universal made any tradition too fragile to bother delimiting because it does not uphold a central doctrine or maintain its purity from other traditions. The ambiguous truth of the secular tradition is far stranger than a simple binary of secular and religious can contain. The middle path I have tried to clear has proven useful for answering many of my own questions, so I hope it might also prove useful for others.

One of the benefits of recognizing that the secular discursive tradition is religion-like is that it provides strong evidence for the colonialist influence on religion and its continued dependence on Christianity as the analogical referent for world religions. With the edited volume *After World Religions*, scholars of religion Christopher Cotter and David Robertson make a compelling case for teaching through the "world religions" paradigm rather than avoiding it. They recount the history of the paradigm, rooted in the efforts of religious and secular scholars, and they draw from it examples that can explain the paradigm's durability, such as in courses on "world religions" and as a structure for academic departments of religion.[105]

The strategy Cotter and Robertson develop is also helpful for understanding secular people and their secularism, which are worthy of critique but also careful attention. Throughout this book, I have observed the secular's misfits, or those who mis-fit religion and its rejection. This chapter concludes by looking at three more examples of secular misfits. Despite their marginalization in the American secular movement, their perspectives offer the greatest insights into the secular paradox, as well as evidence for it. Returning to these misfits demonstrates the usefulness of a generous study of secular people for understanding why "religion" is such a troublesome category and how Christianity structures not only the traditions we call "world religions" but also the secular tradition.

Secular Jewish Tradition

In chapter 2, I described a visit to the headquarters of the Society for Humanistic Judaism, located at the Birmingham Temple in Farmington, Michigan. On that same trip, I met up with a man named Saul at La Strada Cafe in Birmingham. We sat in the back of the cafe, and though no one sat near us, we managed to turn a few heads. Saul founded an atheist Meetup group in the area, and he is also an "intactivist," an activist against male circumcision. Before meeting Saul, I knew that John Kellogg, a Seventh-day Adventist who cofounded the Kellogg Company, had advocated circumcision as a way to prevent masturbation.[106] I did not remember that the Kellogg Company was founded in Battle Creek, Michigan. According to Saul, Kellogg's efforts had lasting effects on circumcision rates in Michigan, which are among the highest in the country.[107]

Saul and I started by talking about his path to atheist activism, and after a while, I asked him about his intactivism. He gave me a quick history of male circumcision and explained his opposition before turning to his frustrations with Jewish deconversion:

> I meet people, and I tell them I'm an atheist. They say, "You're still Jewish." "There's no way you can un-Jew yourself," my wife would say. I would say, "I'm not. I'm not Jewish." She'd say, "You're irrational. You're Jewish." I kept meeting people who would say, "You're an atheist Jew." People from the Society for Humanistic Judaism, they say Judaism is ethnic. It's cultural. You can still claim "Jewish." I said, "What are you talking about? I come from a family with some common traits as myself, but how does that make me Jewish?" I look like my parents. We have common genetic traits. It doesn't make us a people. It doesn't make us a tribe. One of my passions is to write about this: *Why I'm Not a Jew*. I'm a universalist. The nation-state is going to fade gradually. We see that with globalization. Just in a purely economic sense, it makes a lot of sense. From a human

rights perspective, it makes a lot of sense. Like in Africa: "Don't criticize female genital mutilation. That's our practice." It's cutting, whether it's here or there.

Saul told me that his desire to "un-Jew" himself was a source of strife in his marriage. His ex-wife is from an Orthodox family and wanted to raise their children Jewish. She suggested going to the Birmingham Temple, but he refused. "I was an atheist, not a Jewish atheist," he told me. For those who go to the Birmingham Temple, he explained, "What matters are the people, the Jewish values, the family, getting us to be better human beings, to change the world. That's not my position because that's not exclusive to Judaism." After his divorce, Saul became more involved in atheist activism because he felt more free to do so.

According to Saul, he has friends who say, "I hate Judaism," but his own view is, "I have nothing to do with Judaism." He told me about those friends: "They probably have some inner work to do, but they would agree with me. I'm not a Jewish atheist—just an atheist. I'm a minority within the minority." This last phrase—"a minority within the minority"—is fascinating because it still positions him within the tradition he is trying to reject. When I asked Saul if his atheist and anticircumcision activism are connected, he responded in abstract rather than personal terms: "the anticircumcision movement, indirectly, is critical of religion, as well as dogmatic thinking." I did not press further, but given the ways in which the threads of our conversation wove together, it is hard not to read Saul's frustration with having been circumcised into his desire for secular purity and a clean break from Judaism.

In *Becoming Un-Orthodox*, sociologist Lynn Davidman recognizes the Christian-centrism of sociological studies of deconversion, and she attends closely to the bodily challenges that Orthodox Jews face when deconverting, which often get overlooked in accounts that focus on Christians and emphasize belief. Circumcision does not appear to be a challenge that her interlocutors discussed.[108] Saul's position is extreme, but it is also structured by the secular paradox. He wants the secular purity that atheists who deconvert from Christianity can achieve. His body is a site of a struggle over secular conversion, which remains structured by Christian norms but also by Jewish tradition. The same mis-fit of the Jewish discursive tradition, which allows secular Jews to be both secular and Jewish without much need for explanation, frustrates Saul to no end. "People would not let me say, 'I'm not Jewish,'" he told me later in the same interview. Saul wants to become purely secular, to fully reject the Jewish tradition and fully join the secular. His inability to translate every part of his body into the secular leaves him with anxiety about its religious pollution. He wants to be recognized as purely secular by those around him, but people who continue to consider him Jewish make social acceptance of his chosen identity impossible.

Muslimish Tradition

Secular Muslims also face bodily challenges to deconversion that most Christians do not. In chapter 3, I described how blasphemy is a bodily practice for ex-Muslims. Rituals like "Haramadan," at which they eat pork and drink alcohol, blaspheme their formerly religious bodies to make them more secular, while still allowing them to retain celebrations like Eid. In chapter 2, I introduced some of the secular Muslims I went bar-hopping with in Detroit, including Hisham, who grew up in the United Arab Emirates and moved to the United States as a teenager by way of Lebanon. Hisham is a delight, and his intellect sparkles in everything he says. Our long conversation is worth revisiting to emphasize the deep Christianity of the secular discursive tradition and the problems it causes for non-Christian people who want to convert to secularism.

Hisham emphasized several times that being Muslim is a bodily, affective practice: "Islam weaves itself into your emotions, your existential side—I don't want to say spirit." Leaving Islam behind is hard, he said, but he also described how good it feels: "I started a new journey. It's like being reborn: reestablishing all your values, rediscovering everything, reinterpreting everything. It's like losing all your memory and starting as a fresh human. It's a beautiful journey when you feel so free." Hisham is describing his break with the Muslim tradition—the negative half of being secular—and the freedom he feels to explore a new one. He is also describing the process of translating himself into the secular tradition. His new tradition does not always feel like home. When he first started to attend events in atheist communities, he tried to find other former Muslims, but there were none. Wanting to be with people who share his experiences, he helped start new groups for people like him.

One of these groups is Muslimish, a network of communities for Muslims who do not want to become fully secular: "You'll have some Muslimish people who listen to the Qur'an because it makes them feel comfortable. They're used to it. It's passionate in some areas." He also told me that family ties make deconversion hard: "People's relationships with their grandmas, they'll go to the funeral of a young man who died, and they'll feel bad because they prayed with his family. This aspect of not being the asshole in the family is the Muslimish stance." Those who join a Muslimish group or just consider themselves Muslimish "appreciate the positive things [about Islam], the morals, the poetry, the heritage. But they don't want to reckon themselves atheist, and they don't want to call themselves Muslims. Technically, Islam does not consider them Muslims." Hisham was contrasting those who are Muslimish with his own way, which is decidedly secular, though he understands their struggle.

Hisham spends time with Muslimish people and even sides with them in arguments on occasion, but he sees himself as having left Islam behind. Despite his efforts to translate himself into his new discursive tradition—his beautiful journey—the secular tradition cannot fully contain him because it has evolved mostly in Christian-centered cultures. In the stories that Saul and Hisham told me, it is clear that scholars who have critiqued the secular tradition for its Christian bias are correct. Given the peregrination through Christianity of ideas that eventually become associated with the secular, this influence is unsurprising. The same process that made the so-called world religions in the image of Christianity, through the rituals of abstraction and translation, has also formed secularism, both as Christianity's antithesis and as a religion-like tradition of its own. That Saul and Hisham are pioneering their own secular formations challenges us to see how secular people deal with secularism's Christian norms and try to remake the tradition in their own image. Their efforts demand a broader, more inclusive view of the secular tradition.

Secular Native American Tradition

While giving a public lecture on secular people at a university, I mentioned in passing that I had been unable to find any Native Americans involved in the secular movement. After the lecture, a student approached me and told me that I just did. Teresa helped start her campus's secular student group, and she and her brother, Daniel, both identify as atheists. About a week later, I interviewed each of them separately over the phone. The siblings are very bright, and Teresa, in particular, is inquisitive and skeptical. In her responses to my questions, she often pushed back against my latent assumptions, and it was a pleasure to think with her as a cotheorist. Teresa and Daniel's father is Filipino, and their mother belongs to the Potawatomi tribe. Teresa and her brother were raised Catholic, but they both became atheists as teenagers and stopped attending church after being confirmed. The group Teresa created at her university is far more diverse than any other I encountered. She described its members as "mostly Filipino, from the islands, Tongan, Asian, Vietnamese, Korean. There's a couple of Latinx girls too."

Teresa told me that she identifies more with Native American than Filipino culture: "I feel like I've given so much of myself to my Potawatomi side, and I haven't given my Filipino side a chance. I know it's going to be a struggle because it's so deeply engulfed in Catholicism." The siblings visit their tribe in Oklahoma often: "We would go every year, multiple times a year, to discuss what was going on with the tribe. We'd make art, weave baskets, stuff connected with the culture, learning the language. We have to grip onto our culture, relearn it, and teach it to future generations. It's a top priority." She described in detail her naming ceremony, which took place in Oklahoma in the summer of 2017. Her uncle led the ceremony, she told me: "Because he's so involved in the tribe, he's more knowledgeable about creation stories and stuff like that. He sees the value in preserving the culture, but it's not something my other family members have looked into."

I was surprised to learn that Teresa's uncle is, in her words, "deeply Catholic." Given Teresa's rejection of Catholicism, I asked her how she understands the relationship between her secularism and her Native side. Her answers were thoughtful and fascinating. She said that she and her brother had already talked about this question after her naming ceremony:

> There's this whole part: you're offering tobacco to enter the circle, in each direction, toward each spirit, of north, south, east, and west. I asked Daniel, "Hey, what did you think about that part when you were supposed to

be saying your prayer?" He said, "I wasn't thinking about anything." So how do we balance these identities out? I was thinking about my ancestors. This is so cool that I get to be a part of this ritual that my ancestors were a part of hundreds of years ago. This is what they practiced, what they did. They honored the earth around them, the spirits around them. The reason why I was tolerating it is because I knew that the way that I was taking it, once again, was just me enjoying my culture and honoring my ancestors. This is a part of what I am.

Thinking about her tribe, Teresa recognizes that many members are Christian and she is secular, but none of them see a conflict with their Native tradition: "Even though there a lot of Christian and Catholic members, the culture in itself is pretty—you can consider it kind of secular." By secular here, she means "not religious," which is to say, not in conflict with a religion-like tradition such as Christianity or secularism.

Teresa saw in my questions that I was probing how she draws boundaries: "It has to do with the attitudes that our family has toward what you would consider the religion of our tribe. It's all taken with a grain of salt." Describing her relatives who are Christian, she said, "That's their *personal* religion. Daniel and I have that common ground with [the Native side] as well. We appreciate these observations [about nature], but we don't necessarily feel it necessary to worship." Because Teresa's relatives have already established ways to be both Christian and Native, she can be both secular and Native. The traditions have been strategically configured to complement one another. Her Native tradition has been made "secular" so that it conflicts neither with her relatives' Christianity nor with the secularism of her and her brother.

As I listened to Teresa, it was clear that she had considered some of these questions before but not in great depth. There is nothing wrong with this, of course, but it made us both aware that she was working out descriptions as we were talking. She told me that other than her brother, she had "never met anyone else who identifies as Native and atheist." I asked more questions, and Teresa became increasingly self-conscious of the language she was using:

> I consider the Native American side "culture": looking to nature and a connection in an appreciation sort of way. I wouldn't consider it "spiritu-

ality," but I know that it was "sacred," as in, I see it from a secular perspective. Obviously when I think of land being sacred, I think of it as being how you would treat a historical landmark in a sense. It's not touchable because this was a home to other people. The place meant a lot to people going back centuries and centuries. It's more a historical sacred than a spiritual thing.

Teresa uses abstraction and translation in clever ways. She finds categories that can contain others like history and aesthetics, and she translates "sacred" into a secular meaning. Teresa even theorized the aestheticization of religion as a purification strategy: "I would draw a line [with my acceptance of Catholicism] somewhere with aesthetics. There's such beauty in the opulence of the Catholic Church. It's aesthetically pleasing." She then told me a story about going to the Vatican and meeting the pope: "Because I'm from a Catholic family, I was there getting things blessed by his general blessing. He was riding his Popemobile around, and he blessed me, so everything I was wearing was blessed. I have some sweet Doc Martens that were blessed that day. I wear that coat basically every day of my life. I'll gladly rep that thing, but it doesn't have that significance for me." For Teresa, the pope's blessing has significance, but not the way it would for a devout Catholic. Even translated into her secular ontology, meeting the pope and getting his blessing is momentous. I would feel the same.

After we talked a little more, I invited Teresa to think with me about what I was learning from her. She and I both see no inherent conflict between her secularism and her participation in her Native culture. We were both aware of the threat, however, that a certain kind of secularism would prohibit her from engaging with it. In this threat lies an entire history of Christian assumptions about religious purity, secular assumptions about secular purity, and a colonialist configuration of Native traditions to try to sequester them to "secular" categories like culture and aesthetics.[109] In this case, the sequestration allows Native practices to coexist with a religious commitment to Christianity—or a religion-like commitment to the secular. The work of abstraction and categorical sequestration is part of the secular discursive tradition but also part of the Christian tradition and the Native tradition that Teresa participates in and maintains. As with being Jewish, being Native mis-fits the secular, though in different ways. Because they are different kinds of traditions than Christianity, in part because of their relationship *to* Christianity, they can coexist with the secular. This middle space is harder to find in secular Islam as it stands today, but Hisham and his secular friends are changing that and making it work. The relationship among these traditions is being reconfigured, and new hybrid forms are emerging.

A Place in the Pantheon

I have found that a secular tradition is this book's most controversial claim. It is no accident that this chapter is its last and that it refers back to previous chapters often. I have built the evidence for my argument slowly and deliberately in the same way I convinced myself. I began with the fact of secular people and their odd relationship with religion, and I have tried to make sense of how things came to be this way. I am grateful to historians like Palmer and Kors, who have done research I never could, and to postmodern philosophers like Taylor, who have taken a more rationalist, Hegelian approach to the same history and arrived at many of the same insights. Hopefully I have introduced their scholarship to more researchers who study secular people.

In the spirit of social science, I have tested the notion that there is a secular tradition in many different fora. I have argued for it in panel presentations and scholarly lectures, at public talks for nonbelievers and in podcast interviews, in my classroom and in publications. My experiments, though badly run, have taught me that the secular tradition makes many people feel anxious. For some, it is too religious. Because it situates secular people's beliefs and practices in a long history and categorizes them with quasi-secular and religious forebears, it contaminates their secular purity. Inasmuch as this book is about the anxiety that secular people feel when too proximate to religion, it is also about the distinctively secular anxiety of being part of a religion-like secular tradition.

Perhaps more unsettling, if we define the secular discursive tradition broadly, its subterranean current courses through almost everyone.[110] Avowedly secular people are its primary inheritors, but its reach extends much further. This extended reach we might fairly call "secularity" because it describes a secular condition that we experience without necessarily averring secularism. An analogy to Christianity is revelatory. In French, "Christianity" takes a different suffix: *le christianisme*. The "-ity" suffix used in English blurs the boundary between a particular tradition, consciously affirmed—an ism—and a broader inheritance in which even non-Christians find themselves.[111] Christians inherit the Christian tradition, but even as a non-Christian, so do I. The secular tradition is no different. Just as there is Christianism, there is Christianity; just as there is secularism, there is secularity. Recovering a secular discursive tradition helps make this distinction, which in turn helps us see that the secular tradition imbricates all of us in secularity, even if we are not all followers of secularism.

The secular paradox explains how and why the secular discursive tradition has remained mostly subterranean. It is both a rejection of religion and a religion-like tradition of its own; each half can be concealed when its generative pendulum swings far enough in one direction or the other. Spending time with and learning from very secular people has allowed me to glimpse the secular tradition and its constitutive paradox. I have built from what secular people have shown me. Because the secular paradox structures the secular tradition, it has the greatest impact on those who are most secular; it has less of a hold on those who are within secularity but not committed to one of many secular worldviews. This means that the secular paradox works differently on those who are less secular or merely influenced by secularity than it does on the very secular. More narrowly, all secular people, including the indifferent, regulate their lives to avoid religion, often unconsciously, while embracing parts of life that are religious or religion-like. The secular paradox helps make sense of their ambiguous religiosity and their ambivalence toward religion. It shows how the knots that bind them to religion grow tighter as they struggle against them. It also shows that they remain bound even if they ignore their knots.[112] A secular discursive tradition gives secular people a history of their practices, feelings, and ways of belonging. Setting secular people in their tradition makes them one among many. It denies the eternity of our truth but provides us a place in the pantheon.

Epilogue

The Helmet of Mambrino

"Lord save me!" said the barber who was the target of the joke. "Is it possible that so many honorable people are saying that this is not a basin but a helmet? This seems to be something that could astonish an entire university, no matter how learned. Enough: if it's true that this basin is a helmet, then this packsaddle must also be a horse's harness, just as the gentleman said."
—Miguel de Cervantes, *Don Quixote* (1605)

I started this book with a story about visiting an Ethical Culture society in part because I continue to find the intensity of Ethical Humanists' rejection of religion as surprising as the intensity of their embrace. Ethical Culture is one of the institutional inheritors of the secular tradition, and like humanists who attend the First Unitarian Society of Minneapolis, its adherents are well attuned to their paradoxical relationship with religion. Early on in my field research, I met Marty, an Ethical Culture Leader in New York. Marty works as a therapist, and though he avoids peppering his speech with language from psychology, he speaks in full paragraphs that often include paraphrased quotes. We bonded over an affection for John Dewey, and he won me over with his sweet, gentle nature and his care for everyone around him. I am glad we have stayed in touch.

In a conversation at Henry's, a restaurant on the Upper West Side, Marty told me that Ethical Culture "lacks the barnacles of tradition," but "every community needs a tradition. Rituals are traditions which are freighted with symbolic meaning." Explaining how he perceives Ethical Culture's relationship with religion, he continued,

> I use the *American College Dictionary* 1949 definition of religion. I can quote it. Definition one—this is a pretty good paraphrase: religion is the

quest for the ideal life, involving three parts: the ideal itself, the practices that attain to the ideal, and the theology or worldview that relates the ideal to the environing universe. So I tell people we're religious humanism. We're religious. We have an ideal. The ideal is our highest calling. It's to create a more just world. Practices, well, no secret handshakes. Our practices are like karma, yoga—like Gandhi talked about. Worldview is action in the world. We don't have a theology. You can if you wish, but we as an institution, we don't. The worldview is naturalistic, scientific humanism. That's how we connect to the universe. To me that's a very rich posture to take. Being a humanist, I'm so relieved I don't have to have the truth. My Christian colleagues are hanging onto the truth with their fingernails. I can relax. I can be a pragmatist in the philosophical sense. That to me is a very rich and satisfying posture in life. And it's fun.

Like other very secular people, Marty embraces aspects of religion and also rejects them. He abstracts from a Christian-centered notion of religion and imagines analogues for its component parts. He told me that humanists have practices and rituals, but some think too many: "I get requests from people who want more ritual, and I get complaints about too much." They have a tradition, but not the bad kind. They have a worldview, but not a theology. They have rituals, but just enough. The humanist tradition purifies itself by holding itself at arm's length.

During the years I have spent trying to understand secular people, I have thought often about Miguel de Cervantes's masterpiece *Don Quixote*. One subplot, in particular, contains insights that have shaped this book deeply. Cervantes's novel tells the story of a Spanish gentleman of modest means who leaves his farm, his housekeeper, and his niece and wanders through the countryside of Spain acting out scenes from chivalric novels and insisting that he is a knight-errant of great renown. Don Quixote entangles those whom he meets in his fictions, often by the point of his lance, though he and his squire, Sancho, receive many beatings of their own. In a typical encounter, while traveling on a rural road, Quixote sees a barber wearing a shiny new basin atop his head to cover it from the rain. Without a hint of willingness on the part of the barber, Quixote narrates the man into his story and attacks him for having stolen the famed Helmet of Mambrino. The barber flees on foot and leaves the basin in the road. When Quixote approaches the barber's basin, he admits to Sancho that up close it appears to be just that—a basin—but he quickly concludes that someone must have failed to recognize the true value of the helmet and melted down its other half for gold. "Be that as it may," he insists, "I recognize it, and its transmutation does not matter to me."[1]

Near the end of the novel, Quixote, Sancho, and many of the novel's other characters encounter one another at a rural inn. In a climactic scene, the barber also arrives, and he accuses Quixote of stealing his basin (and Sancho of stealing his donkey). At stake is not only whether the helmet is a basin but also whether Quixote is a noble knight or a common thief. Because Quixote has endeared himself to the others at the inn, the reality of the "basihelm," as Sancho calls it, becomes a matter of perception. After a debate about the item's essence, the exasperated barber asks aloud, "Is it possible that so many honorable people are saying that this is not a basin but a helmet?"[2] A priest defers to Quixote's judgment, and a wealthy nobleman sides with Quixote for sport. The barber's basin, the narrator tells the reader, "had been transformed into the helmet of Mambrino before [the barber's] very eyes."[3] In the end, members of the Holy Brotherhood—officers of the law—mediate the dispute. By their authority, the basin becomes a helmet, which Quixote keeps, and the priest pays the barber in secret to settle Quixote's debt. The reality of the basihelm is a question not only of perspective but also of authority.

Questions about secular people too often assume an essence. Our adverbs tell a story of suspicion. What is *really* secular? Are secular people *actually* religious? Who are they *truly*? The basin can only become the helmet because they share certain qualities, at first at a distance but again up close. The basin becomes a helmet because of Don Quixote, but the transmutation also requires the authority of religion, wealth, noble birth, and the law. Secular and religious transmutations are no different. With the modest authority of a researcher, I have tried to observe these transmutations and see the secular from many perspectives. In the end, it is neither essentially religious nor essentially not. The empirical fact of the secular is that it is both, depending on who claims its essence, in what context, and with what authority. By studying a strangely ambiguous part of life that we can and often do narrate both ways, I have tried to capture the ambiguity of being secular. I hope I have made moot the question of whether something is *really* secular or *actually* religious by describing the secular paradox and its many consequences. And I hope an awareness of this paradox can change how others understand the secular as it has changed my own.

ACKNOWLEDGMENTS

To write this book I've learned from more people than I can possibly thank. Courtney Bender, Mark Taylor, Gil Anidjar, and Josef Sorett gave me the freedom, support, and criticism I needed at Columbia University. They'll find their influence woven throughout. Jerry Stein, Harvey Sarles, and Richard Leppert inspired me to go to graduate school when I was a first-generation college student at the University of Minnesota. At the University of California, Irvine, George Marcus, Michelle Molina, Gaby Schwab, and Achille Mbembe gave me the confidence I needed to become a scholar. Fellow graduate students who became good friends—George Zhu, Lee Laskin, Terressa Benz, Patton Burchett, Dan Vaca, Todd French, Matt Pereira, Susie Andrews, Greg Scott, Tori Gross, Alf García, Sarah Dees, James Robertson, and Liron Mor—have kept me grounded and afloat. John Modern, Sylvester Johnson, Sally Promey, Robert Yelle, Randy Balmer, Jonathan Sheehan, Vincent Pecora, Jonathan VanAntwerpen, Chuck Mathewes, Udi Greenberg, Brad Onishi, Danny Steinmetz-Jenkins, Donovan Schaefer, Katharine Gerbner, Matt Cressler, Samira Mehta, Chris Cantwell, Jamil Drake, Shari Rabin, Alexis Wells-Oghoghomeh, and Melissa Borja gave sage advice and much-needed encouragement along the way.

In 2015 I joined a wonderful intellectual community at the University of California, Santa Barbara. Kathie Moore, Roger Friedland, Tom Carlson, Randy Garr, Dominic Steavu, and Dusty Hoesly have supported me, personally and professionally. Greg and Kari Johnson have given me a home away from home. Dave Walker is a wonderful friend who continues to make me a better teacher and scholar. Several brilliant graduate students have also helped me realize this book, including Matt Harris, Courtney Applewhite, Damian Lanahan-Kalish, and Shakir Stephen. Luke McCracken appears in its footnotes because our conversations have shaped my arguments deeply. Outside Religious Studies, Terence Keel, David Pellow, Lisa Park, and Sameer Pandya welcomed me to Santa Barbara and helped me feel like I belong. Mayanthi Fernando and Sangseraima Ujeed provided valuable friendship and advice during a difficult time to finish a book: a pandemic.

The research on which this book relies has been supported by the Institute for Religion, Culture, and Public Life and the Center for Democracy, Toleration, and Religion at Columbia University; the Social Science Research Council; the Institute for Social, Behavioral, and Economic Research at the University of California, Santa Barbara; and the Hellman Foundation. Conversations and mentorship that have shaped its ideas have been supported by the Center for the Study of Religion and American Culture and the National Endowment for Humanities. I am also grateful to the Multicultural Center at the University of California, Santa Barbara for creating a wonderfully supportive community and for changing how I think.

Parts of this book have been presented to insightful audiences at the University of Pennsylvania, the College of William & Mary, Middlebury College, Cal-State Bakersfield, Harvard University, Yale University, Goethe University in Frankfurt, the University of Toronto, the University of Bern, Princeton University, Stanford University, Brown University, McGill University, Oxford University, the University of California, Berkeley, and the University of California, Los Angeles. Their comments and questions have been invaluable, and most importantly, they have helped me see the forest for the trees.

More than a hundred very secular people sat down with me for interviews, invited me into their homes and offices, took me to dinner, drove me around, and shared their most personal thoughts. They have made this book possible. I'm grateful, and I hope I've described their lives with the care and generosity they deserve.

Those close to me know I do my best thinking out loud. My friends who are not scholars will surely hear our conversations echo throughout this book. Eli Geminder, Tomás Nazal, Joseph Meyers, Nick Kraus, Rob Bosworth, Jeremy Dennison, Jacob Kraemer, David Cole, and Coleman Moore have believed in me, distracted me, and asked me the best questions. Vlad Tsyrklevich, Nick Sadler, Ben Stein, Andrew Boyd, and Eric Kamerman held me up when I was down. Tyler Carlson encouraged me to finish and insisted we celebrate when I did.

My family knows how much I love them, but I can't miss this opportunity to remind them in print. Janet Figueroa, Luis Figueroa, Carina Figueroa, Jacob Figueroa, and Jedidiah Figueroa always have my back. Thank you for everything.

NOTES

INTRODUCTION

1. Olds, *American Religious Humanism*, 174.
2. Radest, *Toward Common Ground*, 14.
3. Chuman, "Between Secularism and Supernaturalism," 150–69.
4. Schmidt, *Village Atheists*; Warren, *American Freethought*; Jacoby, *Freethinkers*.
5. Radest, *Toward Common Ground*, 58–59.
6. "Leader" is capitalized because it is a formal title applied by Ethical Culture to its movement's trained, clergy-like leaders. Adler, *Our Part in This World*, 68. The volume is a collection of undated selections that Friess compiled from transcripts of lectures given by Adler. King's Crown Press is a now-defunct division of Columbia University Press.
7. García and Blankholm, "Social Context of Organized Nonbelief."
8. Flaccus, "Atheist 'Mega-Churches' Take Root."
9. The anthropologist Mary Douglas uses the concepts "purity" and "pollution" to help explain the boundaries that people draw in all parts of life. Her concepts find their origin in Émile Durkheim's *The Elementary Forms of Religious Life*, in which he draws a distinction between sacred and profane. He argues that these distinctions structure not only religion but all social life. Things that are sacred must be kept apart because they reflect value-based distinctions in the social order; their sequestration maintains that order. In *Purity and Danger*, Douglas extends Durkheim's framework, arguing that the distinction between clean and unclean structures all of social life because cleanliness is order and pollution is disorder. Order, or cleanliness, requires the clarification of boundaries through a process of purification, which excises or avoids that which is disordered and thus polluted.
10. Douglas's approach can only explain the negative half of secular people's ambivalence to religion. Robert Yelle argues in his analysis of her work that structuralists like Douglas inherit their semiotic ideology from Deism and older forms of Protestantism that share "a bias against the supra-legal or disorderly dimensions of the Holy." Yelle, *Semiotics of Religion*, 156. In Yelle's reading, secular people are no different. They receive from their Protestant inheritance a fear of disorder, which drives them to order or, in their case, secular purity. It is "fear of arbitrariness," according to Yelle, that drives us to divide secular and religious into a tidy binary. On the secular's Protestant inheritance, see also Yelle, *Language of Disenchantment*.

11. In *Modernity and Ambivalence*, Zygmunt Bauman observes, "Modern mastery is the power to divide, classify and allocate—in thought, in practice, in the practice of thought and in the thought of practice. Paradoxically, it is for this reason that ambivalence is the main affliction of modernity and the most worrying of its concerns. . . . If modernity is about the production of order then ambivalence is the waste of modernity" (15). Bauman is right. It is the modern pursuit of tidy division that necessarily produces excess that cannot be tidied as the world overflows any attempt to describe it. That secular people, modern par excellence, should be ambivalent toward their ostensible antithesis is thus, by Bauman's logic, entirely unsurprising.
12. In taking this approach, I draw on the work of Mark C. Taylor, who has explored in numerous books the immense productivity of constitutive negation in Christian and post-Christian culture. For the foundations of his approach, see Taylor, *Erring*; Taylor, *Altarity*; Taylor, *Nots*.
13. Hout, "Religious Ambivalence"; Drescher, *Choosing Our Religion*.
14. This third sense of "secularism," as religion-making, is of more recent conceptual coinage. In the twenty-first century, its inquiry was pioneered by Talal Asad (*Formations of the Secular*) and Janet Jakobsen and Ann Pellegrini (*Secularisms*). It is curious and noteworthy that the Asadians rarely cite Jakobsen and Pellegrini. Perhaps the clearest statement of secularism as religion-making can be found in a volume edited by Markus Dressler and Arvind Mandair, *Secularism and Religion-Making*. Other senses of "secular," such as secularity, have spawned their own related literature. See, for example, the wide-ranging discussion in C. Taylor, *Secular Age*; Warner, VanAntwerpen, and Calhoun, *Varieties of Secularism in a Secular Age*; and Gorski et al., *Post-secular in Question*.
15. Kosmin et al., *American Nones*.
16. Lim, MacGregor, and Putnam, "Secular and Liminal."
17. The percentage of Americans with no religious affiliation was stable for decades until doubling during the 1990s, after the end of the Cold War. Hout and Fischer, "Why More Americans Have No Religious Preference"; Hout and Fischer, "Explaining Why More Americans Have No Religious Preference."
18. Derrida, "Faith and Knowledge."
19. Anidjar, "Of Globalatinology"; Fitzgerald, *Religion and the Secular*; Masuzawa, *Invention of World Religions*.
20. Darren Sherkat has argued that growth in belief in a nonagentive higher power is a symptom of the declining hold of "Abrahamic" religions (*Changing Faith*).
21. Bender and McRoberts, "Mapping a Field."
22. On the challenges of measurement and some practical responses, see Voas, "Afterword." On the usefulness of religion as it relates to politics, see Campbell and Putnam, *American Grace*; Layman, "Religion and Political Behavior in the United States"; Castle et al., "Survey Experiments."
23. Todd Weir has published significant research on the Monist movement and the concept of "worldview" in the German context. Weir, *Monism*; Weir, *Secularism and Religion*; Weir, "Germany and the New Global History of Secularism."

24. Kennedy, "Ideology."
25. Fitzgerald, *Religion and Politics in International Relations*; Hurd, *Beyond Religious Freedom*.
26. See, for instance, Keel, *Divine Variations*.
27. Fessenden, *Culture and Redemption*; Yelle, *Language of Disenchantment*; Nongbri, *Before Religion*.
28. Mahmood, *Religious Difference in a Secular Age*; Dressler and Mandair, *Secularism and Religion-Making*.
29. Mahmood, *Religious Difference in a Secular Age*, 3.
30. Löwith, *Meaning in History*; Blumenberg, *Legitimacy of the Modern Age*.
31. In recent years, Samuel Moyn has been at the center of a debate regarding the Christianity of human rights, which echoes in many ways the debate between Löwith and Blumenberg. Moyn, *Christian Human Rights*; Scott, *Politics of the Veil*.
32. Latour, *We Have Never Been Modern*.
33. Horkheimer and Adorno, *Dialectic of Enlightenment*.
34. Voas and Chaves, "Is the United States a Counterexample to the Secularism Thesis?"
35. Hurd, *Beyond Religious Freedom*, 122–27.
36. McKinnon, "Sociological Definitions," 80.
37. Blankholm, "Secularism and Secular People."
38. Political theorist Matthew Scherer has tried to do the same in his excellent book on secularism as conversion, *Beyond Church and State*.
39. Marcus, "Ethnography in/of the World System."
40. Since I began conducting this research, a number of other scholars have published important books and essays on organized secularism in the United States. Cimino and Smith, "Secular Humanism and Atheism"; Cimino and Smith, *Atheist Awakening*; Smith and Cimino, "Atheisms Unbound"; Jesse Smith, "Becoming an Atheist in America"; Jesse Smith, "Creating a Godless Community"; LeDrew, "Discovering Atheism"; LeDrew, *Evolution of Atheism*; Guenther, Mulligan, and Papp, "From the Outside In"; Guenther, "Bounded by Disbelief"; Kettell, "Faithless"; Kettell, "Divided We Stand"; Cragun, Manning, and Fazzino, *Organized Secularism in the United States*.
41. Bourdieu, "Sociologists of Belief and Beliefs of Sociologists."
42. Wuthnow, *God Problem*.
43. Wilson, *Mindful America*; Helderman, "Drawing the Boundaries."
44. Kurtz, *Meaning and Value in a Secular Age*. See also Kurtz's earlier book in which he spells the term differently, Kurtz, *Eupraxophy*. Kurtz founded the first organization for *secular* humanism in the United States after breaking away from the American Humanist Association.
45. Barad, "Posthumanist Performativity"; Barad, *Meeting the University Halfway*.
46. For instance, Matthew Engelke has observed this ambivalence as a potential site of inquiry and written, "We need more ethnographies of atheism, of secular humanism, of ambivalent non-religiosity" ("On Atheism and Non-religion," 138).

47. Campbell, *Toward a Sociology of Irreligion*, 43–44.
48. Jesse Smith, "Becoming an Atheist in America"; Jesse Smith, "Creating a Godless Community"; LeDrew, "Discovering Atheism." Smith and LeDrew also exchanged responses in the same issue of *Sociology of Religion* in which LeDrew's article appeared. LeDrew argues explicitly that nonbelievers have beliefs. Smith's forthcoming research on the Sunday Assembly focuses more on what nonbelievers share. LeDrew, *Evolution of Atheism*; Frost, "Rejecting Rejection Identities."
49. Smolkin, *Sacred Space Is Never Empty*, 5.
50. Flew, *God, Freedom, and Immortality*, 13–30. For a criticism of this distinction, see Kenny, *Faith and Reason*. A century earlier, John Stuart Mill drew a similar distinction between positive and negative atheism, where the former is "the dogmatic denial of his existence," and the latter is "the denial that there is any evidence on either side, which for most practical purposes amounts to the same thing as if the existence of a God had been disproved." Mill, "Theism," 242.
51. G. Smith, *Atheism*; M. Martin, *Atheism*, 281.
52. Layman and Weaver, "Religion and Secularism."
53. Bullivant, "Defining 'Atheism,'" 11.
54. Minois, *Histoire de l'athéisme*, 34. The translation is my own.
55. What Mark C. Taylor writes on money, so too applies to atheism: "Whatever its form, money's intermediate status is what lends it an ambiguity that provokes ambivalence" (*Confidence Games*, 60). And in Camus's words, "To will is to stir up paradoxes" (*Myth of Sisyphus*, 25).

CHAPTER 1. BELIEF

1. The term "ideology" was first coined as a name for the "science of ideas" developed by Count Antoine Destutt de Tracy in the late eighteenth century. Kennedy, "Ideology." Intended as a moral and political science, "ideology" provided a replacement for church teachings as "a foundation for public morality" in the wake of the French Revolution. Calhoun, Jurgensmeyer, and VanAntwerpen, introduction to *Rethinking Secularism*, 8; De Tracy's "ideology" would later influence Auguste Comte's development of Positivism and his Religion of Humanity, whence the term "humanism" emerges to name the belief system of some nonbelievers. Derided as a sect and a "College of Atheists," the *idéologues* were attacked so successfully by Napoleon and Chateaubriand that their positive appellation became Marx's term for "false class consciousness" within just fifty years of its coinage. Kennedy, "Ideology," 353–54.
2. The IRS agrees, as have US courts. See Blankholm, "Secularism and Secular People." Federally, the American Ethical Union, like its member societies, is a religious 501(c)3 nonprofit. Because it is a "church," in the parlance of the IRS, it need not file financial-disclosure statements. GuideStar, "American Ethical Union Inc." See Washington Ethical Society v. District of Columbia, 249 F.2d 127 (B.C. Cir. 1957).
3. A vast literature argues for converting to nonbelief and, in the process, specifies the proper beliefs of nonbelievers. The most prominent examples in recent years

are the writings of the so-called New Atheists, whose worldview and antireligious sentiments are not so new but whose targets have been timely. Harris, *End of Faith*; Harris, *Letter to a Christian Nation*; Dawkins, *God Delusion*; Dennett, *Breaking the Spell*; Hitchens, *God Is Not Great*.

4. Fazzino and Cragun, "Splitters!"
5. This book is an empiricist investigation of the secular paradox. For a superb example of a philosophical approach, see Alexandre Kojève's *Atheism*. Kojève also begins by inquiring into the paradox of "atheistic religion" (1). His *Atheism* is unfinished, however; it is a sketch more than a monograph. Though he never completes his inquiry, he recognizes the importance of moving from abstract philosophical arguments to the experience of the atheist and, eventually, to the variety of ways in which atheists actually live in the world: "Further on I would like to supplement concretely in this direction the 'demonstration' given by me, the phenomenological description and the ontological analysis of atheism. To this end, I will have to speak about different life attitudes (scientific, active, aesthetic, religious, and philosophical) of the 'human being in the world,' above all the atheistic, alongside this the theistic as well since here too the contrast with theism will help us to clarify the essence of atheism. Finally, I will have to describe and analyze the fullness of the givenness of the atheistic 'human being in the world' to herself (of course, all this will be superficial and incomplete)" (114). My inquiry into the lived experience of the secular paradox works toward Kojève's aim, though surely in ways he would not expect.
6. Robbins, "Continuity Thinking."
7. On creeds and baptism as distinctively Christian attempts to produce uniformity of belief, which in turn structure the category of "belief" and its applicability to other cultures, see Ruel, *Belief, Ritual and the Securing of Life*.
8. Robbins argues that anthropologists should be more inclusive when deciding whether groups that convert to Christianity are in fact Christian ("Continuity Thinking," 16–17). See also Bielo, "Belief, Deconversion, and Authenticity"; Cannell, *Anthropology of Christianity*, 1–50; Garriott and O'Neill, "Who Is a Christian?" New Atheists like Sam Harris and Richard Dawkins also engage in debates over who is a true Christian, arguing that religious moderates are hypocrites who enable more genuine Christians the cover of reason. See Harris, *Letter to a Christian Nation*; Dawkins, *God Delusion*.
9. For an opposing perspective on the efficacy of belief for understanding religion, see Lopez, "Belief." Such criticisms of "belief" have become canon among scholars of religion, but they offer little help in explaining ontological communities like organized nonbelievers in the United States, who take beliefs seriously even as they disavow having them. On the aversion to "belief" among scholars of religion and the category's usefulness for understanding people who organize themselves in terms of belief, see Hungerford, *Postmodern Belief*. For a critical but sympathetic response to Hungerford, see Rubenstein, "Twilight of the Doxai." Rubenstein is part of a tradition of skepticism that considers criticism of assertions of belief to

be the process of pursuing truth. Surely, this a/theological tradition is at least a cousin of atheism, though not one I found prevalent among organized nonbelievers in the United States. I was trained in this tradition as a decades-long reader of Continental philosophy and as a graduate student at Columbia University, working with Mark C. Taylor. See M. Taylor, *Erring*. One might call a/theological skepticism my subterranean religion, if the latter could be queered enough to contain its ostensibly secular opposite. In turn, this book could fairly be called an a/theological anthropology of secularism or an empiricist a/theology.

10. Freedom From Religion Foundation, "Billboards in Action!"
11. On "positive" and "negative" or "active" and "passive" versions of atheism, see Flew, *God, Freedom, and Immortality*, 13–30; G. Smith, *Atheism*; M. Martin, *Atheism*, 281.
12. Blumenberg, *Legitimacy of the Modern Age*.
13. Fahmy, "Key Findings about Americans' Belief in God."
14. On the role of a "higher power" in Alcoholics Anonymous and other related movements, see Travis, *Language of the Heart*; Taves, *Revelatory Events*.
15. This was also the approach of the Free Religious Association (FRA), founded in 1867, mostly by Unitarians. The FRA was a precursor to Ethical Culture, a movement founded by Felix Adler. Adler was president of the Free Religious Association before deciding to found his own movement, which was also influenced by his father's Reform Judaism. Persons, *Free Religion*. That contemporary members of Ethical Culture should espouse these ideas—or that those who do would gravitate to the movement—is a testament to their long-standing influence.
16. A Unitarian minister I interviewed in Minneapolis told me that "spirituality" is "a hard word to avoid." See also Sam Harris's appropriation of the term to describe Buddhism's phenomenological approach to consciousness, which Harris considers secular, in *Waking Up*.
17. Post, *Popular Freethought in America*; Warren, *American Freethought*.
18. Jacoby, *Freethinkers*, 4.
19. Warren, *American Freethought*, 4.
20. New York Freethinker's Association, "Proceedings and Addresses," 116.
21. New York Freethinker's Association, 125.
22. Gaylor, *Women without Superstition*; Jacoby, *Freethinkers*.
23. "Tell Us Why You're a Freethinker," 5. The editorial prompt to readers does not cite its dictionary source.
24. Freedom From Religion Foundation, "Greater Sacramento FFRF Chapter."
25. On the importance of individualism and "freethinking" in Unitarian Universalism, see Leitgeb, "Building Theology, Reinscribing Subjectivity"; and Hoop, "Being a Community of Individuals." Leitgeb relies on Foucault, Asad, and Connolly to characterize subjectivity formation among members of UU: "Unitarian Universalism relies on these discourses of individualism, personal sovereignty, freedom of belief, and the process of evaluating truth claims through properly educated senses of reason." ("Building Theology, Reinscribing Subjectivity," 7). On

creed aversion and the concern over "creeping creedalism" among UU members, see Leitgeb, "Building Theology, Reinscribing Subjectivity," 33–39, 103–28.
26. Matthew Engelke observes the same self-discovery among British humanists, in "On Atheism and Non-religion."
27. I explore the history of humanism and its relationship with secularism at greater length in my contribution to the *Oxford Handbook of Secularism*: Blankholm, "Secularism, Humanism, and Secular Humanism."
28. Olds, *American Religious Humanism*; E. Wilson, *Genesis of a Humanist Manifesto*, 10. W. Creighton Peden presents a longer and more scholar-centric history of the rise of humanism by emphasizing Ralph Waldo Emerson, Octavius Brooks Frothingham, Francis E. Abbot, William James, Potter, George Burman Foster, Edward Scribner Ames, and A. Eustace Haydon ("Rise of American Humanism").
29. Olds, *American Religious Humanism*, 59, 97; Dietrich, *What Is an Atheist?*, 14.
30. Olds, *American Religious Humanism*, 33, 56, 205n5; C. Winston, *This Circle of Earth*; Walter, *Humanism*, 66; Royle, *Victorian Infidels*, 55, 59–106, 126–29; Budd, *Varieties of Unbelief*, 70–71. The Rationalist Press Association has persisted through various transformations, and in 2002 it became the Rationalist Association.
31. Olds, *American Religious Humanism*, 127–33; Straton, *Famous New York Fundamentalist-Modernist Debates*.
32. American Humanist Association, "Humanist Manifesto I"; E. Wilson, *Genesis of a Humanist Manifesto*.
33. American Humanist Association, "Humanist Manifesto I."
34. Fazzino and Cragun, "Splitters!," 69–71.
35. Today, AHA avoids qualifying its humanism as either secular or religious, though it is willing to argue in court that it is a religion. Blankholm, "Secularism and Secular People."
36. For more on the construction of the secular humanism bugaboo by the Religious Right in the 1960s, '70s, and '80s, see Toumey, "Evolution and Secular Humanism"; Pfeffer, "How Religious Is Secular Humanism?," 14.
37. Whitehead and Conlan, "Establishment of the Religion of Secular Humanism."
38. Whitehead and Conlan, 12.
39. LaHaye, *Battle for the Mind*, 27–30; Schaeffer, *How Should We Live Then?*
40. Fellowship of Humanity v. County of Alameda, 153 Cal. App. 2d 673 (1957); *Washington Ethical Society*, 249 F.2d. 127.
41. "Having It Both Ways," 40; Speckhardt, "Humanist Tax Exemption."
42. For a recent and prominent example in the field of US religion, see Schmidt, *Village Atheists*.
43. Edgell, Gerteis, and Hartmann, "Atheists as 'Other.'"
44. Flipping the notion of this contradiction on its head, filmmaker Jeremiah Camara has made a documentary about the contradiction he sees in Black Americans' continued support for religion: *Contradiction*. The documentary has been screened in local nonbeliever communities throughout the United States.

45. Evans, *Burden of Black Religion*.
46. I discuss this problem at greater length in chapter 2. For historical criticism of the Black church and the role of Christianity in Black life, see Frazier, *Negro Church in America*; and Hart, "One Percenters." For a recovery of the presence of Protestantism in Black life in the middle of the twentieth century that tries to evenhandedly engage what this inheritance enables and forecloses, see Sorett, *Spirit in the Dark*.
47. Edgell, Frost, and Stewart, "From Existential to Social Understandings of Risk"; Schnabel et al., "Gender and Atheism." For an ethnographic study of stigma management among nonbelievers, see Loren and Rambo, "God Smites You!"; Pond, "Living without God."
48. Whitmarsh, *Battling the Gods*.
49. Palmer, *Reading Lucretius in the Renaissance*, 21–22.
50. Kors, *D'Holbach's Coterie*; Kors, *Atheism in France*; Kors, "Atheism of D'Holbach and Naigeon."
51. J. Butler, *Bodies That Matter*, 172–75.
52. Loren and Rambo, "God Smites You!"
53. Gaylor, *Women without Superstition*; Ginzberg, "Hearts of Your Readers"; Block, "Going to Church"; Pinn, *By These Hands*; Floyd-Thomas, *Origins of Black Humanism*; Cameron, *Black Freethinkers*.
54. Joan Scott supports her analysis, in *Sex and Secularism*.
55. Quack, "Outline of a Relational Approach to 'Nonreligion.'"
56. Holland, "Agnosticism"; LePoidevin, *Agnosticism*, 21.
57. Huxley, "Agnosticism," 237–38.
58. García and Blankholm, "Social Context of Organized Nonbelief." The essay relies on a database that García and I built of all the local nonbeliever groups in the United States.
59. Ritchey, "One Nation under God"; Jesse Smith, "Becoming an Atheist in America"; Jesse Smith, "Creating a Godless Community"; LeDrew, "Discovering Atheism."
60. Descartes, *Discourse on Method*; Spinoza, *Spinoza Reader*.
61. Bourdieu and Wacquant, *Invitation to Reflexive Sociology*; Quack, "Outline of a Relational Approach to 'Nonreligion.'"
62. I published an essay on this briefing: Blankholm, "Political Advantages of a Polysemous Secular."
63. C. Brown, *Healing Gods*; Bender, "Review of Healing Gods."
64. Harris, *End of Faith*; Harris, *Letter to a Christian Nation*.
65. Husserl, *Ideas*; Heidegger, *Being and Time*; Sartre, *Being and Nothingness*.
66. James, *Varieties of Religious Experience*; Proudfoot, *Religious Experience*; Taves, *Religious Experience Reconsidered*.
67. Harris, *Waking Up*, 6.
68. Mark C. Taylor discusses this conceptual trauma as constitutive of the a/theological in *Erring*. See also Caruth, *Unclaimed Experience*.

CHAPTER 2. COMMUNITY

1. Engelhart, "After a Schism, a Question"; "Atheist Church Schism."
2. Sunday Assembly New York City, "Assemblies Are on Hiatus."
3. "Godless Revival."
4. This quote is from a private Google group to which I had access.
5. This quote is also from the same private Google group. On the different uses of "secular" and "secularism" and the productivity of their confusion for secular activists, see Blankholm, "Political Advantages of a Polysemous Secular."
6. Hoesly, "Your Wedding, Your Way"; Calhoun, Jurgensmeyer, and VanAntwerpen, introduction to *Rethinking Secularism*, 9–10.
7. American Humanist Association, "Humanist Manifesto I"; American Humanist Association, "Humanist Manifesto II"; Kurtz, *Humanist Manifesto 2000*; American Humanist Association, "Humanism and Its Aspirations."
8. Humanist Society, "About the Humanist Society"; P. Smith, "Spitting with the Wind."
9. K. Winston, "Federal Prisons Will Now Recognize Humanism."
10. On the importance of mimetic play in the history of "religion," in the positivistic sense of the long history of that which now bears its name, see Bellah, *Religion in Human Evolution*; Burchell, Gordon, and Miller, *Foucault Effect*.
11. Lipka, "10 Facts about Religion in America."
12. Sehat, *Myth of American Religious Freedom*; Crapanzano, *Serving the Word*.
13. Paul DiMaggio and Walter Powell describe governmental prescriptions that shape an organizational landscape as "coercive isomorphism," and they contrast it with "mimetic isomorphism," which is an organizational response to uncertainty, and "normative isomorphism," which results from organizational professionalization. DiMaggio and Powell acknowledge that in empirical reality these types of isomorphism overlap, which is the case with nonbeliever organizations. The gamesmanship of those who lead nonbeliever groups is more akin to mimetic play that models itself after the strategies of religious groups than to submission or coercion. Surely, the US government and its tax code are coercive, but nonbelievers play the game in more than one way, sometimes by refusing to play, as in the case of the Freedom From Religion Foundation. Nonbeliever organizations can respond to governmental coercion by modeling their strategies on religious groups, i.e., by copying them mimetically, or they can refuse to do so in order to maintain their secular purity. All of this work requires professionalization in the form of an expert class of leaders, including attorneys, who understand the stakes and share with one another potential strategies in response to coercion. See DiMaggio and Powell, "Iron Cage Revisited."
14. Sullivan, *Impossibility of Religious Freedom*; Sullivan, *Ministry of Presence*; Stahl, *Enlisting Faith*.
15. Bialecki and Hoenas del Pinal, "Beyond Logos"; Keane, *Christian Moderns*; Derrida, "Faith and Knowledge."

16. Harrison, *Territories of Science and Religion*; McCutcheon, "They Licked the Platter Clean"; Storm, "Superstition, Secularism, and Religion Trinary"; Wheatley, "US Colonial Governance of Superstition and Fanaticism"; McCrary, "Superstitious Subjects"; Storm, *Invention of Religion in Japan*.
17. McKinnon, "Sociological Definitions"; Wittgenstein, *Philosophical Investigations*.
18. Doe v. Acton-Boxborough Regional School District, 468 (Mass. 64 2014).
19. Quack, "Outline of a Relational Approach to 'Nonreligion.'"
20. "Forum: Recovering the Immanentist Tradition."
21. Brad Gregory's criticisms of nominalism and the story he tells about the rise of secular modernity are typical of a long history of Catholic critique of secularism (*Unintended Reformation*). On the coincidence of Asadian and Catholic critiques of secularism, see Greenberg, "Is Religious Freedom Protestant?"
22. The "Protestant-Secular" is a way of describing the close affinities between Protestantism and secularism. Careful analyses show their similarities, Protestantism's influential role in shaping secularism, and their common ancestors or shared structuring conditions. Less careful understandings lump the two together as if there is no substantive difference. Anidjar, "Secularism"; Fessenden, *Culture and Redemption*; Modern, *Secularism in Antebellum America*; Sorett, *Spirit in the Dark*; McCrary and Wheatley, "Protestant Secular."
23. Robert Yelle toes this line well by identifying a residuum from Protestantism that carries over into secularism. This debt or inheritance does not make secularism inherently Protestant, but it has consequences that are apparent in colonialism and in the laws of secular states, so it must be reckoned with. Yelle, *Language of Disenchantment*.
24. García and Blankholm, "Social Context of Organized Nonbelief."
25. For a volume that surveys a range of groups and approaches to studying them, see Cragun, Manning, and Fazzino, *Organized Secularism in the United States*.
26. Freedom From Religion Foundation, "Chapters."
27. Grayling, *God Argument*, 16. For critiques of how Grayling and the New Atheists imagine religion, see Eagleton, *Reason, Faith and Revolution*; and Beattie, *New Atheists*.
28. In *The God Problem*, Robert Wuthnow provides a concise summary of the criticisms that Grayling and the New Atheists level against religion. In their view, religion is irrational, uninformed, antidemocratic, destructive, and fraudulent. See Wuthnow, 7–44.
29. Asad, *Formations of the Secular*; Dressler and Mandair, *Secularism and Religion-Making*.
30. Veer, *Modern Spirit of Asia*.
31. Wenger, *Religious Freedom*; Wheatley, "US Colonial Governance of Superstition and Fanaticism"; Crosson, "Impossibility of Liberal Secularism."
32. Fernando, *Republic Unsettled*; Oliphant, "Circulations of the Sacred."

33. Levitt, "What Is Religion Anyway?" See also Levitt, "Impossible Assimilations." The same is arguably true for Mormons, which is a roundabout way of demonstrating their nonnormative Christianity. Brooks, *Disenchanted Lives*.
34. "Forum: Recovering the Immanentist Tradition."
35. Quack, *Disenchanting India*; Kaviraj, "Disenchantment Deferred."
36. For instance, the Bharatiya Janata Party's use of the term "secularism" in India would sound strange to the ear of many Europeans and Americans. See Veer, *Modern Spirit of Asia*, 161–62.
37. Sugrue, *Origins of the Urban Crisis*.
38. "Atheist Rabbi"; Wine, "Unbelief within Judaism," 455.
39. Wine, "Unbelief within Judaism," 455.
40. Epstein and Croft, "Godless Congregation."
41. See, for instance, Wine, *Judaism beyond God*.
42. Blankholm, "Secularism, Humanism, and Secular Humanism."
43. Biale, *Not in the Heavens*, 5.
44. Spinoza was not an avowed atheist like Marx and Freud. The French materialists appear to be the first people to have taken on the label as a self-appellation and did so in the late eighteenth century. The pantheism for which Spinoza was excommunicated from his synagogue in Amsterdam had a significant influence on freethinkers in succeeding centuries and is at the very least a monism in which the single substance of reality is coextensive with nature. For an account of the Enlightenment in which Spinoza figures prominently, see Israel, *Radical Enlightenment*. On Marx's relationship to secularism, see Blankholm, "Remembering Marx's Secularism."
45. Radest, *Toward Common Ground*, 14.
46. Goldman, "Philosophy of Atheism."
47. Stern, *Jewish Materialism*. Stern means several things by "materialism," but ontological materialism is certainly part of the movement he describes.
48. Stern, 106, 187.
49. Kaplan wanted to take "tradition seriously without taking it literally" (*Judaism without Supernaturalism*, 29).
50. Secular Judaism's relationship with the Reform tradition is complicated. Though Wine's nontheism did not cause him to be expelled from the Reform rabbinate, Reform holds individual humanistic congregations at arm's length. Gonzalez, "Temple with No Place for God." The Union of American Hebrew Congregations, the national Reform organization, refused to accept a humanistic congregation in Cincinnati that applied for membership in 1994 ("Atheist Rabbi").
51. "Dawkins: I'm a Cultural Christian."
52. Bowers, "Q&A with Richard Dawkins." Belief in the supremacy of Christian culture and the unique relationship between Christianity and democracy can be found across the political spectrum in Europe and North America, though especially among far-right cultural conservatives. Accetti, *What Is Christian Democracy?* Stephen Prothero has written on the white-supremacist terrorist Anders

Breivik's relationship to Christianity, in "My Take." The arch-conservative Steve Bannon is also an advocate of Christian culture: Steinmetz-Jenkins and Pheiffer, "Steve Bannon's Would-Be Coalition." Stern and Biale argue that those like Kaplan who developed a notion of "Jewish peoplehood" helped to distinguish Jewish identity from Jewish religiosity. This in turn undergirds the national identity of Israel, which relies on a conception of Jewishness that transcends the particulars of religious observance. Stern, *Jewish Materialism*; Biale, *Not in the Heavens*.

53. Levitt, "What Is Religion Anyway?," 108.
54. Levitt, "Revisiting Jewish Secularism in America."
55. Levitt, "Impossible Assimilations."
56. Anidjar, *Blood*.
57. Mehta, *Beyond Chrismukkah*. See also Alba, "Sociological Significance of the American Jewish Experience."
58. On the ways in which in some nonbeliever groups in the United States have approached the ministerial housing allowance, see Blankholm, "Secularism and Secular People."
59. On religious individualism, especially as it relates to what gets called "spirituality," see Altglas, *From Yoga to Kabbalah*. More research is needed on secularism and spirituality as practices that can be mediated by both individualism and institutional life—and, in turn, how this challenges the facile distinction between religion as institutional or communal and spirituality or secularism as individualist. Courtney Bender describes a way forward in *New Metaphysicals*.
60. Masuzawa, *Invention of World Religions*.
61. There is a rich tradition of atheist socialism in Mexico, though none of the nonbelievers I spoke with placed themselves within it. Lomnitz, "Secularism and the Mexican Revolution."
62. Fernando, "Belief and/in the Law"; Keane, *Christian Moderns*.
63. Evans, *Burden of Black Religion*; Savage, *Your Spirits Walk beside Us*; Masci, "5 Facts about Blacks and Religion in America."
64. Evans, *Burden of Black Religion*.
65. Raboteau, *Slave Religion*; Gerbner, *Christian Slavery*. Whether and how long these "retentions" survived is a subject of significant debate in African American studies.
66. See also the preface to Mintz and Price, *Birth of African American Culture*; Gerbner, "They Call Me Obea"; Evans, *Burden of Black Religion*; Du Bois, *Negro Church*.
67. Frazier broke with Du Bois, who described the Black Church as "the only social institution among the Negroes which started in the African forest and survived slavery." Du Bois, *Negro Church*, ii, quoted in Frazier, *Negro Church in America*, 13. Herskovits countered Frazier's argument that slavery completely destroyed any significant "retentions" from African culture, though he also promoted the idea that Black people are innately religious (*Myth of the Negro Past*). Raboteau acknowledges that both sides of the debate have merits, paving the way for later

studies that observe African "retentions" or "survivals" in African American culture without relying on the trope of innate religiosity (*Slave Religion*, 86). See also Chireau, *Black Magic*; Frazier, "Rejoinder"; Fauset, *Black Gods of the Metropolis*, 98–106.
68. Raboteau offers a careful perspectivism in his reading of the Herskovits-Frazier debate that is also useful for the study of the secular and its relationship to Christianity: "The resolution of the Herskovits-Frazier debate lies in recognizing the true aspects of both positions. It is not a debate with a winner and a loser, for using differing perspectives, both are right" (*Slave Religion*, 86).
69. Atheist activist Debbie Goddard has talked about Black atheists as a "double minority." Josephs, "Black Atheists Explain What It's Like."
70. Harris, "Forbidden Knowledge"; Amarasingam and Brewster, "Rise and Fall of the New Atheism."
71. Foundation Beyond Belief, "Interview: Sikivu Hutchinson."
72. On the double minority of Black atheism, see Josephs, "Black Atheists Explain What It's Like." On Afro-pessimist Black negativity, see Jared Sexton interviewed by Daniel Colucciello Barber, "On Black Negativity."
73. Sikivu Hutchinson makes the same point using the word "magically," in *Moral Combat*, 213.
74. Hart, "One Percenters," 686.
75. Sorett, *Spirit in the Dark*.
76. Crawley, *Blackpentecostal Breath*.
77. Hart, Sorett, and Crawley elaborate the tensions within Black life, but they also describe well the generative contradictions of the secular paradox. Blackness and secularism both struggle against claims to their innate religiosity, which overdetermine the power of their ambiguity. In *Divine Variations*, Terence Keel describes how Christian ideas fueled the racism of nineteenth-century race science. Sometimes Christian influence on race science was direct, and sometimes it structured the questions that scientists asked and how they narrated their explanations. Reading Hans Blumenberg, Keel shows that modernity often recapitulates Christian questions by "reoccupying" them (15–17). To be secular—to assert oneself as such—is also an answer to Christian questions under Christian conditions, though almost always in rejection of Christianity. Tidy arguments about the Christianity of science and secularism or the unique spiritual aesthetic of the Black tradition only superficially resolve the paradoxes that such a messy inheritance bequeaths. Care and honesty reveal a much more complicated and, for some people, less satisfying picture of a thing that is both/ and but not fully either, like the excesses of Blackpentecostalism that Crawley describes so well.
78. On the bodily discipline of Muslim practice, see Mahmood, *Politics of Piety*; and Hirschkind, *Ethical Soundscape*. On the distress and excitement of transgressing the bodily disciplines of traditions people have left, see Brooks, *Disenchanted Lives*; and Davidman, *Becoming Un-Orthodox*.

79. Alfredo García's doctoral dissertation describes the economic motivation for this aesthetic homogenization through an analysis of the gentrification of the Wynwood neighborhood of Miami, which took place with the guidance and investment of those who developed parts of Brooklyn, New York. García, "Walls of Wynwood."
80. Simon Cottee describes similar upheaval among ex-Muslims in *The Apostates*.
81. Lean, "Dawkins, Harris, Hitchens."
82. Harris, *End of Faith*.
83. Amarasingam and Brewster, "Rise and Fall of the New Atheism."
84. For example, "Fighting Allah, Defending Muslims" was the name of a panel featuring EXMNA members hosted by the Secular Panthers secular student group at Georgia State University in 2018. Ex-Muslims of North America, "Fighting Allah, Defending Muslims."
85. For more on the affective turn and its impact on the study of religion, see Schaefer, *Religious Affects*. On the secular body and its sensorium, see Hirschkind, "Is There a Secular Body?"; and Asad, "Thinking about the Secular Body."
86. On the feeling of being secular, see Scheer, Fadil, and Johansen, *Secular Bodies, Affects, and Emotions*.
87. For another zoological analogy to explain the secular, see Seales, *Secular Spectacle*, 1. Seales likens southern US secularism to "a greasy pig."

CHAPTER 3. RITUAL

1. KCET, "La Fonda Restaurant"; Colker, "Musician Nati Cano Dies at 81."
2. On the use of Spanish revival architecture in southern California, see Sagarena, *Aztlán and Arcadia*.
3. In Mexico, the event is often called El Día de Muertos, but as is common in the Anglophone United States, the event's organizers titled it without the definite article: Día de los Muertos. In the plural, Los Días de los Muertos refers to the period from October 31 through November 2. In the singular, El Día de Muertos refers to November 2.
4. On the complexity of Latinx identity and its unique mixture of influences, or *mestizaje*, see Anzaldúa, *Borderlands / La Frontera*. For a more contemporary overview, see Avalos, "Latinx Indigeneities and Christianities."
5. Freud, *Uncanny*.
6. Among scholars of ritual, these are also called "rites of passage," following the nomenclature of van Gennep, *Rites of Passage*. For more on secular weddings as life-cycle rituals, see Aston, "Formations of a Secular Wedding." See also Kasselstrand, "We Still Wanted That Sense of Occasion."
7. In "Coffin Question," Matthew Engelke finds the same to be true among British humanists, who prefer not to have the body present and want a "memorial service" rather than a "funeral." The presence of the body encourages people to address it as if it were still the person, while in a materialist ontology, that person

is now dead. Humanists seek to avoid the challenge this poses, which Engelke dubs "the coffin question." I discuss this issue more in chapter 5, on tradition.
8. Engelke finds that British humanists use the same distancing strategy (37–38).
9. Sarah Pike observes similar cultural appropriation among Neopagan ritual creators. They "claim that their usefulness is judged by the needs of the self—'what works,' to use their words. Neopagans turn to the self as a measure for moral certitude in response to ethical disputes about borrowing and the attacks of some Native American critics. What is 'good' or 'bad' is measured by effects on the self, rather than against any absolute standards of judgment" (*Earthly Bodies, Magical Selves*, xxi).
10. Asad, *Genealogies of Religion*; Geertz, *Interpretation of Cultures*, 90.
11. Asad, *Genealogies of Religion*; Masuzawa, *Invention of World Religions*.
12. Jonathan Z. Smith, *To Take Place*, 96–103. Lofton describes how debates among Protestants effected a discourse of ritual specialization, which she calls *scientia ritus*. This specialized discourse laid the ground work for the abstraction of "ritual" and "Ritualism" as interreligious and even secular categories. "*Scientia ritus*," Lofton writes, "describes the near-obsessive definitional precision by which ritual became a subject for lay appropriation and for social scientific study" (*Consuming Religion*, 67).
13. Taves, "Camp Meeting," 121. Taves analyzes the evangelical Camp Meeting to show that Protestants can reject what they consider ritual while embracing what scholars would consider ritual.
14. Bell, *Ritual*, 264.
15. Sarah M. Pike's research on ritual among Neopagans in the United States indicates that the nonbelievers I spent time with are representative of a larger American trend toward self-conscious ritual creation. Pike, *Earthly Bodies, Magical Selves*.
16. Bell, *Ritual*, 265.
17. Wade Clark Roof develops the concept of "reflexive spirituality," which describes how late-twentieth-century seekers recognize their own perspective as one among many and engage with religion in the abstract, as a sociologist would (*Spiritual Marketplace*, 74–76). Roof's theory of reflexivity among seekers applies just as well to twenty-first-century secular people who engage with religion self-consciously, interpreting rituals in order to abstract their gist and then creating rituals anew from the pieces they have appropriated.
18. Harris, *Waking Up*.
19. On the homogeneous time of the secular, see Asad, *Formations of the Secular*, 2–5. Asad draws this concept from Charles Taylor, who gets it from Benedict Anderson. C. Taylor, "Modes of Secularism"; Anderson, *Imagined Communities*.
20. Freedom From Religion Foundation, "FFRF Urges Atlanta to Abandon the Supernatural."
21. FFRF v. Geithner, No. 11-CV-626, Defendant's Brief in Support of Its Motion for Summary Judgment, at 17 (W.D. Wis. 2011).

22. For an analysis of the lawsuit and its implications, see Blankholm, "Secularism and Secular People."
23. Along the same lines, Dipesh Chakrabarty analyzes "the practice of abstraction that helps us to universalize": "We need universals to produce critical readings of social injustices. Yet the universal and the analytical produce forms of thought that ultimately evacuate the place of the local. It does not matter if this is done in an empirical idiom, for the empirical can often be a result of the universal, just as the particular follows from the general. Such thought fundamentally tends to sever the relationship between thought and modes of human belonging" (*Provincializing Europe*, 254–55).
24. See Asad, "Toward a Genealogy of the Concept of Ritual"; Asad, *Secular Translations*.
25. C. Taylor, *Secular Age*, 26–29.
26. Many scholars have in recent years critiqued the use of "religion" as an analytic category. For a paradigmatic example, see Arnal and McCutcheon, *Sacred Is the Profane*.
27. This is Talal Asad's "more modest endeavor: An inquiry into what is involved when 'the secular' is invoked—who tries to define it, in what context, how, and why" ("Thinking about the Secular Body," 673). Asad echoes the method that Linell Cady and Elizabeth Shakman Hurd describe: "One must track the diverse ways the insistent claims to being secular are made" (*Comparative Secularisms*, 12).
28. Bourdieu, "Genesis and Structure of the Religious Field"; Bourdieu, *Field of Cultural Production*.
29. Quack, "Outline of a Relational Approach to 'Nonreligion.'"
30. Nietzsche, *On the Genealogy of Morals*, 119. Emphasis in original.
31. The secular paradox is also a "not," which is Mark C. Taylor's term for the aporia of constitutive negation (*Nots*). During Courtney Bender's fieldwork among spiritual practitioners in Cambridge, Massachusetts, she observed that scholars who study spirituality are deeply entangled with those who practice it (*New Metaphysicals*, 5–18). Like nonbelievers, people who call themselves "spiritual" often read the work of scholars, and they appropriate its theories and technical terms for their own ends. Bender found herself "caught . . . in a web of relations" when studying spiritual people (15). She urges scholars to make entanglements objects of their research—to study the knots in which they find themselves. See Bender, "Things in Their Entanglements," 67. I have mostly adopted this reflexive approach, which binds my analytic voice with empirical strands from interviews and field anecdotes, as well as other scholars' research.
32. See, for instance, Selby, "Required Romance."
33. Kathryn Lofton offers a contemporary approach along these lines in *Consuming Religion*.
34. Through transposition, decontextualization, and rearticulation, the a/theological tradition preserves the religious through processes of blasphemy and transforma-

tion. It transposes, decontextualizes, and recontextualizes elements of the religious into a secular framework in order to demonstrate how Christianity haunts the secular but also to make Christianity ventriloquize secularism. See M. Taylor, *Erring*; Onishi, *Sacrality of the Secular*.
35. See Blankholm, "Self-Critique and Moral Ground"; Mahmood, "Cultural Studies and Ethnic Absolutism"; Mahmood, "Brief Response to Stuart Hall's Comments"; Hall, "Culture, Community, Nation"; Hall, "Response to Saba Mahmood."
36. Blankholm, "No Part of the World."
37. Protestantism and secularism negate—they disenchant—but they also affirm. Secularism is more paradoxical because it negates itself and its own religion-like qualities, whereas Protestantism negates those aspects of religion it associates with Catholicism but not all religiosity. In other words, Protestantism approaches a paradox where it is most like the Catholicism it negates, and secularism approaches a paradox where it is most like religion. See Yelle, *Language of Disenchantment*.
38. When translating into English from Arabic, "blasphemy" captures a range of concepts that have no perfect analogues in Christian and post-Christian cultures. Because Christianity is the source of "blasphemy" as a concept, it retains Christian particularity at the expense of non-Christianity. See Asad, "Free Speech, Blasphemy, and Secular Criticism." See also Asad, "Reflections on Blasphemy and Secular Criticism."
39. Lucas McCracken, a PhD student in the Department of Religious Studies at the University of California, Santa Barbara, drew my attention to the valuable term "transpose" in an essay he wrote for a seminar on secularism. I borrow it, by way of McCracken, from Martin Heidegger's reading of René Descartes in *Introduction to Phenomenological Research*. As McCracken notes, Ryan Coyne explores Heidegger's use of the term "transpose" in *Heidegger's Confessions*, 116. In Heidegger's use, as in Coyne's, "transpose" refers to the translation from one ontological domain to another, namely, from Christian theology to secular philosophy.
40. On the blasphemy of ex-Mormons, see Brooks, *Disenchanted Lives*. On ex-Muslims, see Cottee, *Apostates*.
41. Foucault, *History of Sexuality*.
42. Derrida, "Faith and Knowledge."
43. Hirschkind, *Ethical Soundscape*; Mahmood, *Politics of Piety*.
44. Durkheim, *Elementary Forms of Religious Life*; Douglas, *Purity and Danger*.
45. Freud, "On Narcissism," 74.
46. The *New York Times* organizes an archive of stories that it associates with the "Danish cartoon controversy" and its aftermath, which includes articles published through 2015 ("Danish Cartoon Controversy").
47. Wendy Brown captures their ambivalence well when summarizing Talal Asad's argument about the cartoon controversy: "The modern Western opposition between freedom and blasphemy permits Westerners to believe that they are free of the restrictions a discourse of blasphemy imposes, while denying the belonging

to a particular way of life that secularism must protect in other, less forthrightly religious terms" (introduction to *Is Critique Secular?*, 15).
48. Barker does not help his case with this blurb that he gave for Peter Boghossian's 2013 book *A Manual for Creating Atheists*: "Since atheism is truly Good News [i.e., literally, the 'gospel'], it should not be hidden under a bushel. Peter Boghossian shows us how to take it to the highways and the byways. I love it!" Federal attorneys making their case against Barker and FFRF appear to have been unaware of this blurb. FFRF v. Geithner, Defendant's Brief in Support of Its Motion for Summary Judgment, at 17 (W.D. Wis. 2011).
49. Mayanthi Fernando shows how Muslim French cannot be fully abstracted into French citizens because they continue to be interpellated as bearing their religious and cultural particularity. The contradiction of being Muslim and French is the displaced contradiction of the French Republic's self-understanding, which depends on an inclusive, abstract notion of citizenship and a specific notion of the authentic Frenchman (gender intended). Fernando elaborates the role of abstraction most fully in chapter 2 of *Republic Unsettled*. On the gendered binaries of French Republicanism, see Scott, *Sex and Secularism*. In *Secular Translations*, Asad focuses at length on the practice of secular abstraction and the ways in which particulars cling to abstract concepts despite their ostensible removal.
50. Avery Gordon analyzes critically how this process works among sociologists, in *Ghostly Matters*. I agree with Gordon that we should engage the past that haunts, neither disavowing it nor attempting to escape it through abstract categories that only appear to be free of ghosts because they seem to be free of particulars. All inheritance is haunted.
51. On Pythagoras, see Russell, "Pythagoras." On the ways in which transhumanism can appears secular, spiritual, or religious, see Farman, "Mind out of Place."
52. For a comparative study that highlights how the low countries have embraced humanism and even secular humanism as a religion-like worldview or life stance, see Nutte and Gasenbeek, *Organised Humanism in the World*.
53. Schwartzman, "What If Religion Is Not Special?" Secular activists in the United States are acutely aware of the differences between these modes of abstraction, and they calibrate their legal strategies accordingly. For an analysis of three lawsuits filed by nonbelievers' groups that show the role abstraction plays in producing legal secularism and framing secular people, see Blankholm, "Secularism and Secular People."
54. Holley, "How the Satanic Temple Forced Phoenix Lawmakers"; "Satanists Get Phoenix to Drop Council Prayer."
55. Town of Greece v. Galloway, 572 U.S. 565 (2014).
56. Victoria Smolkin's excellent history of Soviet atheism demonstrates this idea well. She divides Soviet attempts to promote atheism into three stages. In the first, the state tries to create an atheist population by eliminating religion. Recognizing the failure of this eliminative approach, it then tries to indoctrinate the Soviet people with a materialist worldview. When state researchers realize that this attempt pro-

duces indifference rather than committed materialists, the state begins promoting atheism as an entire way of life, including rituals and other elements that would have previously been considered too religious. Soviet efforts demonstrate that successful conversion to atheism or secularism is not merely the elimination of religion or even simply indoctrination into a new set of beliefs but the remaking of an entire way of life. Smolkin, *Sacred Space Is Never Empty*.

57. "Transubstantiation" is a more accurate term for ontological change, but I have chosen "translation" for two reasons. "Translation" is less theologically technical than "transubstantiation" and thus better able to express that secular translation is a quotidian practice for secular people. "Translation" is also better because it can capture discourse, which includes ontological and epistemological assumptions. "Translation" is a more everyday word and also more capacious. Talal Asad uses "translation" to refer to movement across discourses, in *Secular Translations*. According to Asad, "when verbal models are used to discipline the religious body (or techniques used to write and play a piece of music) they are not strictly speaking *replaced* by nonverbal sign systems because signs as signs gradually disappear into *the way* a particular life is expressed and lived" (5–6). For more on discourse and discursive tradition, see Asad, "Idea of an Anthropology of Islam." Noreen Khawaja has criticized "translation" for being too literal and triumphant. "Secular translation," she argues, is inadequate for describing atheistic existentialism's complex relationship with Christianity. The existentialisms of Heidegger and Sartre are not merely secularized versions of Kierkegaard, shorn of their religiosity; their imbrication with Christianity goes much deeper. Clearly, I agree, though I also recognize that from the perspective of secular people, "secular translation" is a mode of purifying the secular of its religious pollution, even if it remains impure from other perspectives like Khawaja's "subthematic" approach. Khawaja, *Religion of Existence*, 19–20.

58. Talal Asad describes the discursive translation of Christian concepts into secular ones to show that in their rearticulation, there is a rupture, and they are transformed: "Thus, when Jürgen Habermas argues that the Christian concept of *imago Dei*, 'Man created in the image of God,' can be translated into the political demand that all human beings be treated equally, he ignores a semantic rupture. In order for the idea of man created in the image of God to be given a worldly sense, it must first be purged of the belief (much emphasized by Protestant theologians) that the Fall, leading to Adam's expulsion from Eden into the world, rendered man corrupt—and therefore redeemable only by divine grace. That idea must then be put into a context in which rights and dignity are assumed to be universal and unconditional—an a priori assumption with *no* connection whatever to otherworldliness or divine grace" (*Secular Translations*, 17).

59. Harris, *Waking Up*. On the secular translation of Buddhism into US psychotherapy, see Helderman, "Drawing the Boundaries between 'Religion' and 'Secular'"; For a history of the integration of Buddhist mindfulness practices into secular therapy and cognitive science research, see J. Wilson, *Mindful America*.

60. When organized nonbelievers have invited me to present my research at their events, I have found that they appreciate the way I talk about their ambivalence and accept my caveats that they are not *actually* religious but are by definition in a condition in which they cannot help but appear as both religious and not.

61. This is, in essence, the Epicurean position. See, for instance, Stephen Greenblatt's introduction to *The Swerve*, in which he discusses his mother's death anxiety and the way in which the philosophy of Lucretius helped him overcome it. Greenblatt is a twenty-first-century secular American who has drawn on the Epicurean tradition as if he found it anew in order to announce his affirmative way of life, which is most often construed as an absence. He is part of a long tradition of secular people who have found themselves already present in Epicureanism. I discuss his role in the shaping of this tradition in chapter 5. See also Kors, *Epicureans and Atheists in France*.

62. For a beautiful phenomenological analysis of secular finitude, love, and death, see Carlson, *With the World at Heart*.

63. For more examples, see *Atheist Nomads*, "Hispanic Atheists with Jose Alvarado."

64. Charlton, *Secular Religions in France*.

65. Gordon, *Ghostly Matters*.

CHAPTER 4. CONVERSION

1. Launched by the Richard Dawkins Foundation in 2007, the Out Campaign encourages atheists and other kinds of nonbelievers to announce their nonbelief in public. I discuss the campaign at greater length later in this chapter. The red "A" is a "scarlet letter" that stands for "Atheist" and symbolizes the stigma that nonbelievers experience. The campaign's aim is to normalize atheism by encouraging self-identity and awareness.

2. On the growth of the religiously unaffiliated in the United States and the complex factors that have led to it, see Hout and Fischer, "Explaining Why More Americans Have No Religious Preference."

3. "Pakistan Honour Killings on the Rise."

4. Brighenti, Xu, and Yaffe-Bellany, "Worker Smashes 'Racist' Panel."

5. Brighenti and Yaffe-Bellany, "Yale Gags Rehired Cafeteria Worker."

6. The Organization of America States was founded in 1948 as an intercontinental effort to oppose the threat of communism in the Western Hemisphere and promote capitalist interests, especially those of the United States. With the creation of the Inter-American Commission on Human Rights, an autonomous adjunct of the OAS, the organization's mission evolved. As with any international body, power is not distributed evenly among the member states, and despite its ostensible defense of human rights and the pressure it applies on governments that violate them, it continues to reflect the vested power interests of the Western Hemisphere. See Farer, "Rise of the Inter-American Human Rights Regime." On human rights as a relatively recent discourse in international politics, see Eckel and Moyn, *Breakthrough*.

7. There has been no press release announcing the initiative, it does not appear on the group's website, and neither Alfredo nor his group appears in Pro Publica's database of lobbying arrangements. Merrill, "Lobbying Registrations."
8. Camus writes, "There exists an obvious fact that seems utterly moral: namely, that a man is always prey to his truths. Once he has admitted them, he cannot free himself from them. One has to pay something" (*Myth of Sisyphus*, 35).
9. Dillahunty raises the question of whether religion is a cancer, but he argues against that equation as a bad analogy. Aaron's attempt stands regardless because he wanted to start a conversation about an active debate rather than take a particular side. Dillahunty, "Don't Be a Dick."
10. Writing on Soren Kierkegaard, Howard Hong identifies the paradox of a good joke: "Laughter arises essentially from an awareness of contradiction, opposites, basic contrasts. Laughter means the distinction between appearance and reality, what is expected and what is, what is and what ought to be" ("Comic, Satire, Irony, and Humor," 99). Thank you to Lucas McCracken for this reference and for long conversations about humor and philosophy.
11. New York City Skeptics, "Drinking Skeptically."
12. On the history of the antivaccination movement in the United States, see Willrich, *Pox*; Colgrove, "Science in a Democracy"; Davidovitch, "Negotiating Dissent."
13. Jonathan Simmons calls skepticism a "lifestyle movement" to contrast it with the secular "social movement." He argues that the former is a weaker collective identity that advocates individual lifestyle change as the path to social change. "Critical thinking" is the key to a skeptic's "conversion" process. Though Simmons uses the term "conversion" twice in his essay, he puts it in single quotes, reflecting the religion-like ambiguity of the secular paradox. Simmons, "Not That Kind of Atheist."
14. Hammer, "New Age Religion and the Sceptics"; Hecht, *Doubt*. See also Walker, "Humbug in American Religion."
15. For a history of the modern skeptic movement and its antecedents, see Hammer, "New Age Religion and the Sceptics."
16. See Albanese, *Republic of Mind and Spirit*; and Hammer, *Claiming Knowledge*, especially chapter 5 on scientism.
17. Blankholm, "Political Advantages of a Polysemous Secular."
18. Popkin, *History of Scepticism*.
19. Hammer, "New Age Religion and the Sceptics," 382.
20. Sextus Empiricus deals deftly with the question of whether "skepticism" is an ism in his *Outlines of Skepticism*: "We take the same attitude to the question: Do Sceptics belong to a school? If you say that a school involves adherence to a number of beliefs which cohere both with one another and with what is apparent, and if you say that belief is assent to something unclear, then we shall say that Sceptics do not belong to any school. But if you count as a school a persuasion which, to all appearances, coheres with some account, the account showing how it is possible to live correctly (where 'correctly' is taken not only with reference to virtue, but

more loosely, and extends to the ability to suspend judgement)—in that case we say that Sceptics do belong to a school. For we coherently follow, to all appearances, an account which shows us a life in conformity with traditional customs and the law and persuasions and our own feelings" (7).

21. Boghossian, *Manual for Creating Atheists*, 39–40.
22. Boghossian, 51.
23. Boghossian, 13–14.
24. For the most pointed critique, see Hurd, *Beyond Religious Freedom*. The academic literature in this area is now robust; see, for example, Masuzawa, *Invention of World Religions*; Curtis, *Production of American Religious Freedom*; Fernando, *Republic Unsettled*; Storm, "Superstition, Secularism, and Religion Trinary"; Storm, *Invention of Religion in Japan*. See also Greenwald, "Sam Harris"; Lean, "Dawkins, Harris, Hitchens"; Hussain, "Scientific Racism."
25. Boghossian, *Manual for Creating Atheists*, 52.
26. Saba Mahmood dedicated her career to this sort of self-inquiry, as I make an effort to show in an essay on her influence on the study of religion and secularism: Blankholm, "Self-Critique and Moral Ground."
27. Hammer, "New Age Religion and the Sceptics," 382.
28. In *Prisms*, Theodor Adorno describes immanent criticism: "A successful work [of] immanent criticism is not one which resolves objective contradictions in a spurious harmony, but one which expresses the harmony negatively by embodying the contradictions, pure and uncompromised, in its innermost structure. Confronted with this kind of work, the verdict 'mere ideology' loses its meaning. At the same time, however, immanent criticism holds in evidence that the mind has always been under a spell. On its own it is unable to resolve the contradictions under which it labours. Even the most radical reflection of the mind on its own failure is limited by the fact that it remains a reflection, without altering the existence of which its failure bears witness" (31–32).
29. Kors, *Atheism in France*, 49. The morality of atheists has long been in question. Pierre Bayle, for instance, includes an essay titled "Atheism—Atheists" in his groundbreaking *Dictionnaire historique et critique*, published in several editions in the early eighteenth century. The essay is chiefly a defense of atheists' morality. Bayle, *Dictionary Historical and Critical*. See also Holbach, *System of Nature*. Kantians, like Felix Adler, the founder of Ethical Culture, find room for moral universals in an otherwise materialist ontology. On Adler and Kant, see Chuman, "Between Secularism and Supernaturalism." For a different attempt at grounding atheist morality, see Harris, *Moral Landscape*.
30. Edgell, Gerteis, and Hartmann, "Atheists as 'Other'"; Edgell et al., "Atheists and Other Cultural Outsiders."
31. Holyoake, *Origin and Nature of Secularism*.
32. Radest, *Toward Common Ground*, 303–4.
33. Humanists International, "Amsterdam Declaration 1952."
34. Humanists International, "Amsterdam Declaration."

35. Boghossian, *Manual for Creating Atheists*, 38.
36. McCreight, "How I Unwittingly Infiltrated the Boys Club." See also McCreight, "How I Started Boobquake."
37. Anne, "'Humanism' and 'Atheism+'"; Croft, "What Humanism Is."
38. Simmons, "Not That Kind of Atheist."
39. "Letter on Justice and Open Debate."
40. "More Specific Letter on Justice and Open Debate."
41. Harris, "Forbidden Knowledge."
42. The amorality of the gods in Ovid's *Metamorphoses* demonstrates well this gap between power and authority. Desire transforms, manifest as power, but no authority judges because the transgressors are the gods. Though Ovid's account is too self-aware to count as an endorsement of this ethos, the dynamic he depicts is captured in the aphorism "Might is right." See also Agamben, *State of Exception*.
43. Palmer, *Reading Lucretius in the Renaissance*; Kors, *Naturalism and Unbelief in France*; Kors, *Epicureans and Atheists in France*.
44. Alasdair MacIntyre traces the influence of Aristotle and debates about him through the Christian and secular traditions in *After Virtue*. MacIntyre is especially attentive to the challenge that Aristotle has posed for Enlightenment thinkers.
45. Kant, *Groundwork for the Metaphysics of Morals*.
46. Camus, *Myth of Sisyphus*; Sartre, *Being and Nothingness*.
47. Mill, *Utilitarianism*.
48. Harris, *Moral Landscape*; Harris, "Brain Science and Human Values."
49. In Weber's influential lecture-cum-essay "Science as a Vocation," the sociologist meditates on the tension between the pursuit of goals, or instrumental rationality, and the judgment of those goals' value. As a vocation, or way of life, science can only judge effectiveness and not morality or value, so it can lead to the improvement of a goal's pursuit but cannot determine whether that goal is worthy of pursuing. This produces for Weber a melancholy, which grows from a uniquely modern disappointment. Secular but human, the quintessentially modern academic walks a hard road, tempted always by religion's naive certainties: "To anyone who is unable to endure the fate of the age like a man we must say that he should return to the welcoming and merciful embrace of the old churches—simply, silently, and without any of the usual public bluster of the renegade. They will surely not make it hard for him" (*Vocation Lectures*, 30). The normativity of all descriptions belies the ostensible sequestration of norms from values that is constitutive of modernity's self-understanding.
50. Mead, *Mind, Self, and Society*; Rorty, *Achieving Our Country*.
51. Nietzsche, *On the Genealogy of Morals*; Foucault, "Nietzsche, Genealogy, History"; J. Butler, *Bodies That Matter*; Mahmood, *Politics of Piety*.
52. Cultural relativism has a long history in the lineage of anthropology pioneered by Franz Boas. See Boas, "Principles of Ethnological Classification," 61–66; Marcus and Fischer, *Anthropology as Cultural Critique*.

53. This is, for instance, the core problem of existentialism, which grows from Kierkegaard's astute analysis of the inability to know the mind of a Calvinist God. Kierkegaard, *Fear and Trembling*; Khawaja, *Religion of Existence*.
54. John Rawls coined the phrase "reflective equilibrium" in *Theory of Justice*, 18. Julia Galef, who moderated the conversation between Pigliucci and Shermer, has drawn the distinction between instrumental rationality and epistemic rationality in order to clarify that the latter has expressly secular goals, whereas the former can be the rational pursuit of a nonsecular goal, as in the discipline of theology. See Galef, "3 Ways CFAR Has Changed My Perspective."
55. "Black without God."
56. Partly to address this vacuum, Roy Speckhardt, executive director of AHA, announced his intention to resign in early 2021 and called for his replacement to be a person of color. The American Humanist Association has at times sided with nonbelievers who align themselves with social justice causes, but a controversy over who would get to participate in the process of hiring Speckhardt's replacement has spurred still more disagreement. E. Miller, "American Humanist Leader Roy Speckhardt"; American Humanist Association, "AHA Affirms Commitment to Social Justice Advocacy."
57. Hart, "One Percenters," 693.
58. Camp Quest, "Our Mission."
59. Manning, "Unaffiliated Parents," 160.
60. Manning, *Losing Our Religion*.
61. One example is Barry Kosmin, who has served on the board of directors of the Center for Inquiry and has made major contributions to the study of secular people, primarily through the American Religious Identification Survey (ARIS). The ARIS pioneered the contemporary study of the diversity of worldviews among the nonreligious and helped draw attention to the "rise of the nones," or the religiously unaffiliated. Kosmin and Keysar, "American Religious Identification Survey."
62. For more on the history of the sociology of religion, see Wuthnow, *Inventing American Religion*.
63. Bourdieu, "Sociologists of Belief and Beliefs of Sociologists."
64. Hunsberger and Altemeyer, *Atheists*. The book's publisher, Prometheus Books, was founded by Paul Kurtz, the founder and former leader of several of the major nonbeliever and skeptic organizations in the United States. Kurtz's son, Jonathan, now runs the publishing house. Until the boom in interest in nonbelief and the secular that emerged over the past decade, Prometheus was the sole publisher of many books related to atheism and freethought, and this book contains numerous references to its titles.
65. Zuckerman, *Society without God*, 4–5.
66. Zuckerman, *Faith No More*.
67. Cimino and Smith, "Secular Humanism and Atheism"; Cimino and Smith, "New Atheism and the Formation of the Imagined Secularist Community"; Smith and Cimino, "Atheisms Unbound."

68. Jesse Smith, "Becoming an Atheist in America"; Jesse Smith, "Creating a Godless Community"; LeDrew, "Discovering Atheism." Smith and LeDrew also exchanged responses in the same issue of *Sociology of Religion* in which LeDrew's article appeared.
69. Guenther, Mulligan, and Papp, "From the Outside In." See also Guenther, "Bounded by Disbelief"; Kettell, "Faithless"; Kettell, "Divided We Stand."
70. Writing in *Bookforum* in 2005, Wayne State University professor Ronald Aronson coined the term "new atheists" to describe an emerging set of authors who develop an atheism that could "absorb the experience of the twentieth century and the issues of the twenty-first" ("Faith No More?," 19). In the opening pages of his essay, Aronson reviews Alister McGrath's *The Twilight of Atheism*, granting McGrath the argument that "disbelief" is in decline and needs new ways of understanding itself that are free of the teleology of the secularization thesis and more focused on "the vital questions about how to live one's life" (19). Aronson emphasizes the "newness" of the new atheism to argue that it differs from older forms that he and McGrath believe are out of step with contemporary concerns. Half prescriptive in his tone, Aronson argues that this new atheism "has made a beginning, but much remains to be done" (19). Of the authors whom Aronson dubs the "new atheists," only Sam Harris has achieved widespread popularity in the United States. The other works Aronson reviews include the French philosopher Michel Onfray's *Le traité d'athéologie*, published in the United States as *The Atheist Manifesto*; Julian Baggini's *Atheism: A Very Short Introduction*; Erik Wielenberg's *Value and Virtue in a Godless Universe*; and Daniel Harbour's *An Intelligent Person's Guide to Atheism*. Writing again in 2007, this time in the *Nation*, Aronson capitalized and canonized the "New Atheists" with a review of four works in addition to Harris's *The End of Faith*: Richard Dawkins's *The God Delusion*, Christopher Hitchens's *God Is Not Great*, Daniel Dennett's *Breaking the Spell*, and Harris's *Letter to a Christian Nation*. Though Aronson does not explain what makes these atheists "new" besides their dates of publication, he describes the four authors as sharing in a passionate attack on religion that "speak[s] to and for" a segment of nonbelieving Americans who "feel beleaguered" and "voiceless in the public arena" ("New Atheists," 12–13).
71. Cimino and Smith, "New Atheism and the Formation of the Imagined Secularist Community," 27, 33.
72. Cimino and Smith, "New Atheism and the Empowerment of American Freethinkers."
73. Guenther, Mulligan, and Papp, "From the Outside In."
74. K. Winston, "New 'Openly Secular' Group."
75. I have written on this lawsuit in greater detail in Blankholm, "Secularism and Secular People."
76. Goodridge v. Department of Public Health, 798 N.E.2d 941 (Mass. 2003).
77. Niose, *Nonbeliever Nation*, 197–202.

78. Niose, 127–29; Richard Dawkins Foundation for Reason & Science, "Richard Dawkins Explains His 'Scarlet A' Lapel Pin."
79. Niose, *Nonbeliever Nation*, 207.
80. I borrow this notion of entanglements from Bender, "Things in Their Entanglements."
81. Putnam and Campbell write, "Perhaps close, morally intense, but nonreligious social networks could have a similarly powerful effect. . . . We cannot exclude that possibility, because we have not found a significant number of such groups nationwide to study. While we cannot deny that secular equivalents of religiously based social networks might exist, we are confident that in America today religious institutions represent by far the most common site of such communities." Campbell and Putnam, *American Grace*, 361.
82. Sherine, "Atheists—Gimme Five."
83. Reasonable New York, the New York City coalition, is a notable exception. Disagreements among local groups and UnitedCoR resulted in their remaining separate from the national organization.
84. For a current list of coalitions, see United Coalition of Reason, "Find a Local Group."
85. García and Blankholm, "Social Context of Organized Nonbelief."
86. The unification of humanism is an old project. See Blackham, "Definition of Humanism," 35: "I deprecate any definition of Humanism that mutilates it with an epithet—'ethical,' 'scientific,' 'religious.' For this gives exclusive or special right to a selected aspect of human life and maims the body of all-around Humanist concern with human being."
87. On frame alignment in identity-based movements, see Snow et al., "Frame Alignment Processes."
88. Blankholm, "Political Advantages of a Polysemous Secular."
89. The American Ethical Union is the umbrella organization for independently run Ethical Culture societies throughout the United States. The Society for Humanistic Judaism has the same relationship to its independent societies. The Unitarian Universalist Humanists are religious humanists who are part of the Unitarian Universalist Association and operate within UU congregations.
90. Edgell, Gerteis, and Hartmann, "Atheists as 'Other.'"
91. Edgell et al., "Atheists and Other Cultural Outsiders."
92. Faircloth, "Our Secular Decade."

CHAPTER 5. TRADITION
1. Blankholm, "Secularism, Humanism, and Secular Humanism."
2. Ritchie, "Flaming Chalice."
3. Shelton, "Changing the Words."
4. Furst, "Protestors Shut Down I-94."
5. First Unitarian Society of Minneapolis, "Frequently Asked Questions."
6. Olds, *American Religious Humanism*, 3.

7. Lamont, *Philosophy of Humanism*.
8. Potter, *Humanism*, quoted in Olds, *American Religious Humanism*, 3. See also the tentative opening line of N. W. DeWitt's article "Greek Humanism," in which he deploys an anachronistic understanding of the term: "Humanism may be crudely defined for the present purpose as a system of thought in which the interests of mankind are the chief concern, and a social system of which mankind shall be the chief beneficiary" (263). "Greek humanism" receives book-length treatment by one of Corliss Lamont's colleagues at Columbia University: Hadas, *Humanism*.
9. Potter, *Humanism*, 61.
10. Potter, 67. This same quote from Protagoras provides the epigraph of an essay on humanism by the humanist philosopher and leader of several organizations for nonbelievers Howard Radest, "Humanism as Experience."
11. Olds, *American Religious Humanism*, 3. Searching for atheists in ancient Greece, the historian Tim Whitmarsh faces a similar challenge. *Atheos* is a Greek term that meant "heretic" more than "person with a secular worldview," so like any historian of atheism, Whitmarsh must balance a search for doubt and heresy with the search for modern secularism's substance. Like Potter and Olds, he finds in ancient Greece similarity rather than sameness. Whitmarsh, *Battling the Gods*.
12. Potter, *Humanism*, 4.
13. Potter, 70–72.
14. Dietrich, *Humanism*, 6, quoted in Olds, *American Religious Humanism*, 4.
15. Kristeller, "Humanism," 113.
16. Mann, "Origins of Humanism," 1–2.
17. For an example of a work that does partially trace this lineage of reception through the rediscovery of manuscripts, see Greenblatt, *Swerve*. For a more sweeping synthesis organized as a history of "atheism" and its transmission, see Minois, *Histoire de l'athéisme*.
18. Bullough, "Humanism," 403.
19. The organization's name was shortened to the Council for Secular Humanism in 1996.
20. Olds, *American Religious Humanism*, 5–7. Norman Foerster edited an anthology of the "New Humanism," which includes essays from More, Babbitt, and T. S. Eliot: *Humanism and America*.
21. For instance, Potter, *Humanism*, 110–12; and Firkins, "Two Humanisms"; cited in Olds, *American Religious Humanism*, 6n6.
22. Babbitt, "What I Believe," 13.
23. Babbitt, "On Being Original," cited in Olds as a representative work (*American Religious Humanism*, 6n7).
24. Olds, *American Religious Humanism*, 7–9.
25. Olds, 9.
26. Geroulanos, *Atheism That Is Not Humanist*, 252–58.
27. Geroulanos, 255.

28. Blanchot, "On Nietzsche's Side." See also Mark C. Taylor on the concept of denegation: "Denegating God."
29. Levinas, *Sur Maurice Blanchot*, 10; translated in Levinas, *Proper Names*, 127; quoted in Geroulanos, *Atheism That Is Not Humanist*, 5. The phrase is the source for the title of Geroulanos's book.
30. Henri de Lubac draws a worthy distinction between positivist, Marxist, and Nietzschean humanisms in his strongly Catholic treatment of the subject: *Drama of Atheist Humanism*. It is against Lubac that Blanchot defends Nietzsche in "On Nietzsche's Side."
31. Sartre, "Existentialism," 45.
32. Heidegger, "Letter on Humanism," 226.
33. Heidegger, *Being and Time*.
34. Olds, *American Religious Humanism*, 10.
35. Lamont, *Philosophy of Humanism*, 35.
36. For discussions of "naturalism" and "materialism" as they relate to atheism and other forms of nonbelief, see M. Martin, "Naturalism"; and Tuñón, "Materialism, Philosophical." For a discussion of the relationship between the two terms and their compatibility with certain forms of theism, see M. Martin, *Atheism*, 469–470.
37. Olds, *American Religious Humanism*, 10.
38. Lamont, *Philosophy of Humanism*, 41.
39. Olds, *American Religious Humanism*, 11. Olds's echoes of John Dewey's argument in *A Common Faith* are surely intentional. Several humanists mentioned Dewey's book during interviews and casual conversations, and many humanists claim Dewey in the humanist tradition. Paul Kurtz considered himself an intellectual heir to Dewey by way of Sidney Hook, with whom Kurtz studied as an undergraduate at New York University. Corliss Lamont recalls in his memoirs taking "a good course under Professor John Dewey," whom he "regarded as America's greatest philosopher": "He was in essence a Humanist, but preferred the word *Naturalist* to describe his position" (*Yes to Life*, 29).
40. Hart, "One Percenters," 2013.
41. Pinn, *Varieties of African American Religious Experience*.
42. Pinn, *By These Hands*; Pinn, *What Has the Black Church to Do with Public Life?*
43. M. Miller, *Religion and Hip Hop*.
44. Hart, "One Percenters," 682–83.
45. Pinn, "Humanism as Guide to Life Meaning," 31.
46. Hägglund, *This Life*.
47. Radest, "Humanism as Experience," 22.
48. Radest, 23.
49. For a study that connects deism to liberal democracy and contemporary forms of secularism, see Critchley, *Faith of the Faithless*.
50. Hobsbawm, "Introduction: Inventing Traditions," 1.
51. Hobsbawm, 4–5.

52. Hobsbawm, 11.
53. C. Taylor, *Secular Age*.
54. C. Taylor, 159–211.
55. Smolkin, *Sacred Space Is Never Empty*.
56. Engelke, "Coffin Question."
57. Copeman and Quack, "Godless People and Dead Bodies," 56. They call the presence they find "lived materialism."
58. Applewhite, "Institutionalized Individuality."
59. Farman, *On Not Dying*.
60. Farman, "Mind out of Place."
61. José Casanova's "The Secular and Secularisms" is often cited as a turning point among sociologists. Peter Berger has charted the rise and fall of the secularization thesis with a revision of his earlier work: *Sacred Canopy* and *Desecularization of the World*. For my periodization, I rely on Cannell, "Anthropology of Secularism."
62. D. Martin, "Notes for a General Theory of Secularisation"; D. Martin, *General Theory of Secularization*; D. Martin, *On Secularization*. Steve Bruce, Darren Sherkat, and David Hollinger have continued to argue for strong versions of secularization, though especially for Sherkat and Hollinger, this is more a process of de-Christianization than a move away from all forms of religious belief, belonging, and behavior. See Bruce, *Secularization*; Sherkat, *Changing Faith*; Hollinger, *After Cloven Tongues of Fire*. "Value spheres" is Max Weber's term ("Religious Rejections of the World"). On the importance of this essay in Weber's corpus, see Bellah, "Max Weber and World-Denying Love."
63. C. Taylor, *Secular Age*, 2007; Calhoun, Jurgensmeyer, and VanAntwerpen, introduction to *Rethinking Secularism*. See also Bender and Taves, *What Matters?*; Warner, VanAntwerpen, and Calhoun, *Varieties of Secularism in a Secular Age*; Gorski et al., *Post-secular in Question*; Shah, Stepan, and Toft, *Rethinking Religion and World Affairs*; Mendieta and VanAntwerpen, *Power of Religion in the Public Sphere*; Calhoun, Mendieta, and VanAntwerpen, *Habermas and Religion*.
64. Asad, *Formations of the Secular*. Saba Mahmood and Mayanthi Fernando have also taken up Asad's call for an anthropology of secularism. Mahmood, "Secularism, Hermeneutics, and Empire"; Fernando, *Republic Unsettled*.
65. Asad, "Idea of an Anthropology of Islam," 20. See also Ovamir Anjum, who provides a careful, insightful analysis of Asad's use of the concept to describe Islam, in "Islam as a Discursive Tradition."
66. Asad, *Secular Translations*, 144–45.
67. Latour, *We Have Never Been Modern*.
68. Asad, *Secular Translations*, 95.
69. Alasdair MacIntyre has attended carefully to disagreement and embodiment in his writing on the traditions that have shaped European life: *Whose Justice?* and *After Virtue*.

70. Scheer, Fadil, and Johansen, *Secular Bodies, Affects, and Emotions*; Farman, "Speculative Matter"; Asad, "Thinking about the Secular Body"; Hirschkind, "Is There a Secular Body?"
71. Asad, "Idea of an Anthropology of Islam," 24.
72. MacIntyre considers the Enlightenment to be a tradition that intentionally disembodies itself and rejects tradition, understanding itself a break. As I have tried to show, he is only half right. MacIntyre, *After Virtue*.
73. Wootton, "New Histories of Atheism"; Febvre, *Problem of Unbelief in the Sixteenth Century*.
74. Pugh et al., "Book Review Forum: *The Swerve*." Medieval, Renaissance, Enlightenment, and Modern are temporal heuristics that too often conceal conflict and complexity in the homogeneity of an epoch. Skinner, "Meaning and Understanding in the History of Ideas."
75. Nicholas Hudson has written an excellent intellectual history of the Enlightenment concept and its uses and misuses: "What Is the Enlightenment?" See also Gay, *Enlightenment*, vol. 1; Gay, *Enlightenment*, vol. 2; Gillespie, *Theological Origins of Modernity*.
76. On the importance of "lost-found" for the creation of a tradition, see Jackson, *Thin Description*.
77. Palmer, *Reading Lucretius in the Renaissance*; Kors, *D'Holbach's Coterie*; Kors, *Atheism in France*; Kors, "Atheism of D'Holbach and Naigeon"; Kors, *Epicureans and Atheists in France*; Kors, *Naturalism and Unbelief in France*.
78. Palmer, *Reading Lucretius in the Renaissance*, 25.
79. Gerard Passannante likens this piecemeal distribution to the dispersal of atoms in the Lucretian philosophical system (*Lucretian Renaissance*). Palmer discusses Passannante in *Reading Lucretius in the Renaissance*, 40.
80. For an example of a more paranoid style of reading, see Strauss, *Persecution and the Art of Writing*; Strauss, "Notes on Lucretius." For an example of a reading of Spinoza as duplicitous, see Yovel, *Spinoza and Other Heretics*, vol. 1. In a second volume with the same title, subtitled *The Adventures of Immanence*, Yovel charts the influence of Spinoza's philosophy of immanentism on a wide range of Continental philosophers, secular and religious.
81. Palmer, *Reading Lucretius in the Renaissance*, 26–29.
82. Foner and Landor, "Two Neglected Interviews with Karl Marx." The self-identification is on page 15.
83. I have written elsewhere about Marx's place in a religion-like secular tradition and its implications for a critique of the secular. Blankholm, "Remembering Marx's Secularism." See also Smolkin, *Sacred Space Is Never Empty*; Luehrmann, *Secularism Soviet Style*.
84. Althusser, "Le courant souterrain du matérialisme de la rencontre," For analyses of Althusser's late turn, see Bargu, "In the Theater of Politics"; Suchting, "Althusser's Late Thinking about Materialism"; Lewis, "Althusser's Scientism and Aleatory Materialism."

85. Hart, *Afro-Eccentricity*; Deleuze, *Spinoza*; Deleuze, "Immanence"; Hägglund, *Radical Atheism*.
86. Jared Sexton questions the distinction between the two in "Social Life of Social Death." He is in conversation with Moten, "Black Op."
87. Barad, *Meeting the University Halfway*; Haraway, "Manifesto for Cyborgs."
88. Fields and Fields, *Racecraft*; Wynter, "Re-enchantment of Humanism."
89. The most interesting examples of a secular perspective in Butler's work appear in *Parable of the Sower* and *Parable of the Talents*. Shelley, *Frankenstein*.
90. Fanon, *Black Skin, White Masks*; Nguyen, *Sympathizer*; Ellison, *Invisible Man*. See also Lloyd, "Negative Political Theology of James Baldwin."
91. In *Parable of the Talents* and *Parable of the Sower*, Butler's protagonist invents a secular religion that guides its followers through an environmental collapse. I have used some of these examples to draw similar insights in a short essay published on *The Immanent Frame*: Blankholm, "Ghost of Immanentism."
92. For an understanding of what I mean by "liberalism" here, see Laborde, *Liberalism's Religion*.
93. Altizer, *Gospel of Christian Atheism*; Bloch, *Atheism in Christianity*.
94. M. Taylor, *Erring*; M. Taylor, *Confidence Games*; M. Taylor, *Hiding*; M. Taylor, *Moment of Complexity*.
95. Carlson, *Indiscretion*; Carlson, *Indiscrete Image*; Carlson, *With the World at Heart*.
96. Rubenstein, *Pantheologies*, xvii. *Pantheologies* is a wonderful study of ideas that many people in the secular tradition would claim as their own; it attends to the peregrination of these ideas through theological sources and concerns.
97. Rubenstein, *Worlds without End*.
98. Bradley Onishi's *The Sacrality of the Secular* provides a great introduction to the a/theological tradition and its strongest arguments.
99. Vincent Pecora's *Secularization without End* is masterful in drawing out the influences of Calvinism on a set of well-known secular authors. The influence of Epicureanism on Nominalism, Lutheranism, and Calvinism deserves its own study.
100. Yelle, *Language of Disenchantment*.
101. McCrary, "Superstitious Subjects"; Crosson, "Impossibility of Liberal Secularism"; Storm, "Superstition, Secularism, and Religion Trinary"; Wheatley, "US Colonial Governance of Superstition and Fanaticism."
102. Fessenden, *Culture and Redemption*.
103. Modern, *Secularism in Antebellum America*; Scott, *Sex and Secularism*.
104. Schmidt and Promey, *American Religious Liberalism*.
105. Cotter and Robertson, "Introduction."
106. Aggleton, "'Just a Snip'?"
107. Offman-Zavala, "Great Foreskin Debate." On the minimal risks and health benefits of circumcision, see Keatley, "Should You Circumcise Your Baby Boy?"
108. Davidman, *Becoming Un-Orthodox*. Davidman mentions circumcision in passing on page 76.

109. For a wonderful analysis of indigenous people's struggle to define their tradition as a "religion" and secure protections under American religious freedom laws, see Wenger, *We Have a Religion*. See also Johnson, "Materialising and Performing Hawaiian Religion(s)."
110. Asad's genealogy of the secular is especially expansive in *Secular Translations*, though many others have begun to use "secularism" as a name for almost any large-scale cause of harm, like capitalism, corporations, or law. Farman follows Asad in construing the secular tradition more broadly. Their tradition focuses more on secular institutions: "law, science, statecraft, and social governance" (Farman, "Speculative Matter," 738). See also Coviello, *Make Yourselves Gods*.
111. I owe thanks to Lucas McCracken for this elegant insight.
112. Rubenstein, "Twilight of the Doxai"; M. Taylor, *Nots*.

EPILOGUE

1. Cervantes, *Don Quixote*, 155.
2. Cervantes, 390.
3. Cervantes, 393.

BIBLIOGRAPHY

Accetti, Carlo Invernizzi. *What Is Christian Democracy? Politics, Religion and Ideology.* New York: Cambridge University Press, 2019.
Adler, Felix. *Our Part in This World.* Edited by Horace L. Friess. New York: King's Crown, 1946.
Adorno, Theodor W. *Prisms.* Translated by Samuel Weber and Shierry Weber. Cambridge, MA: MIT Press, 1997.
Agamben, Giorgio. *State of Exception.* Translated by Kevin Attell. Chicago: University of Chicago Press, 2005.
Aggleton, Peter. "'Just a Snip'? A Social History of Male Circumcision." *Reproductive Health Matters* 15, no. 29 (2007): 15–21.
Alba, Richard. "On the Sociological Significance of the American Jewish Experience: Boundary Blurring, Assimilation, and Pluralism." *Sociology of Religion* 67, no. 4 (2006): 347–58.
Albanese, Catherine L. *A Republic of Mind and Spirit: A Cultural History of American Metaphysical Religion.* New Haven, CT: Yale University Press, 2007.
Altglas, Véronique. *From Yoga to Kabbalah: Religious Exoticism and the Logics of Bricolage.* New York: Oxford University Press, 2014.
Althusser, Louis. "Le courant souterrain du matérialisme de la rencontre." In *Ecrits philosophiques et politiques*, vol. 1, 539–79. Paris: Le Livre de Poche, 1982.
Altizer, Thomas J. J. *The Gospel of Christian Atheism.* Philadelphia: Westminster, 1966.
Amarasingam, Amarnath, and Melanie Elyse Brewster. "The Rise and Fall of the New Atheism: Identity Politics and Tensions within US Nonbelievers." In *Annual Review of the Sociology of Religion*, vol. 7, *Sociology of Atheism*, edited by Roberto Cipriani and Franco Garelli, 118–36. Leiden: Brill, 2016.
American Humanist Association. "AHA Affirms Commitment to Social Justice Advocacy." Press release. February 25, 2016. https://americanhumanist.org.
———. "Humanism and Its Aspirations: Humanist Manifesto III, a Successor to the Humanist Manifesto of 1933." August 8, 2019. https://americanhumanist.org.
———. "Humanist Manifesto I." August 8, 2019. https://americanhumanist.org.
———. "Humanist Manifesto II." August 8, 2019. https://americanhumanist.org.
Anderson, Benedict. *Imagined Communities: Reflections on the Origin and Spread of Nationalism.* New York: Verso Books, 2006.
Anidjar, Gil. *Blood: A Critique of Christianity.* New York: Columbia University Press, 2014.

———. "Of Globalatinology." *Derrida Today* 6, no. 1 (2013): 11–22.
———. "Secularism." *Critical Inquiry* 33, no. 1 (2006): 52–77.
Anjum, Ovamir. "Islam as a Discursive Tradition: Talal Asad and His Interlocutors." *Comparative Studies of South Asia, Africa, and the Middle East* 27, no. 3 (2007): 656–72.
Anne, Libby. "'Humanism' and 'Atheism+': What's the Difference?" *Love, Joy, Feminism* (blog), August 20, 2012. www.patheos.com.
Anzaldúa, Gloria. *Borderlands / La Frontera: The New Mestiza*. San Francisco: Aunt Lute Books, 1987.
Applewhite, Courtney. "Institutionalized Individuality: Death Practices and Afterlife Beliefs in Unity Church, Unitarian Universalism, and Spiritualism in Santa Barbara." Master's thesis, University of California, Santa Barbara, 2019.
Arnal, William E., and Russell T. McCutcheon. *The Sacred Is the Profane: The Political Nature of "Religion."* New York: Oxford University Press, 2012.
Aronson, Ronald. "Faith No More? Against the Rising Tide of Rejuvenated Religion, a Number of Writers Make the Case for Disbelief." *Bookforum* 12, no. 3 (October 2005): 16–19.
———. "The New Atheists." *Nation* 285, no. 24 (2007): 11–14.
Asad, Talal. *Formations of the Secular: Christianity, Islam, Modernity*. Cultural Memory in the Present. Stanford, CA: Stanford University Press, 2003.
———. "Free Speech, Blasphemy, and Secular Criticism." In *Is Critique Secular? Blasphemy, Injury, and Free Speech*, edited by Wendy Brown, Judith Butler, and Saba Mahmood, 20–63. Berkeley: University of California Press, 2009.
———. *Genealogies of Religion: Discipline and Reasons of Power in Christianity and Islam*. Baltimore: Johns Hopkins University Press, 1993.
———. "The Idea of an Anthropology of Islam." *Qui Parle* 17, no. 2 (2009): 1–30.
———. "Reflections on Blasphemy and Secular Criticism." In *Religion: Beyond a Concept*, edited by Hent de Vries, 580–609. New York: Fordham University Press, 2008.
———. *Secular Translations: Nation State, Modern Self, and Calculative Reason*. New York: Columbia University Press, 2018.
———. "Thinking about the Secular Body, Pain, and Liberal Politics." *Cultural Anthropology* 26, no. 4 (2011): 657–75. https://doi.org/10.1111/j.1548-1360.2011.01118.x.
———. "Toward a Genealogy of the Concept of Ritual." In *Genealogies of Religion: Discipline and Reasons of Power in Christianity and Islam*, 55–79. Baltimore: Johns Hopkins University Press, 1993.
Aston, Katie. "Formations of a Secular Wedding." In *Secular Bodies, Affects, and Emotions: European Configurations*, edited by Monique Scheer, Nadia Fadil, and Birgitte Schepelern Johansen, 77–92. London: Bloomsbury Academic, 2019.
"Atheist Church Schism Illustrates Diversity of Non-Belief." *Huffington Post*, January 23, 2014. www.huffingtonpost.com.
Atheist Nomads. "Hispanic Atheists with Jose Alvarado." Podcast. Episode 23, March 21, 2013. https://atheistnomads.com.
"Atheist Rabbi, The." *Time*, January 29, 1965.

Avalos, Natalie. "Latinx Indigeneities and Christianities." In *The Oxford Handbook of Latino/a Christianities in the United States*. Oxford: Oxford University Press, forthcoming.

Babbitt, Irving. "On Being Original." *Atlantic* 10 (March 10, 1908): 388–96.

———. "What I Believe: Rousseau and Religion." *Forum* 38, no. 2 (February 1930): 80–87.

Baggini, Julian. *Atheism: A Very Short Introduction*. Oxford: Oxford University Press, 2003.

Barad, Karen. *Meeting the University Halfway: Quantum Physics and the Entanglement of Matter and Meaning*. Durham, NC: Duke University Press, 2007.

———. "Posthumanist Performativity: Toward an Understanding of How Matter Comes to Matter." *Signs: Journal of Women in Culture and Society* 28, no. 3 (March 1, 2003): 801–31. https://doi.org/10.1086/345321.

Barber, Daniel Colucciello. "On Black Negativity, or the Affirmation of Nothing: Jared Sexton, Interviewed by Daniel Barber." *Society & Space*, September 18, 2017. www.societyandspace.org.

Bargu, Ban. "In the Theater of Politics: Althusser's Aleatory Materialism and Aesthetics." *Diacritics* 40, no. 3 (2012): 86–113.

Bauman, Zygmunt. *Modernity and Ambivalence*. Cambridge, UK: Polity, 1991.

Bayle, Peter. *The Dictionary Historical and Critical of Mr. Peter Bayle*. 1734. Translated by Pierre Desmaizeaux. 2nd ed. New York: Garland, 2015.

Beattie, Tina. *The New Atheists: The Twilight of Reason and the War on Religion*. Maryknoll, NY: Orbis Books, 2008.

Bell, Catherine. *Ritual: Perspectives and Dimensions*. New York: Oxford University Press, 2009.

Bellah, Robert. "Max Weber and World-Denying Love: A Look at the Historical Sociology of Religion." *Journal of the American Academy of Religion* 67, no. 2 (1999): 277–304.

———. *Religion in Human Evolution: From the Paleolithic to the Axial Age*. Cambridge, MA: Harvard University Press, 2011.

Bender, Courtney. *The New Metaphysicals: Spirituality and the American Religious Imagination*. Chicago: University of Chicago Press, 2010.

———. "Review of *Healing Gods*." *Church History* 83, no. 4 (2014): 1097–1100.

———. "Things in Their Entanglements." In *The Post-secular in Question: Religion in Contemporary Society*, edited by Philip S. Gorski, David Kyuman Kim, John Torpey, and Jonathan VanAntwerpen, 43–76. New York: New York University Press, 2012.

Bender, Courtney, and Omar McRoberts. "Mapping a Field: Why and How to Study Spirituality." Social Science Research Council, October 2012.

Bender, Courtney, and Ann Taves, eds. *What Matters? Ethnographies of Value in a (Not So) Secular Age*. New York: Columbia University Press, 2012.

Berger, Peter. *The Desecularization of the World: Resurgent Religion and World Politics*. Grand Rapids, MI: Eerdmans, 1999.

———. *The Sacred Canopy: Elements of a Sociological Theory of Religion*. New York: Anchor Books, 1967.

Biale, David. *Not in the Heavens: The Tradition of Jewish Secular Thought*. Princeton, NJ: Princeton University Press, 2005.
Bialecki, Jon, and Eric Hoenas del Pinal. "Beyond Logos: Extensions of the Language Paradigm in Global Christianities." *Anthropological Quarterly* 84, no. 3 (2011): 575–93.
Bielo, James. "Belief, Deconversion, and Authenticity among U.S. Emerging Evangelicals." *ETHOS* 40, no. 3 (2012): 258–76.
Blackham, H. J. "A Definition of Humanism." In *The Humanist Alternative*, edited by Paul Kurtz, 35–37. Buffalo, NY: Prometheus Books, 1973.
"Black without God." *The Current* (UC–Santa Barbara), February 23, 2017. www.news.ucsb.edu.
Blanchot, Maurice. "On Nietzsche's Side." In *The Work of Fire*, translated by Charlotte Mandel, 287–99. Stanford, CA: Stanford University Press, 1995.
Blankholm, Joseph. "The Ghost of Immanentism." *The Immanent Frame*, November 14, 2017. https://tif.ssrc.org.
———. "No Part of the World: How Jehovah's Witnesses Perform the Boundaries of Their Community." *ARC* 37 (2009): 197–211.
———. "The Political Advantages of a Polysemous Secular." *Journal for the Scientific Study of Religion* 53, no. 4 (2014): 775–90.
———. "Remembering Marx's Secularism." *Journal of the American Academy of Religion* 88, no. 1 (2020): 35–57.
———. "Secularism and Secular People." *Public Culture* 30, no. 2 (2018): 245–68.
———. "Secularism, Humanism, and Secular Humanism: Terms and Institutions." In *The Oxford Handbook of Secularism*, edited by Phil Zuckerman and John R. Shook, 689–705. Oxford: Oxford University Press, 2017.
———. "Self-Critique and Moral Ground: Saba Mahmood's Contribution to Remaking Secularism and the Study of Religion." *Journal of the American Academy of Religion* 87, no. 4 (December 12, 2019): 941–54. https://doi.org/10.1093/jaarel/lfz082.
Bloch, Ernst. *Atheism in Christianity: The Religion of the Exodus and the Kingdom*. Translated by J. T. Swann and Peter Thompson. 2nd ed. New York: Verso, 2009.
Block, Tina. "'Going to Church Just Never Even Occurred to Me': Women and Secularism in the Pacific Northwest, 1950–1975." *Pacific Northwest* 96, no. 2 (2005): 61–68.
Blumenberg, Hans. *The Legitimacy of the Modern Age*. Translated by Robert M. Wallace. Cambridge, MA: MIT Press, 1983.
Boas, Franz. "The Principles of Ethnological Classification." In *A Franz Boas Reader*, edited by George W. Stocking Jr., 61–66. Chicago: University of Chicago Press, 1974.
Boghossian, Peter. *A Manual for Creating Atheists*. Durham, NC: Pitchstone, 2013.
Bourdieu, Pierre. *The Field of Cultural Production*. New York: Columbia University Press, 1993.
———. "Genesis and Structure of the Religious Field." *Comparative Social Research* 13 (1991): 1–44.
———. "Sociologists of Belief and Beliefs of Sociologists." Translated by Véronique Altglas and Matthew Wood. *Nordic Journal of Religion and Society* 23, no. 1 (2010): 1–7.

Bourdieu, Pierre, and Loïc J. D. Wacquant. *An Invitation to Reflexive Sociology*. Chicago: University of Chicago Press, 1992.
Bowers, Paul. "Q&A with Richard Dawkins: 'I Guess I'm a Cultural Christian.'" *Charleston City Paper*, March 4, 2013. www.charlestoncitypaper.com.
Brighenti, David, Qi Xu, and David Yaffe-Bellany. "Worker Smashes 'Racist' Panel, Loses Job." *New Haven Independent*, July 11, 2016. www.newhavenindependent.org.
Brighenti, David, and David Yaffe-Bellany. "Yale Gags Rehired Cafeteria Worker." *New Haven Independent*, July 26, 2016. www.newhavenindependent.org.
Brooks, E. Marshall. *Disenchanted Lives: Apostasy and Ex-Mormonism among the Latter-Day Saints*. New Brunswick, NJ: Rutgers University Press, 2018.
Brown, Candy Gunther. *Healing Gods: Complementary and Alternative Medicine in Christian America*. Oxford: Oxford University Press, 2013.
Brown, Wendy. Introduction to *Is Critique Secular? Blasphemy, Injury, and Free Speech*, edited by Talal Asad, Wendy Brown, Judith Butler, and Saba Mahmood, 7–19. Berkeley: University of California Press, 2009.
Bruce, Steve. *Secularization: In Defense of an Unfashionable Theory*. Oxford: Oxford University Press, 2011.
Budd, Susan. *Varieties of Unbelief: Atheists and Agnostics in English Society, 1850–1960*. London: Heinemann Educational Books, 1977.
Bullivant, Stephen. "Defining 'Atheism.'" In *The Oxford Handbook of Atheism*, edited by Stephen Bullivant and Michael Ruse, 11–21. New York: Oxford University Press, 2013.
Bullough, Vern L. "Humanism." In *The New Encyclopedia of Unbelief*, edited by Tom Flynn, 402–405. Amherst, NY: Prometheus Books, 2007.
Burchell, Graham, Colin Gordon, and Peter Miller, eds. *The Foucault Effect: Studies in Governmentality*. Chicago: Chicago University Press, 1991.
Butler, Judith. *Bodies That Matter: On the Discursive Limits of "Sex."* 1993. Reprint, London: Routledge, 2011.
Butler, Octavia. *Parable of the Sower*. New York: Four Walls Eight Windows, 1993.
———. *Parable of the Talents*. New York: Seven Stories, 1998.
Cady, Linell E., and Elizabeth Shakman Hurd. *Comparative Secularisms in a Global Age*. Basingstoke, UK: Palgrave Macmillan, 2010.
Calhoun, Craig J., Mark Jurgensmeyer, and Jonathan VanAntwerpen. Introduction to *Rethinking Secularism*, edited by Craig J. Calhoun, Mark Jurgensmeyer, and Jonathan VanAntwerpen, 3–30. New York: Oxford University Press, 2011.
———, eds. *Rethinking Secularism*. Oxford: Oxford University Press, 2011.
Calhoun, Craig, Eduardo Mendieta, and Jonathan VanAntwerpen, eds. *Habermas and Religion*. Cambridge, UK: Polity, 2013.
Cameron, Christopher. *Black Freethinkers: A History of African American Freethought*. Evanston, IL: Northwestern University Press, 2019.
Campbell, Colin. *Toward a Sociology of Irreligion*. London: Macmillan, 1971.
Campbell, David E., and Robert D. Putnam. *American Grace: How Religion Divides and Unites Us*. New York: Simon and Schuster, 2010.

Camp Quest. "Our Mission." 2019. www.campquest.org.
Camus, Albert. *The Myth of Sisyphus*. Translated by Justin O'Brien. London: Hamish Hamilton, 1955.
Cannell, Fenella. *The Anthropology of Christianity*. Durham, NC: Duke University Press, 2006.
———. "The Anthropology of Secularism." *Annual Review of Anthropology* 39 (2010): 85–100.
Carlson, Thomas A. *The Indiscrete Image: Infinitude and Creation of the Human*. Religion and Postmodernism. Chicago: University of Chicago Press, 2008.
———. *Indiscretion: Finitude and the Naming of God*. Religion and Postmodernism. Chicago: University of Chicago Press, 1999.
———. *With the World at Heart: Studies in the Secular Today*. Chicago: Chicago University Press, 2019.
Caruth, Cathy. *Unclaimed Experience: Trauma, Narrative, and History*. Baltimore: Johns Hopkins University Press, 1996.
Casanova, José. "The Secular and Secularisms." *Social Research* 76, no. 4 (2009): 1049–66.
Castle, Jeremiah J., Geoffrey C. Layman, David E. Campbell, and John C. Green. "Survey Experiments on Candidate Religiosity, Political Attitudes, and Vote Choice." *Journal for the Scientific Study of Religion* 56, no. 1 (2017): 143–61.
Cervantes, Miguel de. *Don Quixote*. Translated by Edith Grossman. New York: HarperCollins, 2003.
Chakrabarty, Dipesh. *Provincializing Europe: Postcolonial Thought and Historical Difference*. Reissue with a new preface by the author. Princeton Studies in Culture, Power, History. Princeton, NJ: Princeton University Press, 2008.
Charlton, D. G. *Secular Religions in France: 1815–1870*. Oxford: Oxford University Press, 1963.
Chireau, Yvonne P. *Black Magic: Religion and the African American Conjuring Tradition*. Berkeley: University of California Press, 2003.
Chuman, Joseph. "Between Secularism and Supernaturalism: The Religious Philosophies of Theodore Parker and Felix Adler." PhD diss., Columbia University, 1994.
Cimino, Richard, and Christopher Smith. *Atheist Awakening: Secular Activism and Community in America*. Oxford: Oxford University Press, 2014.
———. "The New Atheism and the Empowerment of American Freethinkers." In *Religion and the New Atheism: A Critical Appraisal*, edited by Amarnath Amarasingam, 139–56. Leiden: Brill, 2010.
———. "The New Atheism and the Formation of the Imagined Secularist Community." *Journal of Media and Religion* 10, no. 1 (January 31, 2011): 24–38. https://doi.org/10.1080/15348423.2011.549391.
———. "Secular Humanism and Atheism beyond Progressive Secularism." *Sociology of Religion* 68, no. 4 (December 1, 2007): 407–24. https://doi.org/10.1093/socrel/68.4.407.

Colgrove, James. "'Science in a Democracy': The Contested Status of Vaccination in the Progressive Era and the 1920s." *Isis* 96 (2005): 167–91.
Colker, Daniel. "Musician Nati Cano Dies at 81; Leader of Mariachi Los Camperos." *Los Angeles Times*, October 5, 2014. www.latimes.com.
Contradiction: A Question of Faith. Directed by Jeremiah Camara. Documentary film. 2013. www.imdb.com.
Copeman, Jacob, and Johannes Quack. "Godless People and Dead Bodies: Materiality and the Morality of Atheist Materialism." *Social Analysis* 59, no. 2 (2015): 40–61.
Cottee, Simon. *The Apostates: When Muslims Leave Islam*. New York: Oxford University Press, 2015.
Cotter, Christopher, and David G. Robertson. "Introduction: The 'World Religions' Paradigm in Contemporary Religious Studies." In *After World Religions: Reconstructing Religious Studies*, edited by Christopher Cotter and David G. Robertson, 1–20. London: Routledge, 2016.
Coviello, Peter. *Make Yourselves Gods: Mormons and the Unfinished Business of American Secularism*. Chicago: Chicago University Press, 2019.
Coyne, Ryan. *Heidegger's Confessions: The Remains of St. Augustine in "Being and Time" and Beyond*. Chicago: University of Chicago Press, 2015.
Cragun, Ryan T., Christel Manning, and Lori L. Fazzino. *Organized Secularism in the United States: New Directions in Research*. Berlin: De Gruyter, 2017.
Crapanzano, Vincent. *Serving the Word: Literalism in America from the Pulpit to the Bench*. New York: New Press, 2001.
Crawley, Ashon T. *Blackpentecostal Breath: The Aesthetics of Possibility*. New York: Fordham University Press, 2016.
Critchley, Simon. *Faith of the Faithless: Experiments in Political Theology*. New York: Verso, 2012.
Croft, James. "What Humanism Is—and Isn't." *Temple of the Future* (blog), August 22, 2012. www.patheos.com.
Crosson, J. Brent. "The Impossibility of Liberal Secularism: Religious (In)Tolerance, Spirituality, and Not-Religion." *Method and Theory in the Study of Religion* 30, no. 1 (2017): 37–55.
Curtis, Finbarr. *The Production of American Religious Freedom*. North American Religions. New York: New York University Press, 2016.
"Danish Cartoon Controversy." *New York Times*, 2015. www.nytimes.com.
Davidman, Lynn. *Becoming Un-Orthodox: Stories of Ex-Hasidic Jews*. New York: Oxford University Press, 2014.
Davidovitch, Nadav. "Negotiating Dissent: Homeopathy and Antivaccinationism at the Turn of the Twentieth Century." In *The Politics of Healing: Histories of Alternative Medicine in Twentieth-Century North America*, edited by Robert D. Johnston, 11–28. New York: Routledge, 2004.
Dawkins, Richard. *The God Delusion*. London: Black Swan, 2007.
"Dawkins: I'm a Cultural Christian." *BBC News*, December 10, 2007. http://news.bbc.co.uk.

Deleuze, Gilles. "Immanence: A Life." In *Two Regimes of Madness: Texts and Interviews 1975–1995*, edited by David Lapoujade, translated by Ames Hodges and Mike Taormina, 385–93. New York: Semiotext(e), 2006.

———. *Spinoza: Practical Philosophy*. San Francisco: City Lights Books, 1988.

Dennett, Daniel C. *Breaking the Spell: Religion as a Natural Phenomenon*. London: Penguin, 2006.

Derrida, Jacques. "Faith and Knowledge: The Two Sources of 'Religion' at the Limits of Reason Alone." In *Acts of Religion*, edited by Gil Anidjar, translated by Samuel Weber, 40–101. New York: Routledge, 2002.

Descartes, René. *Discourse on Method and Meditations on First Philosophy*. Indianapolis: Hackett, 1998.

Dewey, John. *A Common Faith*. New Haven, CT: Yale University Press, 1934.

DeWitt, Norman Wentworth. "Greek Humanism." *Classical Journal* 28, no. 5 (1933): 263–70.

Dietrich, John H. *Humanism*. Boston: American Unitarian Association, 1934.

———. *What Is an Atheist?* Humanist Pulpit 2. Minneapolis: First Unitarian Society, 1928.

Dillahunty, Matt. "Don't Be a Dick—New from Jezebel!" *Freethought Blogs* (blog), July 18, 2013. https://freethoughtblogs.com.

DiMaggio, Paul J., and Walter W. Powell. "The Iron Cage Revisited: Institutional Isomorphism and Collective Rationality in Organizational Fields." In *The New Institutionalism in Organizational Analysis*, edited by Paul J. DiMaggio and Walter W. Powell, 61–82. Chicago: University of Chicago Press, 1991.

Doe v. Acton-Boxborough Regional School District, 468 Mass. 64 (2014).

Douglas, Mary. *Purity and Danger: An Analysis of Concepts of Pollution and Taboo*. New York: Routledge, 1966.

Drescher, Elizabeth. *Choosing Our Religion: The Spiritual Lives of America's Nones*. Oxford: Oxford University Press, 2016.

Dressler, Markus, and Arvind Mandair, eds. *Secularism and Religion-Making*. New York: Oxford University Press, 2011.

Du Bois, W. E. B., ed. *The Negro Church*. Atlanta: Atlanta University Press, 1903.

Durkheim, Émile. *The Elementary Forms of Religious Life*. Translated by Karen E. Fields. New York: Free Press, 1995.

Eagleton, Terry. *Reason, Faith and Revolution: Reflections on the God Debate*. New Haven, CT: Yale University Press, 2009.

Eckel, Jan, and Samuel Moyn, eds. *The Breakthrough: Human Rights in the 1970s*. Philadelphia: University of Pennsylvania Press, 2014.

Edgell, Penny, Jacqui Frost, and Evan Stewart. "From Existential to Social Understandings of Risk: Examining Gender Differences in Nonreligion." *Social Currents* 4, no. 6 (2017): 556–74.

Edgell, Penny, Joseph Gerteis, and Douglas Hartmann. "Atheists as 'Other': Moral Boundaries and Cultural Membership in American Society." *American Sociological Review* 71, no. 2 (April 2006): 211–34.

Edgell, Penny, Douglas Hartmann, Evan Stewart, and Joseph Gerteis. "Atheists and Other Cultural Outsiders: Moral Boundaries and the Non-Religious in the United States." *Social Forces* 95, no. 2 (December 7, 2016): 607–38. https://doi.org/10.1093/sf/sow063.

Ellison, Ralph. *Invisible Man*. New York: Vintage Books, 1995.

Empiricus, Sextus. *Outlines of Scepticism*. Cambridge Texts in the History of Philosophy. Cambridge: Cambridge University Press, 2000.

Engelhart, Katie. "After a Schism, a Question: Can Atheist Churches Last?" *CNN Belief Blog*, January 4, 2014. http://religion.blogs.cnn.com.

Engelke, Matthew. "The Coffin Question: Death and Materiality in Humanist Funerals." *Material Religion* 11, no. 1 (2015): 26–48. https://doi.org/10.2752/2053932 15X14259900061553.

———. "On Atheism and Non-religion: An Afterword." *Social Analysis* 59, no. 2 (2015): 135–45.

Epstein, Greg M. *Good without God: What a Billion Non-religious People Do Believe*. New York: William Morrow, 2009.

Epstein, Greg M., and James Croft. "The Godless Congregation: An Idea Whose Time Has Come." *Free Inquiry* 33, no. 6 (October 2013). https://secularhumanism.org.

Evans, Curtis J. *The Burden of Black Religion*. New York: Oxford University Press, 2008.

Ex-Muslims of North America. "Fighting Allah, Defending Muslims—Armin Navabi, Imtiaz Shams, Muhammad Syed." YouTube, January 5, 2018. https://www.youtube.com/watch?v=KwnHreJNavE.

Fahmy, Dalia. "Key Findings about Americans' Belief in God." Pew Research Center, April 25, 2018. www.pewresearch.org.

Faircloth, Sean. "Our Secular Decade: Goals and Tactics of the Nontheist Movement." TheHumanist.com, March 10, 2010. https://thehumanist.com.

Fanon, Frantz. *Black Skin, White Masks*. Translated by Charles Lam Markmann. New York: Grove, 1967.

Farer, Tom. "The Rise of the Inter-American Human Rights Regime: No Longer a Unicorn, Not Yet an Ox." *Human Rights Quarterly* 19, no. 3 (1997): 510–46.

Farman, Abou. "Mind out of Place: Transhuman Spirituality." *Journal of the American Academy of Religion* 87, no. 1 (March 6, 2019): 57–80. https://doi.org/10.1093/jaarel/lfy039.

———. *On Not Dying: Secular Immortality in the Age of Technoscience*. Minneapolis: University of Minnesota Press, 2020.

———. "Speculative Matter: Secular Bodies, Minds, and Persons." *Cultural Anthropology* 28, no. 4 (2013): 737–59.

Fauset, Arthur Huff. *Black Gods of the Metropolis*. Philadelphia: University of Pennsylvania Press, 1944.

Fazzino, Lori L., and Ryan T. Cragun. "Splitters! Lessons from Monty Python for Secular Organizations in the US." In *Organized Secularism in the United States*, edited by Ryan T. Cragun, Christel Manning, and Lori L. Fazzino, 57–85. Berlin: De Gruyter, 2017.

Febvre, Lucien. *The Problem of Unbelief in the Sixteenth Century: The Religion of Rabelais*. Cambridge, MA: Harvard University Press, 1985.

Fellowship of Humanity v. County of Alameda, 153 Cal. App. 2d 673 (1957).

Fernando, Mayanthi. "Belief and/in the Law." *Method and Theory in the Study of Religion* 24, no. 1 (2012): 71–80.

———. *The Republic Unsettled: Muslim French and the Contradictions of Secularism*. Durham, NC: Duke University Press, 2014.

Fessenden, Tracy. *Culture and Redemption: Religion, the Secular, and American Literature*. Princeton, NJ: Princeton University Press, 2007.

FFRF v. Geithner, Defendant's Brief in Support of Its Motion for Summary Judgment. W.D. Wis. (2011).

Fields, Karen E., and Barbara J. Fields. *Racecraft: The Soul of Inequality in American Life*. New York: Verso, 2014.

Firkins, O. W. "The Two Humanisms: A Discrimination." *New Humanist* 4 (1931): 1–9.

First Unitarian Society of Minneapolis. "Frequently Asked Questions." Accessed March 1, 2021. https://firstunitarian.org.

Fitzgerald, Timothy. *Religion and Politics in International Relations: The Modern Myth*. New York: Continuum, 2011.

———, ed. *Religion and the Secular: Historical and Colonial Formations*. London: Equinox, 2007.

Flaccus, Gillian. "Atheist 'Mega-Churches' Take Root across US, World." National Public Radio, November 10, 2013. www.npr.org.

Flew, Antony. *God, Freedom, and Immortality*. Buffalo, NY: Prometheus Books, 1984.

Floyd-Thomas, Juan Marcial. *The Origins of Black Humanism in America: Reverend Ethelred Brown and the Unitarian Church*. New York: Palgrave Macmillan, 2008.

Foerster, Norman, ed. *Humanism and America: Essays on the Outlook of American Civilisation*. New York: Farrar and Rinehart, 1930.

Foner, Philip S., and R. Landor. "Two Neglected Interviews with Karl Marx." *Science & Society* 36, no. 1 (1972): 3–28.

"Forum: Recovering the Immanentist Tradition." *The Immanent Frame*, 2017. https://tif.ssrc.org.

Foucault, Michel. *The History of Sexuality*. Vol. 1. Translated by Robert Hurley. New York: Vintage Books, 1976.

———. "Nietzsche, Genealogy, History." In *Language, Counter-Memory, Practice: Selected Essays and Interviews*, edited by Donald F. Bouchard, translated by Donald F. Bouchard and Sherry Simon, 139–64. Ithaca, NY: Cornell University Press, 2019.

Foundation Beyond Belief. "Interview: Sikivu Hutchinson, Humanism at Work Speaker." *Foundation Beyond Belief Blog*, June 17, 2015. https://foundationbeyondbelief.org.

Frazier, E. Franklin. *The Negro Church in America*. New York: Schocken Books, 1974.

———. "Rejoinder." *American Sociological Review* 8 (1943): 402–4.

Freedom From Religion Foundation. "Billboards in Action!" Accessed February 1, 2016. https://ffrf.org.

———. "Chapters." December 28, 2013. http://ffrf.org.
———. "FFRF Urges Atlanta to Abandon the Supernatural." June 13, 2018. https://ffrf.org.
———. "Greater Sacramento FFRF Chapter." Accessed August 13, 2019. http://ffrf.org.
Freud, Sigmund. "On Narcissism: An Introduction." In *The Standard Edition of the Complete Psychological Works of Sigmund Freud*, vol. 14, edited by James Strachey, 67–102. London: Hogarth, 1957.
———. *The Uncanny* [*Das Unheimliche*]. Translated by David McLintock. New York: Penguin Books, 2003.
Frost, Jacqui. "Rejecting Rejection Identities: Negotiating Positive Non-religiosity at the Sunday Assembly." In *Organized Secularism in the United States*, edited by Ryan T. Cragun, Christel Manning, and Lori L. Fazzino, 171–90. Boston: De Gruyter, 2017.
Furst, Randy. "Protestors Shut Down I-94 in St. Paul for Hours." *Minneapolis Star Tribune*, July 11, 2016. www.startribune.com.
Galef, Julia. "3 Ways CFAR Has Changed My Perspective on Rationality." Center for Applied Rationality, 2013. www.rationality.org.
García, Alfredo. "The Walls of Wynwood: Art and Change in the Global Neighborhood." PhD diss., Princeton University, 2017.
García, Alfredo, and Joseph Blankholm. "The Social Context of Organized Nonbelief: County-Level Predictors of Nonbeliever Organizations in the United States." *Journal for the Scientific Study of Religion* 55, no. 1 (2016): 70–90.
Garriott, William, and Kevin Lewis O'Neill. "Who Is a Christian? Further Notes toward an Anthropology of Christianity." *Anthropological Theory* 8, no. 4 (2008): 381–98.
Gay, Peter. *The Enlightenment: An Interpretation*. Vol. 1, *The Rise of Modern Paganism*. New York: Norton, 1995.
———. *The Enlightenment: An Interpretation*. Vol. 2, *The Science of Freedom*. Rev. ed. New York: Norton, 2013.
Gaylor, Annie Laurie. *Women without Superstition: "No Gods—No Masters": The Collected Writings of Women Freethinkers of the Nineteenth and Twentieth Centuries*. Madison, WI: Freedom From Religion Foundation, 1997.
Geertz, Clifford. *The Interpretation of Cultures*. New York: Basic Books, 2000.
Gerbner, Katharine. *Christian Slavery: Conversion and Race in the Protestant Atlantic World*. Philadelphia: University of Pennsylvania Press, 2018.
———. "'They Call Me Obea': German Moravian Missionaries and Afro-Caribbean Religion in Jamaica, 1754–1760." *Atlantic Studies* 12, no. 2 (2015): 160–78.
Geroulanos, Stefanos. *An Atheism That Is Not Humanist Emerges in French Thought*. Cultural Memory in the Present. Stanford, CA: Stanford University Press, 2010.
Gillespie, Michael Allen. *The Theological Origins of Modernity*. Chicago: University of Chicago Press, 2008.
Ginzberg, Lori D. "'The Hearts of Your Readers Will Shudder': Fanny Wright, Infidelity, and American Freethought." *American Quarterly* 46, no. 2 (1994): 195–226.

"Godless Revival, The." Facebook, September 16, 2018. https://www.facebook.com/pg/The-Godless-Revival-532305740178434/posts/.
Goldman, Emma. "The Philosophy of Atheism." *Mother Earth*, February 1916. www.marxists.org.
Gonzalez, David. "Temple with No Place for God Seeks a Place." *New York Times*, June 11, 1994. www.nytimes.com.
Goodridge v. Department of Public Health, 798 N.E.2d 941 (Mass. 2003).
Gordon, Avery. *Ghostly Matters: Haunting and the Sociological Imagination*. Minneapolis: University of Minnesota Press, 1997.
Gorski, Philip S., David Kyuman Kim, John Torpey, and Jonathan VanAntwerpen, eds. *The Post-secular in Question: Religion in Contemporary Society*. New York: New York University Press, 2012.
Grayling, A. C. *The God Argument: The Case against Religion and for Humanism*. New York: Bloomsbury, 2013.
Greenberg, Udi. "Is Religious Freedom Protestant? On the History of a Critical Idea." *Journal of the American Academy of Religion* 88, no. 1 (2020): 74–91.
Greenblatt, Stephen. *The Swerve: How the World Became Modern*. New York: Norton, 2011.
Greenwald, Glenn. "Sam Harris, the New Atheists, and Anti-Muslim Animus." *Guardian*, April 3, 2013. www.theguardian.com.
Gregory, Brad S. *The Unintended Reformation: How a Religious Revolution Secularized Society*. Cambridge, MA: Harvard University Press, 2012.
Guenther, Katja M. "Bounded by Disbelief: How Atheists in the United States Differentiate Themselves from Religious Believers." *Journal of Contemporary Religion* 29, no. 1 (2014): 1–16.
Guenther, Katja M., Kerry Mulligan, and Cameron Papp. "From the Outside In: Crossing Boundaries to Build Collective Identity in the New Atheist Movement." *Social Problems* 60, no. 4 (November 2013): 457–75.
GuideStar. "American Ethical Union Inc." Accessed August 13, 2019. www.guidestar.org.
Hadas, Moses. *Humanism: The Greek Ideal and Its Survival*. New York: Harper, 1960.
Hägglund, Martin. *Radical Atheism: Derrida and the Time of Life*. Stanford, CA: Stanford University Press, 2008.
———. *This Life: Secular Faith and Spiritual Freedom*. Norwell, MA: Anchor, 2020.
Hall, Stuart. "Culture, Community, Nation." *Cultural Studies* 7, no. 3 (October 1, 1993): 349–63.
———. "Response to Saba Mahmood." *Cultural Studies* 10, no. 1 (January 1, 1996): 12–15. https://doi.org/10.1080/09502389600490431.
Hammer, Olav. *Claiming Knowledge: Strategies of Epistemology from Theosophy to the New Age*. Numen Book Series 90. Leiden: Brill, 2003.
———. "New Age Religion and the Sceptics." In *Handbook of New Age*, edited by James Lewis and Daren Kemp, 375–404. Brill Handbooks on Contemporary Religion. Leiden: Brill, 2007.
Haraway, Donna. "Manifesto for Cyborgs: Science, Technology, and Socialist-Feminism in the 1980s." *Socialist Review* 80 (1985): 65–108.

Harbour, Daniel. *An Intelligent Person's Guide to Atheism*. London: Duckworth, 2003.
Harris, Sam. "Brain Science and Human Values." *Sam Harris* (blog), September 9, 2008. https://samharris.org.
———. *The End of Faith: Religion, Terror, and the Future of Reason*. New York: Norton, 2004.
———. "Forbidden Knowledge: A Conversation with Charles Murray." *Making Sense* (podcast), April 22, 2017. https://samharris.org.
———. *Letter to a Christian Nation*. New York: Vintage Books, 2008.
———. *The Moral Landscape*. New York: Free Press, 2010.
———. *Waking Up: A Guide to Spirituality without Religion*. New York: Simon and Schuster, 2014.
Harrison, Peter. *The Territories of Science and Religion*. Chicago: University of Chicago Press, 2015.
Hart, William D. *Afro-Eccentricity: Beyond the Standard Narrative of Black Religion*. New York: Palgrave Macmillan, 2011.
———. "'One Percenters': Black Atheists, Secular Humanists, and Naturalists." *South Atlantic Quarterly* 112, no. 4 (October 1, 2013): 675–96. https://doi.org/10.1215/00382876-2345234.
"Having It Both Ways." *Free Inquiry* 22, no. 4 (Fall 2002): 40.
Hecht, Jennifer. *Doubt: A History; The Great Doubters and Their Legacy of Innovation from Socrates and Jesus to Thomas Jefferson and Emily Dickinson*. New York: Harper Collins, 2003.
Heidegger, Martin. *Being and Time*. Translated by John Macquarrie and Edward Robinson. New York: Harper and Row, 1962.
———. *Introduction to Phenomenological Research*. Translated by Daniel O. Dahlstrom. Bloomington: Indiana University Press, 2005.
———. "Letter on Humanism." In *Basic Writings*, edited by David Farrell Krell, translated by Frank A. Capuzzi and J. Glenn Gray, 213–65. San Francisco: HarperSanFrancisco, 1993.
Helderman, Ira P. "Drawing the Boundaries between 'Religion' and 'Secular' in Psychotherapists' Approaches to Buddhist Traditions in the United States." *Journal of the American Academy of Religion* 84, no. 4 (2016): 937–72.
Herskovits, Melville. *The Myth of the Negro Past*. Boston: Beacon, 1958.
Hirschkind, Charles. *The Ethical Soundscape: Cassette Sermons and Islamic Counterpublics*. New York: Columbia University Press, 2006.
———. "Is There a Secular Body?" *Cultural Anthropology* 26, no. 4 (2011): 633–47.
Hitchens, Christopher. *God Is Not Great: How Religion Poisons Everything*. New York: Twelve Books, 2007.
———, ed. *The Portable Atheist*. Boston: Da Capo, 2007.
Hobsbawm, Eric. "Introduction: Inventing Traditions." In *The Invention of Tradition*, edited by Eric Hobsbawm and Terence Ranger, 1–14. New York: Cambridge University Press, 1983.

Hoesly, Dusty. "Your Wedding, Your Way: Personalized, Nonreligious Weddings through the Universal Life Church." In *Organized Secularism in the United States*, edited by Ryan T. Cragun, Christel Manning, and Lori Fazzino, 253–78. Berlin: De Gruyter, 2017.

Holbach, Baron d'. *The System of Nature or the Laws of the Moral and Physical World*. Translated by H. D. Robinson. Boston: J .P. Mendum, 1889.

Holland, Aaron. "Agnosticism." In *The New Encyclopedia of Unbelief*, edited by Tom Flynn, 33–35. Amherst, NY: Prometheus Books, 2007.

Holley, Peter. "How the Satanic Temple Forced Phoenix Lawmakers to Ban Public Prayer." *Washington Post*, February 5, 2016. www.washingtonpost.com.

Hollinger, David A. *After Cloven Tongues of Fire: Protestant Liberalism in Modern American History*. Princeton, NJ: Princeton University Press, 2015.

Holyoake, George Jacob. *The Origin and Nature of Secularism: Showing That Where Freethought Commonly Ends Secularism Begins*. London: Watts, 1896.

Hong, Howard V. "The Comic, Satire, Irony, and Humor: Kierkegaardian Reflections." *Midwest Studies in Philosophy* 1, no. 1 (1976): 98–105.

Hoop, Katrina C. "Being a Community of Individuals: Collective Identity and Rhetorical Strategies in a Unitarian Universalist Church." *International Review of Modern Sociology* 38, no. 1 (2012): 105–30.

Horkheimer, Max, and Theodor W. Adorno. *Dialectic of Enlightenment: Philosophical Fragments*. Translated by Edmund Jephcott. Stanford, CA: Stanford University Press, 2002.

Hout, Michael. "Religious Ambivalence, Liminality, and the Increase of No Religious Preference in the United States, 2006–2014." *Journal for the Scientific Study of Religion* 56, no. 1 (2017): 52–63.

Hout, Michael, and Claude S. Fischer. "Explaining Why More Americans Have No Religious Preference: Political Backlash and Generational Succession, 1987–2012." *Sociological Science* 1, no. 24 (2014): 423–47.

———. "Why More Americans Have No Religious Preference: Politics and Generations." *American Sociological Review* 67, no. 2 (2002): 165–90. https://doi.org/10.2307/3088891.

Hudson, Nicholas. "What Is the Enlightenment? Investigating the Origins and Ideological Uses of an Historical Category." *Lumen* 25 (2006): 163–74.

Humanists International. "The Amsterdam Declaration." Accessed March 1, 2021. https://humanists.international.

———. "Amsterdam Declaration 1952." Amsterdam: Humanists International, World Humanist Congress, 1952. https://humanists.international.

Humanist Society. "About the Humanist Society." Accessed August 31, 2013. http://humanist-society.org.

Hungerford, Amy. *Postmodern Belief: American Literature and Religion Since 1960*. Princeton, NJ: Princeton University Press, 2010.

Hunsberger, Bruce E., and Bob Altemeyer. *Atheists: A Groundbreaking Study of America's Nonbelievers*. Amherst, NY: Prometheus Books, 2006.

Hurd, Elizabeth Shakman. *Beyond Religious Freedom: The New Global Politics of Religion*. Princeton, NJ: Princeton University Press, 2015.
Hussain, Murtaza. "Scientific Racism, Militarism, and the New Atheists." *Aljazeera*, April 2, 2013. www.aljazeera.com.
Husserl, Edmund. *Ideas: A General Introduction to Pure Phenomenology*. Translated by W. R. Boyce Gibson. New York: Collier Books, 1963.
Hutchinson, Sikivu. *Moral Combat: Black Atheists, Gender Politics, and the Values Wars*. Los Angeles: Infidel Books, 2011.
Huxley, Thomas H. "Agnosticism." In *Collected Essays*, vol. 5, *Science and Christian Tradition*, 209–62. New York: D. Appleton, 1902.
Israel, Jonathan I. *Radical Enlightenment: Philosophy and the Making of Modernity, 1650–1750*. New York: Oxford University Press, 2001.
Jackson, John L. *Thin Description*. Cambridge, MA: Harvard University Press, 2013.
Jacoby, Susan. *Freethinkers: A History of American Secularism*. New York: Owl Books, 2004.
Jakobsen, Janet R., and Ann Pellegrini, eds. *Secularisms*. Social Text Books. Durham, NC: Duke University Press, 2008.
James, William. *Varieties of Religious Experience: A Study in Human Nature*. New York: Routledge, 2002.
Johnson, Greg. "Materialising and Performing Hawaiian Religion(s) on Mauna Kea." In *Handbook of Indigenous Religion(s)*, edited by Greg Johnson and Siv Ellen Kraft, 156–75. Brill Handbooks on Contemporary Religion 15. Leiden: Brill, 2017.
Jones, William R. *Is God a White Racist? A Preamble to Black Theology*. Boston: Beacon, 1998.
Josephs, Brian. "Black Atheists Explain What It's Like to Be a 'Double Minority.'" *Vice*, April 22, 2016. www.vice.com.
Kant, Immanuel. *Groundwork for the Metaphysics of Morals*. Translated by Allen W. Wood. New Haven, CT: Yale University Press, 2002.
Kaplan, Mordecai. *Judaism without Supernaturalism*. New York: Reconstructionist Press, 1958.
Kasselstrand, Isabella. "'We Still Wanted That Sense of Occasion': Traditions and Meaning-Making in Scottish Humanist Marriage Ceremonies." *Scottish Affairs* 27, no. 3 (2018): 273–93.
Kaviraj, Sudipta. "Disenchantment Deferred." In *Beyond the Secular West*, edited by Akeel Bilgrami, 135–87. New York: Columbia University Press, 2016.
KCET. "La Fonda Restaurant." Accessed September 26, 2019. www.kcet.org.
Keane, Webb. *Christian Moderns: Freedom and Fetish in the Mission Encounter*. Berkeley: University of California Press, 2011.
Keatley, Susan Reslewic. "Should You Circumcise Your Baby Boy?" *New York Times*, April 17, 2020. www.nytimes.com.
Keel, Terence. *Divine Variations: How Christian Thought Became Racial Science*. Stanford, CA: Stanford University Press, 2018.
Kennedy, Emmet. "'Ideology' from Destutt de Tracy to Marx." *Journal of the History of Ideas* 40, no. 3 (1979): 353–68.

Kenny, Anthony. *Faith and Reason*. New York: Columbia University Press, 1983.
Kettell, Steven. "Divided We Stand: The Politics of the Atheist Movement in the United States." *Journal of Contemporary Religion* 29, no. 3 (September 2, 2014): 377–91.
———. "Faithless: The Politics of New Atheism." *Secularism and Nonreligion* 2 (November 21, 2013): 61–72. https://doi.org/10.5334/snr.al.
Khawaja, Noreen. *The Religion of Existence: Asceticism in Philosophy from Kierkegaard to Sartre*. Chicago: University of Chicago Press, 2016.
Kierkegaard, Soren. *Fear and Trembling*. In *Fear and Trembling; Repetition*, Kierkegaard's Writings 6, edited by Howard V. Hong and Edna H. Hong, 1–123 Princeton, NJ: Princeton University Press, 1983.
Kojève, Alexandre. *Atheism*. Translated by Jeff Love. New York: Columbia University Press, 2018.
Kors, Alan Charles. *Atheism in France, 1650–1729: The Orthodox Sources of Disbelief*. Princeton, NJ: Princeton University Press, 1990.
———. "The Atheism of D'Holbach and Naigeon." In *Atheism from the Reformation to the Enlightenment*, edited by Michael Hunter and David Wootton, 273–300. New York: Oxford University Press, 1992.
———. *D'Holbach's Coterie: An Enlightenment in Paris*. Princeton, NJ: Princeton University Press, 1976.
———. *Epicureans and Atheists in France, 1650–1729*. New York: Cambridge University Press, 2016.
———. *Naturalism and Unbelief in France, 1650–1729*. New York: Cambridge University Press, 2016.
Kosmin, Barry A., and Ariela Keysar. "American Religious Identification Survey (ARIS 2008)." Hartford, CT: Trinity College, 2008. www.americanreligionsurvey-aris.org.
Kosmin, Barry A., Ariela Keysar, Ryan Cragun, and Juhem Navarro-Rivera. *American Nones: The Profile of the No Religion Population; A Report Based on the American Religious Identification Survey 2008*. Hartford, CT: Trinity College, 2009. https://commons.trincoll.edu.
Kristeller, Paul Oskar. "Humanism." In *The Cambridge History of Renaissance Philosophy*, edited by Charles B. Schmitt, Quentin Skinner, Eckhard Kessler, and Jill Kraye, 7th ed, 113–37. Cambridge: Cambridge University Press, 2007.
Kurtz, Paul. *Eupraxophy: Living without Religion*. Amherst, NY: Prometheus Books, 1989.
———. *Humanist Manifesto 2000: A Call for a New Planetary Humanism*. Amherst, NY: Prometheus Books, 2000.
———. *Meaning and Value in a Secular Age: Why Eupraxsophy Matters*. Edited by Nathan Bupp. New York: Penguin, 2012.
Laborde, Cécile. *Liberalism's Religion*. Cambridge, MA: Harvard University Press, 2017.
LaHaye, Tim. *The Battle for the Mind*. Old Tappan, NJ: Fleming H. Revell, 1979.
Lamont, Corliss. *The Philosophy of Humanism*. 8th ed. Washington DC: Humanist Press, 1997.
———. *Yes to Life: Memoirs of Corliss Lamont*. New York: Crossroad/Continuum, 1991.

Latour, Bruno. *We Have Never Been Modern*. Cambridge, MA: Harvard University Press, 1993.
Layman, Geoffrey C. "Religion and Political Behavior in the United States: The Impact of Beliefs, Commitment, and Affiliation From 1980 to 1994." *Public Opinion Quarterly* 61, no. 2 (Summer 1997): 288–316.
Layman, Geoffrey C., and Christopher L. Weaver. "Religion and Secularism among American Party Activists." *Politics and Religion* 9 (2016): 271–95.
Lean, Nathan. "Dawkins, Harris, Hitchens: New Atheists Flirt with Islamophobia." *Salon*, March 29, 2013. www.salon.com.
LeDrew, Stephen. "Discovering Atheism: Heterogeneity in Trajectories to Atheist Identity and Activism." *Sociology of Religion* 74, no. 4 (December 12, 2013): 431–53. https://doi.org/10.1093/socrel/srt014.
———. *The Evolution of Atheism: The Politics of a Modern Movement*. New York: Oxford University Press, 2015.
Leitgeb, Lori E. "Building Theology, Reinscribing Subjectivity: Cultivating a Liberal Identity in Unitarian Universalism." PhD diss., University at Buffalo, State University of New York, 2009.
LePoidevin, Robin. *Agnosticism: A Very Short Introduction*. New York: Oxford University Press, 2010.
"Letter on Justice and Open Debate, A." *Harper's Magazine*, July 7, 2020. https://harpers.org.
Levinas, Emmanuel. *Proper Names*. Translated by Michael Smith. Stanford, CA: Stanford University Press, 1997.
———. *Sur Maurice Blanchot*. Montpellier, France: Fata Morgana, 1975.
Levitt, Laura. "Impossible Assimilations, American Liberalism, and Jewish Difference: Revisiting Jewish Secularism." *American Quarterly* 59, no. 3 (2007): 807–32.
———. "Revisiting Jewish Secularism in America." In *Secularisms*, edited by Janet R. Jakobsen and Ann Pellegrini, 108–38. Durham, NC: Duke University Press, 2008.
———. "What Is Religion Anyway? Rereading the Postsecular from an American Jewish Perspective." *Religion & Literature* 41, no. 3 (2009): 107–18.
Lewis, William S. "Althusser's Scientism and Aleatory Materialism." *Décalages* 2, no. 1 (2016). http://scholar.oxy.edu.
Lim, Chaeyoon, Carol Ann MacGregor, and Robert D. Putnam. "Secular and Liminal: Discovering Heterogeneity among Religious Nones." *Journal for the Scientific Study of Religion* 49, no. 4 (2010): 596–618.
Lipka, Michael. "10 Facts about Religion in America." Pew Research Center, August 27, 2015. www.pewresearch.org.
Lloyd, Vincent. "The Negative Political Theology of James Baldwin." In *A Political Companion to James Baldwin*, edited by Susan J. McWilliams, 174–94. Lexington: University Press of Kentucky, 2017.
Lofton, Kathryn. *Consuming Religion*. Class 200: New Studies in Religion. Chicago: University of Chicago Press, 2017.
Lomnitz, Claudio. "Secularism and the Mexican Revolution." In *Beyond the Secular West*, edited by Akeel Bilgrami, 97–116. New York: Columbia University Press, 2016.

Lopez, Donald S. "Belief." In *Critical Terms of Religious Studies*, edited by Mark C. Taylor, 21–35. Chicago: University of Chicago Press, 1998.

Loren, Degan, and Carol Rambo. "'God Smites You!': Atheists' Experience of Stigma, Identity Politics, and Queerness." *Deviant Behavior* 40, no. 4 (2019): 445–60.

Löwith, Karl. *Meaning in History*. Chicago: University of Chicago Press, 1949.

Lubac, Henri de. *The Drama of Atheist Humanism*. Cleveland, OH: Meridian Books, 1963.

Luehrmann, Sonja. *Secularism Soviet Style: Teaching Atheism and Religion in a Volga Republic*. New Anthropologies of Europe. Bloomington: Indiana University Press, 2011.

MacIntyre, Alasdair. *After Virtue: A Study in Moral Theory*. Notre Dame, IN: University of Notre Dame Press, 2007.

———. *Whose Justice? Which Rationality?* Notre Dame, IN: University of Notre Dame Press, 1988.

Mahmood, Saba. "A Brief Response to Stuart Hall's Comments on My Essay 'Cultural Studies and Ethnic Absolutism.'" *Cultural Studies* 10, no. 3 (1996): 506–7. https://doi.org/10.1080/09502389600490311.

———. "Cultural Studies and Ethnic Absolutism: Comments on Stuart Hall's 'Culture, Community, Nation.'" *Cultural Studies* 10, no. 1 (January 1, 1996): 1–11. https://doi.org/10.1080/09502389600490421.

———. *Politics of Piety: The Islamic Revival and the Feminist Subject*. Princeton, NJ: Princeton University Press, 2012.

———. *Religious Difference in a Secular Age: A Minority Report*. Princeton, NJ: Princeton University Press, 2016.

———. "Secularism, Hermeneutics, and Empire: The Politics of Islamic Reformation." *Public Culture* 18, no. 2 (April 1, 2006): 323–47. https://doi.org/10.1215/08992363-2006-006.

Mann, Nicholas. "The Origins of Humanism." In *The Cambridge Companion to Renaissance Humanism*, edited by Jill Kraye, 1–19. Cambridge Companions to Literature. New York: Cambridge University Press, 1996.

Manning, Christel J. *Losing Our Religion: How Unaffiliated Parents Are Raising Their Children*. New York: New York University Press, 2015.

———. "Unaffiliated Parents and the Religious Training of Their Children." *Sociology of Religion* 74, no. 2 (2013): 149–75.

Marcus, George E. "Ethnography in/of the World System: The Emergence of Multi-sited Ethnography." *Annual Review of Anthropology* 24 (1995): 95–117.

Marcus, George E., and Michael M. J. Fischer. *Anthropology as Cultural Critique: The Experimental Moment in the Human Sciences*. Chicago: University of Chicago Press, 1986.

Martin, David. *A General Theory of Secularization*. New York: Harper and Row, 1979.

———. "Notes for a General Theory of Secularisation." *European Journal of Sociology* 10, no. 2 (1969): 192–201.

———. *On Secularization: Towards a Revised General Theory*. Aldershot, UK: Ashgate, 2005.

Martin, Michael. *Atheism: A Philosophical Justification*. Philadelphia: Temple University Press, 1990.

———. "Naturalism." In *The New Encyclopedia of Unbelief*, edited by Tom Flynn, 557–60. Amherst, NY: Prometheus Books, 2007.

Masci, David. "5 Facts about Blacks and Religion in America." Pew Research Center, February 7, 2018. www.pewresearch.org.

Masuzawa, Tomoko. *The Invention of World Religions; or, How European Universalism Was Preserved in the Language of Pluralism*. Chicago: University of Chicago Press, 2005.

McCrary, Charles. "Superstitious Subjects: US Religion, Race, and Freedom." *Method and Theory in the Study of Religion* 30, no. 1 (2017): 56–70.

McCrary, Charles, and Jeffrey Wheatley. "The Protestant Secular in the Study of American Religion: Reappraisal and Suggestions." *Religion* 47, no. 2 (April 3, 2017): 256–76. https://doi.org/10.1080/0048721X.2016.1244124.

McCreight, Jennifer. "How I Started Boobquake." *Daily Beast*, April 27, 2010. www.thedailybeast.com.

———. "How I Unwittingly Infiltrated the Boys Club & Why It's Time for a New Wave of Atheism." *Blag Hag* (blog), August 18, 2012. http://freethoughtblogs.com.

McCutcheon, Russell. "'They Licked the Platter Clean': On the Co-dependency of the Religious and the Secular." *Method & Theory in the Study of Religion* 19, nos. 3–4 (2007): 173–99.

McGrath, Alister. *The Twilight of Atheism: The Rise and Fall of Disbelief in the Modern World*. London: Rider, 2004.

McKinnon, Andrew. "Sociological Definitions, Language Games, and the 'Essence' of Religion." *Method & Theory in the Study of Religion* 14, no. 1 (January 1, 2002): 61–83. https://doi.org/10.1163/157006802760198776.

Mead, George H. *Mind, Self, and Society: From the Standpoint of a Social Behaviorist*. Chicago: University of Chicago Press, 1934.

Mehta, Samira. *Beyond Chrismukkah: The Christian-Jewish Interfaith Family in the United States*. Chapel Hill: University of North Carolina Press, 2018.

Mendieta, Eduardo, and Jonathan VanAntwerpen, eds. *The Power of Religion in the Public Sphere*. New York: Columbia University Press, 2011.

Merrill, Jeremy B. "Lobbying Registrations." ProPublica. Accessed July 1, 2019. https://projects.propublica.org.

Mill, John Stuart. "Theism." In *Three Essays on Religion*, 2nd ed., 125–257 London: Longmans, Green, Reader, and Dyer, 1874.

———. *Utilitarianism*. Edited by Roger Crisp. New York: Oxford University Press, 1998.

Miller, Emily McFarlan. "American Humanist Leader Roy Speckhardt Stepping Down to Make Room for Diverse Leaders." Religious News Service, February 5, 2021. https://religionnews.com.

Miller, Monica R. *Religion and Hip Hop*. Routledge Research in Religion, Media, and Culture. New York: Routledge, 2013.
Minois, Georges. *Histoire de l'athéisme: Les incroyants dans le monde occidental des origines à nos jours*. Paris: Favard, 1998.
Mintz, Sidney W., and Richard Price. *The Birth of African American Culture: An Anthropological Perspective*. Boston: Beacon, 1992.
Modern, John Lardas. *Secularism in Antebellum America: With Reference to Ghosts, Protestant Subcultures, Machines, and Their Metaphors: Featuring Discussions of Mass Media, Moby-Dick, Spirituality, Phrenology, Anthropology, Sing Sing State Penitentiary, and Sex with the New Motive Power*. Religion and Postmodernism. Chicago: University of Chicago Press, 2011.
"More Specific Letter on Justice and Open Debate, A." The Objective, July 10, 2020. www.objectivejournalism.org.
Moten, Fred. "Black Op." In "Comparative Racialization." Special issue. *PMLA* 123, no. 5 (2008): 1743–47.
Moyn, Samuel. *Christian Human Rights*. Philadelphia: University of Pennsylvania Press, 2015.
New York City Skeptics. "Drinking Skeptically." Accessed July 14, 2014. www.nycskeptics.org.
New York Freethinker's Association. "The Proceedings and Addresses of the Freethinker's Convention Held at Watkins, NY." New York: D. M. Bennett, 1878.
Nguyen, Viet Thanh. *The Sympathizer*. New York: Grove, 2015.
Nietzsche, Friedrich. *On the Genealogy of Morals*. Translated by Walter Kaufmann and R. J. Hollingdale. New York: Vintage, 1967.
Niose, David. *Nonbeliever Nation: The Rise of Secular Americans*. New York: Palgrave Macmillan, 2012.
Nongbri, Brent. *Before Religion: A History of a Modern Concept*. New Haven, CT: Yale University Press, 2013.
Nutte, Niels de, and Bert Gasenbeek, eds. *Organised Humanism in the World: Belgium, Great Britain, the Netherlands, and the United States of America, 1945–2005*. Brussels: Vrije Universiteit Press, 2019.
Offman-Zavala, Alysa. "The Great Foreskin Debate: Why the Midwest Leads the World in Infant Circumcision and What the Hell That Says about Us." *Detroit Metro Times*, October 1, 2014. www.metrotimes.com.
Olds, Mason. *American Religious Humanism*. Rev. ed. Minneapolis: Fellowship of Religious Humanists, 1996.
Oliphant, Elayne. "Circulations of the Sacred: Contemporary Art as 'Cultural' Catholicism in Paris." In *Global Secularisms in a Post-Secular Age*, edited by Michael Rectenwald, Rochelle Almeida, and George Levine, 287–94. Berlin: De Gruyter, 2015.
Onfray, Michael. *The Atheist Manifesto: The Case against Christianity, Judaism, and Islam*. New York: Arcade, 2007.
———. *Le traité d'athéologie: Physique de la métaphysique*. Paris: Grasset, 2005.

Onishi, Bradley B. *The Sacrality of the Secular: Postmodern Philosophy of Religion.* New York: Columbia University Press, 2018.
Ovid. *Metamorphoses.* Dallas: Spring, 1989.
"Pakistan Honour Killings on the Rise, Report Reveals." *BBC News,* April 1, 2016. www.bbc.com.
Palmer, Ada. *Reading Lucretius in the Renaissance.* I Tatti Studies in Italian Renaissance History. Cambridge, MA: Harvard University Press, 2014.
Passannante, Gerard. *The Lucretian Renaissance: Philology and the Afterlife of Tradition.* Chicago: University of Chicago Press, 2011.
Pecora, Vincent P. *Secularization without End: Beckett, Mann, Coetzee.* Notre Dame, IN: University of Notre Dame Press, 2015.
Peden, W. Creighton. "The Rise of American Humanism in the 19th and 20th Centuries." *Essays in the Philosophy of Humanism* 19, no. 2 (Fall–Winter 2011): 27–42.
Persons, Stow. *Free Religion: An American Faith.* New Haven, CT: Yale University Press, 1947.
Pfeffer, Leo. "How Religious Is Secular Humanism?" *Humanist* 48, no. 5 (1988): 13–18.
Pike, Sarah. *Earthly Bodies, Magical Selves: Contemporary Pagans and the Search for Community.* Berkeley: University of California Press, 2001.
Pinn, Anthony B., ed. *By These Hands: A Documentary History of African American Humanism.* New York: New York University Press, 2001.
———. "Humanism as Guide to Life Meaning." In *What Is Humanism, and Why Does It Matter?,* edited by Anthony B. Pinn, 28–41. New York: Routledge, 2014.
———. *Varieties of African American Religious Experience.* Minneapolis: Fortress, 1998.
———. *What Has the Black Church to Do with Public Life?* New York: Palgrave Macmillan, 2013.
Pond, Jamie L. "Living without God: Female Atheists and Stigma Management in the South." PhD diss., University of Kentucky, 2015.
Popkin, Richard H. *The History of Scepticism: From Savonarola to Bayle.* Rev. ed. Oxford: Oxford University Press, 2003.
Post, Albert. *Popular Freethought in America: 1825–1850.* New York: Columbia University Press, 1943.
Potter, Charles Francis. *Humanism: A New Religion.* New York: Simon and Schuster, 1930.
Prothero, Stephen. "My Take: Christians Should Denounce Norway's Christian Terrorist." *CNN Belief Blog,* July 26, 2011. http://religion.blogs.cnn.com.
Proudfoot, Wayne. *Religious Experience.* Berkeley: University of California Press, 1985.
Pugh, Tison, Michael H. Shank, Elaine Treharne, Marjorie Curry Woods, John Parker, David L. Sedley, Lee Morrissey, et al. "Book Review Forum: *The Swerve: How the World Became Modern.* By Stephen Greenblatt. W. W. Norton, 2011." *Medieval, Early Modern, Theory* 25, no. 4 (2013): 313–70.
Quack, Johannes. *Disenchanting India: Organized Rationalism and Criticism of Religion in India.* New York: Oxford University Press, 2011.

———. "Outline of a Relational Approach to 'Nonreligion.'" *Method & Theory in the Study of Religion* 26, nos. 4–5 (November 28, 2014): 439–69. https://doi.org/10.1163/15700682-12341327.

Raboteau, Albert J. *Slave Religion: The Invisible Institution in the Antebellum South.* Oxford: Oxford University Press, 2004.

Radest, Howard B. "Humanism as Experience." In *What Is Humanism, and Why Does It Matter?*, edited by Anthony B. Pinn, 2–27. New York: Routledge, 2014.

———. *Toward Common Ground: The Story of the Ethical Societies in the United States.* New York: Frederick Unger, 1969.

Rawls, John. *A Theory of Justice.* Cambridge, MA: Harvard University Press, 1999.

Richard Dawkins Foundation for Reason & Science. "Richard Dawkins Explains His 'Scarlet A' Lapel Pin—The Out Campaign." December 23, 2008. https://richarddawkins.net.

Ritchey, Jeff. "'One Nation under God': Identity and Resistance in a Rural Atheist Organization." *Journal of Religion and Popular Culture* 21, no. 2 (2009): 1–13.

Ritchie, Susan J. "The Flaming Chalice." Unitarian Universalist Association. Accessed March 1, 2021. www.uua.org.

Robbins, Joel. "Continuity Thinking and the Problem of Christian Culture: Belief, Time and the Anthropology of Christianity." *Current Anthropology* 48, no. 1 (2007): 5–38.

Roof, Wade Clark. *Spiritual Marketplace: Baby Boomers and the Remaking of American Religion.* Princeton, NJ: Princeton University Press, 1999.

Rorty, Richard. *Achieving Our Country: Leftist Thought in Twentieth-Century America.* Cambridge, MA: Harvard University Press, 1998.

Royle, Edward. *Victorian Infidels: The Origins of the British Secularist Movement, 1791–1866.* Manchester: Manchester University Press, 1974.

Rubenstein, Mary-Jane. *Pantheologies: Gods, Worlds, Monsters.* New York: Columbia University Press, 2018.

———. "The Twilight of the Doxai: Or, How to Philosophize with a Whac-a-Mole (TM) Mallet." *Method and Theory in the Study of Religion* 24 (2012): 64–70.

———. *Worlds without End: The Many Lives of the Multiverse.* New York: Columbia University Press, 2014.

Ruel, Malcolm. *Belief, Ritual and the Securing of Life: Reflexive Essays on a Bantu Religion.* Leiden: Brill, 1997.

Russell, Bertrand. "Pythagoras." In *The History of Western Philosophy*, 29–37. New York: Simon and Schuster, 1945.

Sagarena, Roberto Ramón Lint. *Aztlán and Arcadia: Religion, Ethnicity, and the Creation of Place.* New York: New York University Press, 2014.

Sartre, Jean-Paul. "Existentialism." In *Basic Writings*, edited by Stephen Priest, 20–57. New York: Routledge, 2001.

———. *Being and Nothingness.* Translated by Hazel Barnes. New York: Washington Square Press, 1956.

"Satanists Get Phoenix to Drop Council Prayer." *Freethought Today*, March 2016. https://ffrf.org.

Savage, Barbara. *Your Spirits Walk beside Us: The Politics of Black Religion*. Cambridge, MA: Harvard University Press, 2008.

Schaefer, Donovan O. *Religious Affects: Animality, Evolution, and Power*. Durham, NC: Duke University Press, 2015.

Schaeffer, Francis A. *How Should We Live Then?* Old Tappan, NJ: Fleming H. Revell, 1976.

Scheer, Monique, Nadia Fadil, and Birgitte Schepelern Johansen, eds. *Secular Bodies, Affects, and Emotions: European Configurations*. London: Bloomsbury Academic, 2019.

Scherer, Matthew. *Beyond Church and State: Democracy, Secularism, and Conversion*. Cambridge: Cambridge University Press, 2013.

Schmidt, Leigh Eric. *Village Atheists: How America's Unbelievers Made Their Way in a Godly Nation*. Princeton, NJ: Princeton University Press, 2016.

Schmidt, Leigh Eric, and Sally M. Promey, eds. *American Religious Liberalism*. Religion in North America. Bloomington: Indiana University Press, 2012.

Schnabel, Landon, Matthew Facciani, Ariel Sincoff-Yedid, and Lori Fazzino. "Gender and Atheism: Paradoxes, Contradictions, and an Agenda for Future Research." In *Sociology of Atheism*, edited by Roberto Cipriani and Franco Garelli, 75–97. Leiden: Brill, 2016.

Schwartzman, Micah. "What If Religion Is Not Special?" *University of Chicago Law Review* 79, no. 4 (2012): 1351–1427.

Scott, Joan Wallach. *Politics of the Veil*. Princeton, NJ: Princeton University Press, 2007.

———. *Sex and Secularism*. Princeton, NJ: Princeton University Press, 2018.

Seales, Chad E. *The Secular Spectacle: Performing Religion in a Southern Town*. New York: Oxford University Press, 2013.

Sehat, David. *The Myth of American Religious Freedom*. New York: Oxford University Press, 2011.

Selby, Jennifer. "Required Romance: On Secular Sensibilities in Recent French Marriage and Immigration Regulations." In *Secular Bodies, Affects, and Emotions: European Configurations*, edited by Monique Scheer, Nadia Fadil, and Birgitte Schepelern Johansen, 157–69. London: Bloomsbury Academic, 2019.

Sexton, Jared. "The Social Life of Social Death: On Afro-Pessimism and Black Optimism." *Intensions*, no. 5 (2011). www.yorku.ca.

Shah, Timothy Samuel, Alfred Stepan, and Monica Duffy Toft, eds. *Rethinking Religion and World Affairs*. New York: Oxford University Press, 2012.

Shelley, Mary. *Frankenstein; or, The Modern Prometheus*. London: Lackington, Hughes, Harding, Mavor, and Jones, 1818.

Shelton, Jason. "Changing the Words: An Historical Introduction to Unitarian Universalist Hymnody." *Unitarian Universalist History (Online)*, May 24, 2002, 1–12.

Sherine, Ariane. "Atheists—Gimme Five." *Guardian*, June 20, 2008. www.theguardian.com.

Sherkat, Darren E. *Changing Faith: The Dynamics and Consequences of Americans' Shifting Religious Identities*. New York: New York University Press, 2014.

Shermer, Michael. "Science is universal, international, inclusive, nonpartisan, a-political, a-gender, a-race, & a-ideological. Don't inject identity politics." Twitter post, March 22, 2017. https://twitter.com/michaelshermer/status/844714652420493313?s=20.

Simmons, Jonathan. "'Not That Kind of Atheist': Scepticism as a Lifestyle Movement." *Social Movement Studies* 17, no. 4 (2018): 437–315.

Skinner, Quentin. "Meaning and Understanding in the History of Ideas." *History and Theory* 8, no. 1 (1969): 3–53.

Smith, Christopher, and Richard Cimino. "Atheisms Unbound: The Role of the New Media in the Formation of a Secularist Identity." *Secularism and Nonreligion* 1, no. 0 (February 21, 2012): 17–31.

Smith, George H. *Atheism: The Case against God*. New York: Prometheus Books, 1980.

Smith, Jesse M. "Becoming an Atheist in America: Constructing Identity and Meaning from the Rejection of Theism." *Sociology of Religion* 72, no. 2 (July 1, 2011): 215–37. https://doi.org/10.1093/socrel/srq082.

———. "Creating a Godless Community: The Collective Identity Work of Contemporary American Atheists." *Journal for the Scientific Study of Religion* 52, no. 1 (March 1, 2013): 80–99. https://doi.org/10.2307/23353892.

Smith, Jonathan Z. *To Take Place: Toward Theory in Ritual*. Chicago: University of Chicago Press, 2000.

Smith, Per. "Spitting with the Wind." The New Humanism. Accessed August 31, 2013. http://thenewhumanism.org.

Smolkin, Victoria. *A Sacred Space Is Never Empty: A History of Soviet Atheism*. Princeton, NJ: Princeton University Press, 2018.

Snow, David A., E. Burke Rochford Jr., Steven K. Worden, and Robert D. Benford. "Frame Alignment Processes, Micromobilization, and Movement Participation." *American Sociological Review* 51, no. 4 (1986): 464–81.

Sorett, Josef. *Spirit in the Dark: A Religious History of Racial Aesthetics*. New York: Oxford University Press, 2016.

Speckhardt, Roy. "The Humanist Tax Exemption." Institute for Humanist Studies, February 7, 2007. http://archive.li.

Spinoza, Benedict de. *The Ethics*. In *A Spinoza Reader: The "Ethics" and Other Works*, translated by Edwin Curley, 85–265. Princeton, NJ: Princeton University Press, 1994.

Stahl, Ronit. *Enlisting Faith: How the Military Chaplaincy Shaped Religion and State in Modern America*. Cambridge, MA: Harvard University Press, 2017.

Steinmetz-Jenkins, Daniel, and Brittany Pheiffer. "Steve Bannon's Would-Be Coalition of Christian Traditionalists." *Atlantic*, March 24, 2017. www.theatlantic.com.

Stern, Eliyahu. *Jewish Materialism: The Intellectual Revolution of the 1870s*. New Haven, CT: Yale University Press, 2018.

Storm, Joseph Ānanda Josephson. *The Invention of Religion in Japan*. Chicago: University of Chicago Press, 2012.

———. "The Superstition, Secularism, and Religion Trinary: Or Re-theorizing Secularism." *Method & Theory in the Study of Religion* 30, no. 1 (January 2, 2018): 1–20.

Straton, John Roach. *The Famous New York Fundamentalist-Modernist Debates: The Orthodox Side*. New York: George H. Doran, 1925.

Strauss, Leo. "Notes on Lucretius." In *Liberalism Ancient and Modern*, 76–139. Chicago: University of Chicago Press, 1995.

———. *Persecution and the Art of Writing*. New York: Free Press, 1952.

Suchting, Wal. "Althusser's Late Thinking about Materialism." *Historical Materialism* 12, no. 1 (2004): 3–70.

Sugrue, Thomas J. *The Origins of the Urban Crisis: Race and Inequality in Postwar Detroit*. Princeton, NJ: Princeton University Press, 2014.

Sullivan, Winnifred Fallers. *The Impossibility of Religious Freedom*. Princeton, NJ: Princeton University Press, 2007.

———. *A Ministry of Presence: Chaplaincy, Spiritual Care, and the Law*. Chicago: University of Chicago Press, 2014.

Sunday Assembly New York City. "Assemblies Are on Hiatus, but We Aren't Stopping." January 19, 2016. http://nyc.sundayassembly.com.

Taves, Ann. "The Camp Meeting and the Paradoxes of Evangelical Protestant Ritual." In *Teaching Ritual*, edited by Catherine Bell, 119–32. New York: Oxford University Press, 2007.

———. *Religious Experience Reconsidered: A Building-Block Approach to the Study of Religion and Other Special Things*. Princeton, NJ: Princeton University Press, 2009.

———. *Revelatory Events: Three Case Studies of the Emergence of New Spiritual Paths*. Princeton, NJ: Princeton University Press, 2016.

Taylor, Charles. "Modes of Secularism." In *Secularism and Its Critics: Themes in Politics*, edited by Rajeev Bhargava, 32–53. New Delhi: Oxford University Press, 1998.

———. *A Secular Age*. Cambridge, MA: Harvard University Press, 2007.

Taylor, Mark C. *Altarity*. Chicago: University of Chicago Press, 1987.

———. *Confidence Games: Money and Markets in a World without Redemption*. Religion and Postmodernism. Chicago: University of Chicago Press, 2008.

———. "Denegating God." *Critical Inquiry* 20, no. 4 (1994): 592–610.

———. *Erring: A Postmodern A/Theology*. Chicago: University of Chicago Press, 1984.

———. *Hiding*. Religion and Postmodernism. Chicago: University of Chicago Press, 1998.

———. *The Moment of Complexity: Emerging Network Culture*. Chicago: University of Chicago Press, 2001.

———. *Nots*. Religion and Postmodernism. Chicago: University of Chicago Press, 1993.

"Tell Us Why You're a Freethinker." *Freethought Today*, March 1, 2011.

Toumey, Christopher P. "Evolution and Secular Humanism." *Journal of the American Academy of Religion* 61, no. 2 (July 1, 1993): 275–301. https://doi.org/10.1093/jaarel/LXI.2.275.

Town of Greece v. Galloway, 572 U.S. 565 (2014).

Travis, Trysh. *The Language of the Heart: A Cultural History of the Recovery Movement from Alcoholics Anonymous to Oprah Winfrey*. Chapel Hill: University of North Carolina Press, 2009.

Tuñon, Alberto Hidalgo de. "Materialism, Philosophical." In *The New Encyclopedia of Unbelief*, edited by Tom Flynn, 524–28. Amherst, NY: Prometheus Books, 2007.

United Coalition of Reason. "Find a Local Group." Accessed April 15, 2014. https://unitedcor.org/.

van Gennep, Arnold. *The Rites of Passage*. Translated by Monika B. Yizedom and Gabrielle L. Caffee. Chicago: University of Chicago Press, 1960.

Veer, Peter van der. *The Modern Spirit of Asia: The Spiritual and the Secular in China and India*. Princeton, NJ: Princeton University Press, 2014.

Voas, David. "Afterword: Some Reflection on Numbers in the Study of Religion." *Diskus* 16, no. 2 (2014): 116–24.

Voas, David, and Mark Chaves. "Is the United States a Counterexample to the Secularism Thesis?" *American Journal of Sociology* 121, no. 5 (2016): 1517–56.

Walker, David. "The Humbug in American Religion: Ritual Theories of Nineteenth-Century Spiritualism." *Religion and American Culture: A Journal of Interpretation* 23, no. 1 (2013): 30–74.

Walter, Nicolas. *Humanism: Finding Meaning in the Word*. London: Rationalist Press Association, 1994.

Warner, Michael, Jonathan VanAntwerpen, and Craig Calhoun, eds. *Varieties of Secularism in a Secular Age*. Cambridge, MA: Harvard University Press, 2010.

Warren, Sidney. *American Freethought: 1860–1914*. New York: Columbia University Press, 1943.

Washington Ethical Society v. District of Columbia, 249 F.2d 127 (B.C. Cir. 1957).

Weber, Max. "Religious Rejections of the World and Their Directions." In *From Max Weber: Essays in Sociology*, edited by H. H. Gerth and C. Wright Mills, 323–59. New York: Oxford University Press, 2013.

———. *The Vocation Lectures*. Edited by David S. Owen and Tracy B. Strong. Translated by Rodney Livingstone. Indianapolis: Hackett, 2004.

Weir, Todd H. "Germany and the New Global History of Secularism: Questioning the Postcolonial Genealogy." *Germanic Review: Literature, Culture, Theory* 90, no. 1 (January 2, 2015): 6–20. https://doi.org/10.1080/00168890.2014.986431.

———. *Monism: Science, Philosophy, Religion, and the History of a Worldview*. New York: Palgrave Macmillan, 2012.

———. *Secularism and Religion in Nineteenth-Century Germany: The Rise of the Fourth Confession*. New York: Cambridge University Press, 2014.

Wenger, Tisa Joy. *Religious Freedom: The Contested History of an American Ideal*. Chapel Hill: University of North Carolina Press, 2017.

———. *We Have a Religion: The 1920s Pueblo Indian Dance Controversy and American Religious Freedom*. Chapel Hill: University of North Carolina Press, 2009.

Wheatley, Jeffrey. "US Colonial Governance of Superstition and Fanaticism in the Philippines." *Method and Theory in the Study of Religion* 30, no. 1 (2017): 21–36.

Whitehead, John W., and John Conlan. "The Establishment of the Religion of Secular Humanism and Its First Amendment Implications." *Texas Tech Law Review* 10, no. 1 (1978): 1–66.

Whitmarsh, Tim. *Battling the Gods: Atheism in the Ancient World*. New York: Penguin, 2016.

Wielenberg, Erik J. *Value and Virtue in a Godless Universe*. New York: Oxford University Press, 2005.

Willrich, Michael. *Pox: An American History*. New York: Penguin, 2011.

Wilson, Edwin H. *The Genesis of a Humanist Manifesto*. Edited by Teresa Maciocha. Amherst, NY: Humanist Press, 1995.

Wilson, Jeff. *Mindful America: The Mutual Transformation of Buddhist Meditation and American Culture*. Oxford: Oxford University Press, 2014.

Wine, Sherwin T. *Judaism beyond God: A Radical New Way to Be Jewish*. Farmington Hills, MI: Society for Humanistic Judaism, 1985.

———. "Unbelief within Judaism." In *The New Encyclopedia of Unbelief*, edited by Tom Flynn, 455. Amherst, NY: Prometheus Books, 2007.

Winston, Carleton. *This Circle of Earth*. New York: G. P. Putnam, 1942.

Winston, Kimberly. "Federal Prisons Will Now Recognize Humanism." *HuffPost*, July 29, 2015. www.huffpost.com.

———. "New 'Openly Secular' Group Seeks to Combat Anti-Atheist Discrimination." *Washington Post*, May 2, 2014. www.washingtonpost.com.

Wittgenstein, Ludwig. *Philosophical Investigations*. Edited and translated by G. E. M. Anscombe, P. M. S. Hacker, and Joachim Schulte. 4th ed. Malden, MA: Blackwell, 2009.

Wootton, David. "New Histories of Atheism." In *Atheism from the Reformation to the Enlightenment*, edited by Michael Hunter and David Wootton, 13–53. Oxford: Oxford University Press, 1992.

Wuthnow, Robert. *The God Problem: Expressing Faith and Being Reasonable*. Berkeley: University of California Press, 2012.

———. *Inventing American Religion: Polls, Surveys, and the Tenuous Quest for a Nation's Faith*. Oxford: Oxford University Press, 2015.

Wynter, Sylvia. "The Re-enchantment of Humanism: An Interview (with David Scott)." *Small Axe* 8 (2000): 119–207.

Yelle, Robert A. *The Language of Disenchantment: Protestant Literalism and Colonial Discourse in British India*. New York: Oxford University Press, 2013.

———. *The Semiotics of Religion: Signs of the Sacred in History*. London: Bloomsbury, 2013.

Yovel, Yirmiyahu. *Spinoza and Other Heretics*. Vol. 1, *The Marrano of Reason*. Princeton, NJ: Princeton University Press, 1992.

———. *Spinoza and Other Heretics*. Vol. 2, *The Adventures of Immanence*. Princeton, NJ: Princeton University Press, 1992.

Zuckerman, Phil. *Faith No More: Why People Reject Religion*. Oxford: Oxford University Press, 2011.

———. *Society without God: What the Least Religious Nations Can Tell Us about Contentment*. New York: New York University Press, 2008.

INDEX

abstraction: into aesthetics, 82, 83, 94, 124, 217; from Christianity, 7, 8, 116–117, 132, 135, 144–145, 147, 214, 222; of community, 93; into culture or nonspecificity, 21, 81, 115, 126, 133, 136–138; description of the process of, 114; as emptiness, 132, 135, 139; haunted by source, 249n50; moment of silence, 134, 136; as neutrality, 131–133, 135, 139, 150; not inherently secular, 132; of prayer, 133–134, 136–137; of ritual , 111–113, 136–138, 141, 243n12, 243n17; as secular purification, 18, 75; 113–119, 127–128, 131–139, 142, 144–145, 214, 217–218, 246n49, 249n53; of tradition, 202; as universalization, 112–113, 116, 118, 132, 244n23; zeroing out through a cipher, 114, 116–118, 127, 139. *See also* analogy; community; culture; neutrality; ritual; secular purification; tradition

affect, affective, 5, 82 101, 115, 119, 127, 242n85, 242n86. *See also* emotion; feelings

agnostic, agnosticism, 6–7, 11, 35–39, 51–53, 69, 155, 160. *See also* nonbelievers; secular people

Alcoholics Anonymous, 30. *See also* higher power; spirituality

ambiguity: of atheism, 20, 49; of "ethical," 156–157; of "secular," 72, 180, 182–183, 187, 210, 224; of secularism, 66, 76, 148; of secular people, 10, 13, 22, 28, 71, 80, 121, 168, 188, 219

ambivalence: of being secular, 30, 66, 104, 118, 131, 162, 189, 231n46, 245n47, 248n60; modern, 230n11; semantic, 34; toward

belief, 28, 34, 56; toward religion, 3–4, 6, 16–20, 62, 68, 71, 74, 80, 82, 126, 138, 148, 219, 229n10

American Atheists, 14, 182

American Ethical Union, 15, 46, 178, 181, 254n89. *See also* Ethical Culture movement

American Humanist Association (AHA), 45–46, 60–62, 65, 69, 108, 135–136, 149, 164, 178, 252n56. *See also* Celebrant; humanism

analogy, 17–18, 82, 102, 108, 114, 134; to Christianity, 8, 72, 77, 135, 139, 219, 245n38; role in creating "religion," 7, 63, 71, 210, 222

Anidjar, Gil, 77, 238n22

apostasy, 48. *See also* heresy

Asad, Talal, 111–112, 154, 199–202, 230n14, 244n27, 246n49, 247n57, 247n58, 260n110

astrology, 72. *See also* woo-woo

atheism: affirmative, 20, 57, 142; anthropology of, 15, 231n46; Black (see atheist, Black); death, 198; father's, 105; gospel of, 131, 246n48, 259n93; history and emergence, 49, 130, 203–208; negative 5, 43, 58, 142; not a choice, 146–148, 154; ethical or not, 154–155, 157–160, 165–166, 191–192; ontological certainty of, 51, 150, 152, 210; philosophy of, 233n5; public resurgence of, 55, 172–173; stigma of, 49, 172–173, 181; strategic term and identity, 46–51, 58–59; tension within, 17, 19–20, 159–160, 232n50; whiteness of, 81, 92. *See also* a/theology; atheist; New Atheists; whiteness

289

atheist, 11, 16, 47–51, 57–58; atheist community, 58, 68, 91–92; atheistic worldview, 18, 20, 35, 39, 42, 52–53; aversion to use of term "atheist," 11, 16, 25, 39, 51; Black atheists, 31, 50, 71, 86–94, 101, 164–165; Hispanic atheists, 41, 145; as immoral person, 84, 155; Jewish atheists, 212; Native American atheists, 216; as self-identifier, 5–6, 22, 30, 172; White atheists, 81–82, 90, 92, 99. *See also* atheism; a/theology; community: mis-fit; New Atheists; secular misfits; whiteness

a/theology, 120, 208–209, 233n9. *See also* Taylor, Mark C.

avoidance, of religion, 113–117, 120–127, 147, 150, 202. *See also* secular purification

baptism, 8, 108, 233n7; de-baptism, 116, 130–131

Bell, Catherine, 112–113

belonging, 3, 7–8, 10, 16, 18, 57, 162, 219

Bender, Courtney, 240n59, 244n31, 254n80

blasphemy, 113–116, 127–131; ambiguity of, 114, 130–131, 244n34; Blasphemy Day, 130; Christianity of, 127, 245n38; as a mode of purification, 101; my own with this book, 119–120; as a bodily practice for secular Muslims, 96–98, 128–129; 213. *See also* ambiguity; humor and jokes; secular purification

Boghossian, Peter, 151–154, 157–158, 162–163, 166–167, 183, 246n48

Bourdieu, Pierre, 118. *See also* religion-related field

Catholicism, 64, 83–86, 110–112, 146, 215–217, 238n21; anti-Catholic, 112, 245n37. *See also* Christianity

Celebrant, 18, 60–63, 108–109, 113. *See also* humanism; Humanist Celebrants

Center for Inquiry (CFI), 14, 30, 61, 65–66, 69, 120–121, 130, 149, 167, 179–180

certainty: ontological, 51–52; moral, 159; uncertainty, 237n13. *See also* feelings: anxiety of uncertainty

Christianity, 77, 116–117, 127, 139, 156, 193, 203–205, 208–211, 212–214, 216–218, 233n8; and the category of religion, 63, 65, 71–72, 78, 112–113, 154, 200, 211; Christian inheritance, 7–10, 12, 22, 26, 30, 56, 120, 122, 125–126, 154, 219, 245n38; Christian-like, 49, 66, 72, 82, 159–160; Christian missionaries, 88; Christian roots, 40, 45; critique of, 93; early Christians, 49; leaving, 67, 131; non-Christian, 60, 63, 213, 219. *See also* abstraction: from Christianity; analogy; Catholicism; evangelical; haunting; Protestant

colonialism, 7, 50, 71–72, 82, 154, 200, 208, 238n23

community, 116, 118; ambivalence towards, 42, 101, 104, 147; secular, 5, 19, 21–22, 59, 68, 81–82, 90–93, 107–108, 165, 172

conversion, 88, 233n8; deconversion, 43, 84, 88, 98, 131, 135, 166–167, 211, 212, 213–214; secular, 43, 84, 89, 95, 127, 148, 151, 166–169, 178, 183–184, 198, 212, 249n13. *See also* translation

cosmology, 41, 206

Crawley, Ashon T., 93, 102, 241n77

critical thinking, 27, 145–146, 169; and ethics, 21, 90, 163; and skepticism, 36, 54, 150, 249n13

critique: affectionate, 22, 154, 202; immanent, 22, 93, 102, 154, 202; of religion, 244n36; of science, 159; of secularism, 153–154, 200, 202, 214; of Western feminism, 161

culture, 7, 21, 73, 126, 207, 215–217, 233n7; African-American or Black, 88–89, 93–94, 240n67; American, 16, 77, 152, 158, 170; Christian-centered, 8, 30,

49, 56, 71–72, 77, 125, 155, 158, 184, 195, 205, 214; Islamic or Muslim, 98–100; preservation of, 80–84, 88–89, 99, 100; purification of, 80–84, 86, 98, 100; secular, 9, 33, 101; of white people, 81–82, 89, 96, 101. *See also* discursive tradition; whiteness

Darwin, Charles, 28, 104, 176; theory of evolution, 52
Dawkins, Richard, 67, 77, 86, 90, 95, 99, 152, 172, 201, 233n8. *See also* New Atheists
deism, 37, 196, 229n10
Dennett, Daniel, 172. *See also* New Atheists
Derrida, Jacques, 207, 230n18
Descartes, René, 53, 245n39
discursive tradition, 115–116, 119, 199–200, 212, 214, 247n57. *See also* secular discursive tradition
dogma, opposition to, 15, 36–37, 39, 70–71, 101, 160, 196, 212, 232n50
doubt, 67, 88, 150; as purification, 37
Douglas, Mary, 229n9, 229n10
Durkheim, Émile, 119, 229n9

emotion, 82, 107, 114, 124; distrust of emotions, 21, 101. *See also* affect; feelings
empiricism, 54, 72, 119, 150–152, 161, 233n5, 233n9; limits of, 11, 51, 55; skepticism of, 154, 184; strict, 25, 52
Epicureanism, 161, 203–204, 206–207, 248n61
Ethical Culture movement, 2–6, 10, 14–15, 19, 25, 28, 32–33, 68, 76, 156–157, 178, 181, 221, 229n6, 234n15, 250n29, 254n89
ethics, 159–160, 245n86; and atheism, 156–158; personal, 42; as a process, 162; and religion, 2, 39; secular, 142, 148, 155–156, 165–166, 175; Spinoza's, 161. *See also* Spinoza, Baruch

evangelical, 46, 54, 67, 168, 183; evangelical atheist, 10, 50, 167. *See also* Christianity
Evans, Curtis J., 88, 102
Ex-Muslims of North America (EXMNA), 14, 96, 100, 128, 159, 242n84

faith, 52, 151–152; absence or avoidance of, 37, 39, 55; crisis of, 67; in science, 28; vs. reason or empirical evidence, 26, 38, 184; interfaith, 64, 78, 109–110; secular faith, 142
Farman, Abou, 198, 200, 209, 246n5, 260n110
feelings, 3, 6, 18, 30, 101, 110–111, 118, 126, 196, 219; anger, 44, 48, 114, 163, 168, 205–206; anxiety about religious pollution, 5, 118, 131, 140, 175, 213, 218; anxiety about inauthenticity, 85; anxiety about breaking bodily habits, 96, 126; anxiety about Jewishness, 138; anxiety about the absence of authority, 160–161; anxiety about death, 198, 248n61; anxiety of uncertainty, 209; confusion, 6, 11, 16, 20, 25, 71, 105, 237n5; crying, 105; depression, 95; familiarity, 14, 25, 86, 101, 106, 138; happiness, 64, 83–84, 162, 168, 171; joy, 42, 57, 67, 79, 114, 137; my own, as an object of inquiry, 16, 25, 105, 120–121. *See also* affect; emotion; religious pollution
feminism, 21, 99, 158, 161, 208
Fernando, Mayanthi, 85, 238n32, 240n62, 246n49, 257n64
Foucault, Michel, 161, 196, 201, 234n25
Freedom From Religion Foundation (FFRF), 3, 14–15, 27, 38–39, 64–65, 69–70, 116, 180, 237n13
freethinker, 52, 101, 110, 127; freethought movement, 4, 47, 70, 180; Hispanic freethinkers, 71, 80, 82; history of freethought, 36–38; as self-identifier, 6, 8, 11, 38–40, 51, 155, 169. *See also* misfit; secular misfits: Hispanic nonbelievers; secular people
Freud, Sigmund, 76, 239n44

García, Alfredo, 66, 236n58, 242n79
gender, 22, 50, 90, 164, 209, 246n49

Harris, Sam, 99, 172, 233n8, 253n70; and morality, 159, 161–162; and spirituality, 54–55, 234n16. See also New Atheists
Hart, William David, 93, 165, 194, 207, 236n46, 241n77
haunting (residue of religion), 116–120, 134, 136, 143, 199, 234n34, 246n50. See also Christianity: Christian inheritance
Hegelian idealism, 120, 218
Heidegger, Martin, 192–193, 195, 207–208, 245n39, 247n57
herding cats, 60, 101, 179
heresy, heretic, 17, 27, 48–50, 255n11. See also apostasy
higher power, 29–31, 33, 148, 230n20. See also spirituality
Hirschkind, Charles, 241n78, 242n85
Hispanic American Freethinkers, 80, 82
Hitchens, Christopher, 99, 104, 172. See also New Atheists
Hobsbawm, Eric, 196–198, 200
homosexuality, 31
humanism, 41–47, 109–110, 158, 165–169, 194–197, 222, 254n86, 256n39; history of, 44–47, 156–157 185, 188–193, 232n1, 255n8; humanistic Judaism, 74, 76–80, 85–86, 90, 93, 101, 138, 211, 239n50; humanist as self-identifier, 8, 11, 41, 155, 169, 180; and inclusion, 207–208; religious humanism, 32, 178, 185, 203, 209; secular humanism, 35, 39, 48, 52, 81–82, 202–203, 209, 231n44; Unitarian humanist tradition, 187. See also Humanist Celebrants; misfits; Nietzsche: Nietzschean Humanism; secular misfits: humanistic Jews; Unitarian Humanist Celebrants, 60–64, 108–109
humor and jokes: about atheism, 37, 51–52, 67, 172; about conference etiquette, 163; about Christianity, 114, 131, 144–145; about death, 105, 198; about Islam, 21, 97–98, 128–129, 144; about race, 107; my own laughter as an object of inquiry, 147–148, 221, 2489n10; tired of 206. See also affect; emotions; feelings: my own as an object of inquiry; herding cats
Hutchinson, Sikivu, 90–91, 163–164, 194, 241n71, 241n73

iconoclasm, 8, 82, 101, 182
identity: Black identity, 88–89, 93, 165; identity-based groups, 73; identity politics, 159; Jewish identity, 77–78, 138, 213, 239n52; Muslim identity, 24, 48; secular identity, 6, 20, 51, 66, 119, 134, 149–150, 170–173, 182, 188, 200, 203, 205, 209
ideology, 8, 24, 70, 232n1, 250n28; history of the term, 232n1; religious, 92; secular, 156; semiotic, 229n10. See also language
imperialism, 50. See also colonialism
indifference, 2, 136, 175, 219, 246n56; affect of, 115; the religiously indifferent, 3, 7, 20, 169. See also affect; emotion
Internal Revenue Service (IRS), 46, 60, 62, 67, 78, 116, 131, 231n2
intersectionality, 91, 94
Islamophobia, 99–100

Kant, Immanuel, 4, 161, 250n29
Kors, Alan Charles, 204, 207, 218, 250n29

lacuna, 132, 134, 143
language, 9–10, 97, 114, 139–140, 229n10; polysemy, 150; shift in my own register, 118, 139. See also ideology: semiotic; semiotics
liberalism, 162, 204, 207–208, 259n92
Lofton, Kathryn, 112, 244n12, 244n33
Lucretius, 203–204, 206–207, 248n61, 258n79

magic, 63, 72, 92
Mahmood, Saba, 8, 120, 161, 231n28, 231n29, 241n78, 250n26, 257n64
maleness, 30, 50, 81, 90–91, 193
Marx, Karl, 76, 192, 207, 232n1, 239n44, 258n83; Marxism, 207, 256n30
materialism, 146, 160, 165–166, 193, 207–208, 256n36; French materialists, 49, 239n44; Jewish materialism, 76, 239n47; materialist ontology, 53, 139, 150, 193, 242n7, 250n29; materialist tradition, 72. See also secular discursive tradition
meditation, 18, 30, 115, 140–141
mis-fit, 91, 94, 126; of religion, 71, 210, 212; of secularism, 3, 22, 73, 86, 127, 209, 217; examples of mis-fitting, 77, 91, 94, 126. See also secular misfits
modernity, 199, 203–204, 205, 230n11; modernization, 197–198; modern science, 151; modern skepticism, 149–151, 154; myth of modernity, 204. See also science; skepticism
monism, 40–41, 139, 161, 193, 230n23, 239n44
myth, 27, 121, 140–141, 204; mythos, 195–196

neutrality, as a mode of the secular, 109, 116–117, 131–136, 139, 142, 200, 209
New Atheists, 54–55, 152, 166, 172–173, 183, 232n3; origin of the phrase, 253n70. See also Dawkins, Richard; Dennett, Daniel; Harris, Sam; Hitchens, Christopher
Nietzsche, Friedrich, 119, 161, 191, 206–207; Nietzschean humanism, 188, 191–192, 256n30. See also humanism
nonbelievers, 63–64, 71–73, 178–183; beliefs of, 17–18, 29–31, 232n48; definition of, 6, 11, 107, 150; labels for, 36, 155; language of, 26, 53–55; organized, 8, 10, 19–21 15–16, 47, 160, 170–173, 237n13; paradox of, 25. See also community: secular; secular people
nones, 7,164, 230n17, 252n61

Palmer, Ada, 204–207, 218
Pentecostal, 21, 42, 80, 83, 92–93
perspectivism, 79, 119, 221–224
Pew Research, 6, 30, 86, 182
phenomenology, 55, 140, 192, 233n5, 234n16, 248n62
Pinn, Anthony, 194–195, 207, 236n53, 256n41, 256n42, 256n45
pollution. See religious pollution
Protestant: Black Protestantism, 86, 93, 236n46; post-Protestant, 85–86, 111, 113; Protestant game, 60, 65, 78; Protestantism, 45, 50, 63, 65–66, 82, 113, 126–127, 229n10, 245n37; Protestantism and religious studies, 112–113; Protestant Reformation, 49; Protestant secularism, 8, 77, 209, 238n22, 238n23. See also Christianity
proximity, to religion, 5, 17, 44, 47, 128, 136, 142, 218. See also religious pollution
purification, 37, 70, 229n9; modes of secular, 113–115, 119, 127–128, 136, 200–201; rituals of, 141–142. See also abstraction; avoidance; blasphemy; religious pollution; translation
purity, 229n9; linguistic, 9; religious, 217; secular, 5, 27, 39, 43–44, 60, 71, 77, 116, 119, 122–123, 143, 210, 212, 217–218, 229n10, 237n13. See also purification; religious pollution; secular purification

queerness, 49–50, 164

race, 22, 73, 90; antiracism, 91–92, 146, 154, 165; racism, 86, 88, 90–92, 94, 145–146, 158–159, 164–165, 186–187, 194, 208–209, 241n77; secularism as racializing, 22. See also science: scientific racism rationality, 32, 39, 91, 195, 251n49, 252n54; irrationality, 37; rationalist, 53–54, 161, 203, 218

reason, 20, 28, 38, 118, 143, 146, 151–152, 184

religion: antireligion, 11, 25, 114, 138, 142, 150, 204, 232n3; antireligious groups, 3, 27, 39; antireligious speech, 105, 114, 131, 144; burden of, 86, 90, 101; examples of antireligion, 116; religious excess, 19, 2, 77–78, 80, 82, 86, 100, 148, 179, 196, 203, 218, 246n56; inherently religious, 89, 240n67; as private, 34, 37, 166, 199; religion-like, 17, 22, 68–69, 90, 107, 117, 119, 147, 184, 249n13; religion-like behavior, 10, 60, 124–125, 150; religion-like secular, 134–136, 166, 217, 218, 245n37, 258n83; religion-like tradition; 43, 59, 114, 200, 209–210, 216, 218–219, 246n52. *See also* analogy

religion-related field, 118, 119, 170, 230n21, 231n28, 244n28, 244n29

religiosity, 7, 10, 17–18, 22, 49, 72, 85–86, 101, 115, 122, 123, 124–125, 127–128, 219, 235n37

religious pollution, 5, 17, 115, 119, 124, 143, 229n9, 229n10, 247n57; anxiety about, 175, 188, 213; danger of, 37, 39, 64, 77, 195; fear of, 210; of language, 120–122; of meditation, 140; proximity of, 44–45, 128, 131, 136, 142; purification of, 82, 101, 113, 119–120, 127–128, 140, 142; stigma of, 86; 140. *See also* affect; emotion; feelings; language; meditation; purification; purity

ritual: abstract category of, 8, 82, 85, 107, 110–113, 116–117, 124–125, 132, 141, 221–222; aversion to, 122–124; bar and bat mitzvahs, 80, 137–138, 141; Catholic, 84–86, 110–112, 124; Christmas, 60, 78, 83–84, 86, 125–126, 128, 132, 140–141, 143; creating, 27, 80, 108, 197; Día de los Muertos, 103–107, 110, 113, 131, 141–143, 242n3; Easter, 78, 124; Haramadan, 129, 213; invocations, 108, 133–136; life-cycle, 8, 61, 78–79, 108, 113; memorial services, 61, 108, 113, 200, 242n7; Mullahween, 96; naming ceremonies, 108, 215; Native American, 214–216, 243n9; Protestant, 110–111; Satanic, 66, 133–135; secular, 110–111, 131, 142; skepticism toward, 8. *See also* baptism; Catholicism; satanism; weddings

Roof, Wade Clark, 243n17

satanism, 41, 133–135

science: belief in, 28, 166–167; donation to science, 197; pseudoscience, 54, 88, 149; science fiction, 208; science and morality, 159, 162, 251n49; scientific empiricism, 161; scientific knowledge, 157; scientific method, 51–52, 149–150, 193; scientific racism, 90, 159, 241n77; scientific spirit, 45; and scientism, as a practice and way of knowing, 2, 11, 25, 31–33, 54, 63, 65, 91, 95, 141, 149–150, 152, 154, 193, 198, 205 ; social science, 7–8, 10, 16, 19–20, 79, 218. *See also* empiricism; race: racism

secular. *See* lacuna

Secular Coalition for America, 11, 14, 40, 159, 173, 180–183, 187

secular discursive tradition, 160, 162, 196, 202, 207–208, 210, 217–219; and Christianity, 213; critique of, 154; effects of, 119, 135, 219; participants in, 169, 184, 198, 203; translation into, 170. *See also* discursive tradition; tradition

secular misfits 3–4, 20–22, 71–73. Black atheists, 31, 50, 71, 86–94, 101, 164–165; Hispanic nonbelievers, 80–86, 144–145; humanistic Jews, 73–80, 114; secular Muslims, ex-Muslim, 21, 95–

100, 127–129, 213–214; secular Native American tradition, 214–217 *See also* mis-fit; women, secular
secular paradox, 4, 26, 44, 55–56, 59–60, 66, 71–72, 91, 100–102, 107, 126, 195, 208, 210, 212, 224, 233n5, 241n77; definition of, 3, 19, 244n31; effects of, 3, 6, 34, 43, 136, 147, 149, 158, 179, 184, 202–204; negative half, 117, 142, 169, 200, 206, 229n10; origin of, 3, 6, 27, 143; positive/affirmative half, 117, 142
secular people, 2–3, 5–6, 8–12, 15–23, 60, 136, 184, 219, 223, 229n10. *See also* nonbelievers
secular purification, 201, 217, 229n9, 229n10; extreme purification, 136; modes of, 113–115, 119, 127–128, 142, 200; of religious pollution, 70, 113, 140, 247n57. *See also* abstraction; avoidance; blasphemy; translation
Secular Student Alliance (SSA), 14, 43, 164, 178, 180
secularism, 3–6, 71, 260n110; critique of, 126, 153, 198–200; diversity within, 50–51; Hispanic, 83–84; history of, 65–66, 156; as religion-making, 8, 142, 153, 230n14; as separation of church and state, 6, 69, 153, 180–182; as system of belief, 31–32, 119, 146, 167; as traditiona, 219. *See also* secular discursive tradition
secularity (as a condition), 127, 219; definition of, 8, 218–219, 230n14; of misfits, 71, 129; of secular people, 4–5, 114, 142
secularization: as a process 8, 46, 72, 93, 175; as a theory and narrative, 197–199, 253n70, 257n61
semiotics, 229n10. *See also* language
skepticism, 8, 36, 54, 149–151, 160, 202, 233n9, 249n13, 249n20
Smith, Jonathan Z., 112, 243n12

Society for Humanistic Judaism (SHJ), 14, 74, 77–79, 181, 211
Sorett, Josef, 93–94, 102, 236n46, 238n22, 241n77
Spinoza, Baruch, 53, 76, 161, 207, 239n44, 258n80
spiritual force. *See* higher power
spirituality, 5, 9, 33, 44, 54–55, 63, 72, 124, 140, 169–170, 180, 234n16, 240n59, 244n31; spiritual but not religious, 7, 72; spiritualists, 11, 38
Sunday Assembly, 19, 57–59, 100, 232n48

tarot, 72. *See also* woo-woo
Taylor, Charles, 117, 197, 243n19
Taylor, Mark C., 208, 230n12, 232n55, 233n10, 236n68, 244n34
theology, 120, 209, 222, 245n39, 247n57
tradition, 22, 110; discursive, 115–116, 119, 135, 169–170, 196, 198–202, 202–205, 207–210, 247n57, 257n65, 258n72; Epicurean, 72, 76, 160–161, 204–207, 209; humanist, 187–191, 193–194, 196, 256n39; invented, 196, 198; secular, 3, 72, 76, 160, 162, 248n61, 260n110. *See also* Epicureanism; humanism; secular discursive tradition
translation, 113–117, 120, 127, 139, 166, 200, 214, 217, 247n57, 247n58; incompleteness of, 117, 249n50; into whiteness, 141. *See also* secular purification

uncanny, 17, 106, 136, 138; self-estrangement 16, 231n41
Unitarian, 122–123, 196, 234n25; Unitarian Universalist church, 33, 44, 162, 185–187, 189, 194, 221; Unitarian Universalist Humanist Association, 14, 40, 181, 194

Weber, Max, 161–162, 251n49, 257n62
weddings, 2, 5, 8, 61–65, 108–111, 242n6. *See also* ritual

whiteness, 26–27, 73, 80–89, 96–107, 194; of atheism, 49–50; culture of, 21–22, 42, 81–82, 89, 96, 101; of secularism, 3–4

woo-woo, 33–34, 72

women, secular, 3, 21–22, 48–51, 60, 99–100, 158, 163, 193–194, 208. *See also* secular misfits

worldview, 49, 139, 150, 198, 230n23; construction of, 31; definition of, 8; and ethics, 155, 157, 165, 184; expression of, 35; humanistic, 43, 47, 155; religious, 40–41; secular, 20, 29, 33–34, 39, 55–56, 72–73, 101, 109, 115, 152, 154, 252n61

yoga, 5, 18, 222

ABOUT THE AUTHOR

JOSEPH BLANKHOLM is Assistant Professor of Religious Studies at the University of California, Santa Barbara.

www.ingramcontent.com/pod-product-compliance
Lightning Source LLC
Chambersburg PA
CBHW020355080526
44584CB00014B/1029